The
Arabists

The
Arabists

THE ROMANCE OF
AN AMERICAN ELITE

ROBERT D. KAPLAN

THE FREE PRESS
A Division of Macmillan, Inc.
NEW YORK

Maxwell Macmillan Canada
TORONTO

Maxwell Macmillan International
NEW YORK   OXFORD   SINGAPORE   SYDNEY

The Free Press
A Division of Macmillan, Inc.
866 Third Avenue, New York, N.Y. 10022

Maxwell Macmillan Canada, Inc.
1200 Eglinton Avenue East
Suite 200
Don Mills, Ontario M3C 3N1

Macmillan, Inc. is part of the Maxwell Communication
Group of Companies.

Printed in the United States of America

printing number

   2   3   4   5   6   7   8   9   10

Library of Congress Cataloging-in-Publication Data

Kaplan, Robert D.
    The Arabists : the romance of an American elite / Robert D.
Kaplan.
        p.   cm.
    Includes bibliographical references (p.   ) and index.
    ISBN 0-02-916785-X
    1. Arab countries—Foreign relations—United States.   2. United
States—Foreign relations—Arab countries.   3. United States.   Dept.
of State.   Bureau for Near Eastern and South Asian Affairs—Biography.
4.   Orientalists—United States—Biography.   I. Title.
DS63.2.U5K35   1993
327.730174927—dc20   93-4321
                                                        CIP

For my wife
MARIA
and my son
MICHAEL

Contents

Preface and Acknowledgments

A s with my previous books on Ethiopia, Afghanistan, and the Balkans, this one began as a magazine article for the *Atlantic Monthly,* under the editorial guidance of Cullen Murphy and with the advice and support of Bill Whitworth. However, this book is no mere extension of the article "Tales from the Bazaar," which ran as a cover story in the August 1992 issue of the *Atlantic.* That piece was a horizontal exercise, where I meandered on a flat plane from personality to personality, giving the reader a taste of the subculture of State Department Arabists. This book is a vertical project—that is to say, historical—and, therefore, ultimately more critical. Though large sections of the article have been adapted for use in this book, especially in the later chapters, even those parts contain much additional information that has influenced my conclusions.

This is neither pure history nor pure journalism but a mixture of both. I have tried to see various individuals in terms of the historical and social milieu in which they were fated to work. I could sleep a lot easier had I been able to make everyone in this book appear a hero. Unfortunately, that has not been possible since it would have involved a complete suspension of judgment on my part. However, I am still in some awe of Arabists as a group of unambiguous, nation-state Americans, for whom patriotism is a more clear-cut enterprise than it is for those of my own Vietnam-age generation. I have, therefore, tried with all my heart to be fair. And being fair, in this case, means presenting information in its proper context. Thus, as regards my analysis, I make no apologies.

This book could not have been written without the financial assistance of The Lynde and Harry Bradley Foundation in Milwaukee, whose funds were administered by the Foreign Policy Research Institute in Philadelphia. In this regard, I would like to thank Dianne Monroe, Hillel Fradkin, Alan Luxenberg, and Daniel Pipes, who provided me with help whenever I asked but otherwise gave me the intellectual freedom I needed to reach my own conclusions. Adam Bellow has been a wise editor, always able to see things in their larger context. Carl Brandt, my literary agent, continues to steer me gently through confusing straits to the landfall of one book after another.

I also wish to pay special tribute to several works that I relied heavily on in writing this book:

Legacy to Lebanon by Grace Dodge Guthrie and *Lebanon's Child* by Anne Byerly Moore, two poignant memoirs of Lebanon in the earlier part of the century, certainly deserve a wider readership than the private printings so far available. They opened my mind up to a world and a Lebanon that I, as someone born after World War II, never knew existed. David H. Finnie's *Pioneers East: The Early American Experience in the Middle East* is the finest general study available about American missionaries in the Levant. Leo J. Bocage's *The Public Career of Charles R. Crane* goes into detail about a figure that is given only superficial treatment in other books about the history of the modern Middle East. H. W. Brands's *Inside the Cold War: Loy Henderson and the Rise of the American Empire 1918–1961* is exceptional in its cool objectivity and insight regarding a very controversial and talented diplomat. Finally, the Foreign Affairs Oral History Program of the Association for Diplomatic Studies and Georgetown University made it possible for me to check the opinions of several individuals discussed in this book. I wish to thank the librarians at the Foreign Service Institute in Arlington, Virginia, for making these Oral Histories available to me.

One last word: in this project, I've tried to be a writer whose aim is to empathize, rather than sympathize, with my subjects. The information in this book is therefore based on interviews I've conducted—both on and off the record—mainly with people described in these pages, and from the books that are mentioned in the bibliography. In cases where quotes come from an interview conducted under the abovementioned Oral History Program, I have signified this with a note.

In Syria, and Palestine, and Egypt, you might as well dispute the efficacy of grass or grain as of Magic. There is no controversy about the matter. The effect of this, the unanimous belief of an ignorant people, upon the mind of a stranger, is extremely curious, and well worth noticing. A man coming freshly from Europe is at first proof against the nonsense with which he is assailed; but often it happens that after a little while the social atmosphere of Asia will begin to infect him, and, if he has been unaccustomed to the cunning of fence by which reason prepares the means of guarding herself against fallacy, he will yield himself at last to the faith of those around him; and this he will do by sympathy, it would seem, rather than from conviction."

—Alexander Kinglake, *Eothen*

To work for Syria is to work among a splendid people in the land which gave us Christianity, the one faith which can make a man or a nation an uplifting force in the world.

—Margaret McGilvary, *A Story of Our Syria Mission*

For this cruel land can cast a spell which no temperate clime can match.

—Wilfred Thesiger, *Arabian Sands*

How partial is the evidence on which great decisions are often made.

—Richard Crossman, *Palestine Mission*

Prologue

Three generations,
Three wars,
Three marriages

It was 1960, the height of the Cold War, and Yemen was hurtling into the thirteenth century. While Francis Gary Powers flew a U-2 spy plane over the Soviet Union, Bill Stoltzfus was fighting Communism with home movies. "The Russians and Chinese were showing double features on consecutive nights at their embassies," his wife Janet recalls. "So Bill crossed the Red Sea to Ethiopia—where the U.S. had an air base—and came back with the reel of *Seven Brides for Seven Brothers*." Bill set up a 16-mm projector on the roof of a crumbling fort and organized separate seating for men and women, out of deference to Moslem tradition. The movie played every night for a week. The Imam of Yemen saw it twice. "Victory was ours!"

There were no schools, no radios, no telephones, no cars in Yemen then. The gates of the city walls closed at dusk. The only currency was the Maria Theresa thaler, a heavy silver coin that was the legacy of nineteenth century European traders. "The wrongdoers were in chains, beheadings were commonplace. We had a few barefoot servants and a Jeep that Bill and I would take turns driving to Aden for provisions. We subsisted on cans of baked beans from the U.S. military base in Ethiopia. Bill would take the day off before each embassy dinner party to go into the desert to shoot guinea fowl. We had a lot of liquor, though. We were drunk much of the time," laughs Janet, openly exaggerating.

Bill, a tall and athletic man in his seventies with a full crop of white hair,

1

breaks into a deep smile at the recollection, then adds: "Whenever I'd go up to Sukhna, where the Imam was, I'd wait in isolation for days for an audience. I remember the mud-walled castle where the Imam kept his hostages. Hostage taking, of course, was a tradition in Yemen. The Imam would incarcerate the sons of royal pretenders in order to ensure their loyalty. Yes, I remember kneeling with the Imam on a carpet. The Imam had his big wildcat brought to him. He opened the cage and stuck his hand in for the wildcat to stroke. After the Imam withdrew his hand, the servant handed him a cloth. The Imam took the cloth and, with a look of contentment, wiped the blood off his hand."

Bill goes silent, then says: "I thought that was really something, the way the Imam liked to feel the wildcat scratch him—to feel the cat's rage, I mean."

This causes Bill to talk about "Moslem rage."

"The Moslems don't accept our technology. And why should they? They don't believe that we're better off simply because we're more modern. What is "modern," by the way? We Americans are so wrapped up in ourselves, we don't take the time to understand other cultures."

Bill's belief is that "the Moslems and their culture will be a force in the next century." In Bill's view, conditions in Yemen, while medieval, were never primitive. "*Primitive*," Bill intones, "is a word we don't use in this house. It implies a value judgment. We prefer to say *basic*."

Janet cuts in, to complete the memory of Yemen: "Don't forget Amadeo Guillet, dear." Guillet, an Italian aristocrat, had ridden equestrian in the Olympics and was a cavalry officer with Mussolini's troops in Ethiopia. When Emperor Haile Selassie put a price on Guillet's head, Guillet escaped on a boat to Yemen, disguised as an Arab madman. The Imam hired him as a riding instructor for his sons. Guillet then became a close friend of Bill and Janet's. "Amadeo always wore native dress." Janet's voice trails off.

Welcome to the Princeton, New Jersey, home of Ambassador and Mrs. William A. Stoltzfus, Jr., the former first couple of the United States of America in no less than six Arab countries: Yemen, Bahrein, the United Arab Emirates, Qatar, Oman, and Kuwait. Nowadays, with an oriental carpet shop in many a suburban mall, the acquisition of eastern rugs may not signify much. But in this house the rugs are grand, and set, as they are, amid Byzantine crosses from Ethiopia, copperware from Iran, royal Arabic seals from Bahrein, a brass chest and a tall, exquisite coffeepot from Saudi Arabia, and a massive, hand-carved door from Kuwait serving as the living room table, the force and hold of a life experience vastly different from one's own begins to impress itself upon the visitor, a life in which Yemen was just a small chapter, deserving of one oil canvas of a native street scene near the foyer.

In Arabia, writes the British diplomat and traveler Freya Stark, "one never gets away from that strange sensation of being not in real life, but in some picture or story. It has the quality of things read or told in childhood." In Bill and Janet's case, this storybook Arabia was quite real. Its basic settings formed the backdrop for the major events of their lives.

Bill Stoltzfus was born in Beirut in 1924, the son of Protestant missionaries from the Midwest (his father was a Mennonite from Ohio, his mother a Presbyterian from Minnesota). "My birth certificate reads "Beirut, Syria," not "Beirut, Lebanon," because that's what it was. We always thought of Beirut as part of Syria. Modern Lebanon is a French invention," Bill explains.

Bill's father and mother met in an orphanage in Sidon, a Mediterranean coastal town south of Beirut, where both were doing humanitarian relief work after World War I. And it was in Beirut, after World War II, that Bill, a Princeton graduate taking an advanced course in Arabic, met Janet, a Wellesley graduate doing humanitarian work among the Arabs. Two of Bill and Janet's five children were born in the Arab world. One of their sons, Philip, a Princeton graduate like his father and his grandfather before him, met his American bride-to-be—a Dartmouth alumna and humanitarian relief worker—in Lebanon after the 1975–76 civil war. "Three generations, three wars, three marriages," notes Bill with reverence.

After Bill and Janet married in 1954, Bill was posted to Kuwait as the American vice-consul. In those days Kuwait was just a walled medieval city with its back to the desert. There was no air-conditioning. In the hundred-degree summer nights Bill and Janet slept outside on the roof. Their first son, William A. Stoltzfus III, was the first non-Arab baby born in the local hospital, built by American missionaries of the Dutch Reformed Church almost half a century before.

Bill's days were taken up with Palestinian refugees applying for visas to the United States. Because the Palestinians had come from a densely populated zone near the Mediterranean that had undergone rapid modernization by the British, they were better educated and harder working than the indigenous Kuwaitis. Forty years later the aptitude and determination of those refugees remain a standard that Janet, a teacher in a Princeton secondary school, still applies: "These days, whenever you see a Korean or a Japanese or a Chinese name on a class roster, you just know that child is going to excel—just like the Palestinian children I knew in Kuwait."

Given the circumstances of their lives to that point, for Bill and Janet not to have sympathized with the Palestinians would have been a thing inhuman. Janet wants to put this in context, however. A professional educator, she is impressively smooth and relaxed about what is a tender subject.

"You're young," she tells her visitor. "You simply cannot realize how powerful and unconscious a force anti-Semitism was in America at the middle of this century, when Bill and I were in school. At Princeton and Wellesley, at the prep schools we went to, you almost never encountered Jews. It was a different America then. God, was it different! Why, the Holocaust—because of all the books and films and articles of recent years—seems a lot closer to us now than it was right after it happened."

Bill explains: "When the first photos and stories about the concentration camps appeared, I remember reading about it and being shocked, horrified. Sure, I felt sympathy for the Jews. But it was an abstract sympathy. Like the kind others feel when reading about the Cambodians or the Ethiopians. If you don't know people personally who have been affected, it's very hard to stay continually worked up over what has happened to them. The Jews were a distant, unreal world to us then, but the Palestinians were individuals we knew."

From Kuwait, in 1956, Bill was posted to the U.S. embassy in Damascus as the political officer. For other Americans Syria in the 1950s was the dark side of the moon, an unstable netherworld of chilling coups and political incorrigibility. For Bill and Janet it was akin to a homecoming.

Bill had grown up in Aleppo, an historic bazaar city in northern Syria, after his missionary father became president of Aleppo College when Bill was a year old. Aleppo was also where Bill and Janet had gone to celebrate their engagement. There was also Beirut, only a few hours by car from Damascus, where Bill's parents had recently returned. As for the Damascus of that era, "What a pretty place," recalls Janet, referring to a small town of colorful markets steeped in biblical lore. Bill adds, "The Syrians had always been tolerant of Americans. We trusted them and they trusted us."

For Beirut-born and Aleppo-raised Bill Stoltzfus, therefore, American-Syrian relations were never the hostile spectacle of recent decades but rather the network of personal friendships between an educated stratum of Arab society and American missionaries and educators who began coming to Syria in the early nineteenth century.

Back then, when the Ottoman Turks ruled the Middle East, borders did not really exist. There was just the limestone plateau region of the north, called Syria, and everything else—a sandstone desert reaching all the way south to Yemen. *Syria,* a Greek word derived from the Semitic *Siryon,* first appears in Deuteronomy in reference to Mount Hermon, a mountain straddling the current frontiers of Syria, Lebanon, and Israel. Not only was Lebanon then part of Syria, but so was Palestine, Jordan, western Iraq, and southern Turkey. In truth, it was American missionaries like Bill's parents, through their letters home, their cultural societies, and their printing presses, who led the movement to legitimize the term *Syria* not only in the West but among the local Arabs, who until the coming of those Protestants simply referred to the region as *Ash-Sham,* "the North."

So for Bill, Syria constituted much more than a home. It was almost a transplanted version of New England itself: a glorified tableau of Ivy League Brahmins, each with a foothold in the Lebanese mountains, a magical kingdom of Protestant families brimming with a spirit of adventure, rectitude, and religious idealism, where the twentieth century would not fully arrive until 1948. When it came, it came with a vengeance.

Not every Foreign Service officer, no matter how talented, becomes an ambassador. Some luck is usually required, and Bill Stoltzfus is no exception. Bill's lucky moment came in 1971, when as second-in-command at the U.S. embassy in Jidda, Saudi Arabia, he was given the task of organizing the visit to Jidda of then–Vice President Spiro Agnew.

In some ways this was unpleasant work. "The Secret Service agents were so insensitive to the local culture," Bill explains. "For example, they peeked behind the curtains in the women's area of the palace before the vice president arrived." Playing tennis with Agnew was not unpleasant, though. Bill had been warned that the vice president was "a guy who hated to lose." So for a while Bill kept hitting the ball meekly. " 'This is ridiculous,' I finally said to myself. Then I polished him off." Rather than take offense, the vice president was impressed. A friendship ensued, and Bill imparted to Agnew some of what he knew about the Middle East. "Agnew was a great guy, a real decent sort, though, of course," Bill lifts his white eyebrows, "he had his problems."

Not long after Agnew returned to Washington, Bill was promoted to the rank of ambassador.

When a scandal forced Agnew to resign the vice presidency in 1974, he began frequenting the Middle East as a businessman and publicly espousing the Arab cause against Israel. What is not known, however, is that some of Agnew's first tutorials on Middle East politics came from Bill Stoltzfus. "You see," explains Bill, "it is domestic concerns that subvert our foreign policy. And it's pretty clear to me that the powerful, vested interest of a certain group of people, concentrated in the big cities in big states, determines our Middle East policy. If you're looking for some kind of a plot, that's where to look."

Bill says all this while his visitor takes notes. Bill has invited his visitor into the privacy of his own home in order to put such things in their proper perspective. The visitor therefore has a responsibility to do so:

What Bill means to say is that while the decades-long political conflict between American Jewish lobby groups and diplomats like himself cannot be denied—and is something that he, quite candidly, still has strong feelings about—it is nevertheless very unfortunate. To be at odds with another group of Americans is the last thing Bill wants. With their youngest daughter in the Peace Corps in Africa, Bill and Janet are people with a keen and self-reflective sense of American idealism. That much should be clear.

Bill Stoltzfus is an *Arabist,* one of the most loaded words in America's political vocabulary. In the Middle Ages an Arabist was only a physician who had studied Arab medicine, then much more advanced than the kind practiced in Europe. In the late nineteenth and twentieth centuries an Arabist was merely a student of Arabic, like a Hellenist or a Latinist. But with the birth of Israel in 1948, the term *Arabist* quickly gathered another meaning. Richard Murphy, a former assistant secretary of state for the Middle East and a former ambassador to Syria and to Saudi Arabia, says the word "became a pejorative for *he who intellectually sleeps with Arabs*," someone, that is, assumed to be politically naive, elitist, and too deferential to exotic cultures. The word almost *presumes* guilt. The very syllables resonate with sympathy and possession—*of and with the Arabs*—in a way that a word like Sinologist does not. Murphy's wife, Anne, nods sadly. "If you call yourself an Arabist," she says, "people may think you're anti-Semitic."

Bill admits that "to a man, the American community in Syria and Lebanon remained opposed to the State of Israel and some even crossed the line into anti-Semitism. The community finally had to accept Israel, sure, but not in its heart: the way conservatives finally had to accept Communist China."

If people like Bill are associated with anything, it is usually with a group of sand-mad Britons, such as Sir Richard Francis Burton, Charles Doughty, T. E. Lawrence ("of Arabia"), Harry "Abdullah" Philby, Wilfred Thesiger, and Gertrude Bell, who went native in the Arabian desert and around whom hovers a gust of fantasy and sexual perversion and nihilism. "I wanted colour and savagery," Wilfred Thesiger cries, "a cleanness which was infinitely remote from the world of men. . . . I craved for the past, resented the present, and dreaded the future."

In fact, few American government officials over the decades have been so vilified as a group while remaining so mysterious and unknown as individuals as the Arabists. In most cases, Arabists are not the handful of upper-level State Department officials savaged by columnists. Nor, usually, are they the Middle East policy types who appear on talk shows. Arabists are men and women, like Bill, who read and speak Arabic and who have passed many years of their professional lives, with their families, in the Arab world, whether as diplomats, military attachés, intelligence agents, or even scholar-adventurers.

Arabists also represent the most exotic and controversial vestige of the East Coast Establishment. Francis Fukuyama, a former member of the State Department's Policy Planning Staff and a renowned political philosopher, says Arabists are "a sociological phenomenon, an elite within an elite, who have been more systemically wrong than any other area specialists in the diplomatic corps. This is because Arabists not only take on the cause of the Arabs, but also the Arabs' tendency for self-delusion."

Nicholas Veliotes, another former assistant secretary of state for the

Middle East, as well as a former ambassador to Jordan and to Egypt, sharply disagrees. "Whenever I hear someone criticizing Arabists I shoot back, 'Arabists are men and women who have mastered a difficult language and have spent years of their lives in a difficult foreign environment in service to the United States. I wish I were one of them. Unfortunately, because my Arabic was never very good, I'm not.' "

The reader may think that he already understands Bill Stoltzfus, but he doesn't. There are levels of his personality that one can only penetrate through access to a certain historical experience.

To start with, one should not confuse Bill with the sand-mad Britons. Whatever the individual traits of the British Arabists, they all operated against a backdrop of imperialism. It was the advantages of power and privilege that imperialism offered that allowed these British men and women to work out their personalities and fantasies upon such an exotic stage. Their myriad eccentricities notwithstanding, men such as Lawrence and women such as Gertrude Bell were in Araby as British government agents, and thus it was the mechanics of imperial power that primarily concerned them.

While British Arabists were imperialists, American Arabists were originally—and, therefore, most significantly—missionaries. Mission work defines the American Arabist, much as imperialism defines the British Arabist.

Truly there are few social species as authentically American as the missionary and, by extension, the missionary-Arabist: a person concerned less with political power than with the doing of good deeds in order to improve the world and to be loved by less-fortunate others. The British sought to dominate, to acquire a culture and a terrain as one acquires a rare and beautiful book.* But Americans like Bill's parents sought something more tantalizing. They sought to change this terrain, to improve upon it, using their own model. They manifested a psychology that grew out of the American Revolution and that would finally culminate in the tragedy of one American ambassador in Iraq more than two hundred years later.

As we shall learn, the famous encounter in July 1990 between U.S.

---

* This metaphor can be taken quite literally: D. G. Hogarth, who ran the British Arab Bureau in Cairo during World War I, accumulated three hundred books on Arab subjects during the course of the war.

ambassador April Glaspie and Iraqi president Saddam Hussein was, in reality, two centuries in the making. Miss Glaspie entered Saddam's lair freighted with the baggage of a venerable Arabist tradition. The real Iraqgate was never a banking scandal but an epic human story that parallels the history of the American Republic.

Oddly, though, Americans know more about British imperialism than they know about what motivated their own countrymen in the Middle East, men and women whose influence was prodigious. Indeed, never before in the American or British experience has there been an expatriate culture quite like the American missionary colonies in the Moslem world. It is a story that first needs to be addressed before we can even begin to discover who, exactly, Bill Stoltzfus is and who, exactly, the other people are who have been the secret drivers of America's Middle East policy since the end of World War II.

Part I
Dream

Chapter 1

Home to Lebanon

" "The engines throbbed, the ship shuddered and finally we were on our way down the Hudson River, past the Statue of Liberty, past Staten Island and out into the great Atlantic bound for home." Home for eight-year-old Anne Byerly was the Lebanese coastal town of Sidon.* In 1931 Sidon was a drowsy, picturesque hamlet, known for an ancient tree where Job rested and "scratched his boils" and a spot on the beach where Jonah was cast up by the whale.

The small, redheaded Anne, returning to Sidon after a year at school in America, came from dignified Anglo-American stock. Anne's great-great-great-grandfather, Andrew Byerly, fought in the French and Indian War (there is a trail named for him in a state park west of Pittsburgh). Her grandfather, Andrew Robertson Byerly, was a Union captain in the Civil War. Her father, the Reverend Robert Crane Byerly, was born in the Pennsylvania Dutch country and went out to Lebanon (then part of Syria) as a Presbyterian missionary at the outbreak of World War I, where he met Anne's mother, a second-generation missionary from London. The two, like Bill Stoltzfus's parents, would pass their adult lives in humanitarian service to the Arabs.

---

* While the French Mandate of 1920 had given Lebanon a separate legal identity, until the present Syrian state came into being after World War II, the missionaries continued to think of Lebanon as Syrian territory.

For an American child in Lebanon between the two world wars, Anne's blood-and-soil Protestant background was entirely typical, as was her exotic sense of national identity. Anne grew up "speaking a mixture of English, Arabic, and French." At the family table breakfast was American, tea English, and dinner "the tasty Arab dishes we all loved." Anne "unconsciously absorbed the cultures" of the people around her. Still, she "felt great surges of patriotism" when joining fellow Americans in singing "O beautiful for spacious skies" on the Fourth of July.

What Anne, like the other American "children of Lebanon," especially remembers are the picnics by the Mediterranean. "When the moon was full we stayed until after dark, splashing and playing in the water, and marveling at the sparkling phosphorus that clung to our bathing suits." The Arab servants would lay out *samboosik* (pastry triangles stuffed with meat and cooked vegetables) on steamer rugs for the children and their families. Afterwards, everyone would toss the crumbs to the crabs. Following one such evening, a friend of Anne's, Louise Plummer, sent Anne a poem, entitled "The Syrian Crabs":

> *A camel caravan in miniature I saw at dusk*
> *While bathing in the sea off Sidon's shore,*
> *It slowly wound its way to water's edge*
> *And disappeared beneath the blue.*
> *The moon, a golden ball, arose*
> *Behind the Lebanons nearby*
> *And we, so like Aeneas sung by bards of old,*
> *Our supper ate and then our plates devoured.*
> *What matter that the plates were bread*
>   *and camels only crabs,*
> *It is a treasured memory of pleasant days*
>   *in Sidon spent.*

Grace Dodge, the daughter of the president of the American University of Beirut and another of Anne's childhood acquaintances, remembers her walks home from school by the "deep blue and green" Mediterranean, "mottled with brown silt" from a river egress that the ancients called "the blood of Adonis." Mount Sannin was in the background, wearing "a mantle of snow which at sunset would glow pink." Along the way were a series of coves that Grace and her school chums often explored. Grace's brother, David Stuart Dodge, remembers the hiking and skiing on Cedar Mountain, where the same cedar trees had stood since antiquity. In the summers Grace and David pitched tents with their family in a cedar grove protected by the Maronite church. "The Lebanon I knew as a boy was such a peaceful place," says David, who like his father and great-grandfather grew up to become president of the American University of Beirut. Indeed, "peaceful" and "sleepy" are words frequently applied to the Lebanon of this era.

Talcott Seelye, a future U.S. ambassador to Tunisia and to Syria, will always recall the beautiful sound of the Christian hymns every morning at chapel and the "sleepy, peaceful" quality of Beirut. David Zimmerman, another future U.S. diplomat, remembers the Saturday baseball games, the Cub Scout meetings in sight of Beirut harbor, and picking thistles to throw in the Fourth of July bonfires. "We lived like English feudal lords with servants, all on our own mountains, in houses which were like those on the New England lakes," says Bill Stoltzfus.

Arthur and Ray Close, later to become pioneer intelligence officers in the Middle East after Word War II, were part of the gang, too. The two brothers grew up in Moslem Beirut, in a family of missionaries that had lived in Lebanon since the mid-nineteenth century. "Unlike other American families, we had only one servant. In a given week, we'd have four Arab meals and three American ones. My mother spoke fluent Arabic. She loved the Arabs. The Lebanese in those days were such an easy people to love and we were brought up to love the country and what it had to offer. I'll always remember the hikes through the Moslem and Druse villages. It was a somewhat false, idyllic existence we all lived," Arthur recalls.

False, it might turn out to be, depending on one's opinion. But so was it idyllic. Seen through the mists of time—more than a decade of cinematic urban violence in the 1970s and 1980s, preceded by three decades of political conflict caused by the rise of Arab nationalism and encompassing four wars with Israel—these exquisite memories of a Lebanon that no longer exists, and in a sense may never have existed, seem distant, trivial, and unreal. Yet the memories are important, since enough of the people who hold them were later to become influential.

It is hard to think of a luckier bunch of kids than Anne Byerly, Grace and David Dodge, Talcott Seelye, Bill Stoltzfus, David Zimmerman, Arthur and Ray Close, and their friends. Physically, there are few places on earth as lovely as Lebanon: it's one of those sacred spots in which winter and summer, sea and desert, occident and orient all come together for a stirring synthesis amidst a sylvan backdrop of cedars and cypresses, where one can swim and windsurf in sight of the mountain snows. To have known it not only before the Lebanese civil war but before the seaside glitz and simmering tensions of the 1950s and 60s would have been heaven enough. But to have known it as an American child in the 1920s and 30s would have been to inhabit a rustic paradise where you were not only on a social and economic pedestal but on a moral one, too.

The American expatriate community in Lebanon prior to World War II was the result of a stunning exception to Lowell Thomas's "traditional order" of conquest: "the explorer, the missionary, the soldier, and then the merchant."* In Lebanon the explorer and the missionary had been one and the same, the soldier had never arrived, and instead of the merchant—of which there were to be only a benign handful—there came the educator.

In marked contrast to the conduct of European colonials in the underdeveloped world or American expatriates in the Panama Canal Zone and the Pacific holdings, imperialism and commercial exploitation were entirely missing from the baggage carried by the missionaries in Lebanon. Nor did the Americans even present a threat to the local religious culture, as the missionary colonies in India, China, Burma, and Siam would. For if truth be told, compared to the missionaries in the Far East, who won over significant numbers of Chinese to Protestant Christianity, the American missionaries in the Middle East were complete failures. The intractability of Islam quickly forced them to give up any hope of converting souls to Christ. In an acute observation of just how harmless the Americans were seen to be, Mrs. Eli Smith, a Beirut missionary wife, noted in 1839 that through Moslem eyes, "Americans did not lie, nor steal, nor quarrel, nor do any such thing; but, poor creatures, they have no religion!"

It would be only as purveyors of Western education that the Americans in Lebanon were to succeed. And for that the local Arabs would learn to love them.

The first American citizen ever to walk among the Arabs was John Ledyard of Groton, Connecticut. A Dartmouth College dropout, Ledyard

---

* See Thomas's introduction to *The Golden Milestone*, listed under Zwemer in the bibliography.

explored the New Hampshire wilderness and trekked by foot across Siberia in 1786 before accepting an offer from London's Africa Society to sail up the Nile to explore Central Africa. Ledyard arrived in the Egyptian Mediterranean port of Alexandria in July 1788, a year before George Washington was inaugurated president. Ledyard never got further than Cairo, dying there a few months later of some vague ailment, complicated by an overdose of medicinal drugs. Ledyard was 37, and except for a curious description of the Nile as "no bigger than the Connecticut River"—motivated, it is said, by patriotism—he was immediately and completely forgotten.

It was in western Massachusetts, however, two decades later, where America's dramatic relationship with the Moslem world, and with the Arabs in particular, had its true beginning. In 1808, on the campus of Williams College, five students led by one Samuel J. Mills, Jr., met and prayed beside a dry haystack during an electric storm to demonstrate their belief in Christ. The event, known as the Haystack Incident, passed into legend, and the details became obscured. What is known is that the five vowed to spread the Good News to millions of heathens in Asia and Africa who were without the benefit of hearing His message.

This peculiar demonstration of faith did not occur in a vacuum but was the culmination of one process and the start of another. Protestantism, had, by that time, emerged as the paramount social and cultural institution of the young United States. The late eighteenth and early nineteenth centuries "was a time of camp meetings, revivals, conversions," notes the missionary historian David Finnie, "of Protestant vigor" such as the world had never known, all borne within a framework of extraordinary pioneer optimism. Protestant evangelicals of every stripe, each of whom thought he had the true revelation, were fanning out over New England in a fierce competition for souls. For the first time in human history, faith became purely a matter of choice. It was in this way that the various Protestant denominations—Presbyterian, Congregationalist, Methodist, Baptist, Unitarian, Episcopalian—all came into being. As the religious historian Martin E. Marty points out, the American Revolution was in truth three revolutions, only one of which was a shooting war. The second revolution was the separation of church and state, an idea that was less a noble inspiration than a practical outgrowth of newly diversified Protestantism, which now made it impossible to identify the new nation and its founding elite with any single church. The third revolution made religion more a matter of reason than of heart, "something accessible to all, whether or not they believed in the Bible," writes Marty. It is this third revolution that became associated with the Great Awakening, whose driving force was missionary work.

The Great Awakening, according to one of its spokesmen, the Reverend Samuel Hopkins of Newport, Rhode Island, sought to scatter the Glory of God from the happiness of one man to that of the greatest number of men. "Only the extension of Christian love," the Reverend Hopkins explained, "could bring nearer to humankind the millennium that would wipe out poverty, injustice and oppression." This represented the religious voice of young America in all its dynamism, egalitarian purity, and self-assurance, the direct by-product of the new nation's heady experience with freedom as a solution to man's ills. It was such beliefs that made "the true Puritan," according to Randolph Bourne, writing in 1917, at once "the most unselfish and the most self-righteous of men." It is also what motivated Samuel Mills and his disciples to meet beside the haystack while lightning flickered all around.

In a sense, almost all of the Protestant denominations began as missionary movements whose leaders scoured New England in a competition for converts. It was only logical, therefore, that the next step would be to seek new disciples farther afield. At the turn of the nineteenth century, the Baptists had already begun their conquest of the American South, and the Methodists their conquest of the border states. But these victories for God in the New World had barely commenced—almost the entire native American Indian population was still unconverted—when the Congregationalists, led by Mills, soon to be joined by the Presbyterians and the Dutch Reformed Church, became suddenly enamored of the prospect of mission work abroad.*

Compared with the dangerous and largely unsuccessful labors among the native Indian population, the Congregationalists assumed that abroad "the difficulties" would be "the least," the competition for souls less, and the possibilities for prestige and glory more. The impulse driving men and women overseas was no different then than it is now. Going abroad was a way to improve one's social status, which in the clergymen's case had already begun slipping as the first heavy waves of European immigrants began arriving in New England, changing the face of the countryside. Villages

---

* The Congregationalists were to dominate missionary activities in the Middle East until 1870, when a friendly division of labor emerged: the Congregationalists became responsible for Turkey, the Presbyterians for Egypt, Syria, and Iran, and the Dutch Reformed Church for the Arabian Gulf.

became bustling towns, and ministers became just one of the many voices competing for attention in a more culturally diverse and economically expanding America.

The Sandwich Islands (Hawaii), China, and the west coast of Africa were the first foreign shores invaded by the New England Protestants. But the Holy Land beckoned above all, and not just because of the importance that went with its being the Lord's birthplace. The missionaries saw their movement as nothing less than a new Crusade, one that would finally rescue the land of the Bible from Moslem backwardness. "What are your marching orders?" one Congregationalist asked himself, just the way a soldier would. The Congregationalists truly felt it was the Americans—not the Europeans—who were destined to bring the Western Bible to the Holy Land. The Americans certainly invested themselves with a mantle of purity. They lived in a virginal land untainted by the hate and other iniquities of the Old World, best exemplified, they felt, by the fact that the new United States was the "only Christian nation, which has never persecuted the descendants of Israel." Anti-Semitism would one day become a critical issue for Americans in the Arab world. But it all began rather differently.

These early Congregationalists were, in the strictest sense, the ultimate Wasps: "the direct spiritual descendants of the original Puritans," according to the historian Finnie. They bestowed biblical Hebrew names on their children: Daniel, Isaac, Elnathan, Levi. Their religion, like that of the Arabs, was a complete social system that featured abstinence from alcohol, frugality, charity, and severe dress. But it was their self-conscious tolerance of Jews, common to this day among some evangelicals, which would help launch the first American missionary stations in the Moslem world.

The Congregationalist elders had at first rejected Mills's plan for missions abroad, but pleas by him and others continued unabated. One must bear in mind that it was an era of excitable idealism. Newly established colleges such as Williams and Middlebury (and soon Hamilton and Amherst), in addition to theological seminaries like Andover and Union, were producing the kind of supremely self-confident and self-sacrificing young men for whom a life abroad in mission work guaranteed instant status. In 1810, only two years after the Haystack Incident, collegians and parishioners had collected enough funds to organize an American Board of Commissioners for Foreign Missions, dominated by Congregationalists and headquartered in Boston.

It wasn't until 1819, however, during the presidency of James Monroe, nine years after the Mission Board was established and six years after the first missionaries set out for the Far East, that the first American missionaries sailed for the Holy Land. It quickly became apparent that the Holy Land of reality was a different place from the one of the Protestants' imaginations.

Pliny Fisk was a graduate of Middlebury College in Vermont and the Andover Theological Seminary, north of Boston. At Middlebury he befriended Levi Parsons, another pious young man who buried his head in Scriptures. Fisk had an aversion to foreign languages. Parsons was "moody, introspective," and had a weak stomach. In 1820 this sorry pair reached Smyrna, a Greek city on the western coast of Turkey then known as the "Pearl of the Levant," whose Orthodox Christian population and community of Western traders provided a Westernized beachhead in the Moslem Orient (much as Beirut would later become) that could ease newcomers like the two Americans into the baffling ways of the East.

Parsons spent most of the time in Smyrna sick in bed. Fisk spent his time attending to Parsons and praying. In 1822 the two sailed for Alexandria in the hope that Parsons's health would improve. But Parsons died the month after their arrival in Egypt. Though Fisk did manage several visits to Jerusalem in 1823 and 1824, in 1825 he died of illness in Beirut at the age of thirty-three, in utter agony on his deathbed, exactly like that of his friend Parsons.

Then there was William McClure Thomson, twenty-eight, and his bride Eliza, thirty-four, both of whom fared little better than Fisk and Parsons. The Thomsons had met at Princeton, establishing a tradition for Middle East missionaries and Arabic specialists that would carry through to the present day. Soon after they arrived in the Holy Land in 1834, the Arab inhabitants of Jerusalem rebelled against their Egyptian overlord, Mohammed Ali, who ruled Palestine for a time in place of the Turks. Due to the outbreak of fighting, Thomson, momentarily on the coast at Jaffa, was cut off for two months from his wife in Jerusalem. Eliza Thomson, alone amid the "roar of cannon, falling walls, the shrieks of the neighbors, the terror of servants and constant expectation of massacre," gave birth to a son, William, Jr. Less than two weeks after her husband's return, she died of fever.

William Thomson remained in the Middle East, but it was not as a missionary but as a travel writer, with the publication of a best-selling adventure, *The Land and the Book,* that he gained success. In the book Thomson admits that of the handful of Arabs who expressed any interest in the Western Gospel, almost all did so because they figured there was money to be made off the bewildered and naive foreigners. Indeed, the first missionaries must have struck the Arabs the way traveling hippies struck Asians in the 1960s and 1970s or the way the greenest of Western relief workers appear to people in the Third World they are intent to help: as pathetically out of their depth.

But because these abject failures were occurring half a world away, the details became obscured and suffused with glory. "One might rewrite the eleventh chapter of Hebrews with well-known names from modern annals of Christian workers in Bible lands. . . . Foremost among these should come the names of Pliny Fisk, Levi Parsons," writes a clergyman of the day. The Mission Board in Boston was undaunted. It dispatched more missionaries to the Levant. The fact that similarly disastrous experiences with the American Indians caused the Protestant churches to cease all efforts on behalf of the native Americans did not affect fund-raising for the overseas missions, even after it became clear that in the Middle East, at least, the majority of Moslems stood absolutely no chance of being converted.

But by 1830 the Boston Mission Board was desperate enough that it targeted an obscure sect of Oriental Christians, the Nestorians in faraway Iran, as a possibility for conversion. Their initial experiences in Smyrna, Alexandria, Jerusalem, and Beirut had taught the Congregationalists that the Eastern Christians were no less in need of Christ than the Moslems. If anything, they needed him more.

The very impossibility of converting the Moslems—or the Eastern Jews, for that matter—forced the missionaries to accept these two peoples as unalterably different: part of the exotic Oriental milieu requiring serious study.* But to arrive in Jerusalem nearly at death's door, as Fisk and the Thomsons did, only to see the Church of the Holy Sepulchre and the other Holy Places guarded by a dirty and superstitious rabble of Greeks and Byzantinized Arabs, all kissing icons and burning incense amid gold-leaf finery, scandalized these well-bred and puritanical New Englanders. In the eyes of the missionaries, it was the Oriental Christians—the Greek Orthodox, the Egyptian Copts, the Lebanese Maronites, and others—who had

---

* Ottoman law, in fact, forbade Christian missionary work among the Moslem population.

truly usurped the Holy Land, by emphasizing the hypnotic mechanics of liturgy over the *Word* of God! The Protestant missionary animus toward these strange Eastern rite churches, products of Byzantine rule in the Middle East from the fourth through sixth centuries A.D., was never to dissipate. In fact, it would grow. In 1920 a Beirut missionary, Margaret McGilvary, writes: "The Oriental Church is the canker at the heart of Christianity, and inasmuch as it is the chief point of contact with Islam, it behooves the Christian world to renovate the system which so unworthily represents its cause in the Near East."

To investigate the Nestorians, the Mission Board chose Harrison Gray Otis Dwight and Eli Smith to make the difficult journey across Anatolia to the wild and freezing mountainous region where Turkey, Armenia, Iran, and Georgia intersect. Both men were twenty-nine. Otis Dwight had graduated from Hamilton College in upstate New York and the Andover Theological Seminary; Eli Smith had graduated from Yale and Andover. Dwight was pleasant if superficial company, physically tough, and unflappable in the face of danger; the perfect traveler, in other words. Like William Thomson, Dwight was to succeed as an explorer and travel writer, not as a missionary. Eli Smith was of a more delicate disposition and prone to repeated illnesses, but he would eventually realize much more. Eli Smith became America's first Arabist.

One could even date the beginning of the American Arabist tradition to 1827, when Eli Smith, the Connecticut Yankee from Yale, struck out from the relative safety of a nascent mission community in Beirut for the surrounding mountains, to live for several months with the Moslem and Druze villagers, studying their language. (Richard Francis Burton, the first of the great British Arabists, was a boy of six at the time.) Unlike Pliny Fisk, who quickly gave up on Arabic, Smith kept at it daily for three years, establishing the groundwork for his later scholarship, until he received word from the Mission Board to rendezvous with Dwight for the journey to Iran.

Smith and Dwight began their trip in Smyrna, traveling north on horseback to Constantinople, wearing native robes and turbans, carrying pistols, and sleeping out on the Oriental carpets they brought with them. The beards they grew completed the native attire. Already, these Americans—products of a brand-new and therefore somewhat superficial culture—were finding the old and deeply textured culture of the East to be irresistible.

It took more than three weeks for the pair to cross the windy dust bowl of northern Anatolia, from Constantinople to Erzurum in the Armenian-inhabited region of eastern Turkey. They slept in stables, amid the horses and the manure. By summer Smith and Dwight were in Tiflis, in Georgia, where Smith contracted cholera. Too weak to mount a horse, Smith rode behind Dwight in an oxcart as the pair pressed southeast through the mountains toward Iran. Smith was by now deathly ill and unable to sleep due to constant swarms of mosquitoes. "I lay and wept like a child," he recalled.

For three months Smith and Dwight remained at a Swiss mission outpost in Armenia while Smith recovered. It was now November, and snow was beginning to fall on the steppe as the two set out once more for Tabriz, in northwestern Iran. Spending a night in a dust-ridden cell without a fireplace, Smith again fell ill. On another occasion, sleeping amid "every species of dirt, vermin, and litter," Smith and Dwight were forced to subsist on bread, filled with dead "crawling creatures," baked from the fuel of dried cow dung. Finally, on December 18, 1830, with Smith so weak he could "neither walk nor stand," the Iranian city of Tabriz saw its first Americans.

The following March, Smith had sufficiently improved so that he and Dwight could make the journey to the western shore of nearby Lake Urmia, home of the Nestorians. Perhaps it was the very difficulty of the journey to this far-off band of Christians, plus the miracle of his own survival, that drove Smith to wax enthusiastic about the suitability of Urmia as a site for mission work.

So it was in 1833 that the Boston Mission Board dispatched twenty-eight-year-old Justin Perkins of Holyoke, Massachusetts, and his new bride, Charlotte, to set up housekeeping in the mountains west of Tabriz. Perkins, a graduate of Amherst and the Andover seminary, was a typical Congregationalist Brahmin, with a reputation for "highly polished and courtly manners, an iron will, and a robust constitution." The Perkinses made their journey easier by sailing along northern Anatolia's Black Sea coast to eastern Turkey, before starting out overland. They also brought along their own tent and cooking utensils. Just as Eliza Thomson was giving birth under miserable conditions in Jerusalem, so was Charlotte Perkins in Tabriz. Charlotte survived, but her newborn daughter did not.

The Boston board realized that missions in such primitive places were doomed without the presence of a trained physician. So in the first weeks of 1835, a twenty-eight-year-old medical doctor, Asahel Grant of Marshall, New York, and his wife, Judith, stepped into a boat on the Erie Canal, bound for Iran.

Grant, unlike the other missionaries, was no upper crust New Englander. A small, excitable, dark-complexioned man, he had never attended college or even a proper medical school. His only credentials were that he had apprenticed under a physician in upstate New York and had been brought up on a heavy diet of Scripture. Grant's enthusiasm was driven by his belief that the Nestorians numbered among the lost tribes of Israel.

The first winter in Iran, the Grants and the Perkinses slept on muddy straw, in bedclothes "stiffened" by snow and frost. In January 1836 the Americans opened a mission school by Lake Urmia, teaching the pupils to read the Lord's Prayer. But it was the low-born and unschooled Grant, though ill with cholera, whose medical work quickly won over Urmia's population of Moslems, Nestorians, and Jews. They began calling him *Hakim Sahib* ("Noble Doctor").

The clinic, along with the school, grew and thrived. Grant was soon treating thousands upon thousands of patients. The Boston board next sent out a printing press for the community, which produced the Lord's Prayer and the Book of Psalms in Syriac (the Nestorian tongue similar to the Aramaic spoken by Jesus).

The toil and abysmal conditions took their toll, however. Judith Grant and two of her children died of disease, as did all four of the Perkins children. In addition, Justin's wife, Charlotte, developed epilepsy. The Mission Board's reaction was simply to dispatch more missionaries to Urmia. It wasn't long before new American missions opened in nearby Mosul (now in northern Iraq) and at Ashitha (near the current Turkish-Iraqi border).

This was American frontiersmanship at its bravest and most extreme, thoroughly deserving of mention in our schoolbooks, even if current political correctness precludes the addition of more White Anglo-Saxon Protestant heroes. Back in America in 1835, the Illinois of young Abraham Lincoln had only three years earlier subdued the local Indian tribes in the Black Hawk War and would not have a railroad for two decades yet; Nebraska and Wisconsin had only a handful of tiny, fortified towns in the wilderness; the first white settlers were just filtering into Oregon's Willamette Valley; and Oklahoma was still an Indian-inhabited terra incognita. Yet here were two American couples, the Justin Perkinses and the

Asahel Grants, establishing a settlement by a mountain lake in Iran, near Armenia, Kurdistan, and Azerbaijan, a region that in the 1990s would still—in the words of Judith Grant in an 1835 letter home—be among the world's most "dreadfully wicked." As eccentric as this whole enterprise may have been, it was early proof that America's much-trumpeted isolationism was tempered by an optimism and dynamism that knew no territorial bounds.

Of the Nestorians in Urmia, there turned out to be only six hundred, compared with two thousand Jews and over twenty-seven thousand Moslems. Though the Nestorian community, as well as elements of the Jewish and Moslem ones, became loyal friends and defenders of the missionaries on account of the humanitarian help they provided, the missionaries converted only a handful to Protestantism.

But more significantly, by setting up schools and medical clinics in remote areas where governmental services had never existed, the Congregationalists were, in essence, administering America's first foreign aid program. And by identifying with and learning the languages of the region they served in, the Congregationalists were starting to become more like romantic explorers and Peace Corps workers than real missionaries. Asahel Grant, for instance, after establishing his clinic in Urmia, set out on foot to make an ethnographic study of the Kurdish mountains on the excuse that he might find some Nestorians to convert.

But it was in Beirut, Syria's small but fast-developing port city, walled in by the cedar-clad mountains of the Lebanon range, where the true personality of the American missionary community in the Middle East was to take firm hold.

When in November 1823 the first Americans arrived in Beirut harbor and a suave and worldly wise British consul, Peter Abbott, rescued the bewildered Massachusetts newcomers—Mr. and Mrs. William Goodell and Mr. and Mrs. Isaac Bird—from the devious clutches of a hookah-smoking Turkish governor and invited them to stay at his home until they could find suitable lodgings, a pattern was established. Though the American Revolution had occurred only four decades previously and the War of 1812 had ended only eight years earlier, in 1815, with hatreds still raw, in the hostile foreign environment of the Middle East, the New England Congregationalists found themselves becoming natural and immediate allies of the British.*

Not only were the British the only ones other than the Americans who spoke English, they were also Protestants, who had recently been dispatching missionaries of their own to the Middle East. And having been already established in the Orient, they were able to lead the American neophytes by the hand. For many years thereafter, the official protector and representative of the American missionaries in Syria was the British consul.

Values, too, propelled the Americans into the British camp. Given their missionary calling and their own recent experience in freeing themselves from a foreign tyranny, the Americans quickly came to sympathize with the local Arab population in its survival struggle against the Ottoman sultanate. And the British, who were also enlightened rivals of the Turks, did so, too.†

Besides an affinity for the British, the American Protestants were developing a loyalty for the place: Beirut and "the Lebanon"; that is, Lebanon as a distinct region of Syria, not as a country. From the standpoint of Boston and the nearby Andover Theological Seminary, Jerusalem may have loomed as the most glorious of postings. But in reality, Jerusalem was a cold and stony Turkish provincial rat hole, while Beirut was a modernizing harbor town with a gem-like climate and lovely, European-like mountain scenery. As the Goodells and the Birds were joined by Eli Smith and others in the late 1820s, Beirut started to take on the role of a real expatriate community, however tiny, rather than a mission outpost like Jerusalem or Urmia. By the time Smith returned to Beirut after his near-fatal foray with Otis Dwight into Iran (and a trip back to the East Coast to marry), he was in every way returning "home."

Smith's bride, Sarah Huntington, was, like Smith himself, from a prominent Connecticut family. Sarah's grandfather had helped found the Boston Mission Board. Once in Beirut this New England aristocrat became an avid Anglophile. The site of "English noblemen" in chapel made her realize that only America's "best"-bred citizens belonged on display in Syria. "The plain, independent manners of some of our good republican

---

* Goodell and Bird, the first two Americans in Beirut, had the usual Protestant missionary educations. Goodell was a graduate of Dartmouth and the Andover seminary, Bird of Yale and Andover.

† Syria got a brief respite from Turkish rule in 1833 when Mohammed Ali's Egyptian forces occupied Syria. The period of Egyptian control, which lasted until 1841, saw a more enlightened administration in Beirut that improved public security and made it easier for the first missionaries to settle in.

citizens, would be offensive to foreign taste," Sarah wrote. The New England religious gentry in Beirut displayed a remarkable proclivity for looking up to the British, particularly the fantastic kind. For example, it became a badge of honor for an American in 1830s Beirut to be granted an audience with the Mad Nun of Lebanon, Lady Hester Stanhope, the daughter of an earl who had survived on her own with the Bedouin and now occupied a ruined castle above Sidon, studying magic and astrology.

After Sarah set up house for him in Beirut, Eli Smith promptly got back to his Arabic studies, which he continued full-time for the next twenty-three years, until he died in 1857. He interspersed this activity with methodical travels throughout Syria and Palestine. Smith's mastery of Arabic was so complete that by the time of his death he was a good way through the first-ever translation of the Protestant Bible from English to Arabic.* Smith also compiled an encyclopedic list of Syrian towns and villages that formed the basis of geographic knowledge for later Middle East specialists. With Eli Smith, the meaning of what a missionary was began to change from a proselytizer and woefully ill-prepared traveler and explorer to a rarefied Orientalist and scholar-educator who defined himself through an exotic culture and sensuous Arabic calligraphy.

The missionaries were slowly but surely adapting to their environment. Jonas King, a Williams College graduate, prayed in his heart for a deliverance from the despotic Islamic rule of the Turks but wore a turban and grew a beard in order to more easily socialize with the Arabs. Yet while the missionaries were able to work out a modus vivendi with the local Moslem Arabs, their relations with the Eastern Christians went from bad to worse.

On account of trying to convert some Christians to Protestantism, William Goodell and Isaac Bird were each declared persona non grata among the Greek Orthodox and the Maronites. It was the Maronites that particularly irritated the missionaries. In the Protestants' eyes, Greek Orthodoxy was the idolatrous and corrupt East, pure and simple. But because the issue with the Maronites was more complex, the hatred dug deeper roots.

Named after a fifth-century hermit saint, Maron, the Maronites originated in north central Syria, near the town of Hama, as a renegade offshoot from the traditional Christianity of the Byzantine Empire, which was Greek Orthodoxy. When the Moslem Arabs invaded in the seventh cen-

---

* A fellow Beirut missionary, Dr. Cornelius Van Dyck, completed the translation.

tury, the Maronites welcomed them and eventually adopted Arabic as the language of their liturgy, which they use to this day. It remains unclear exactly when and why the Maronites migrated from northern Syria into the mountains north and northeast of Beirut. As a small sect surrounded by enemies, they survived by making deals with whoever had the power at the moment. Though claiming religious seniority over the Church in Rome, the Maronites sent congratulations to the Pope and joined with the Crusaders the moment that the First Crusade conquered Jerusalem. When Crusader strength ebbed, the Maronites switched allegiance to the Egyptian Mamluks, who soon drove out the Crusaders. As Mamluk dominance in the Middle East weakened, the Maronites resumed ties with the Catholic Church on the eve of the Ottoman Turkish invasion, thus assuring themselves a protective alliance with France, a powerful Catholic nation. Tough mountaineers, the Maronites were in every way the ultimate survivors. Moreover, it was about this time that they began developing their own nationalist ideology. Unlike the other inhabitants of Syria, the Maronites, in a political sense at least, were already on their way to becoming a modern people. And because the Protestant missionaries were obviously not a political power to be taken seriously, the Maronites never treated them with the elegant and polite deference that the Moslem Arabs did.

French Catholic missionaries had been in Syria, working with the Maronites for 150 years before the New England Protestants arrived. It was thus not surprising that the French government and the Maronite hierarchy reacted angrily to attempts by both the British and the Americans to proselytize among Maronite villagers. Tensions worsened in 1840 when Mohammed Ali's Egyptian troops began withdrawing from Syria. Because the Maronites had, in their typical manner, ingratiated themselves with the Egyptian soldiery during its brief occupation, they were now in an exposed position. The returning Turks gave military support to the Maronites' principal enemy, the Druze, a heretical Moslem sect that also lived in the Lebanese mountains. The French reacted to the Turkish provocation by increasing their support for the Maronites. This caused the British, and to some extent the American missionaries, to support the Druze. Thus, for the Protestant missionaries both the Maronites and their French protectors had become "the enemy."

By the middle of the nineteenth century, the New England Protestants in Beirut had battled disease and death—albeit on a smaller scale than their brethren in Iran—and taken on a variety of attitudes and prejudices, all for the sake of converting some thirty local Syrians to Protestantism. But character is destiny, and the character of one man, a Vermonter, soon to arrive in Beirut, would pull together the disparate and superficial strands of missionary good deeds in Syria and give them a dynamic direction, thus affecting American politics in the region through the end of the twentieth century. That man was Daniel Bliss.

Chapter 2

The Finest Site in All Beirut

If there is such a thing as the archetypal early American Protestant, it was Daniel Bliss—a Congregationalist whose family had come over from England a few years after the Pilgrims did, who grew up in a lonely farmhouse in Vermont's Champlain Valley in much the same way that Abraham Lincoln had grown up a few years earlier in Indiana, who as a thirteen-year-old boy migrated to Ohio by covered wagon and by boat on the Erie Canal, and who came back east to study Latin, Greek, and theology at Amherst College.

Bliss, like so many Americans who settled in Beirut, had a kind of idealized childhood; that is not to say an easy one, but the kind blessed with beautiful memories yet of the prerequisite strictness and hardship that breeds iron character and good manners. "The most vivid 'scenes of my childhood' are the cold spring near the tall balsam tree; the gathering of beechnuts and butternuts in the autumn; checkerberries, blueberries, blackberries, strawberries, raspberries, in their season," writes Bliss in his *Reminiscences*. Little Daniel prepared for the winter by storing potatoes and making apple cider. He rode the horse while ploughing, carried the water from the spring, and brought wood to the stove. Like Lincoln, Bliss as a young boy experienced the death of his mother. It was from his mother that he learned the love of Scriptures, which he would frequently quote and whose lessons he would frequently apply to the situation in Lebanon.

31

Bliss craved education every bit as much as Lincoln had. While a teenager, he admits to weeping "like a baby" when his father and older brother
refused him permission to attend a boys' academy in Austinburg, Ohio. He
soon located a school on his own, then found work as a farmhand nearby
so he could pay the fees. Later, Bliss bounced around the Lake Erie region,
knocking on farmhouse doors in search of any available opportunity that
might result in a chance to return to school. He worked as a tanner and a
tree grafter in order to finance his studies at another academy, in Kingsville,
not far from Austinburg in northeastern Ohio (by this time—1846—Bliss
was already twenty-three). At Kingsville Academy his talent was spotted
immediately, and the principal asked him to be a pupil teacher. Now nearly
twenty-six, Bliss was finally able to return to New England to enter Amherst.

Amherst, like many other prestige schools in nineteenth-century New
England, functioned as a small and intimate institution—it had fewer than
a dozen professors—whose main purpose was to prepare its students for
"civilizing and evangelizing the world." Given his ambition, plus the wan-
derlust he evinced as a youth in Ohio, it seemed ordained that Bliss would
gravitate toward mission work abroad.

Bliss stood out at Amherst as he did at Kingsville. In a commencement
address he called for permanent "agitation" in religion and politics, since
there would be "no finality this side of the gates of the New Jerusalem"
until enlightenment and "liberty like day breaks" out everywhere in the
world.

For Bliss the word *Protestant* meant what it was originally supposed to:
someone in protest against a calcified religious and moral order. Protestant
religious idealism, invigorated by political activism and intensified by intellectual introspection, dominated the atmosphere at Amherst and also at
Bliss's next stop, the Andover Theological Seminary. Bliss was taught by
the husband of Harriet Beecher Stowe, the author of *Uncle Tom's Cabin.*
The woman Bliss married, Abby Wood, had been a close friend of Emily
Dickinson. The thirty-five-year-old man who sailed out of Boston harbor
in December 1855 with a bride of under three weeks, bound for Syria, was
thus the quintessential Protestant missionary.

Daniel Bliss not only had the right background but, more important, he
was a self-starter and a bit of an outsider, who rose to the top of his class at
the best of New England schools. Because of his own life course of success
through hardship, Bliss was a man without doubts, devoted to the twin

American revolutionary ideals of progress and human perfectibility. He was absolutely convinced that exposure to the right values and the right education was all that was required to steer even the most intractable of peoples and cultures toward the New Jerusalem, as he put it in his Amherst commencement speech.

Bliss's face reflected it all. It was a visage straight out of a Grant Wood painting, harsh and angular, the clear New England eyes radiating a dead certainty and belief leavened by an attitude of benevolent superiority.

Bliss's first mission station in Syria was at Abeih, high in the mountains above Beirut; his second was a few miles north in Suq al-Gharb. At Abeih, on account of its rarified climate and European-style beauty, Bliss learned to love the Lebanon. In Suq al-Gharb, he acquired a distaste of the Greek Orthodox and the Maronite Christians, whom the "agitator" Bliss immediately recognized as the very incarnations of a calcified religious and social order. Not only did the Greek Orthodox monks dissuade the local children from attending Bliss's mission school, but they soon managed to close it down. In his *Reminiscences,* Bliss cites the example of one student who braved the taunts of the monks to come to his school. This boy eventually became a physician as well as a court judge. If Bliss needed any proof of the power of Western education in the corrupt Levant, it was the determination of that boy. For Bliss the boyhood pain of once being deprived of the benefit of schooling was still fresh, and so he could intuit the intensity with which some of the Arab children craved it.

During the outbreak of fighting in 1860 between the Maronites and the Druze, Bliss learned another thing: a distrust of statecraft, even the British or American variety. While Bliss labored to rescue a group of Christian civilians caught in the middle of hostilities, the British consul refused assistance, as it might complicate Britain's relations with the Druze and the Moslems. Missionaries should be a force apart, Bliss thought, rather than be tainted by the cynical demands of international politics.

But apart to do what? Merely to proselytize? Or to dole out charity here and there after a massacre or an outbreak of plague? No, the results of such activities in Syria had proved to be far too meager to have any permanent effect. The missionaries required a larger role than that. And it was clear to Bliss, as it was to William Thomson, Isaac Bird, and others, that Western education was their most potent weapon.

By 1860 the American missionaries were operating thirty-three schools in Syria. Because the missionaries' ultimate aim was to "civilize" Syrian society, after many discussions and discarded ideas they realized that what they needed was a nondenominational college, open to all races, and run on New England's best standards, which should have a dynamic effect on the direction of Syrian culture. This was a goal that could only be achieved by integrating the college with the local environment, something the British and French schools had not done.

To do this, Arabic, naturally, rather than English would have to be the language of instruction. The Boston Mission Board had always emphasized the importance of Arabic in its battle to win Middle Eastern converts. Still, the decision to instruct Arabs in their own language was especially brave, and not just because of the inherent difficulty of the enterprise. While the Jesuits were able to draw large numbers of students to the French Catholic schools due to the Lebanese desire to learn a European language, the Boston Board, backed by Bliss, did not succumb to the temptation to compete with the Jesuits by offering English at the American schools. The New England missionaries were willing to sacrifice what little clout they had in Syria for the sake of influencing the values of Syrian society. They knew that by teaching in English they would only create an elite stratum of Arabs, divorced from their own people, many of whom would end up emigrating to America or England.

Stephen Penrose, a leading American educator in Beirut, writes that his missionary forebears had "no desire, as others had, to 'Frankify' the natives for imperialistic purposes, and realizing the untold wealth of the rapidly vanishing Arab culture," decided "to make use of it."

The Protestants' choice of Arabic as the language of their new college, though it would turn out to be ill-fated, was symptomatic of their never-ending struggle to convert Syrian society from *within,* as partners, rather than as self-declared outsiders like the French or British. While the French and British in Syria chose to compete and position themselves on a political level, the Americans concentrated on the social and educational level. This would eventually earn the Americans the love and respect of the Arabs. In *The Arab Awakening,* the seminal work of Arab nationalism published in 1938, George Antonius, the book's Christian Arab author, writes:

"The educational activities of the American missionaries in that early period had, among many virtues, one outstanding merit: they gave the pride of place to Arabic, and, once they had committed themselves to teaching in it, put their shoulders with vigour to the task of providing an adequate literature. In that, they were the pioneers ... the intellectual effervescence which marked the first stirrings of the Arab revival owes most to their labours."

The missionaries' altruism had other repercussions, too. It ripened their hostility, strengthened by an assumption of moral superiority, toward the French and the heavily Francophone Maronites. Years later, Margaret McGilvary, the secretary of the Beirut chapter of the American Red Cross, would fume that while the Americans in Syria operated "from purely humanitarian motives," French priests were "agents of political propaganda." And it deepened the alienation of American expatriates in Beirut toward the realpolitik of British diplomacy and also toward the diplomacy of their own country, which, occupied as it was with a Civil War between North and South, completely failed to see the moral issues at stake in the Middle East.

This sense of being alone, of carving out America's destiny on truly holy ground, with neither the help nor the hindrance of the American government, was added psychological fuel to the numerous practical reasons for mastering Arabic—for becoming Arabists, in other words. As Stephen Penrose observes, the missionaries "themselves learned Arabic and taught, preached, wrote or translated articles and books in Arabic."

December 3, 1866, was the end of one era for Americans in the Middle East and the beginning of another. On that day the Syrian Protestant College in Beirut officially opened with sixteen students and Daniel Bliss as the college's first president.* A Congregationalist minister, the Reverend David Stuart Dodge, became the president of its board of trustees (which included Reverend Dodge's brother, William Earl Dodge). The American community in Beirut was now no longer centered around a diverse group of missionaries but around a college.

Initially the Syrian Protestant College consisted of only a few rooms in a few nondescript buildings. Meanwhile Bliss and the Dodge brothers searched all over the Beirut area for a permanent campus. Finally, after a year of looking, they found "the finest site in all Beirut if not in all Syria,"

---

* Three years earlier, in 1863, a former member of the Mission Board opened Robert College in Constantinople (now Istanbul). In 1865 the United Presbyterian Church of America opened Assiut College in central Egypt. But the influence of both those colleges on the American-Arab relationship was marginal.

which they secured with a five thousand dollar down payment. The site lay, fatefully, in the Moslem part of the city, on a hill with a sweeping view of the Mediterranean and St. George's Bay, by the spot where the Christian saint was said to have slain the evil dragon.

On December 7, 1871, Bliss and the Dodge brothers laid the cornerstone of College Hall. The few words he uttered before the small gathering would henceforth become enshrined in Arabist lore, gaining in power as the decades rolled on. And no wonder, for on that day Bliss articulated a vision of the Syrian Protestant College that not only represented a summation of the egalitarian spirit of the Great Awakening but was also to be a forerunner of Wilsonian internationalism:

"This College is for all conditions and classes of men without regard to colour, nationality, race or religion. A man white, black or yellow, Christian, Jew, Mohammedan or heathen, may enter and enjoy all the advantages of this institution for three, four, or eight years; and go out believing in one God, or in many Gods, or in no God. But it will be impossible for any one to continue with us long without knowing what we believe to be the truth and our reasons for that belief."

In other words, though the missionaries were finally willing to concede failure at converting the Jews, the Moslems, and the Eastern Christians to Protestantism, they were nevertheless determined to have victory on the secular battlefield by instilling in the Syrians the Protestant values of democracy, hard work, and free intellectual inquiry.

It turned out, after seventeen years of trying, that teaching exclusively in Arabic proved impractical, mainly due to the impossibility of obtaining up-to-date textbooks in the language. Though English henceforth became the principal language of instruction, Arabic courses remained part of the curriculum, nurturing the Syrian Protestant College's democratic and nationalist personality, whose consequences would be apparent in the following century.

Bliss understood that in the East "memory was usually well developed"—in fact too well developed—but abstract reasoning was not. Filling the students' heads with facts was not what the Arabs needed. The college's success or failure could rest only on its ability to teach its students how to organize and interpret facts. There was no real method for doing this, Bliss knew, except by forcing students to think aloud in class while pointing out their inconsistencies and encouraging free discussion on every issue. Bliss, writes Stephen Penrose, "had a rare ability to reach his pupils' minds—those typical Oriental minds which think in pictures and parables. . . . He was a past master at the apt illustration, the telling example, the story with its own moral. His was the teaching method of Jesus."

Progress was, of course, in this regard difficult to measure. Asking himself in 1912, "Who made the College?" Bliss said, "The answer might be the same as Topsy, in *Uncle Tom's Cabin,* made when asked, 'Who made you, Topsy?' She said, 'Nobody, I jist growed.' "

The Syrian Protestant College, Daniel Bliss's brainchild, was probably the most inspired idea in the history of foreign aid. Not only was it a quintessential cottage industry project for filtering Western values into the Arab world over time, but it also provided a permanent aesthetic monument to America in the region, a monument that posed no threat to anyone else's sovereignty. In fact, the school became an agent for the promotion of Arab sovereignty. Explains David Stuart Dodge, the great-great-grandnephew and namesake of the first president of the college's board of trustees:

"The College fostered an atmosphere of free thought and free discussion which helped give birth to Arab nationalism, and allowed Arab nationalism to develop. You could almost say that Arab nationalism grew up out of the College."

Woodrow Wilson was an eighteen-year-old freshman at Davidson College in North Carolina in 1874 when faculty and students hoisted the bell to the college tower in Beirut, but the most appealing symbol for his internationalist dream of self-determination, rising out of the ashes of a dying colonialist order, was already in place.

That same year, a rural school run by French Jesuits moved to Beirut and was renamed the Jesuit College. Later it became the French University of Saint Joseph. After World War I the Syrian Protestant College would change its name to the American University of Beirut, becoming popularly known as AUB. Over the decades the rivalry between Saint Joseph and AUB got so intense that the two institutions would emerge as symbols for two polar-opposite Lebanons: Saint Joseph emblemizing the intellectual and ideological heart of a Lebanon that saw itself as French, Maronite, Christian, pro-Israeli, and Western, a Lebanon that claimed descent from ancient Phoenicia and looked down upon—spat upon even—the Arab Moslem masses; AUB, on the other hand, became the heart of an Arab nationalist awakening that viewed Lebanon as an integral element of Syria and the wider Arab world, a world for whom the State of Israel was a provocative remnant of British colonialism, just as Maronite-dominated Lebanon was a remnant of French colonialism.

In addition to the French and the Americans, the British, the Russians, the Germans, the Spanish, and the Italians all had their schools and concomitant influences upon rival sectors of the Syrian population (the British schools upon the Druze, the Russians upon the Greek Orthodox, and so on). Thus, the foreigners, while bringing western values to the Arabs—especially the values of modern nationalism—were at the same time, paradoxically, reinforcing deep ethnic and political divisions within Syrian society that were to prevent the region of Syria from ever truly becoming the modern nation of Syria. Bliss's AUB, despite its considerable achievements, was about to be swept up in a large historical drama whose story line the missionaries were, tragically, never quite able to discern.

In 1903 Daniel Bliss, now in his eighties, handed over the presidency of the Syrian Protestant College to his son, Howard Sweetser Bliss, a Congregationalist minister born at his father's mission post of Suq al-Gharb and educated, like his father, at Amherst. Also like his father, before returning to the Syria of his birth, Howard Bliss got a taste of the American frontier by teaching for two years in Topeka, Kansas, in the early 1880s.

In 1910 Howard Bliss escorted two strapping twin brothers, Bayard and Cleveland Dodge, on their first visit to Beirut. Great-grandsons of one of the original members of the college's board of trustees, the Dodge boys—each six feet tall, slender, and handsome, with light blue eyes—had just graduated from Princeton University and were on a world tour when Howard Bliss went to Egypt to fetch them.

Bayard Dodge's daughter, Grace Dodge, "can vividly imagine" her "father's first sight of Beirut as he stood in the ship's prow which sliced through the Delft-blue sea. . . . He would have swept by the coast of ancient Canaan to Phoenicia, passing Jaffa, Caesarea, Tyre, and Sidon. At last his eyes would have caught sight of the yellow ribbons of beaches and the lighthouse on Beirut's point. . . . As they slowed down near the harbor, Howard Bliss would have pointed out the campus, its tawny buildings set like cameos in pools of greenery, balanced by spires of dark cypress trees and the angular tower of College Hall."

How idyllic and hopeful the world, and especially the Middle East, must have looked at that sunny moment for the Bliss and Dodge families and all the other Americans in Araby! The gruff utterances of a German Kaiser, the buildup of armies across northern Europe, and Austria's recent annexation of Bosnia must have appeared to the American community in Beirut as mere disconnected happenings, belonging to a colder and gloomier clime, obscured by distance and uncertain significance. Even the Young Turk Revolution of two years earlier still held out the hope of a democratized Ottoman Empire, whereby subject peoples like the Arabs could peacefully aspire to self-rule.

"These were years of great optimism among the missionaries, who hopefully interpreted scattered evidence to mean that they were at last breaking through the barriers of Islamic society to reach a wider Moslem audience," observes John A. DeNovo, one of a handful of scholars dealing with Americans in the turn-of-the-century Middle East. "Certainly many missionaries rhapsodized [that] a new day was dawning," DeNovo adds, as they anticipated the "evangelization" of the region to American Protestant values.

The missionaries could think this because it was they—more than the Europeans or even the Syrians themselves—who were a guiding, behind-the-scenes force in the development of vital Syrian institutions. The first Arabic printing press in Syria was the press that American missionaries brought to Beirut from Malta in 1834, utilizing a printing font developed by Eli Smith that was known in Syria as American Arabic. The first nationalist Arab cultural group, the Syrian Society of Arts and Sciences, established in 1847, was a joint venture of Syrians and early American missionary-Arabists such as Eli Smith and Cornelius van Dyck. Ibrahim Yazeji, the son of one of the society's founders, wrote what is considered to be the first Arab nationalist verse, *Arise ye Arabs, and awake!* Appearing in both Latin and Arabic letters, it adorns the cover page and inspired the title of Antonius's *The Arab Awakening*. Also, as Antonius points out, "'The first organised effort in the Arab national movement can be traced back to the year 1875 . . . when five young men who had been educated at the Syrian Protestant College in Bairut formed a secret society."

By 1900 the Americans were operating ninety-five schools in Syria and teaching five thousand three hundred students. Even more visible to the Syrian population at large were the contributions being made by Americans in the medical and relief spheres. In 1908, the year of the Young Turk Revolution, Dr. Mary Eddy, the daughter of a Williams College missionary, opened near Beirut the first tuberculosis clinic in the Ottoman Empire. Within a few years American missionaries were treating forty thousand patients annually at hospitals and clinics located throughout the Ottoman Empire. The Syrian Protestant College's medical school, opened in 1867, and its school of pharmacy, opened in 1871, were becoming the hub of a rudimentary rural extension service that brought medicine to Arab villages. Instead of the sixteen students when Daniel Bliss opened the college, there were now six hundred enrolled from throughout the Arab world. Moreover, an increasing percentage of the students were Moslems who remained in the Middle East to assume leadership roles in their own communities. This was especially true of the medical school graduates. Many a village doctor, often the fellow that the community most looked up to, owed his position to his American education, a mark of distinction that everyone in contact with him soon knew about. As the final embers of the nineteenth century were being extinguished, there were few pieces of foreign soil where Americans appeared to the local inhabitants so pure and perfect as they did in Syria.

The American presence in Turkey and western Iran was even larger. The enterprise that had begun in 1830 with the hazardous trek of Otis Dwight and Eli Smith to the mountain redoubt of the Nestorians had grown by 1900 to include 149 mission stations with 206 American missionaries and 1,150 native assistants, who were running nine hospitals and teaching in 542 schools that offered a secular education to nearly 17,000 Turkish, Iranian, Kurdish, Nestorian, Jewish, and other children. Prior to the outbreak of World War I, that figure would rise to over 25,000 students.* If a village youngster in eastern Anatolia or western Iran was lucky enough to get a decent education back then, it was very likely that his teachers were American Congregationalists or Presbyterians.

The American operation in Egypt, run by the Presbyterians, was almost as extensive as the one in Turkey and Iran, with the missionaries teaching fourteen thousand pupils in two hundred schools. When the Presbyterians opened the American girls school in Cairo in 1910, it was none other than former president Theodore Roosevelt—just emerged from the jungles of Africa on an elephant hunting expedition—who presided at the ribbon-cutting ceremony.

---

* These statistics do not include the Sunday schools and theological centers run by the missionaries. See DeNovo entry in the bibliography.

Then there was Arabia itself—that empty sandstone vastness that loomed everywhere south of the limestone plateau of Syria. In 1889 two missionaries supported by the Dutch Reformed Church, Samuel M. Zwemer and James Cantine, organized a mission for the entire Arabian Peninsula. Zwemer and Cantine were the true outriders of the Middle East missionary movement as it gathered steam at the turn of the century. Neither was a New England Wasp or Ivy Leaguer. Zwemer was a Dutch immigrant's son from Michigan. His father and oldest brother were circuit riders for the Dutch Reformed Church throughout the midwest and prairie states. Anther brother was a missionary pioneer in the Dakota territories. Zwemer claims his parents "consecrated me to foreign service before my birth." Both he and Cantine, from the Catskill Mountain region of New York, "were fully persuaded that God wanted us in Arabia." After a stint in Beirut to study Arabic, Zwemer and Cantine boarded a steamship for the Yemeni port of Aden, intent on spying out the land, with only the Book of Joshua for guidance. Upon entering Aden's walled native quarter, their "first real Arabian experience," according to Cantine, the two men immediately came down with malaria. Yet it was the words of the Hebrew God to Joshua that gave Cantine cause to think that their enterprise would eventually succeed: "Ye shall compass the city seven times . . . and the wall of the city shall fall down flat."*

Zwemer and Cantine were true believers, pioneers, and soldiers of God if ever any existed. For fifty years, from 1889 to the outbreak of World War II, these hearty preachers tramped back and forth, up and down the yawning trapezoidal shores of Arabia; from Mesopotamian Baghdad down the reedy, mosquitoed waters of the Tigris to Basra, the legendary home of Sinbad the Sailor at the top of the Arabian Gulf; from Kuwait and the other sheikhdoms down to Muscat; and around the Gulf of Oman to Aden near the mouth of the Red Sea. In these sweaty, lice-infested ports and villages Zwemer and Cantine passed their adult lives, with no servants or the other trappings of privilege that softened the existences of the New England Congregationalists and Presbyterians in the urbanized environments of Beirut and Cairo. The two spent many a night "reading Hebrew Scriptures in Arabic by the dim candlelight amidst all the baggage and beasts of an Oriental inn." Sleeping on barges, inhabiting dirt-floored rooms in mud-

---

* For Cantine, see Zwemer entry in the bibliography. They were co-authors of *The Golden Milestone*.

brick hovels, sick most of the time, the pair lived like down-and-out hippies, suffused with happiness for weeks on end whenever they managed to convince an Arab to accept a copy of Scripture and take it home with him. Through all the years of daily failure, the first chapter of Joshua always sustained them. "Every place that the sole of your foot shall tread upon, to you have I given it."

Zwemer and Cantine's born-again, evangelical spirit and the guiding influence of their New Jersey seminary professor, John Lansing, a scholar of both Hebrew and Arabic, nurtured the pair's philo-Semitism. Zwemer writes of his visits to Jewish synagogues in Yemen and of Moslem oppression of the Jews: "At Taiz, as everywhere in Yemen, the Jews have been so long oppressed and taxed that they have grown content under great injustice. Many of the old Moslem laws against infidels, as regards their being forbidden to ride or carry arms or wear fine clothes in public, were still rigorously enforced." Zwemer goes on to describe the beating of a Jew and the trouble he himself got into "by mentioning that Jesus Christ and Moses were *Jews*—which was an insult to them as God's prophets, the Arabs said. Anti-Semitism existed there, as in Palestine today." When the time would come for the two to write their memoirs of fifty years in Arabia, they would point out that the "idea of celebrating the end of a half-century goes back to Israel and the Book of Leviticus."

Like the Congregationalist and Presbyterian missionaries in Syria, Egypt, Turkey, and Iran, the Dutch Reformed Church would convert only a handful of Arabian Peninsula Moslems to Christ. Nevertheless, like the others, Zwemer and Cantine established a moral universe of a different sort. Besides a network of schools, the two men laid the groundwork for seven missionary hospitals that would one day treat 237,000 patients a year in the Arabian Gulf. The hospital where Bill Stoltzfus's son was born in Kuwait was part of the bounty of the Dutch Reformed Church.

Thus as Howard Bliss gave the Dodge boys their first view of Beirut and Lebanon, the situation could not have seemed more optimistic. American Protestants seemed to be on the verge of achieving the inverse of colonialism and imperialism: they had built a foundation of goodwill and influence on strategic foreign shores, solely through the doing of good works. Back in America Teddy Roosevelt was among the college's most enthusiastic supporters. And the missionaries were about to get another friend in the White House. In 1913 Woodrow Wilson became president—the son of a Presbyterian minister and an old pal of Cleveland Dodge, Sr., the twins' father, as well as an internationalist in favor of self-determination.

The time was not far off, the Americans in Syria felt, when the Arabs would wrest themselves from the clutches of the Turks and the designs of the French. It was even conceivable that one day in the future, public squares in Beirut and Damascus could be named after the likes of Daniel Bliss and Eli Smith, who had delivered Western teaching and Arabic language books, Arab nationalism even, to the Arabs. A synthesis, a cultural interpenetration was about to be consummated. As Howard Bliss himself would write, by sharing "with the people of the East the best things we have in the West," the West had "not a little to receive" too, including "the mystical element so prominent in Eastern religions."

Then at the end of June 1914, a Bosnian Serb protesting Austria's annexation of Bosnia assassinated the Habsburg Archduke Franz Ferdinand, and World War I started, bringing the problems and power relationships of the modern world, essentially for the first time, to the Holy Land. The first of two great cataclysms was about to break over the heads of these pioneer preachers, educators, and relief workers, changing the way the Arabs saw them, the way they saw the Arabs, and the way other Americans saw their own countrymen in the Middle East.

Chapter 3

Sand-Mad Englishmen

O n July 27, 1916, Daniel Bliss died. He was almost ninety-three years old. Less than seven weeks earlier, Hussein, the Grand Sherif of Mecca, stuck a rifle through a window in his house and fired on the nearby Turkish barracks. The famous Arab Revolt against the Ottoman Turks had begun.

While Bliss's family and friends were burying him in the Mission Cemetery in downtown Beirut, a twenty-seven-year-old Arabic scholar and graduate of Jesus College, Oxford, Thomas Edward Lawrence, assigned to British military intelligence in Cairo, was preparing to sail down the Red Sea to the Meccan port of Jidda in order to sound out Sherif Hussein and his sons about an alliance with the British, the aim of which was to drive the pro-German Turks from the Middle East.

Among the items in Lawrence's traveling gear was a two-volume set of *Travels in Arabia Deserta* by Charles M. Doughty, the only Briton ever to have penetrated to the interior of western Arabia where Lawrence was headed. Lawrence had recently purchased the books from Samuel Zwemer, the Dutch Reformed missionary, who was in Cairo for a rest from his own Arabian wanderings when he bumped into Lawrence. It was later reported that Lawrence learned the two volumes of Doughty by heart. Though no doubt an exaggeration, Lawrence himself always referred to the books as his bible for dealing with the Arabs.

Lawrence, of course, was destined to write a much more famous memoir, *Seven Pillars of Wisdom*. And there would soon be other books by other Britons in Arabia, people who may not have spoken Arabic or understood the Arabs any better than a Samuel Zwemer or an Eli Smith or a Daniel Bliss. But these Britons did write more cleverly and more elegantly about their experiences, and that would make all the difference. For it was not just a political upheaval that was about to overwhelm and transform the American expatriates in the Middle East, but a literary one, too.

Who were these romantic English travelers, whom T. E. Lawrence himself called "a band of wild men"? How did they find themselves in such a position of influence? And what, exactly, was their effect upon the Americans?

While the American missionaries Samuel Zwemer and James Cantine were passing out bibles in turn-of-the-century Arabia, Englishmen there were consolidating a regional power structure to guard the sea route to British India.

It had been Napoleon who first quickened Britain's interest in the Middle East by threatening to launch an attack on India from Egypt, which his forces occupied from 1798 to 1801. A hundred years later, when it was the Kaiser's turn to threaten India, Britain's hold on Arabia forced Wilhelm II to go through Turkey, by planning a German railway across Asia Minor to Baghdad. This strategic advantage, and the newly acquired need for oil, gave the British in Arabia the impetus to expand their influence northward into Syria and Mesopotamia.

Imperialism thus brought Englishmen to the Middle East, where they found a fabulous tableau of native culture that offered a respite from their own mechanistic existences in a society undergoing rapid industrialization. Observes the English writer, David Pryce-Jones, "The British imagination was captivated by its peculiar but deep-rooted trait that things different or picturesque should be preserved and cherished." In other words, the English mind can hold dear the beauty of a Bedouin encampment the way it could hold dear the beauty of a garden back home. And like the garden, which was regularly pruned, the detailed image of the tents and robed figures on the sand was to be refined and memorialized by descriptive writing.

The responsibilities of imperialism stimulated this activity. In order to rule over the natives, one had to understand them and their language. This process led to an appreciation of both. And since the other great powers—France, Germany, and Russia were competing with Britain for influence in this fabulous terrain, stealth was also required. That meant the ability to pass unnoticed among the natives, to act and look like them, in order to find out what was going on. The predilection of certain upper-class Englishmen toward eccentricity and playacting lent itself well to this endeavor. This is why Rudyard Kipling's *Kim,* a story about spying and going native in the Northwest Frontier of British India, is judged the supreme artistic achievement of imperialism.

No character in *Kim* so deftly captures the fantasies and eccentricities that imperialism encouraged as Lurgan Sahib, the sinister shopkeeper who could pass for Indian or several other oriental nationalities and from whom the fair-complexioned Irish boy Kim learns the secrets of the spy trade amid old books, Eastern carpets, devil masks, gilt Buddhas, Tibetan prayer wheels, and assorted other gongs and bric-a-brac. It is said that Lurgan and the other characters in *Kim* are all based in varying degrees on one man, that monument in the flesh to nineteenth-century British overseas conquest, Sir Richard Francis Burton.

"Darkly handsome," with "questing panther eyes . . . like a wild beast," and "the brow of a god and the jaw of a devil," Burton spoke twenty-nine languages plus an assortment of dialects. His ability to pass unnoticed as an Afghan in forbidden Mecca and as a Gypsy laborer in a work gang plying the Indus River earned Burton the nickname of the White Nigger.* Burton discovered the Indian sex manual, the *Kama Sutra.* He led the first European expedition into the heart of Africa to search for the sources of the Nile. He also explored the interior of Brazil, the forbidden city of Harar in Abyssinia, and the west coast of Africa. He translated *The Thousand and One Nights* from Arabic. Still, he was first and foremost a secret agent for the British crown, a vocation that permitted many of his other activities.

Throughout Burton's varied life Arabia and Islam remained his lodestars. However, in addition to Burton of Arabia, there was Burton of the Nile and indeed many other Burtons. That is principally why, though he is referred to as Britain's first and greatest Arabist, he was really neither. Burton was never obsessed with Arabs and Arabia to the exclusion of other terrains of the imagination. After visiting Mecca, he turned his attentions to Central Africa because Arabia now offered him "nothing except more

---

* See Rice's biography of Burton, listed in the bibliography.

discovery of deserts." Obsession with the Arabs, as we shall see, would become a defining Arabist trait.

In the Middle East, more than elsewhere in their empire, the British imagination and intelligence work spawned an intense fascination with archaeology, language, and tribal culture that had no precedent. There were several reasons for this phenomenon. Of all the pieces of Great Britain's worldwide imperial domain, the Middle East was geographically the closest and therefore the easiest to get to. Moreover, as the Palestinian scholar Edward W. Said points out in his study *Orientalism,* the "Islamic lands sit adjacent to and even on top of the Biblical lands. . . . Arabic and Hebrew are Semitic languages, and together they dispose and redispose of material that is urgently important to Christianity." This made Islam both a dangerous and a voluptuous "provocation" to the British (and to American missionaries too). It was Islam's usurpation of the Holy Land that had led to the Crusades. Moreover, Islam was familiar enough to be understood (unlike the religions of India or Africa) but still different enough to be bewitching. Islam was like an exotic woman, redolent of perfume, within breathing range of the British: meaning, she would have to be mastered.

And there was something indefinably else. Something about the desert, whose stark and cubistic monotony fostered annihilation and nihilism, as well as a cleanness and perfection. In the desert, there was no edifice or other evidence of man's vanity. Here amid the stifling sand was a garden where Innocence flowered, where everything remained exactly as it had been before the Fall. Part of what drew the biblical patriarchs and prophets into the wilderness would also draw men and women of less fixed principle, motivated more by aesthetics. These were the Arabists.

T. E. Lawrence provides the finest example of this. In *Seven Pillars of Wisdom,* he revels in a description of a clay ruin in northern Syria, where one room smelled of jasmine, another of violet, and a third of rose. But the room that particularly stirred Lawrence's Arab guide, and obviously Lawrence himself, was the room filled only with the "empty, eddyless wind of the desert," a smell "in which mankind had no share or part." That was the smell of nothing, the best smell of all.

While American Arabists were one day to fall under the spell of the books of Lawrence and other Britons, Lawrence, throughout his sojourn in the

Middle East, was under the spell of *Travels in Arabia Deserta:* a twelve-hundred-page account of a two-year odyssey, between 1876 and 1878, in what is today the northwestern part of Saudi Arabia, written by the Oxford don, Charles Montagu Doughty. This tome, which took Doughty a decade to write, is so powerful and all-engrossing in its effect and so completely defines the Arabs and the Middle Eastern desert that the book's influence on Arabist thought cannot be exaggerated.

Travels in Arabia Deserta makes Doughty, truly, Britain's first and greatest Arabist. Burton was sui generis. He was like a star exploding brilliantly everywhere at once, leaving only a black void in its wake. And Burton came along too early. When he died in 1890, the Turkish Empire in the Middle East still had another twenty-six years to run. But Doughty's book started a literary and psychological movement among Westerners drawn to the Arabs, which Burton's incognito journey to Mecca and Medina and his translation of *The Thousand and One Nights* did not. *Travels in Arabia Deserta,* more than Doughty himself, therefore becomes an important character in this story. Lawrence went so far as to refer to *Travels in Arabia Deserta* as, simply, *Doughty.*

Doughty's Arabia was the anvil and crucible through which the character of an Englishman might be tested and forged. It is a land of "cloud-like strange wasted ranges," "horrid sandstone desolation," "rhomboid masses," and repetitive "ghastly grinning" shapes. It is a universe of Old Testament cruelty, where thieves are slowly beaten to death, where dying men are stripped bare on the road before expending their last breath, where men march forth "in a purgatory of aching fatigue," where there is often nothing to eat but locusts and nothing to drink but water "full of swimming vermin." In the course of two years of wandering amid these vast lava fields and slag heaps offering not an inch of shade from the sun, Doughty is periodically robbed, left stranded without food or water, and threatened with death on an almost daily basis because of his refusal to deny his Christian religion and submit to Islam. Upon reaching the Turkish garrison town of Taif at the end of his ordeal, Doughty describes himself thus:

> The tunic was rent on my back, my mantle was old and torn; the hair was grown down under my kerchief to the shoulders, and the beard fallen and unkempt; I had bloodshot eyes, half blinded, and the scorched skin was cracked to the quick upon my face. A barber was sent for, and the bath made ready: and after a cup of tea, it cost the good colonel some pains to reduce me to the likeness of the civil multitude.

Doughty's criticism of the Arabs is scathing: "spotted guile is in their Asiatic hearts more than religion." In the 1880s he foresees that "the nations of Islam, of a barbarous fox-like understanding, and persuaded . . . that 'knowledge is only of the koran,' cannot now come upon any way that is good." As for the holy Moslem city of Mecca, Doughty wonders, "Why have they [our Christian governments] not occupied the direful city in the name of the health of nations . . . ?" From beginning till end, Doughty denounces the very notion of going native, warning that "the longer one lives in a fabulous . . . country, the weaker will become his judgment." For himself, he declares that "the sun made me an Arab, but never warped me to Orientalism." Lawrence notes that the book's strength lies in Doughty's briar-root English character, which was unyielding and uninfluenceable. Yet this is surely a romantic book, and Lawrence's whole attitude toward it, as revealed in an introduction he wrote for a 1921 reprint, is a romantic one.

Doughty describes his journey with the emotional detachment of a scientist. Armed with notebook and aneroid barometer, he wondrously recreates an entire environment: geological, linguistic, cultural, and psychological. He describes, for example, the beauty and practicalities of the moon over the desert, how young camels are named according to the number of their teeth, the various kinds of pumice, basalt, and other desert rock formations, and why the humanity of men's greetings in the wilderness become hypocritical once these same salutations are imported into the towns. Here, specifically, lies the romance; the desert, in all its awesome beauty, horror, and sameness, is completely conveyed. And what is more, it is conveyed in a sonorous voice that has recalled for many the cadences of the sixteenth-century Tyndale Bible.* What reader of Doughty, for instance, could forget his likening of the desert Semites "to a man sitting in a cloaca to the eyes, and whose brows touch heaven." Doughty even admitted that he had gone to Arabia partly "to redeem the English language from the slough into which it had fallen since the time of Spenser."

Thus, as it happened, the very intention of *Doughty* became subverted. The cold and analytical observer warning against identifying too closely with the environment was in time transformed into the sage and unflappable protagonist in an epic and timeless tale of Arabia. The abstract and dehumanizing landscape that had such a deleterious effect upon men's

---

* William Tyndale, the translator, was an English religious reformer executed for heresy.

characters had been turned for the first time ever by Doughty, into a literary landscape, making it, therefore, perversely appealing.

Lawrence himself suggested that the very hideousness of the physical and human terrain caused Doughty's Arabia to become a masochistic measure of manhood. Doughty, writes Lawrence, "had experienced it himself, the test of nomadism, that most deeply biting of all social disciplines, and for our sakes he strained all the more to paint it in its true colours, as a life too hard, too empty, too denying for all but the strongest and most determined men."* Lawrence, as he sailed down the Red Sea from Egypt to Jidda in the summer of 1916 with *Travels in Arabia Deserta* beside him, was determined to prove himself in Doughty country. And because of the nature of British imperialism in the Middle East at that moment, this private libidinal desire did not conflict with—rather it abetted—Lawrence's professional responsibilities.

Before he became known as Lawrence of Arabia, Thomas Edward Lawrence was known simply as Ned or "the little fellow," on account of his being only 5′ 5½″. But the little fellow had, according to Robert Graves, "great physical strength: he has been seen to raise up a rifle at arm's length, holding it by the barrel end, until it was parallel with the ground." Graves, one of Lawrence's biographers, remarked that "the upper part of his face [was] kindly, almost maternal; the lower part . . . severe, almost cruel." Perhaps the most perceptive description of this man, around whom so much controversy and legend swirls, came from a colleague in the British Arab Bureau, Harry St. John B. Philby, who labeled Lawrence as "that curious mingling of a woman's sensibility with the virility of the male."

That, in fact, was what made Lawrence, whatever else one may say about him, great. For this diminutive man, with small hands and feet, was able to survive a regimen as brutal as the one survived by Doughty and write about it with a sensitivity and attention to detail that captivated the post-World War I world, a world that craved an individualistic, sun-filled, and romantic commemoration of a war that had until then been defined by mass and impersonal death in the mud and freezing rain of Flanders field.

While Doughty's book became an obscure work known only to Arab

---

* See Lawrence's introduction in the Dover edition of Doughty's *Travels in Arabia Deserta*.

hands, Lawrence's *Seven Pillars of Wisdom* became one of the most widely read books in the English language, transmogrifying him—with the help of American publicist Lowell Thomas—into Lawrence of Arabia. Lawrence, of course, had an obvious advantage over Doughty, whose adventure in northwestern Arabia occurred during a period of relative political tranquility, with the sleepy Turk still firmly in command, though not for long. Lawrence's adventure, on the other hand, took place in the maelstrom of a war whose consequences are still being felt in the Middle East. This gives *Seven Pillars of Wisdom* an enduring relevance.

But Lawrence had another advantage too, a literary one. The English of Tyndale's Bible may have been fine for connoisseurs, but not for the general public. In truth, the most memorable passages in *Seven Pillars of Wisdom* are based on perceptions first realized by Doughty but translated by Lawrence into plainer, more pointed English for the common man of the day. Doughty's image of the desert Arab as a "man sitting in a cloaca to the eyes, and whose brows touch heaven"—an image that, according to Lawrence, "sums up in full measure their [the Arabs'] strength and weakness, and the strange contradictions of their thought"—was elaborated by Lawrence into perhaps the most famous Arabist analysis of the Arab mind, considered brilliant by some and racist by others:

> In the very outset, at the first meeting with them, was found a universal clearness or hardness of belief, almost mathematical in its limitation, and repellent in its unsympathetic form. . . . They were a people of primary colours, or rather of black and white, who saw the world always in contour. They were a dogmatic people, despising doubt, our modern crown of thorns. They did not understand our metaphysical difficulties, our introspective questionings. . . . They were at ease only in extremes. They inhabited superlatives by choice . . . they never compromised: they pursued the logic of several incompatible opinions to absurd ends, without perceiving the incongruity. . . . They steered their course between the idols of the tribe and of the cave.

While from the vantage point of the late twentieth-century, the Oxbridge English of *Seven Pillars of Wisdom* appears rich and magisterial, by the standards of Doughty, Lawrence's book was, to a significant degree, a souped-up and condensed version of *Travels in Arabia Deserta*. This, unfortunately, became a trend. British Arabism as a subculture has always been dominated by literature, and the literature has gone steadily downhill, becoming more personal, more psychosexual, and more romantic by generational stages. The "I" in *Doughty* is memorable on account of the strength of Doughty's own character, naturally emerging as he immovably chronicles every detail of the desert. But the "I" in *Seven Pillars of Wisdom*, as Professor Elie Kedourie rightly notes, "conforms to the canons of dramatic art: the small, accidental beginnings, the vision in the desert, the years of organising, contriving, fighting, willing and imposing mastery, culminating at last in the investment and capture of Damascus . . . as if this event were the preordained consummation through which all the past incidents of the desert war acquire their meaning and coherence."

The pattern is set at the very beginning with a dedicatory poem by Lawrence, presumably written for his Arab lover:

*I loved you, so I drew these tides of men into my hands
    and wrote my will across the sky in stars . . .*

What follows is the famous saga of how the fair-haired Lawrence (part Irish, just like Kipling's Kim) stripped himself of his British army khakis, donned not just the white robes but the psychological identity of a desert Arab, and, all alone, led these noble savages to victory over the Ottoman Turks.

Of course, Lawrence's Arabs never really liberated Damascus. The Allied regular armies, who did the real liberating, permitted the Arabs to march victoriously into the city as a sop to their pride. Lawrence virtually admits this in a letter to Robert Graves, remarking that the section on Damascus in *Seven Pillars of Wisdom* "is full of half-truth." And of course, the whole Arab Revolt, which Lawrence led, was "a side show of a side show" in World War I: the Middle Eastern theater was of far less significance than the European theater, and the Arab Revolt was a minor element in the Middle Eastern theater. It consisted of little more than Lawrence's guerrilla band blowing up Turkish railway track here and there, causing more inconvenience than destruction.

And then there is the famous incident at Deraa, south of Damascus, where Lawrence describes in meticulous and, one could say, loving detail, how he is physically degraded and then whipped by a Turkish Bey. More than a few have claimed that this never happened, that Lawrence fantasized the beating, just as he got carried away with life in the desert, where "Man in all things lived candidly with man," taking "savage pride in degrading the body . . . in any habit that promised physical pain or filth." While Doughty went into the desert as a scientific explorer, Lawrence—conflicted

by his homosexuality and the illegitimacy of his birth—went there in search
of a very peculiar form of emotional peace.

Nevertheless, at his funeral in 1935, Winston Churchill wept, saying
about Lawrence that "whatever our need we shall never see his like again."*
And Churchill was right. For despite Lawrence's personal failings, and
however exaggerated his role and that of *his* Arabs, Lawrence was a real-life
Kim, who acted out his fantasies while gathering valuable intelligence.
During his whole period in Arabia, Lawrence's official status was always
that of a political intelligence officer, who in the end did deliver the Arabs
to Great Britain.

Lawrence thought as an imperialist. He favored the Balfour Declaration
and the Zionist enterprise as a means to keep the French out of Palestine
and perhaps out of the rest of Syria. He championed ill-fated negotiations
between the Sherif of Mecca's son, the Emir Feisal, and Chaim Weizmann
(whom Lawrence genuinely admired). Lawrence's prejudices were impe-
rially motivated. He loathed Turks and Frenchmen, and he respected Jews.
"The sooner the Jews farm it [Palestine] the better," wrote Lawrence in a
letter home. In *Seven Pillars of Wisdom,* he notes that "only in . . . the
everlasting miracle of Jewry, had distant Semites kept some of their identity
and force" in the greater world.

Still, Lawrence's emotional commitment to the Arabs (who at that time
were principally in conflict, not with the Jews, but with the Turks, and
with the French over Syria) was so unqualified that at the Versailles peace
conference, where Lawrence was part of the British delegation, he dressed
up in full Arab regalia. As a secret agent Lawrence was credible. But how
did someone so obviously sentimental and self-dramatizing attain such a
high policy-making position?

The answer is that as important as the Middle East was in comparison,
say, to Africa and other imperial dominions, compared to Europe it was a
distant and mysterious realm for most high-ranking Britons. Back then,
the number of Britons with language skills and other kinds of area expertise
was so small that there was no distinction between scholar, diplomat, or
military intelligence agent. If one "had" Arabic, one could be all three
interchangeably. At Oxford Lawrence became a protégé of David George
Hogarth, a widely known archaeologist and Orientalist, fluent in Turkish
and Arabic, who had excellent contacts in the British imperial establish-

---

* Lawrence died in a motorcycle accident at the age of 46.

ment. Hogarth arranged for Lawrence to work on an archaeological dig at Carchemish, in the Turkish-Syrian border area. (Archaeological work had long been a traditional cover for intelligence work.) Then, after Hogarth became head of the Arab Bureau in Cairo when World War I began, he found Lawrence a place in military intelligence at the start of the Arab Revolt. By war's end Lawrence, having lived with and led a Bedouin army for two years, had acquired such contacts and expertise that he found himself advising Prime Minister Lloyd George. After all, how many men and women were there like Lawrence?

Several, actually. Lawrence's Arabs weren't the only Arabs in the desert. Lawrence went to Arabia to advise a specific ruler—Hussein, the Sherif of Mecca. Lawrence formed an especially close bond with one of the Sherif's sons, Feisal, and it was Feisal's Arab guerrillas that Lawrence came to lead. These fighters were all from the area of western and northwestern Arabia called the Hejaz, where the Moslem holy cities of Mecca and Medina were situated. While the Hejazis, and particularly the Sherif of Mecca's family, known as Hashemites, enjoyed enormous prestige throughout the Arab world (owing to their role as keepers of the Holy Places and their claim of direct descent from the Prophet Mohammed), the Hejaz did not, in the opinion of some, breed the best warriors or even the best Moslems. That distinction belonged to the tribesmen of central Arabia—the region known as Nejd. Here lived the Wahabis, the followers of Mohammed Ibn Abdul Wahab, an eighteenth-century fundamentalist who believed in a severe and aesthetic interpretation of the Koran. By the Wahabis' strict standards, the Hejazis were effeminate idol worshipers, tainted by their proximity to the Red Sea and its links to the outside world. The foremost tribal leader in Nejd Arabia was Abdul Aziz Ibn Saud.

On the eve of World War I, the British had a political agent attached to Ibn Saud's tribe, Captain William H. I. Shakespear. This Shakespear, distantly related to his namesake, the playwright, was an accomplished explorer and the first European to cross the width of the Arabian peninsula from Kuwait to Suez; quite a feat for those days. But Shakespear, unlike Lawrence, did not believe in dressing up like an Arab, and this cost him his life. During a battle in 1915 between Ibn Saud and the tribesmen of a rival, pro-Turkish Arab sheikh, Ibn Rashid, Shakespear's British uniform made an easy target for Ibn Rashid's shooters. Had Shakespear lived, it is likely that he, not Lawrence, would have led the Arab Revolt against the Turks, the Arabs in such a circumstance being those of Ibn Saud rather than those of Feisal.

Britain's replacement for Shakespear in Nejd Arabia was Harry St. John Bridger Philby; Jack Philby to his English colleagues. While Lawrence's principles often wavered between support for Britain's imperial interests and for what seemed to him Feisal's legitimate claims in Syria, Jack Philby suffered no such pangs of conscience over the issue of dual-loyalty. He always knew that his true allegiance lay with Ibn Saud and the Wahabis.

The English writer Robert Lacey describes Philby as "conceited, irascible, and thoroughly perverse." Jack Philby was, of course, the father of the British double agent, Kim Philby, who defected to the Soviet Union in 1963 while a high-ranking member of British intelligence. It is strange that with all the books written about Cold War spy operations, not one author has methodically addressed the tantalizing relationship between this father and son—both graduates of Trinity College, Cambridge, both spectacular traitors to their country—especially since Kim Philby's Arabist upbringing and subsequent journalistic career in the Middle East did not result in the same love for the Arabs his father had. Drunk one night in a Beirut bar, Kim Philby blurted: "The Arabs are the only people I know of who combine ignorance with arrogance." Although Kim Philby rejected his father and his father's Arabs, like many such sons he ended up replicating his father's conduct.

Jack Philby's career began near the turn of the century in India as a British colonial agent dealing with such mundane matters as tax collection and flood control in the Punjab. Philby quickly displayed a remarkable ability with languages and dialects, easily mastering Hindustani, Pushtu, Bengali, and other tongues. He was clearly happiest when immersing himself in any culture other than his own. When World War I began and Mesopotamia became a strategic battleground between Britain and the Turks, who had just aligned themselves with the Kaiser, Philby was one of several officers recruited to the British Mission in Basra, where he soon added Arabic to the list of languages in which he was fluent. Suddenly India was forgotten, and Philby became an addict of Arab tribal culture, spending long hours poring over tribal genealogies that he admitted had little to do with his work as a diplomat but were "merely a by-product of my linguistic studies." In Mesopotamia, though, Philby was just a small fish in a sizable pond of talented British officials. It was Shakespear's death that provided Philby the chance to "adopt" a major Arab leader.

That was what one did to make an impact. Lawrence had Feisal and the Hejazis, and now Philby would have Ibn Saud and the Wahabis. "Clientitis" was a flaw that began as a necessity in an age when Arab states did not officially exist and there was no formal mechanism for tribal leaders to make known their feelings except through sympathetic British officers whose career fortunes rose and fell in direct proportion to those of the particular tribesmen they were attached to. Moreover, with communications technology so primitive, a colonial official in World War I Arabia was on a much looser leash from his home office than a diplomat of today. He could go months with only his adopted tribesmen for company, and this fact made his overseas experience that much more intense. And the more intense the experience, the more intense the loyalty that developed from it.

Philby wasted no time ingratiating himself with Ibn Saud. Within a week after his November 1917 meeting with the swarthily handsome and tall Arabian sheikh outside Riyadh, Philby had a bitter row with Colonel R. E. A. Hamilton, the British agent for Sheikh Mubarak Sabah of Kuwait. Hamilton stalked off in disgust after Philby had suggested that Ibn Saud be allowed to take Kuwait away from the Sabah family.

There was little that was controlled or modest about Jack Philby. Even his friend and Arabist colleague Gertrude Bell thought him "too domineering and difficult." Philby soon appeared in full Arab dress, atop a camel, with Ibn Saud's Wahabi warriors, announcing himself as "the new star in the Arabian firmament." As he writes in his autobiography, *Arabian Days,* "I was able to add enormously to our existing knowledge of conditions in Arabia, and to start a new hare which has made me infamous ever since. I had the temerity to report . . . my conviction that Arabia's man of destiny was Abdel Aziz Ibn Saud and not Hussein Ibn Ali [the Sherif of Mecca]," the darling of both Lawrence and the British colonial establishment.

The argument of the Colonial Office, which nearly every Arabist save Philby subscribed to, was the following: when the Turks disappear from the scene, only the Hashemite family of the Sherif of Mecca—the direct descendants of Mohammed—would have the requisite political and religious prestige to rule stably in Arabia. But in 1925, Ibn Saud's forces swept westward out of central Arabia and overran Hejaz. The Sherif of Mecca went into exile. The holy cities of Mecca and Medina became part of a newly expanded kingdom to be known as Saudi Arabia. Jack Philby had proved all of his British colleagues wrong. To say it went to his head would be an understatement.

Philby emerged not only as King Ibn Saud's right-hand man—with whom Ibn Saud shared slave girls and held long discussions about the Koran—but also as the king's gatekeeper. Every Westerner who came to Riyadh over the next quarter century seeking oil concessions and other commercial contracts had to do business with Jack Philby. Beyond the accumulation of wealth that this activity allowed, Philby took advantage of his privileged position to travel constantly in regions where foreigners were not normally permitted and to produce over a dozen books about Arabian culture, ethnography, and geographic exploration that to this day rank as classics, invaluable for area specialists. In 1929, after ceasing his official relationship with the British government, Philby moved into Beit Bagh-dadi, a sandcastle-type pile with overhanging balconies by the Red Sea in Jidda, where he lived with a "growing collection of Arabian baboons," who occupied cages on the terrace.

In 1930 Philby was ready to take the final step in what had been a gradual process of slipping off one personality and acquiring a new one, or as he put it, "to go all the way with the Arabs." In early August, dressed as an Arab sheikh, he signed a document signifying his "acceptance of Islam" and adopted the name Abdullah, "slave of God." Abdullah Philby then journeyed for the first time to Mecca, to preform the rite of *Umra,* the lesser pilgrimage, where he circumambulated the *Ka'aba,* the holy black stone, with his coreligionists. "It was an impressive and even awe-inspiring experience . . . all very familiar and intimate, like something vaguely re-membered from a forgotten past," Philby wrote. Now he was able to par-ticipate fully in the revelry of the king's court. The following year Ibn Saud gave Philby a slave girl, Mariam, as a gift in honor of his conversion.

But it would be his friend and hero Ibn Saud who was to betray Philby. As the power of Nazism increased in Europe, Philby despaired of a coming war against Adolf Hitler and began whispering in the king's ear that it would not be such a bad thing if England were to conclude a peace, more or less, on Hitler's terms. Still, the king was careful to play both sides, and in addition to making arms deals with Nazi Germany and fascist Italy, he tipped off the British to an antiwar speaking tour that Philby was about to embark on in 1940. As soon as Philby left Saudi Arabia, he was arrested by British intelligence.

Later Philby was allowed back into the kingdom and again found solace in Wahabism, whose strict adherence to ancient principles shielded him from a fast-changing world. In 1955, at the age of sixty-nine, the dream ended for Abdullah Philby. After he had complained to the new king, Saud, about "appalling corruption" in the kingdom, Saud called Philby into his presence and publicly spat upon him. He then ordered Philby into exile in Lebanon.

When Philby first arrived in Mesopotamia from India in 1916, he quickly struck up a friendship with Gertrude Bell. As Philby put it, "We discovered a common interest in such abstruse things as the genealogies of Arab tribes and potentates." Miss Bell had the classic good looks of an English aristocrat. She was tall and lanky with sharp features and silvery hair. By the time Philby met her, she spoke Arabic with barely the trace of an accent. Officially, Miss Bell was a political officer for the British Arab Bureau in Mesopotamia. In truth, she was emerging as the dominant force behind a new state being assembled from a rump of Kurdistan and the Sunni and Shiite areas of Mesopotamia. It came to be known as Iraq, the Arabic word for "venerable" and "well-rooted."

Gertrude Margaret Lowthian Bell grew up in the English countryside surrounded by wealth and influence. In 1888, by the age of twenty, having graduated from Oxford early, she was fluent in Latin, French, and German and had hobnobbed with British diplomats in Istanbul, where she developed an intense curiosity and longing for what lay on the other side of the Bosphorus, in Asia. In the early 1890s we find her in Teheran, mastering Persian and publishing her Persian travel diaries as well as translating the works of Hafiz, a fourteenth-century Persian poet. From Persia it was a logical next step to venture into Syria and Mesopotamia to master Arabic. In Syria, Mesopotamia, and northern Arabia in the early years of the twentieth century, Miss Bell discovered "the irresistible chivalry of the desert," becoming a full-time traveler and amateur archaeologist who insisted on taking her finest cutlery and evening dresses on all of her wanderings.* By the outbreak of World War I, she had authored a half-dozen books about Oriental exploration, including *The Desert and the Sown,* unsurpassed to

---

* See Winstone's biography of Bell in the bibliography.

this day as a traveler's account of the towns and peoples of Syria. But her love was not only for the desert. She developed a passionate illicit relationship with a married officer of the Royal Welsh Fusiliers, Charles H. Montagu Doughty-Wylie, the nephew and namesake of the author of *Travels in Arabia Deserta*. In April 1915 Lieutenant Colonel Doughty-Wylie was leading a force of Australian ANZACS on a final, heroic charge at Gallipoli when the Turks shot him through the head. Thereafter, Miss Bell channeled all her passions to her adopted people, the Arabs of Mesopotamia, and to the new nation of Iraq she was bent on midwifing for them. They became the family that she never had throughout her adult life.

When war broke out, the British authorities requested Miss Bell's linguistic and ethnographic knowledge for the purposes of diplomacy and intelligence work. Following Doughty-Wylie's death, she became obsessed. Between bouts of malaria, editing a local Arabic newspaper, and writing diplomatic and intelligence reports in the drizzly and mud-soaked winters of Baghdad in the last years of World War I, Miss Bell produced a plethora of ethnographic studies on such topics as Shiite traditions and English transliterations of Arabic. She also entertained, though even her fellow Britons, according to her biographer, criticized her for "status snobbery" and her "dislike" of Arab women unless they were, in Miss Bell's own words, "of the better classes."

Uniting all of these activities was her dream of a future Iraq, which, in her words, would be "a center of civilization and prosperity. . . . When we had made Mesopotamia a model Arab state there was not an Arab of Syria and Palestine who wouldn't want to be part of it." British officials were then in the process of jerry-building this state that, for their strategic purposes, would contain both the oil fields of southern Kurdistan and an outlet on the Arabian Gulf to buttress India. Though this meant uniting several forlorn Ottoman provinces which had little in common with each other except hatred going back to antiquity, it did not in the least bother Miss Bell. Iraq became her experimental plaything. Later, after Iraq was a reality, she admitted that while the arguments she had used in her cables to promote the creation of Iraq to the London Foreign Office were political and economic ones, the "keynote" for Iraq in her eyes had always been "*romance*" (her emphasis).

Miss Bell never did go back to England. She stayed on in Baghdad, alone, becoming the director of antiquities for the new Iraqi state and a confidant of the new King Feisal.* Gradually, as Feisal's rule grew more devious and corrupt, her conversations with the Iraqi king took on the air of a disillusioned admirer toward a former hero:

> I began by asking him (King Feisal) whether he believed in my personal sincerity and devotion to him. He said he could not doubt it. . . . I said in that case I could speak with perfect freedom and that I was extremely unhappy. I had formed a beautiful and gracious snow image to which I had given allegiance and I saw it melting before my eyes.

(Miss Bell's tendency for hyperbole and supplication would bear an eerie resemblance to conversations in 1990 between another Iraqi ruler and another Western diplomat who also spent much of her life in the Arab world.)

Declaring, "I am an Iraqi," Miss Bell later assumed the title of *Umm al-Mumminin* ("Mother of the Faithful"). The Iraqis also called her *Al Khatun*, "Lady of the Court." She died and was buried in Baghdad in 1926, two days before her fifty-eighth birthday, after taking a fatal dose of barbiturates. But the story of British misdeeds in Iraq continues through World War II and will be picked up later in this narrative.

Though there were others, Lawrence, Philby, and Miss Bell are the most memorable of the World War I British scholars-cum-imperial agents who had the financial means to travel at leisure and who fascinated each other as much as they were each fascinated by the Arabs. But their influence was not just a matter of acquired cultural knowledge. The key to their power was their ability as writers. Before the books of Lawrence, Philby, Miss Bell, and other Britons influenced generations of America's own Arabists, their diplomatic cables influenced policymakers in London. H. V. F. Winstone, Miss Bell's biographer, observes that she and Lawrence "provided wartime reading which has certainly never been equalled in intelligence documents" and which Foreign Office officials fought to get their hands on. But while brilliant wordsmiths, they were neither clear nor consistent in their views. And this, according to Winstone, was the British Arabists'

---

* This was the same Feisal who had fought with Lawrence against the Turks and was rewarded by Britain with the throne of Iraq, after the French colonial authorities forced him out of Syria.

tragic flaw: "They were over-articulate . . . the world might have been a more peaceful place for future generations if they and their like had not been such 'able and persuasive' writers."

Lawrence, in particular, was a person overly influenced by setting. Among Arabs in the desert, he became pro-Arab; in Whitehall he was pro-Empire; with Chaim Weizmann he felt himself an avid Zionist. Thus, to read the wartime missives of Lawrence, Miss Bell, and others—where, for instance, on one occasion Arab nationalism is proscribed, while on another Iraqi and Syrian self-rule is cheered on—is to find oneself in a muddle. And a muddle is what the British, with assistance from the French, made of the post-Ottoman Middle East.

The made-in-Britain Kingdom of Iraq came as a sequel to the British-French truncation of Syria, which undid much of what the American missionaries had been trying to accomplish at the Syrian Protestant College and other schools.

The Arab Revolt, which Lawrence wound up leading, was merely the military corollary to the American missionary-led Arab Awakening that took place in the cities of Syria in the nineteenth century with the formation of secret cultural and political societies. This legacy made Damascus a hotbed of pan-Arab sentiment by the end of World War I: "the throbbing heart of Arabism," as it came to be known. To quite a few missionaries Syria seemed finally poised to follow in America's footsteps as an independent, united, liberal, and democratic society. But this *borderless* Arab nationalism that the missionaries supported was sympathized with only by the majority Sunni Moslems, who lived mainly along the south-north axis of Damascus, Homs, and Hama. Otherwise, Syria was a hodgepodge of every warring sect, religion, and tribal interest in the Middle East, a term that Miss Bell, in a lucid moment early in her career (before the death of her beloved Doughty-Wylie), said "is merely a geographical term corresponding to no national sentiment in the breasts of the inhabitants."

Besides the Maronites and the Greek Orthodox, there were pockets of Armenians, Jews, and Circassians and the various inbred, heretical sects left behind by the tide of Shia Islam that had swept westward from Iran into Syria and receded a thousand years before: the Druze, the Isma'ilis, and the Alawites. As was earlier stated, the various groups of foreign missionaries—working at cross-purposes through their educational institutions that each catered to a specific sect—were in fact dividing the populace while striving to unite it. When Allied forces, helped by Lawrence's Arab guerrillas, overran Damascus in 1917 and ejected the Ottoman Turks, the British and French proceeded to harden these ethnic divisions into stone, while cutting off the majority Sunni Arabs from each other.

The formerly Ottoman territory of Syria was divided into six different zones. A sliver of northern Syria got amalgamated into a new Turkish state that Mustafa Kemal Ataturk was beginning to carve out of the rump of the old Ottoman Sultanate. Southern Syria was split into two new British territories: a mandate in Palestine (which the British promised twice over, to the Jews and to the Arabs) and a kingdom in Transjordan ruled by one of Lawrence's World War I allies, Abdullah, the brother of Feisal and the son of the Sherif of Mecca. Eastern Syria became part of British Iraq. The French got the hole in the map that was left, which they in turn subdivided by proclaiming an enlarged Lebanese state, known as *Grand Liban,* in order to strengthen their friends, the Maronite Christians, who would now have a large Sunni Moslem population under their thumb.

Meanwhile, Lawrence's World War I comrade-in-arms Feisal the son of the Sherif of Mecca, required a reward for his services; so the British set him up as the king of Syria in 1920. His kingdom lasted a hundred days until the French forced him out. Lawrence and company then proceeded to dump Feisal on Iraq, where his Hashemites from western Arabia enjoyed no local support. An enthusiastic Miss Bell then volunteered to help build a power base for him.

But while the British and French were drawing lines on the map and switching rulers around like chess pieces, the American Protestants were suffering alongside the victims of famine and massacre, which were the mundane consequences of World War I. While Britons like Lawrence, Philby, and Miss Bell were falling in love with the Arabs, the missionaries were learning—more than they ever had before—what it actually felt like to *be* an Arab. It is in the hospices and soup kitchens of World War I Syria, far from the tents of kings and the power centers of London, where we now rejoin the American Protestants.

Chapter 4

End of the Rainbow

When it comes to World War I in the Middle East, modern memory registers the photos of desert camel corps and Lawrence dressed in flowing robes and Arabian headgear. But it doesn't register the haunted faces of three hundred thousand Syrians, many of them children, who starved to death in one of the great forgotten famines of the century.

Bayard Dodge, the Princeton graduate who along with his twin brother had first seen Beirut from the prow of a boat in 1910, returned to the city to study Arabic and to aid in the wartime relief effort. Independently wealthy, he personally supported a network of soup kitchens that fed twelve thousand Arabs in the mountains above Beirut. "The air was filled with the sound of bells tolling for funerals and children crying for a crust to eat," writes Dodge. "Clothing was so scarce that the Americans turned their suits and the women used curtains to make dresses. . . . Kerosene was so scarce that the people used olive oil lamps, as their Phoenician forefathers had done. . . . People fought over garbage pails, and many mountain houses became vacant, their occupants dead and their doors used to make coffins."*

It was the civilian population of Syria that paid the price for the British-

---

* See bibliography for Grace Dodge Guthrie's *Legacy to Lebanon*, in which excerpts appear from her father's writings.

led Arab Revolt in the Hejaz. They became virtual prisoners of the Turks, who imposed a blockade on food supplies into Syria. The American expatriates, whose government under Woodrow Wilson was pro-British and was soon to declare war against Turkey and the other Central Powers, were prisoners, too, constantly threatened by the Turks with deportation in sealed boxcars into the desert interior, while they tried to do what they could to alleviate the suffering they saw all around them.

Howard Bliss, the president of the Syrian Protestant College—an Arabist every bit as knowledgeable as Lawrence or Bell—spent the war years in a never-ending struggle just to find food for the native members of his staff and to keep the college from sinking into debt from the expense of humanitarian work. Not a day went by between 1914 and 1918 when the Turkish police did not threaten or in other ways make trouble for the college president.

In addition to the relief activities of the Syrian Protestant College, American missionaries in Syria spent sixteen million dollars, an enormous sum for that time, on feeding and clothing needy Arabs. Churchgoers back in America raised the money. Still, with war raging across the face of Europe on a scale never before witnessed and with America about to join in the fray, the public back home was not concentrating on the tragedy in Syria. American expatriates, therefore, like the British political officers assigned to the Arabian tribal leaders, felt themselves alone with a very intense, personal experience. It was as though they were entrusted with a great and heart-rending secret about which few in the outside world were even interested in hearing. This frustrated the Americans in Syria and also deepened their passion for their adopted land. They knew, explains Margaret McGilvary, a Beirut missionary, that "there has been a political result from the American work" which nobody in Washington "even attempted to follow up . . . the truth is that America has given so generously and with so little concern as to whether there would be any returns that the Syrian nation has come to recognize in America her one disinterested friend." Grace Dodge, Bayard Dodge's daughter, recalls that for the Arabs of Syria, America represented the "end of the rainbow."

The American expatriates, for their part, McGilvary writes, drew inspiration from the Arabs' "nationalist tendency," which the expatriates saw as a "hopeful sign that Syria possesses latent elements of strength, and a spark of divine fire." At war's end Bliss sailed off to the Versailles peace conference to give an impassioned speech in favor of the Arab nationalist cause. Unlike Lawrence and the other Britons, the belief of Bliss and the American expatriates in Arab nationalism was total, since they did not represent an imperial establishment with ulterior motives in the region. (The government in Washington, as we will see, did not become truly aware of the Middle East until after World War II.)

While the American community in Syria was united in support of the Arab nationalist cause, four years of brutal Turkish occupation aggravated a growing divergence between the staff of the Syrian Protestant College and the other American missionaries. In *The Dawn of a New Era in Syria*, McGilvary, who worked for the Beirut chapter of the Red Cross, accused Bliss and his coworkers "of ingratiating themselves with" the Turks. And Stephen Penrose, in his history of the college, *That They May Have Life*, wrote how Bliss "maintained a consistent attitude of loyalty to the existing Ottoman Government, 'believing that it had a right to demand from the College, as an institution affiliated with the educational system of the Empire, ready obedience. . . .' " After the war, when McGilvary learned the full extent of Bliss's travails, she apologized. But the conundrum of how to get along with the powers that be in Beirut was to plague the college from then on. Taking a perfect moral position would have meant closure of the school long ago, while dealing with the Ottoman soldiery (and later with the French imperialists and after that with the Palestinian guerrilla movement, as the college was repeatedly forced to do), exposed the administration and teachers to charges of *localitis*. In 1991 William Burns, a key Middle East aide to Secretary of State James Baker, explained this perennial Arabist dilemma: "The Arab world can be a nasty place. But the Arabist is someone who doesn't have the luxury to theorize from the sidelines. He must actually live there and work solo with this intractable reality."

Besides the devastation in Europe, the Syrian famine had to compete for attention with another great human catastrophe, the extermination of in excess of a million Armenians by the Turkish authorities in the eastern part of Asia Minor in 1915. It was American missionaries in the region who, through veiled references in their letters home, first told the world about what was happening.

William Nesbitt Chambers, a Princeton graduate and Congregationalist missionary, recalled "that it was an interesting experience to argue with a mob intent on blood and loot, blood lust in the eye." Chambers described how, as he tried to rescue an Armenian pastor, one member of a Turkish mob shot the pastor in the back while another thrust a dagger into the pastor's side. "He fell from my arms lifeless."

This and similar experiences caused Chambers to write an impassioned letter to another Princeton man, President Woodrow Wilson. "One could wish that such a power as the United States should become so strong on land and sea that such a government as Turkey would never dare to commit such a horrible crime." What was required, advised the white-bearded Congregationalist, was a U.S. foreign policy that brandished "a great gun" in "one hand" and "the Gospel in the other."

And indeed, flushed from victory over Germany and angered by British-French machinations, which Wilson described as "the whole disgusting scramble" for Syria, the American president was eager to heed the advice of Chambers and the other missionaries and to join them in remaking the world in America's image. Thus, in 1919, Wilson dispatched Henry C. King, president of Oberlin College in Ohio, and Charles R. Crane, a Chicago millionaire whose father had made a fortune in the manufacture of toilet bowl fittings, to Syria to uncover the political wishes of the local inhabitants. The King-Crane Commission, as it is remembered in history, was in reality the Crane-King commission, with Charles Crane as the overriding factor and driving force and Henry King as the associate.

In the person of Charles Crane, a type of American somewhat different from the missionary invades the Arab world: the gong-and-trinket man. So while the King-Crane Commission is a mere footnote to history, Charles Crane is worth describing.

In a 1950s essay, Christopher Rand, a star foreign correspondent for the old *New York Herald Tribune*, wrote that a "main vice" of his journalistic colleagues "is the tendency" to view the Orient "as merely an interesting background for one's personality . . . a form of egotism—perhaps 'romanticism' " that goes back to the "bower birds . . . men who collected Asiatic trinkets as adornments to their nests—who cluttered their studies with gongs, idols, war clubs, model junks, lacquerware, chinaware and other bric-a-brac. I associate this vogue with Theodore Roosevelt's contemporaries."

Roosevelt, of course, was the originator of the species, bustling home from the African jungles and other exotic places with specimens for his library, the Harvard Club, and the Smithsonian Institution. In Roosevelt's day anyone wealthy enough to travel to such mysterious climes and bring back objects was automatically judged an expert on them. "It was a cheap way of buying a diploma," wrote Rand. "The spell could even be inherited. . . . Franklin Roosevelt thought he knew a good deal about China because an ancestor of his . . . had once done some trading around Hong Kong. It all went with the Golden Age when we had a small, parochial upper class whose members could approach anyone or anything through personal friendship and correct introductions."

Charles Crane was part of that Golden Age. With money inherited from his father, he traveled constantly without the need to work or earn a living. He called his observations on foreign cultures "studies," even though he had no formal training and spoke no foreign language.

Russia was the first object of Crane's fascination. "Friendly gatherings around a samovar gave him so much pleasure that he carried the custom back home with him and took a large measure of pride . . . in serving guests tea from his samovar," wrote Leo J. Bocage, a biographer of Crane. For Crane the major attraction of Russia soon became its churches, gleaming with gold and icons. It wasn't long before collecting Russian religious specimens became a hobby.

As a wealthy American in turn-of-the-century Russia, Crane met Czar Nicholas II and became an emotional supporter of Russia in its war against Japan and its propaganda war against charges of anti-Semitism (Crane considered reports of Cossack-led pogroms against the Jews a nuisance). Crane's cultural passions led him to love and hate easily. His enmity toward Japan for its victory over Russia encouraged his fascination with China, a traditional enemy of Japan. Several visits to China, where he picked up "a few expressions" in the language, established Crane as an authority on the country, leading President William Howard Taft to appoint him America's minister to China.

In those days an ambassadorship to China was considered little more than "an interesting background for one's personality," a way for a gentleman to pass the time. One knowledgeable friend advised Crane "to take up photography as a hobby" because there was little else to do in Peking. But Crane did not, in the end, go to China. President Taft rescinded the appointment partly because, even by the standards of 1909, the State Department considered Crane a dilettante and busybody and partly because Taft himself was shocked by Crane's open hatred of "Japs and Jews," leading the President to conclude that Crane's would have been "a dangerous appointment."

Crane was irrepressible, though. He became the biggest contributor to

Woodrow Wilson's 1912 presidential campaign and eventually became a close friend. (He would be a pallbearer at Wilson's funeral.) Wilson sought Crane's opinions on Russia, which the latter freely gave. The Russians, Crane felt, were a people "entirely free from brutality," and the Bolsheviks were a group not to be taken seriously. Because "they [American Jews] controlled the press and organs of public expression," America was not getting an accurate picture of what was occurring in Russia. In fact, as his biographer makes clear, Crane was never really interested in Russian politics, which for him were a tiresome diversion from his fascination with the Russian Orthodox Church and its artifacts, which he collected.

Wilson offered Crane the ambassadorship to Russia, which Crane turned down. Crane's interest shifted to the plight of the Armenians in Asia Minor, where he became involved with Cleveland Dodge, Sr., Bayard's father, and the Congregationalist missionaries in financing and organizing relief efforts. Crane also joined the board of trustees of Robert College in Constantinople (Istanbul), a school founded by missionaries a few years before the Syrian Protestant College. Crane immersed himself in the Middle East about the same time that, in the midst of great human suffering, British and French intrigue was beginning to undermine President Wilson's goal of self-determination for the Syrians and others. It was natural for Crane to adopt the missionaries' hatred of the British and French and, concomitantly, to develop a loving passion for the Arabs and their culture, of the kind he had developed for the Russians and the Chinese.

In 1919 Wilson dispatched Crane as head of an American commission to document what the people of Syria themselves wanted out of the peace. In a letter to his wife, Cornelia, Crane remarked that there was "a clear feeling" among the Arabs he had interviewed "of the menace about the modern, pushy Jew." Indeed, the King-Crane Commission recommended that the idea of a Jewish homeland be abandoned, that Jewish immigration be severely restricted, and that Palestine be made part of a Syrian state to be governed under an American or British mandate. But in no case should the French be included. Crane, like Chambers, the missionary in Asia Minor, argued for America not to retreat into isolation, but to use its power for the good of the indigenous inhabitants of the Middle East.

That did not occur. France and England divided Syria, and America, which had sent its youth to fight and die in Europe only to see a cynical peace emerge from the victory, found its initial experience as world police-

man bitterly unpleasant and quickly withdrew into itself again, the roar of
the Atlantic immediately silencing the freedom cries in the Middle East
and the Balkans which had briefly engaged the public's attention. This left
Crane and his missionary friends extremely frustrated. But Crane's fascination with the Arabs would not leave him. He began a personal study of
Moslem culture that took him eventually to India and Java, where he continued to collect artifacts for his home. His sympathies were no secret. In
Damascus he once attracted a crowd of several hundred cheering
Arabs, who invited him into their mosque, shouting "Long live independent Syria!" Framed by a black homburg and a white goatee, Crane's benevolent and aloof visage continued to be seen about the Middle East. He
became one of the first Americans to penetrate the walls of medieval Sana'a,
in Yemen, where, as a friend of the Imam, he agreed to finance the first
explorations for oil. Crane also worked with Jack Philby to help King Ibn
Saud, another friend of Crane's, to start oil explorations in Saudi Arabia.

"The most pronounced prejudice which dominated his [Crane's] thinking during [his] later years was his unbridled dislike of Jews," writes his
biographer. Crane "tried . . . to persuade the recently elected President,
Franklin D. Roosevelt, to shun the counsels of Felix Frankfurter and to
avoid appointing other Jews to government posts." Crane "envisioned a
world-wide attempt on the part of the Jews to stamp out all religious life
and felt that only a coalition of Moslems and Roman Catholics would be
strong enough to defeat such designs." In 1933 Crane actually proposed to
Haj Amin Husseini, the Grand Mufti of Jerusalem, that the Mufti open
talks with the Vatican to plan an anti-Jewish campaign.

This led Crane to develop an intense admiration for Adolf Hitler, whose
Germany Crane considered "the real political bulwark of Christian culture." A private audience with the Führer, like the one many years before
with the czar, proved easy for a man of Crane's beliefs and financial means
to arrange. Hitler and Crane found that they shared a hatred of the British
and French as well as of the Jews. Crane's last letter about world affairs
before he died was to Hitler, blaming the Jews for the problems in the
Middle East. Crane, at this time, despite his hatred of the Bolsheviks,
voiced support for Stalin's anti-Jewish purges in Soviet Russia.

A reader might notice that George Antonius's *The Arab Awakening* is
dedicated "To Charles R. Crane, aptly nicknamed Harun al-Rashid affectionately." Crane was a beloved figure among a coterie of Arab intellectuals, both Christian and Moslem, that included Antonius, who occasionally

served as Crane's translator. In fact, Antonius's labors on *The Arab Awakening*, a book which brought for the first time the modern Arab point of view to the Western literary world, were financed by Crane. Crane's great deception, albeit unintended, was to give Antonius and other Arab intellectuals the mistaken impression that most Americans shared his romantic love of the Arabs, coupled with an equally passionate hatred of the Jews. This was certainly not the case among Americans at large, nor was it quite the case among the American expatriate community in Syria.

The pressures of running the Syrian Protestant College under Turkish occupation and afterwards arguing the Arabs' case at the Versailles peace conference proved too much for Howard Bliss, who in 1919 came back to America for medical treatment. Shortly afterward, Bliss died of tuberculosis in Saranac Lake, New York, surrounded by family members. A few hours before his death, Bliss spoke at length in Arabic, the language of the Syria of his birth. He had heard Arabic first as a baby, because his father, Daniel Bliss, had spoken it to his mother in order to learn the language more rapidly.

That same year, the Syrian Protestant College officially changed its name to the American University of Beirut (AUB). After a two-year-search the university's board appointed thirty-four-year-old Bayard Dodge as the first president of the newly christened institution. To an outsider the choice would certainly appear nepotistic. Bayard Dodge was not only the great-nephew of the first president of the college's board of trustees but also the husband of Mary Bliss, who was the daughter of Howard Bliss and the granddaughter of Daniel Bliss. In fact, the choice was both natural and inspired. By 1922 young Dodge was already a hardened veteran of Beirut, with proven leadership abilities in wartime relief work. Moreover, though this would only become clear over time, he was a genius at the art of unspoken compromise and "getting along" in political conditions that were not necessarily friendly to Americans. With Bayard Dodge, the AUB and American missionary-Arabism reach their last stage of pure-hearted accomplishment, before the record becomes clouded by the moral and political challenges that accompanied the birth of Israel.

Unlike his father's friend, Charles Crane, Bayard Dodge was not an extreme offshoot or caricature. With Dodge the various bloodlines of the profession merge, for the most part healthily. He was well born and brought up, perfectly educated at Princeton and Union Theological Seminary, bursting with practical religious idealism, scholarly, and in love with the intellectual and physical aesthetics of Arab culture. Dodge's attitude toward AUB's role in post–World War I Syria is summed up in these words, which are not too different in meaning from those spoken by Daniel Bliss in 1871, when the cornerstone of College Hall was laid:

> We long to teach our students to regard the ideals of their parents with sympathy; to honor all who are charged with the official duties of their sects; to respect the motives for their ceremonies and rites; and to revere places of long-accustomed worship. At the same time we strive to vitalize it all in the light of our modern life, that religion may become something practical . . . a real force in the regeneration of the human soul, and in the reconstruction of our war-ridden world.*

But above all, Dodge felt AUB "forms a link between East and West: a channel for the exchange of ideas between the two. . . ." Dodge was certainly willing to concede a degree of parity between what America had achieved morally and spiritually for its people and what the Arabs of Syria had. Because Syria, despite its truncation by British and French imperialists, was still a place of possibilities, where a reasonable person could be optimistic about its future, Dodge's intellectual orientation was nothing to raise an eyebrow over then.

Under Bayard Dodge AUB became, in a political-cultural sense, more influential than either the British or French governments in the Middle East; a startling achievement considering that the American government had recently retreated from the region and had no real presence to speak of. Then again, AUB in the years between World War I and World War II was forging an identity separate from its American origins.

One of Dodge's first acts as university president was to order teaching appointments made without regard to nationality, which brought many Arab and European professors into the AUB community. While the French University of Saint Joseph in Christian East Beirut was staffed by Jesuits who instilled in their students an allegiance to France, Dodge's AUB in Moslem West Beirut was distinctly internationalist in tone and sympathetic to Arab nationalism.†

---

* See Penrose entry in the bibliography. Quotation is from Penrose's *That They May Have Life.*

† This was at a time when the American International College in Smyrna found the nationalist climate in Mustafa Kemal Ataturk's Turkish Republic so "inhospitable" that it sold its properties and became affiliated with AUB. Smyrna had been the Pearl of the Levant, whose Greek population had provided succor

AUB's interwar growth was spurred by grants from the Rockefeller Foundation, arranged by Dodge, that began flowing in 1924. Much of the money went to the medical faculties, which produced still more of what the Arab man in the street needed most: trained doctors. AUB's reputation in the region rose accordingly. "The influence of the university percolated throughout the Levant and surrounding countries. The friendly attitude of upper-class Arabs testified to the increasing respect the university commanded," writes scholar John DeNovo. In Syria, Iraq, Transjordan, Palestine, Saudi Arabia, the Sudan, and elsewhere in the Arab world, governments sent their brightest students to AUB, which supplied these nascent countries with pharmacists, nurses, accountants, secretaries, and other professionals, as well as with doctors. Throughout the Middle East, AUB under the leadership of Bayard Dodge became affectionately known as "the great Oriental queen." Harvard's distinguished historian George Sarton called the university "a nursery of good men and a perpetual foundation of good will."*

To what extent this was true may be gauged by a poignant memory of a trip to a soccer match in Egypt in 1930, described by Stephen Penrose in *That They May Have Life*. The AUB soccer team went by train to Cairo. Because spring vacation had already commenced, some students were picked up in Palestine. "Had the car been stood on end it might have passed for the Tower of Babel. Arabic, English, Hebrew and French were the principal tongues audible. . . . Moving south from Haifa one worry was on everyone's mind: 'Will Cohen make the train?' Cohen was the star right wing who lived in Tel Aviv some distance from the line. He might miss the connection. . . . So when the train pulled into the junction, the tension was considerable. But Cohen was there and the shout which went up must have startled the good citizens of Lydda. He was lifted on shoulders and passed through the window of the train. . . . Joy was unconfined, for now the American University of Beirut might beat the Egyptians. . . .

"At the time," Penrose continues, "Arab-Jewish feelings ran high . . . but to the Arab students Cohen was not a Jew—he was a team member . . . before the train reached Kantara East, he was to be seen lying in the

---

for the first American missionaries, Pliny Fisk and Levi Parsons. Unfavorably disposed toward Turkey because of the recent Armenian holocaust and the actions of Turkish authorities in Syria during World War I, Americans in Beirut never dreamed that Arab nationalism, put into practice, might prove just as difficult to get along with as Turkish nationalism was already proving to be.

* See Penrose entry in the bibliography.

aisle with his head on the lap of a Moslem sheikh (another student). . . ."

Jews were not uncommon at AUB in the 1930s. The Tel Aviv symphony performed occasionally on campus. The music in daily chapel, remembered so vividly from boyhood by U.S. diplomat Talcott Seelye, was led by the organ playing of a Russian Jew. The Israeli orange industry, even, owes its beginnings in prestate Palestine to help from AUB graduates. Though the growth of the Hebrew University in Jerusalem meant competition for AUB, it was thought of as a friendlier kind than that represented by the French University of Saint Joseph, on the other side of town.

Here were the values of America, and particularly those of New England, in all their glory. Back across the Atlantic in the Massachusetts town of Deerfield, another Congregationalist, Frank L. Boyden, was teaching his boys at Deerfield Academy that the school they belonged to was something greater than themselves; something that constituted a spiritual and ethical universe on a higher level than that of the society at large, and which could therefore be a uniting force for all of them. What Frank Boyden, one of the great headmasters in history, was doing at Deerfield, Bayard Dodge was doing in his own way at AUB. Cohen could lie in the lap of a Moslem sheikh because each knew that as AUB students they were members of a real elite. If one could pick a moment of apotheosis for the missionaries, of achievement impossible to quantify, it might be the one on the train to Egypt with Jews and Moslems united on account of a very American-style team spirit, despite the specter of intercommunal rioting only a few miles away.

AUB's growth and achievements did not come easily. The post–World War I treaties that gave France the mandate over Syria was the worst possible news for an American expatriate community that had been openly and enthusiastically anti-French. Having already watched in horror their beloved Syria chopped up into six pieces by the British and French, the Americans now had to stand by as the French deviously and brutally began to subdivide the remaining rump.

The French, fresh from colonizing experiences in Algeria and Tunisia that had kindled their hostility to Sunni Arab nationalism, deliberately incited sectarian loyalties in order to suppress the rise of such nationalism in Syria. They granted autonomous status to the mountain strongholds of Jabal Druze and Latakia, home to the Druze and Alawites, making these heretical Moslems answerable only to the mandate authorities and not to the Sunni Arabs in Damascus. In addition, the Alawites, the Druze, and the other minorities all paid comparably lower taxes than the majority Sunnis while getting larger development subsidies from the French government. The French also encouraged the recruitment of minorities into their occupation force, the Troupes Speciales du Levant. The majority Sunni Arabs, for their part, were severely repressed. The Damascus region was treated as occupied territory, patrolled by tough Senegalese troops, with help from the Alawites, Druze, and Kurds. The Sunnis, and their American friends, too, in a sense, believed themselves to be still under occupation, as if the Turks had never left, especially since the French had made a separate state out of the Lebanon region, an action that further subdivided Syria and put still more power into the hands of the pro-French and anti-Protestant Maronites.

Dodge wisely turned the other cheek to all of this. Enroute to Beirut to officially assume the presidency of AUB, he made a long stop in Paris to bring his French up to the level of his Arabic. For almost two decades thereafter, until the outbreak of World War II, Dodge courted French officialdom as his late father-in-law, Howard Bliss, had tried to court the Ottoman Turks. In 1940, when the Vichy French took over Syria, Dodge was one of the few Americans or Britons to remain in Beirut during the pro-Nazi occupation, in order to keep AUB operational. A year later, in July 1941, Allied forces liberated the city and Free French leader Charles de Gaulle stopped by the Dodge residence for a tea party.*

As with Daniel and Howard Bliss, there was nothing about Bayard Dodge that did not seem perfect. Like his twin brother, Cleveland, he was tall, fair-haired, austere, and clear-eyed. As with his father's friend, Charles Crane, there was that serene inner glow and aloof benevolence about him that indicated a life of purposeful activity in a field he had chosen, because independent wealth and a fine education had obviated the need for any difficult compromises. What anxious worrying these people did engage in was usually confined to large and heroic matters.

Dodge derived deep satisfaction from his lifelong study of Arabic and the Moslem religion. He devoted many hours to discussing the Koran in

---

* For the Dodge family, though, World War II was not over. On November 22, 1944, one of Dodge's sons, Bayard, Jr., was killed in combat against the Nazis in France, after making a target of himself so as to let the rest of his squad escape. Bayard, Jr. was posthumously awarded the Purple Heart and the Silver Star. After reading the cable notifying him of his son's death, Dodge returned to his seat at a Beirut dinner party, keeping the news from his wife until the following morning, when he was able to take her into the mountains for a day. Discipline and stoicism were evidently family traits.

Arabic with Arabs. "He had so immersed himself in the history of the Arabs
. . . that he realized that there were great things to come from that part of
the world. He had wanted to be part of it, in the same way that the university had been part of the awakening of the Middle East," writes Mounir
Sa'adeh, a teacher in a Beirut secondary school.*

Arthur Close and Bill Stoltzfus grew up in Beirut in the period when Bayard Dodge was president of AUB. Close was born in Beirut in 1925, a year
after Stoltzfus, his boyhood friend. Close's family had been in Syria since
1851, when Close's maternal great-grandfather, William Woodbridge
Eddy, a young Presbyterian minister, sailed into Beirut harbor, fresh from
Williams College. Eddy's life was devoted to mission work and writing a
commentary on the New Testament in Arabic. His son, William King
Eddy, Close's grandfather, also spent his entire life in Syria, except for four
years at Princeton. As Close tells it, his grandfather "adopted the Arab
habit of valuing sons and not daughters, which made life difficult for his
daughter, my mother, that is."

Close's grandmother, Elizabeth Mills Nelson, was the daughter of the
Reverend Henry A. Nelson, who had preached Abraham Lincoln's funeral
service at Lincoln's home church in Springfield, Illinois. Close's mother,
Dora Elizabeth Eddy, like the rest of this very distinguished family, passed
her life in Syrian mission work. Mention should also be made of Close's
maternal uncle, William Alfred Eddy, a star in the Office of Strategic Services (the OSS, precursor to the Central Intelligence Agency) during
World War II, who went on to become American minister to Saudi Arabia.
Eddy interpreted for President Franklin Roosevelt during the President's
meeting with King Ibn Saud in 1945.

"My mother spoke fluent Arabic," Close says. "We lived in the Moslem
half of Beirut, and got along with the Moslems, Druze, and Greek
Orthodox better than with the Maronites. We grew up with an anti-
Catholic prejudice because the French favored the Maronites and the Catholic schools competed with AUB. You see, AUB was the cradle of anti-
French Arab nationalism. We [Americans] basked in being disinterested
good guys. My family was Anglophile, pro-British, and for Arab self-

---

* Quoted in Guthrie; see bibliography.

determination, especially the principles of the King-Crane Commission that supported an Arab state in Palestine."

"The Maronites were extremely arrogant," adds Stoltzfus. "They were tough mountain people who knew how to put people down. To this day, Moslems in Lebanon don't have a completely fair shake. The Maronites were implants, since they didn't consider themselves Arab, but of Phoenician descent."

The Syrian boyhood of Close and Stoltzfus ended upon the outbreak of World War II, when many of the expatriate families returned to the East Coast. This is when Close, Stoltzfus, Talcott Seelye, the two sons of Bayard Dodge (David and Bayard, Jr.), and other "Beiruti" boys were dispatched to Deerfield Academy for their secondary education prior to attending Princeton (or in Seelye's case, Amherst).

There could be no more wholesome place for a teenage boy to have spent four years in the late 1930s and 1940s than at Deerfield, located amid the pastoral charms of western Massachusetts. The progeny of expatriate Beirut and Deerfield Academy grew up high-minded and fine-mannered to a fault. But the America that these teenage boys were introduced to at Deerfield was no less sheltered than the America of expatriate Beirut. Deerfield was an extension of that well-born, white Protestant world. The 1930s and 1940s, in fact, was the period of greatest exclusivity at Deerfield, when three quarters of its students came from private, preprep schools.* Recall Janet Stoltzfus's words: "At Princeton and Wellesley, at the prep schools we went to, you almost never encountered Jews. It was a different America then."

On the eve of World War II, the American community in the Middle East had reached full bloom. There were three American girls schools in Lebanon alone. Besides AUB, the American University of Cairo (AUC) had opened its doors in 1920, headed by Charles R. Watson, whose own Protestant missionary roots in Egypt went back to 1861. With a teacher-training division, a rural extension service, and a school of Oriental studies attached to the main university, AUC quickly became the capstone of American missionary activity in Egypt, just as AUB had become in Syria.

---

* See John McPhee entry in the bibliography.

Like AUB, AUC attracted the sons of the Egyptian establishment, becoming an incubator for Egyptian nationalism as AUB was for pan-Arab nationalism.

But with the chill of war once again sweeping over Europe, Bayard Dodge presciently told AUB's trustees that the Middle East was at the close of an era. Even though America's role in the Arab world was far more beneficial and benign than the roles of France and England, Dodge suggested that the tensions provoked by Arab nationalism would now begin to be felt by America, too. AUB—and by extension the whole American expatriate community in the Arab world—had continued to prosper through World War II because it provided critical services in education and social welfare while abstaining from politics. The expatriates went with the flow of local opinion. They got along with the powers that be. They had no need to apologize for the actions of their government because Washington was not active in the region the way the Europeans were. In truth, Dodge and the other expatriates desired a more visible American government presence to compete with those of the French and the British. Still, they hoped, and indeed assumed, that when Washington did make its presence felt in the Middle East, it would do so in a way that would buttress their private relationships with the Arabs, not complicate them.

What was to take place, of course, would be a cruel, almost divine joke. Another movement, equally liberal, equally well-meaning, and equally humanitarian, yet driven by a human tragedy of a kind and dimension that crushed even the logic of the Protestant Bible, was to crash over the heads of these expatriates, embittering and frustrating them.

In 1948, at the age of sixty, Bayard Dodge retired to Princeton, New Jersey.* That April Dodge published an article in *Reader's Digest* about the Palestine crisis, entitled "Must There Be War in the Middle East?" This six-thousand-word article, while forgotten and obscure, is the definitive statement of American Arabists on the birth of Israel. Though he cautioned, "Not all Jews are Zionists and not all Zionists are extremists," for Dodge the Zionist movement was a tragedy of which little good could come. Dodge was not anti-Semitic. He chided his fellow Christians for

---

* Stephen Penrose succeeded Dodge as AUB president.

behaving "in such a way" as to make the Jews sense of "homelessness . . . more acute." The *Digest* editors, in fact, introduced Dodge as a "distinguished friend of the Arabs and Jews." Dodge's argument against Zionism rests, not on the politics of the movement, but on the Arabs' opposition to it, which in Dodge's view made the Zionist program unrealistic and therefore dangerous. Years and decades of strife would, Dodge knew, follow the birth of a Jewish state. As a result, wrote Dodge, "All the work done by our philanthropic nonprofit American agencies in the Arab world—our Near East Foundation, our missions, our YMCA and YWCA, our Boston Jesuit college in Baghdad, our colleges in Cairo, Beirut, Damascus—would be threatened with complete frustration and collapse. . . . So would our oil concessions," a scenario that Dodge said would help Communist Russia. Dodge then quoted a fellow "American Middle East expert" as saying that "they [the Russians] intend to get many thousands of Russian Communist Jews into the Palestinian Jewish State." Though Dodge made passing reference to the Holocaust (barely three years old at the time he wrote the article), he appeared oblivious to its psychological and historical ramifications upon the European Jewish refugees in Palestine. While admitting that the Arabs would never countenance a Jewish state, Dodge nevertheless exhorted Jews to lay down their arms and talk to the Arabs. The article ends with a quote from the Bible: "Not by might, nor by power, but by my spirit, saith the Lord of Hosts." Dodge did not seem aware that the death-camp-haunted Jews of Palestine read the Old Testament with different eyes from those of a Protestant missionary.

In the 1950s Dodge returned temporarily to the Middle East to live in Cairo, from where he would travel to every single Arab state in the region as well as to Greece, Turkey, Pakistan, and India. Christmasing in Khartoum, writing in his Cairo study about the Al Azhar University, overseeing the publication of learned articles about Moslem medievalism, attending conferences and tea parties hosted by his former AUB students, feted constantly in many an Arab capital, and filling up his diary with descriptions of the bazaars of Lucknow and the exotic birds of Asia, Dodge was reaping the bounty of a life devoted to the Arabs and Moslem culture. Israel is the lone place in the region that never seems to appear in his itinerary.

Upon Dodge's death in 1972, Lebanese Prime Minister Saeb Salam said over Radio Lebanon that "Bayard Dodge understood the Lebanese people, and the Arab peoples. He was one of them and lived their social, educational and national causes. . . ." And like the Arabs, Dodge was unprepared, both emotionally and politically, to deal with the fact of a Jewish state in the part of Palestine awarded it under the UN partition.

Dodge was typical of the entire Beirut community in this regard. The American Protestant missionaries, observes Richard Crossman, a member of Parliament who was part of an Anglo-American team investigating the Palestine problem in 1947, "challenged the Zionist case with all the arguments of the most violently pro-Arab British Middle Eastern officials." So, to a degree, did the sons of these missionaries. Listen to Arthur Close, who after graduating from Deerfield and Princeton became an American official in the Middle East:

"Israel made my job more difficult. I remember the day the Soviet Embassy opened in Damascus. That might not have happened so easily had there been a different solution to the Palestine problem. To be perfectly honest, I thought the creation of the State of Israel was wrong. Logically and morally, I could see how the Jews felt after the Holocaust. But the solution to their problem was arrived at dishonestly. The U.S., the British, and the Soviets railroaded the partition of Palestine through the United Nations."

Part II
Reality

Chapter 5

Mr. Foreign Service

In September 1947 Loy Henderson, the director of the State Department's Office of Near Eastern, African and South Asian Affairs, wrote to the secretary of defense, George Marshall, that the "partitioning of Palestine and the setting up of a Jewish State [is opposed] by practically every member of the Foreign Service and of the Department who has been engaged . . . with the Near and Middle East."* In the Washington political establishment the State Department was not alone in its opposition to Israel. All of President Harry Truman's foreign policy advisers—including many of the so-called wise men: Marshall, Robert Lovett, George Kennan, Charles Bohlen, James Forrestal, and Dean Acheson—were against recognizing the new Jewish state, which they viewed as an oil-poor impediment to good relations with the oil-rich and strategically located Arabs at a time when the United States was embarking on a worldwide struggle with the Soviet Union. But none held so tenaciously to this view as Henderson and his diplomatic colleagues at the State Department's Near Eastern Affairs bureau, known as NEA. When it became clear that Truman was not to be

---

* The terms "Near" and "Middle" East largely overlap and have become virtually indistinguishable. Originally, the Near East meant the Balkans, Turkey, Greater Syria, Arabia, and Egypt; while the Middle East meant Greater Syria, Iraq, Iran, and Arabia. Moreover, the State Department's Office of Near Eastern Affairs would periodically include the Indian subcontinent, Greece, Turkey, Cyprus, and parts of Africa. The title Office Director would later be changed to Assistant Secretary of State for NEA.

swayed from his support for Israel, Lovett, Marshall, and the other wise men withdrew their opposition and got behind the President to a degree that Henderson and the State Department would not. Hearing the news that Truman had recognized Israel, a State Department official assigned to the United Nations in New York, lamented, "It can't be." Another department official, Philip Ireland, who had taught at the AUB, equated Zionism with "Nazi Lebensraum."* Several months later, in the spring of 1948, when the new State of Israel was fighting for its life against five Arab armies, Henderson and his colleagues labored strenuously to prevent arms reaching Israel.

"The area experts to a man were scandalized by what happened in 1948. We had made a tremendous effort to lay the ground for good relations with the Arabs, and all of a sudden, when we were in a good position, all of our hopes were dashed," recalls Parker Hart, an Arabist who later became assistant secretary of state for Near Eastern affairs.† Carleton Coon, Jr., another diplomat, says "the old-time Arabists knew that had the partition vote gone otherwise, the Arab world would have been ripe for American political penetration and intercultural fertilization. But now the days of a beloved American presence were over. In some of their minds, Israel spoiled it all."

Truman had this to say in his memoirs:

"The Department of State's specialists on the Near East were almost without exception unfriendly to the idea of a Jewish state. . . . Some thought the Arabs, on account of their number and because of the fact that they controlled such immense oil resources, should be appeased. . . . Some among them were also inclined to be anti-Semitic."

State Department officials from that era who are still alive take umbrage at that statement. Not only do they deny its validity, but they claim Truman knew full well that Henderson and his men were not anti-Semitic. Truman, these old Arab hands claim, was playing domestic politics, pandering to the fears of American Jews, that is, at the expense of the career Foreign Service.

Nevertheless, not even these officials would deny that they, like the Protestant missionaries and the other American expatriates in the Middle East, were simply not willing, or able, to imagine the Nazi Holocaust to the same

---

* See Baram entry in the bibliography.

† See Kraft entry in the bibliography.

degree that Truman and many Americans were. As Bill Stoltzfus admits, "The Jews were a distant, unreal world to us, but the Palestinians were individuals we knew." Contrast this statement with one about Truman, recalled by his adviser, Clark Clifford: "He [Truman] deplored the existence of Jewish ghettos and the cruel and persistent persecution. He never ceased to be horrified at the murder of some six million Jews by the Nazis. He was fully aware of the miserable status of the hundreds of thousands of Jews who had been displaced by the Second World War."

Of course, emotional responses to the Holocaust in Europe need not have affected one's attitude toward the situation in the Middle East. In abstract moral terms one could well argue that they should not have: why should Arabs be punished for European crimes when traditional Christian anti-Semitism never existed in the Arab world? But such emotional empathy not only affected political attitudes in 1947 and 1948 but, as it would turn out, allowed an insight into what was then unfolding in the Middle East, a development that State Department officials appeared not to grasp. The sheer magnitude of the Holocaust had unleashed a historical process—of which the mass movement of Jewish refugees from Europe to Palestine was only a part—that made the birth of Israel simply inevitable. For most this was plain to see, but not for the Arabists.

However, the State Department variety of this species was different from the Protestant missionary variety. Beginning in the 1950s, these two species would merge into a single brand of Arabist, which would in turn subdivide into a variety of newer strains. It is necessary, therefore, to understand the diplomats who manned the State Department's Office of Near Eastern Affairs in the first years after World War II. That means starting with one man: Loy Henderson.

Loy Henderson was more than a diplomatic archetype: he might be considered the most important and distinguished career diplomat in United States history. That he is little known outside the State Department is testimony to the insider role he played and to the onrush of news events in this century and the speed with which their details are being forgotten. For nearly half a century this man was a behind-the-scenes player in nearly every international drama that involved the United States. The Middle East, as it happens, was only one chapter in Henderson's epic career.

Loy Wesley Henderson came from a small Arkansas town, one of two identical twin boys born in 1892 to a poor Methodist preacher. He went to a small college in a small town in Kansas and afterward transferred to Northwestern University outside Chicago. Due to an arm injury he was rejected for service in World War I, but as a Red Cross volunteer he saw firsthand the social chaos that engulfed Germany and Russia at the end of the war. It was in Latvia in 1920, when he himself was close to death with typhus, that he received a cable informing him that his brother, Roy Henderson, had died from a kidney ailment. Because of Roy's death, Loy's preacher father wrote him, "You must be double as good a man as you had ever planned to be." Henceforth, Loy Henderson's life would be driven forward by the ghost of his dead identical twin. "The eventual result was a near-obsession with duty" that "tended to narrow his field of vision, and . . . discouraged the reflection that allows a person to learn from criticism," observes the scholar H. W. Brands in *Inside The Cold War: Loy Henderson and the Rise of the American Empire 1918–1961*.

Henderson became like a Jesuit priest whose religious order was the Foreign Service, the cadre of diplomats who spend their professional lives representing America at embassies abroad and at the State Department in Washington. But Henderson, unlike other diplomats, was not intellectually curious. He read little aside from the diplomatic cable traffic. According to those who knew him, he lacked a sense of humor and was unable "to share popular emotions." Henderson's attitude toward New York City is telling: the city "was more foreign to me than London, Paris, or Berlin had been. The people in the restaurants and on the subway . . . and those who jostled me in the streets or pushed in front of me in the shops, seemed to have little in common with me." One of Henderson's early jobs in the State Department was to investigate Soviet links to leftist labor organizations in the United States. Given the significant role played by Jews and other ethnics in such organizations in the 1920s, it is possible that this work only deepened Henderson's animosity toward New York City and to the ethnic and political universe it represented.

In some ways Henderson bore an uncanny resemblance to the man who, more than any other, came to epitomize the political power and upper-crust waspdom of the East Coast Establishment: John J. McCloy, Jr. McCloy, a Wall Street titan who helped run the War Department during World War II and was later high commissioner for Germany, president of the World Bank, and chairman of the Chase Manhattan Bank and the

Council on Foreign Relations, was also a consummate insider and narrow, unreflective deal maker, who grew up, like Henderson, in a financially strapped and undistinguished Protestant family. This condition only increased his determination to be more of an American aristocrat—with the typical American aristocrat's devotion to duty—than his colleagues who had been born wealthy. In a photo, taken on the steps of the U.S. legation in Baghdad in 1943, Henderson certainly appears to the manner born: ramrod-straight in a black dinner jacket, hands clasped behind his back, a trimmed moustache, and aloof eyes that reveal not a trace of self-doubt. With his bald head, he even looks like McCloy.

McCloy, the focus of adulation toward the end of his life, has in recent years come under revision as one of the key figures responsible for imprisoning Japanese Americans during World War II and for preventing the U.S. military from bombing the railway tracks leading to Auschwitz. Indeed, McCloy's easy forgiveness of German war criminals immediately after the war, coupled with his vehement opposition to the creation of Israel and to Israeli security long before the Likud came to power, suggests a pattern of possible prejudice. Henderson's life, beginning with his dislike of New York and its leftist ethnic culture, indicates a similar pattern.

But while McCloy's career was full of mistaken judgments, Henderson's judgments—the Middle East aside—were incredibly prescient. And even in regard to the Middle East, Henderson's opinions, though in some cases incorrect, are not impossible to defend.

"Loy Henderson was a big picture man. He saw the world from a global viewpoint. Henderson came to the Middle East relatively late in his career. He placed the Middle East strictly in terms of its impact on the U.S.-Soviet conflict," explains Hermann Eilts, an ambassador to Saudi Arabia and to Egypt, who worked with Henderson as a young Foreign Service officer.

Early in his career, from 1927 through 1942, Henderson worked exclusively on Soviet and Eastern European affairs, including the eight years that he spent living in the Baltic States and Moscow. This experience marked Henderson for life. It permitted him to work alongside George F. Kennan and Charles Bohlen. Together the three of them earned the reputation as the State Department's finest area specialists on the Soviet Union, chalking up a record of prediction and analysis that was never to be surpassed. While many Americans—a group, it must be said, that was to a large degree dominated by Jewish intellectuals—saw the new Communist state in Russia through rose-tinted glasses, Henderson, Kennan, and Bohlen witnessed firsthand the horrific deprivations and terror tactics inflicted by Stalin's regime. Frustrated by Stalin's popularity in liberal circles in America, Henderson, in one diplomatic cable, blamed "international Jewry" for being "an important supporter of" the Soviet Union.*

In Riga Henderson married a Latvian woman, who further encouraged his intense dislike of the Soviet Communists and their sympathizers abroad. As with Charles Crane, it could be said that Henderson's problem with the Jews initiated in Russia. Because he was actually living in Moscow and witnessing the cruelties of Stalinism—he attended the show trials and had the awful experience of having his Russian "contacts" disappear into the gulag—Henderson became more distrustful of Stalin than of Hitler. Consequently, American leftists and Jews publicly attacked Henderson for "fascist" tendencies and anti-Semitism. Nevertheless, Henderson's awareness of the true nature of the Soviet regime led him to predict as early as April 1942 that the American-Soviet alliance against Hitler would be a passing phenomenon, which would break apart the moment the war was over.

In early 1942 with Americans—particularly President Roosevelt—enthralled with their new Soviet wartime allies, Henderson's thinking was not considered politically correct. Pressure on the State Department from Eleanor Roosevelt and others in the White House resulted in Henderson's transfer to the Middle East, a less important part of the world, where it was thought Henderson would not get into trouble by attacking the conventional wisdom. "The Near East! Nothing ever happens there," observed an American diplomat of the day. However, Henderson was fated to arrive in the Middle East at exactly the moment in American history when it became a major strategic concern.

The State Department, though to a much smaller extent than the Protestant missionaries, had a relationship with the Arab world going back to the early days of the Republic. The Alaouite sovereign of Morocco was the first foreign ruler to recognize the United States after the American Revolution. And it was in 1826, during the administration of President John Quincy

---

* Many leftist Jewish intellectuals in the 1930s, being Trotskyites, had a dim view of Stalin, especially given that many of his purge victims were Jewish. But unlike Henderson, these intellectuals still held out hope for communism. For quotations about Henderson, see Brands's book, mentioned in the preface and the bibliography.

Adams, that the first State Department Arabist, William B. Hodgson, received his language training.* But until World War II Washington's diplomatic presence in Araby was exceedingly small. Its policy was to defer to British interests in the region and to support the educational work of the missionaries. The only exception to this rule came in the aftermath of the First World War, when Woodrow Wilson conceived the desire for an American political role in Syria and sent Crane there for that purpose. But Wilson's idea vanished in the face of British and French pressure. Though American oil interests, helped by Crane, had opened relationships with Arab sheikhs prior to World War II, by the time of Pearl Harbor, the United States was still a net exporter of oil, and thus the oil issue was consigned to the future. But from 1939 on, just as Bill Stoltzfus, Arthur Close, and their friends and families were leaving Beirut, the situation began to change dramatically.

Raymond Hare, a young second secretary at the American Legation in Cairo from 1939 through 1942, was one of the handful of Americans who personally experienced this metamorphosis. Born in West Virginia, Hare had taught at Robert College in Istanbul (established by missionaries a few years before AUB). When Hare joined the Foreign Service in the 1920s, there was still no proper facility in Washington for language training; so he, like William Hodgson a hundred years earlier, was dispatched overseas to learn Arabic and Turkish at the Ecole Nationale de Langue Vivant in Paris.

"War was the life of Cairo," recalls Hare in an unpublished memoir. "People were going along having parties and at the same time people were fighting in the desert." The "fast-paced social life" included royalty escaping from Balkan kingdoms and literary luminaries such as Lawrence Durrell, Evelyn Waugh, and Freya Stark. But Washington was not particularly interested in the Middle East, evidenced by the fact that despite the fighting between the British and Germans, the legation lacked a military attaché, a task that fell to Hare, who, except for a source he mysteriously dubs "the Shadow," mainly had to rely on the British embassy for information.

In March 1941, however, Roosevelt persuaded an isolationist Congress to pass the Lend-Lease Act, and the historic shift toward America's recognition of the importance of the Middle East began. Washington immediately poured large quantities of arms into Egypt for use by the British army,

---

* This was in the 1830s. Because Hodgson's study of Arabic was a lone case within the State Department of the time, he cannot be said to have begun the Arabist tradition in the way that Eli Smith did, whose career as an Arabist influenced other Americans in nineteenth-century Lebanon. (Hodgson's career was researched by Hermann Eilts.)

necessitating a considerable logistics, diplomatic, and intelligence presence. Still, Hare was frustrated with Washington's responses to his cables. While he consistently emphasized the importance of the Middle East and especially the Mediterranean to the war against Hitler, Washington—as Roosevelt explained to British prime minister Winston Churchill—replied that "naval control of the Indian Ocean and the Atlantic will in time win the war." The pleas of Hare and his ambassador, Alexander Kirk, for American fighter planes to help the British in Egypt fell on deaf ears in Washington until the 1942 fall of Tobruk in Libya.

Tobruk caused Washington to take action. The American Air Force was involved in the combat by November 1942, when British forces stopped the Afrika Korps's advance at El Alamein in Egypt's western desert. Concomitantly, American troops were landing on the coast of Morocco and dashing eastward across the desert to Tunisia, where in the spring of 1943 they would meet up with British forces marching westward from Egypt and, in a quick series of battles, eject the Germans from North Africa. Though the Americans suddenly found themselves in a position of dominance in the Middle East, Hare reflects that it was "not clear to us" then just how big a role we were very soon to play. It was during this interregnum between the acquisition of regional power and the actual use of it that Henderson was fated to enter the picture.

It is unlikely, given his inclinations and his previous experiences, that Henderson quit Moscow—an exciting World War II nerve center—for mosquito-ridden Baghdad without bearing at least some grudge toward President and Mrs. Roosevelt, the Democratic party liberals, and the American Jews, who at the time were Democrats almost to a man. Henderson was already fifty-one, and he and his wife were childless. His life by then was completely consumed by the Foreign Service, a fact demonstrated by periodic physical breakdowns resulting from overwork.

Baghdad was truly a backwater of a backwater: a supply base for the British, who were in neighboring Iran holding back the Germans and, after a fashion, the Soviets, too. But Iraq was an unstable supply base rather than a calm one. The late Gertrude Bell's dream of making this British-manufactured country "a model Arab state" had gone awry. British domination and the growing dispute between the Jews and Arabs of Palestine had turned many Iraqi Arabs into Nazi sympathizers. In 1941, two years prior to Henderson's arrival, there was an ill-fated pro-Nazi coup in Baghdad led by a group of Iraqi army officers, which involved a pogrom in the Jewish quarter, where an Arab mob murdered over 150 Jewish men, women, and children while British troops stood on the outskirts of Baghdad and did nothing. Freya Stark, a British diplomat and travel writer, who to a certain extent had inherited Miss Bell's mantle as the grand lady of the Iraqi Arabs—Miss Stark saw a great future for democracy in Iraq—defended the British action as necessary to allow time for King Feisal's soldiers "to win their own fight [against the coup plotters] unaided."

Among the surviving Jews was a little boy, Elie Kedourie, whose nightmare memories were crucial to his prodigious outpouring of books and articles against the old British Arab hands. Kedourie saw the 1941 Baghdad pogrom, known locally as the *Farhoud* (Looting), as the direct result of decades of amateurish meddling in Iraq by the likes of Miss Bell and Miss Stark, who, having invented a country and a power base for an Arab Moslem population, should have assumed responsibility for the minorities henceforth threatened by those Arabs. In *The Chatham House Version and Other Middle-Eastern Studies*, Kedourie fumes:

> The right of conquest they [the Jews] could cheerfully acknowledge, for all their history had taught them that there lay safety. . . . It was not by the help of this experience that they would understand the strange, exquisite perversions of the western conscience: the genial eccentricity of Mr. Philby, proposing to make a thug who took his fancy the president of an Iraqi republic; or the fond foolishness of Miss Bell, thinking to stand godmother to a new Abbassid empire; or the disoriented fanaticism of Colonel Lawrence [of Arabia] proclaiming that he would be dishonoured if the progeny of the sharif of Mecca was not forthwith provided with thrones. Yet it was with such people that their [the Jews'] fate rested.

Supporting Kedourie's view was none other than the intelligence officer attached to the British forces in Baghdad, Somerset de Chair:

> . . . the ways of the Foreign Office were beyond my comprehension. . . . Having fought our way, step by step, to the threshold of the city, we must now cool our heels outside. It would, apparently, be lowering to the dignity of our ally, the regent [Feisal], who had fled to Palestine at the *coup d'etat*, if he were seen to be supported on arrival by British bayonets.*

Henderson, after he had arrived in Baghdad and had time to digest all of this history, realized he had little sympathy for the Jews of Iraq. The Jews,

---

* See Kedourie's book.

he felt, bore some responsibility for the violence directed against them, not only because they were "secretly sympathetic to Zionism" rather than to Iraqi nationalism, but also because of "the public dishonesty, profiteering and greed of some of the Jewish merchants who . . . conduct themselves in a manner which gives the impression that they consider themselves socially and culturally superior to the Arabs."

Henderson's instantaneous animus toward the Jewish community in Iraq was more extreme than similar attitudes entertained by the British Arabists or by the missionaries. Perhaps it had different roots. In the case of the British Arabists, it wasn't that they disliked Jews. Some, such as Lawrence, could at times be quite philo-Semitic. But they just liked Arabs more, motivated, as they were, by an aesthetic and scholarly attachment to Arab culture as well as by guilt for betraying Arab aspirations after World War I, particularly in letting the French carve up Syria. The British also had a special affinity for wealthy Arabs. Richard Crossman, a member of Parliament investigating the Palestine problem in 1947, says this about his countrymen: "It is easy to see why the British prefer the Arab upper class to the Jews. The Arab intelligentsia has a French culture, amusing, civilized, tragic and gay. Compared with them, the Jews seem tense, bourgeois, central European or even German."

But Henderson, remember, was a man who read relatively few books, and who had little aptitude for the kinds of cultural aesthetics that the British reveled in. According to Hermann Eilts and others, Henderson was not especially curious about Arab civilization. While Henderson's compatriot Archie Roosevelt, the grandson of Theodore Roosevelt and later a pioneer Arabist at the Central Intelligence Agency, was enthusiastically exploring the archaeological sites and tribal regions of Mesopotamia, Henderson was inside the legation reading political reports.

Unlike the missionaries, Henderson was no idealist. Nor did he, or anyone he was close to, have a vested interest—as the missionaries certainly did—in maintaining a personal relationship with the Arabs. Henderson was, however, both a gifted analyst and a quick study, one who was able immediately to place facts about a region previously unknown to him into a conceptual framework that interlocked with situations elsewhere in the world. And it didn't take him long to figure out that after the war with Germany and Japan was over, the Middle East was bent on a cataclysm. He was absolutely certain by 1943 that the intercommunal situation in Palestine was explosive and nearly impossible to solve, and that its shock effects would fissure throughout the Middle East, distorting the region's politics as it already was doing in Iraq. Because he was also certain that after Hitler was defeated, the Soviet Union would become America's worldwide enemy, he thought that the United States had to look at the Palestine problem through the filter of a global struggle against Communism. This necessitated that the U.S. support the side in Palestine that would better strengthen its hand in dealing with the Soviets. For Henderson there was no contest: the Arabs had oil, strategic locations, and numbers. *And how many oil wells do the Jews have?* Henderson seemed to ask himself. In 1943 this was sheer clairvoyance (even if, as some might assume, Henderson was also motivated by a lack of sympathy for Jews). By 1947 Henderson would realize that recognition of the new State of Israel would buy the United States decades of constant trouble and expense, as well as lead to "the rise of fanatic Mohammedanism" of a kind "not experienced for hundreds of years." Could anyone today argue with this?

Henderson would turn out to be wrong about one thing, however: the U.S. could indeed have it both ways, friendship with the Arabs and with the Jews. But not for three decades, as a consequence of Henry Kissinger's shuttle diplomacy and reestablishment of relations with Egypt and Syria in the 1970s, would this become absolutely clear.

In the end, one's attitude towards Henderson is driven by one's perception of how cold-blooded American policy needed to be back then. Because Henderson had personally experienced Stalinism to a degree that few of his countrymen had, he had no illusions about the enemy they faced and what he thought it would take to eventually defeat that enemy. Henderson was about as different from the missionaries as one could get. He had no special interest in the Arabs, their language, their culture, or their educational and national aspirations. But he did have strong opinions about where the U.S. national interest in the Middle East lay, and these opinions happened to dovetail perfectly with those of the missionaries. This alignment of goals provided the template for the hybrid Arabist culture that would emerge in the 1950s.

Henderson's analytical skills, his determination and energy, and his willingness—with the support of his wife, Elise—to sacrifice much of his personal life on the altar of work and duty resulted in his promotion in 1945. He became the director of the State Department's Near Eastern Affairs office. Henderson's force was felt immediately. When the French government, now controlled by the Free French leader, Charles De Gaulle, began bombing Damascus and other Arab population centers in Syria as a means of retaining control over the Syrian mandate, Henderson went directly to Truman, advising him to force the French to withdraw. Not only, Henderson thought, did French actions mock the spirit of the new United Nations charter, but they threatened to derail the West's relations with Arabs and other Moslems. As Henderson explained to his superiors, Arab hatred of the French would eventually be directed at the entire West and would one day permit the Soviet Union to fill the Great Power void in Syria. This, of course, is exactly what happened.

In early 1946 Soviet troops advanced south to the outskirts of Tabriz in northwestern Iran and were poised to take the city. It was the first crisis in what was to be called the Cold War, and Loy Henderson was ready. It was Henderson who marched into the offices of Undersecretary of State Dean Acheson and Secretary of State James Byrnes, armed with maps to explain how the Soviet troop deployment threatened Turkey, Iraq, and the Iranian oil fields, and prevailed upon the Truman administration to issue a stiff warning to Stalin. Stalin soon pulled back his troops. It was Henderson who, responding to political chaos in Greece later that same year, agitated for a strong U.S. response to prevent a Communist victory there. "The Truman doctrine, which more than any other document served as the blueprint of America's anticommunist empire, took shape in Henderson's office and under his careful direction" as a response to the Greek civil war.

It was in such an atmosphere, with Stalin banging down Greece's door and threatening the northern extremities of Iran, that Henderson confronted the Palestine issue in 1947 and 1948. Henderson, who by now ran NEA in autocratic style and was utterly consumed by the Soviet threat, did everything he could to thwart partition and afterward to thwart U.S. recognition of the part of Palestine awarded to the Jews. Though Marshall and others outside the State Department supported Henderson in this policy, American Jews concentrated their wrath on Henderson alone. "Perhaps Palestine is a new subject for Mr. Marshall. Perhaps he is being briefed by Mr. Loy Henderson, the Arabphile [and] striped-trousered underling saboteur," declared Emanuel Celler, a Democratic congressman from a heavily Jewish area of New York City. By the middle of 1948, with Truman fighting for election, Henderson was a political liability that the Democratic presidential candidate could no longer afford. And so for the crime of challenging the conventional wisdom, Henderson was once again exiled, this time to India as U.S. ambassador.

Henderson regretted nothing. He was willing to be publicly branded an anti-Semite if that was the price he had to pay for fulfilling his responsibilities as a Foreign Service officer. Without missing a beat, he immersed himself in India matters. As he had in the Middle East, Henderson arrived in New Delhi soon after India became a major issue. Again Henderson disrupted both conventional wisdom and political correctness by daring to criticize the new nation of India's celebrated leader, Jawaharlal Nehru. Henderson found Nehru "vain, sensitive, emotional and complicated," as well as ungrateful for America's friendship. Even worse, according to Henderson, Nehru's dislike of America had little to do with policy differences but was driven by his British schoolboy-like snobbery regarding America's commercialism and middle-class culture. Henderson also found Indian neutralism dangerous and intellectually dishonest. Such realizations later became commonplace, but Henderson was the first to point them out.

In 1951 Henderson left India to become Ambassador to Iran just as Mohammed Mosadeq was named prime minister, promising to kick the British and their oil interests out of the country. For almost the next three years Henderson put on a stellar one-man performance in directing U.S. policy toward greater engagement in Iranian affairs and eventually toward overthrowing Mosadeq when his flirtations with the Soviet Union became overt. The Shah's reassertion of power with a strong U.S. presence was thus assured for the next quarter-century, thanks to Henderson, though he took no pleasure in the outcome. He predicted that one day the Iranian people would come to hate America as they did Britain.

The overthrow of Mosadeq led to the creation of the Baghdad Pact, an anticommunist alliance of Near Eastern states to which Henderson was named ambassador in 1955. Henderson was also involved in the Suez, Congo, and other crises. Henderson's last important task in the State Department, as deputy undersecretary of state, was to oversee the reorganization of the Foreign Service in the 1950s, a reorganization that made the service at once more professional and less elite, while laying the groundwork for the true middle-class democratization of the State Department that would occur in the 1980s.

By the end of his career, writes Brands, "peers judged" Henderson "the consummate career officer, a man who did not allow political considerations to color his advice, whose steady advancement owed to solid work and devotion to duty. Subordinates looked up to him as a model of what they might become," particularly because, as Henderson had no children, he adopted a fatherly attitude toward many young Foreign Service officers, seeing them as his heirs.

Loy Henderson, in a sense, invented the political culture of the Foreign Service in the first decades of the postwar era. He was affectionately called Mr. Foreign Service, a title that many of his former colleagues still use when talking about him. While the diplomatic reception rooms on the top floor of the State Department take the names of the Founding Fathers, a large public hall on the ground floor is named after Henderson. Dedicating the hall in 1976, Secretary of State Henry Kissinger lauded Henderson as "the quintessence of what makes our Foreign Service a great and dedicated instrument of national policy."

There could be no greater proof of the immeasurable distance between the State Department and the Jewish state than the fact that the very man who fought hardest to prevent its recognition was thought by his peers to represent the highest standards of their profession. While to Israelis and American Jews Henderson was a "bastard," to Foreign Service officers he was a martyr to public ignorance. Henderson was the classic elitist and insider, who knew popular domestic opinion deserved no place in computing the national interest because the public lacked the facts, the analytical skills, and the living experience overseas that he and his colleagues had in abundance. *Wasn't he right—and all those Jewish intellectuals wrong—about the true nature of communism?*

Though nobody is absolutely sure when the term Arabist was first used in America in a pejorative sense to identify someone as politically pro-Arab, this new and negative definition essentially began with Loy Henderson, who did not speak Arabic and spent only two of his ninety-three years living in the Arab world.*

From the early 1950s onward, two definitions of the word *Arabist* would thus coexist side by side. There would be the Foreign Service and Protestant missionary definition of an Arabist: someone who spoke Arabic well and had substantial living experience in the Arab world. And there would be the public's—particularly the Jewish public's—definition: someone who loved Arabs, often because he hated Jews.

---

* Henderson died in 1986.

This indictment would be festooned with charges of social elitism. Comparing Latin American specialists to Arabists in the State Department, the head of a conservative foundation in Washington lectures: "Spanish—because of our intimate contact with the Latin world—connotes a non-elite, drug-lord, 7-Eleven store culture. Arabic, on the other hand, is a distant, difficult, and thus mysterious language, and fluency in it suggests erudite entry to a ruling class where Jews and other ethnic Americans are not welcome."

Because the State Department Arabists were all individuals who, as time went on, increasingly came from varied backgrounds, the real truth about them is far more subtle, and far more interesting, than either of the two definitions can encapsulate. But their initial political-cultural roots are clear. Upon Israel's creation the State Department Arabists went out to the Middle East with the model of Loy Henderson uppermost in their minds, and once settled in their posts overseas, they began to be influenced by the values of the local missionary communities.

Chapter 6

Old Hands

"I have always believed that you can spot someone whose hobby is bird-watching by a certain remoteness and directness in the way he looks at you. The Arab expert has much the same characteristics," observes Richard Crossman in his diary, *Palestine Mission.*

In 1947 Crossman, a British parliamentarian with no previous involvement in the Middle East or with Jews and Arabs, was made a member of the Anglo-American Committee of Inquiry regarding Palestine. In Jerusalem and Cairo he encountered Arabists—both British and American—for the first time. "Like the bird-watcher," Crossman writes, the Arabist "has escaped from the vulgarity, the tempo and the commercialism of the Western world and found . . . an inner tranquility." He goes on:

> He [the Arabist] is in love with the Arabs because they have given him a contract with ultimate values which he missed at home. There he would have remained an unfulfilled personality; in the Middle East he has found himself. He is determined somehow—he does not yet know the way—to harmonize Western civilization with Arab culture. . . . He himself has learned from the Arabs the most valuable things in his life. But he knows their weaknesses: He is frustrated by their indolence, the corruption of the upper classes, and above all by the bogus Western civilization which the educated Arab often assumes. . . . He is indeed the sharpest critic of the

Arabs because he understands them; but his criticism is that of someone who has identified himself with their cause.

He could easily have been describing Howard Bliss or Bayard Dodge. "The spirit of the AUB was, and is still today, one of celebration of the essential harmony of Western and Arab-Islamic culture," declared Malcolm Kerr, a prominent Arabist and AUB president born in Lebanon, who himself fit into the bird-watcher category before he was assassinated by Moslem extremists in Beirut in 1984.

But there are other men, still around on the east coast of the United States, mainly in the Washington area (to where diplomats often retire), who are also blessed with the inner tranquility Crossman writes about. The youngest of these are in their mid-sixties, the oldest in their nineties. Yet because their eyes shine with the enthusiasm of youth, each looks younger than his age. Some are like boys almost, with white or gray hair and wrinkles. Loy Henderson and John McCloy each lived well into the tenth decade of life, and these men appear blessed with the same longevity.

Almost all went to "good schools" and joined the Foreign Service in their twenties. Many bought prime pieces of East Coast real estate when property was cheap and then were able to live abroad at the government's expense. They all retired with the rank of ambassador or higher and often supplemented their ample pensions with academic or consulting work. Some belong to exclusive clubs, the kind that until a few years ago did not admit women. But genes and financial security may not be the source of their tranquility and eternal youth. Like artists or writers, these men do not have jobs so much as they have a life's pursuit, which is an expression of their aesthetic values and intellectual fascinations. Thus, for them retirement is a meaningless concept. Their life's pursuit is the greater Middle East, where, like the family of Bill Stoltzfus, they passed important years of their lives in storybook settings.

Because these men spent much of their lives abroad, they—rather like the great British Arabists—were able to escape the tedium of modern life, the crowding and industrialization of the American landscape, and, especially, the loss of quaint privilege, which has accompanied the growth of the middle class and the suburbs after World War II. In this way, whatever their financial assets, the life-styles of these men have been more exclusive and more enviable than those of the wealthiest bankers and lawyers. It is impossible not to be charmed by them.

Carleton Stevens Coon, Jr., calls himself "the last nineteenth-century ambassador" in the annals of the U.S. Foreign Service. Sitting in his wood-frame weekend house in Virginia's Shenandoah Valley, with devil masks from India decorating the wall behind him—reminding one of Lurgan Sahib's "laboratory" in *Kim*—Coon describes how, after he had ghostwritten President Ronald Reagan's foreign policy briefing book in early 1981, a number of ambassadorial posts were offered him as a climax to a career spent in the Middle East and the Indian subcontinent.* "I chose Kathmandu because I wanted to be forgotten. It was the 1980s, but there were still no telephones at the embassy in Nepal. The embassy used old-fashioned cables. So Washington didn't care what I did. God, it was wonderful!" Even better, Coon's wife, Jane, another lifelong Foreign Service officer, had been named the ambassador to nearby Bangladesh. "On weekends, I would fly down to Dacca, or Jane would fly up to Kathmandu. Or we would go exploring together in China and Bhutan. We've always enjoyed traveling."

Coon's speech is crisp and welcoming. It exudes a friendly and relaxed circuitry that is vaguely Yankee. In fact, it is the speech of George Bush, albeit grammatical. Coon, like Bush, is a graduate of Phillips Academy in Andover, Massachusetts, situated on the campus of the old Andover Theological Seminary, which in the late nineteenth century moved to the Boston suburb of Newton. While Bush went on to Yale after serving as a fighter pilot in World War II, Coon, who is three years younger than the ex-president, went to Harvard after a short stint in the military. But Coon's story really begins with his father, Carleton Stevens Coon, Sr., who was perhaps the most talented gong-and-trinket man that America ever produced.

Coon, Sr., was born in 1904 in Wakefield, Massachusetts, not far from

---

* The fact that Coon, whose views on foreign policy are quite different from Reagan's, was part of the State Department transition team for the first Reagan Administration, illustrates how the bureaucracy subtly influences even the most ideological of presidents.

Andover. After he was thrown out of Wakefield High School, his parents sent him to Phillips Academy, where he was always in trouble. At Harvard he was an "unguided missile," says his son. But it was at Harvard where Coon, Sr., got involved with a physical anthropologist, Ernest Albert Hooten, whose book *Up from the Ape* fired the elder Coon's imagination. "My father got into racial theory at a time when race theory was respectable. Those were the days when anthropologists ran off to Africa and the Middle East armed with skin color charts and calipers for taking skull measurements. Of course, you can't talk about such stuff today: people would call you a racist. In our society, it has become unfashionable to admit that peoples and cultures can be different."

In particular, Coon, Sr., became attracted to the Riffians, an obscure group of blond, "blue-eyed" Berber tribesmen in the Atlas Mountains of Morocco, then fighting the French colonialists. "Dad liked ferocious fighting types of people. He hated the litigious political types. Dad was in the tradition of the nineteenth-century Brits, who fell in love with the Pathans" (the fierce tribesmen who straddled the border of Afghanistan and British India). So Coon, Sr., and his new wife, aged twenty-two and twenty, found themselves, in the fall of 1926, prisoners of the Riffians, who, thinking that the couple was French, debated how to kill them. Because Coon, Sr., spoke such bad French, the tribesmen finally concluded that they were indeed Americans as they claimed. "Dad then became fast friends with a Riffian named Mohammed Limnibhi, whom he brought back to Massachusetts" for friendship and further study. Coon, Sr., wrote two novels based on Limnibhi's stories, *The Riffian* and *The Flesh of the Wild Ox*. "I remember Limnibhi faintly as a child. He went back to Morocco where he was later poisoned."

While Coon, Sr., and his wife went traveling in distant places, collecting all kinds of objects and specimens, Coon, Jr., was raised by his maternal grandmother. "Our financial situation was precarious. My parents went off on a trip whenever they got money from some foundation or other. When they weren't traveling, the atmosphere in the house was one of ridiculously clownish Harvard drinking bouts.

"Dad was always developing theories. I'll never forget him watching Patrice Lumumba on television during the 1960 Congo crisis. Dad's fingers were moving. You could see how much he wanted to put his fingers all over Lumumba's skull. 'That's not a Congolese skull!' Dad exclaimed."

Coon, Sr., published over thirty books, some of which rank with the most entertaining travel and ethnographic writing of the early and mid-century. He was also a World War II spy for the OSS (the CIA's precursor), and, of course, wrote a book about it, *A North African Story: The Anthropologist as OSS Agent 1941–1943.* "Dad absolutely, instantly volunteered for the OSS. He would have started it himself if it hadn't existed. He was the adventurous, patriotic type."

Were America's a culture like Britain's, where travel writers and ethnographers are truly lionized, Coon, Sr.'s name would be known to every literary sophisticate. Take, for example, *Measuring Ethiopia and Flight into Arabia,* published in 1935. The title refers to Coon, Sr.'s attempts to measure large quantities of heads in Ethiopia and how he was hounded out of the kingdom for this activity, escaping to Yemen where he had better luck in finding live specimens. "I am a magician, slapstick comedian, and father-confessor rolled into one, for my incomprehensible droning [while taking skull measurements] is at times mistaken for prayer, and it often satisfies some inner feeling of importance for an otherwise insignificant person to have his lineaments gone over . . . most of them consider me demented, but fortunately the attitude toward madness in these countries is more tolerant than in our own." Here is high comedy to rank with Evelyn Waugh's *Scoop* and satire on a par with Robert Byron's *The Road to Oxiana.* But there is also something else that recalls the British writing tradition: a longing for Arabia, whose "very bleakness and emptiness appealed strongly" to Coon Sr.

His optimism about Arabia was well founded. Soon, thanks to the services of a Yemeni Jew named Israel, Coon, Sr., was experiencing "bonanza days," working "from sunup to sundown measuring" Semitic heads. "Truly, if we had not met Israel, I do not know what we should have done in the Yemen," for the Jews "know more about Arabs than the Arabs about themselves," Coon, Sr., writes.

Though Coon, Sr., loved exotic eastern Jews *in situ,* he was less fond of the new State of Israel. In *Caravan* he writes that in "1948, the decolonizing trend was reversed when the Israelis anachronistically succeeded the British in Palestine, and are still there." *Caravan* is judged Coon, Sr.'s best book: a work that many American Arabists cut their teeth on, employing geography to explain the cultural characteristics of the Middle East's various peoples. In *Caravan* Coon, Sr., lauds Islam as having made "possible the optimum survival and happiness of millions of human beings in an increasingly impoverished environment." Here too is where Coon, Sr., articulates a fearful disdain of the modern world that is common among Arabists as well as among other literary travelers:

"Geography permits independence, technology defeats it. This is why the idea of One World, into which technical science is forcing us, leaves some people uneasy. If the world is to be one, what place will there be in it for rebels, and without rebels, who will keep the rest of the world on its toes?"

Caravan was published in 1951. But by today's standards "it reads like Herodotus," Coon, Jr., laments. As much as he may try to deny it, Coon, Jr., appears to a visitor like a chip off the old block. His Washington, D.C., home, even more so than the Shenandoah retreat, is a place where his father, or Rudyard Kipling for that matter, would have felt at home. The walls, from floor to ceiling, are lined with the friendly tawny colors of the old book bindings, and the huge floor space, even more so than Bill Stoltzfus's home, is covered with fabulous Eastern rugs. "FSOs [Foreign Service officers] like rugs for the same reason Turkic tribesmen do," Coon explains. "They are a form of nomadic furniture you can carry around the world and that creates its own intimate space."

After following in his dad's footsteps at Phillips Academy and Harvard, Coon decided on a Foreign Service career because it was similar enough to his father's field while still being different. "Dad was pleased at my decision."

And so it was that on September 1, 1952, Coon arrived at Damascus airport. He remembers the date because there to greet him was another foreign service neophyte, William Eagleton. "It was the first time Eagleton and I met. We have been the closest of friends ever since." (In the 1980s Eagleton would play an important role in America's relationship with Iraq. He will be fully introduced later.)

Coon spent the next four years in Syria, a long period for a youth in his twenties. Not only were Coon and Eagleton there, but so were Stoltzfus, Arthur Close, and a number of other Arabists. Because Syria in the 1950s—a universe that included not only the cities of Damascus and Aleppo but the AUB in nearby Beirut (by then part of the independent nation of Lebanon)—was a defining experience for this first generation of post–World War II Arabists, a few details about the political atmosphere of the place will need to be filled in.

"It was a new experience for the Syrians to be mad at us," says Coon. Indeed, rarely has a relationship between two countries been so negatively transformed in so short a time as that between the United States and Syria. From 1946, when Loy Henderson was defending the rights of the Syrians against De Gaulle's French forces (just as Woodrow Wilson and his friend, Charles Crane, had earlier tried to defend the Syrians against the French and British), to 1947, when Truman came out in favor of a Jewish state, the American-Syrian relationship turned upside down. Over a century of loving kindnesses bestowed upon the Syrian Arabs by the American missionaries had collided in the night with another ideal grounded in Western liberalism: the birth of a Jewish state in Palestine. The Syrians, who had seen Americans only in the most exalted of lights through 1946, now saw America as the agent of their further dismemberment. The French had amputated Lebanon, the British Transjordan, and now the Jews, with American support, had finalized the hacking away of Palestine begun by the British. Cries for Arab unity against the Jews were, at least initially, meant as cries for the reconstitution of Greater Syria. However, while Syrians yearned for the return of Palestine as well as other areas taken from them, they were having considerable trouble getting along with themselves: after World War I the French had granted autonomy to the Alawites in the northwest and to the Druze in the south, but at independence a quarter century later these regions suddenly were reintegrated into Damascus's rule, bedeviling the body politic.

A myth persists about Syria, perpetuated by an American media that lacks historical memory and by supporters of Israel, who try to draw as sharp a distinction as possible between the democracy of the Jewish state and the nondemocracy of Arab states. The myth is that Syria is a country whose Arab inhabitants have no experience in democracy or in the rule of law. This is simply not true, as any Arabist who lived in Syria in the 1950s can certify. No Arab country experimented so doggedly and in such good faith against such great odds with Western-style democracy in the late 1940s and 1950s as did Syria. And the record shows that democracy's failure had as much to do with the legacy of European colonialism—of which the creation of Israel was seen to be a part—as with the innate historical and cultural characteristics of the Syrians themselves.

In July 1947, after Henderson had helped force the French military to cease its attacks but with France's divisive influence still strong, Syria held general elections. The results were predictable for a county that had only just been created out of rival political communities. The Damascus-based National Party, led by Shukri al-Quwatli, got more votes than any other group but was still able to form only a minority government. The lion's share of the ballots went to various "independents" representing ethnic and regional interests. Beneath the surface the reality was worse. "I look around me," writes Habib Kahaleh in *Memoirs of a [Syrian] Deputy*, "and see only a bundle of contradictions. . . ." Israel's humiliation of Arab armies in the 1948 war of independence further weakened the democratically elected government. When Syrian chief of staff Husni al-Za'im staged a coup d'état on March 30, 1949—the first of what were to be many military putsches in the post-colonial Arab world—crowds danced in the streets of Damascus.

Za'im had no coherent strategy for reconciling the various local nationalisms of what used to be French Syria. He was soon overthrown in another military coup, court-martialed, and shot. The next military regime restarted the process of scheduling new national elections, which in fact took place later in 1949. But the ballot results were just as fractured as in 1947, leading this latest democratic experiment to collapse into anarchy on account of competing sectarian interests that had matured under French rule. Strikes and demonstrations of the kind that occur in democratic societies were a frequent feature of this period. But so were political murders. The chaos ended in December 1949, when Colonel Adib al-Shishakli took power in another coup.

Shishakli's ability to restore order caused foreign observers to hail him as the Arab world's Ataturk, who could mold Syria into a nation on the Turkish model. But it was Shishakli himself who disabused foreigners of the notion that Syria could now find stability. In 1953 he publicly lamented that Syria was merely "the current official name for that country which lies within the artificial frontiers drawn up by imperialism." The trouble was, he was right.

In 1954 Shishakli was overthrown. Once again it was various sectarian elements within and outside the military: Druze soldiers, Alawites, Kurds, Armenians, and other minority groups, angered at Shishakli's Arabization program, who got rid of him.

A few months after Shishakli's overthrow, in the autumn of 1954, the Syrians held free and unfettered parliamentary elections. The results—as much as the results of Algeria's 1992 elections, which brought Moslem fundamentalists to the brink of power—constituted proof that Western democracy offered no quick solution for the ills of Arab societies. The largest number of seats went to the tribal and sectarian independents, while the biggest gains since the 1949 ballot were registered by the Baath ("Renaissance") party, a new group that attempted to paper over ethnic and religious fissures through an appeal to Communist-style economics and a pro-Soviet foreign policy.

Just as Henderson and company had witnessed firsthand the ravages of Stalinism, this new generation of Foreign Service officers was witnessing another painful spectacle that few in America could appreciate. Coon and his colleagues saw the Syrians struggling and ultimately failing to shake off the crushing weight of Ottoman and European colonial history, a history that the new Zionist state next door was a constant reminder of. Less than an hour's drive from Damascus, it was composed largely of European immigrants whose aggressive Western ways challenged, rather than harmonized with, the indigenous Arab-Islamic culture. And like the Maronites outside Beirut, these Jewish immigrants did not need missionary schools and printing presses to teach them about nationalism. That the Israelis could so quickly and easily construct a nation-state along classic Western liberal lines, while the Arabs of Syria, despite over a century of help from Protestant missionaries, could not, only rubbed salt in the wounds of the American expatriate community. And this had its effect on the American diplomats (some themselves from missionary families) whom the community interacted with.

Israel was the most visible cause not only of Syria's political agony but also of the Syrians' hatred of America, a hatred that was intense because it was so new and unexpected and that was beginning to drive the Syrians toward America's number-one enemy, the Soviets.

This hatred wasn't blind. The diplomats knew something that other Americans did not: the Israelis were not such knights in shining armor, nor were the Syrians such savages. For instance, Alfred Leroy Atherton, Jr., who along with Coon, Eagleton, and Stoltzfus was a young American diplomat in Syria in the 1950s, observed that the Israeli kibbutzniks being shot at by Syrian soldiers upon the Golan Heights were not the innocent victims portrayed by the American media. "Sure, the Syrians were firing on the

Israeli farmers. But these weren't ordinary farmers. They were paramilitary types, and they weren't in Israeli territory, but over the armistice line, deliberately testing and provoking the Syrians. That's why I argued the Syrians' case when I returned to Washington. At that time, I clearly felt a sympathy for the Arabs, knowing that the Israelis had enough sympathizers, and were more than able to take care of themselves." Nevertheless, daily living in Syria was also a lesson in how the Arab national character was helping to make a bad situation worse. Back to Carleton Coon:

"The Syrians had a well-deserved inferiority complex. I remember a military parade where a tank got out of control and killed a bystander. Because there was an American tourist in the area with a camera, they arrested him. . . . Both the Syrians and the Israelis have an extraordinary capacity for perceived injustice. On the Richter scale of emotional disturbances, they need to invent new points on it for the Semitic peoples of the Middle East."

Coon goes on:

"I remember a reception in Damascus where this Syrian journalist lectured me about how America was 'spreading a cancer eating into the heart of the Arab world.' I exploded, replying that 'Israel is here to stay because nobody outside the Middle East is going to get rid of it, and you people don't have the guts or the will to do it yourself.' The other Arabists in the room just stared at me and whispered, 'Coon's cracked.' I'd lost my cool. That's when I knew that I didn't really want to go the last step and become a real Arabist, which is what I should have become given my father's background."

Coon told another interviewer that Israel was ruining the atmosphere for American diplomats in the region. "It was pretty obvious to those who were closely attuned to the facts that the creation of the State of Israel was probably the single most damaging thing to U.S. policy and interests abroad that's happened since the Second World War, and with a long-term aftereffect. What it was doing to our credibility and our position—not only in the Arab states but throughout the Third World—was already evident to anybody who was thinking about it, and looking at it."*

Also, "there were other parts of the East I wanted to see during my

---

* This quote is taken from Coon's *Oral History*, a Foreign Service Institute program whereby retired ambassadors review their careers in a taped interview.

career." So in the summer of 1956, Coon packed up his Ford station wagon and drove across Iraq, Iran, Afghanistan, and Pakistan en route to his new post in New Delhi. "We had thirteen flat tires along the way." But Coon was back in the Middle East in 1963, as the U.S. consul in the northwestern Iranian city of Tabriz. "It was wonderful. Tabriz was at the high point of an eight-hundred year decline."

Coon later returned to the Arab world to serve in Morocco. After he retired, he spent part of his time editing the memoirs of Daniel Bliss, the founder of AUB. Because Coon never properly learned Arabic and spent much of his career outside the Arab world, he is known as an "NEA type," which is a close cousin of the Arabist. Coon calls NEA the best bureau in the State Department. "The East European people never had a riot on their hands until 1989. They never had an ambassador killed. Near East hands know what it's like to be shot at and in the media hot seat."

These things are said casually, without a trace of ill will or bitterness. Coon knows that he has had a successful career in the Foreign Service. He observes his visitor from a serene and detached distance, as though examining him through binoculars. His life overseas, he explains, has endowed him with a certain wisdom by inoculating him against "intellectual fads" and "domestic politics" in America. Coon calls this the "Rip Van Winkle syndrome," and he considers it a blessing.

Talcott Williams Seelye, like his boyhood acquaintances Bill Stoltzfus and Arthur Close, is another welcoming, George Bush sound-alike. Seelye's Washington-area home holds the material effects of a lifetime spent in the Arab world: Oriental carpets, miniature paintings, lithographs of the Holy Land, old books about the Middle East. "I don't read much of the new stuff about the area. I go back to the old books, like George Antonius's *The Arab Awakening*." When his visitor tells Seelye that he wants to write about Arabists, Seelye, a lanky gentleman born in 1922 in Beirut, smiles deeply and answers with a question: "Have you read *The Wilder Shores of Love?*"

The Wilder Shores of Love by Lesley Blanch is a somewhat obscure book about four Victorian-age women who, one might say, fill out their personalities in exotic backgrounds, searching for what, in Blanche's prose, "was vanishing from the West, something to which they were all subconsciously drawn. Repose: the Eastern climate of contemplation, of *Kif*, of nothingness, brought to its quintessential state of voluptuous, animal stillness was a state wholly alien to the West." But Seelye is no sybarite. Despite an at-times stormy career that, after he left the Foreign Service, brought him into head-on clashes with pro-Israel groups, he seems to have reached his own state of *Kif*, though, of course, he strongly denies being a romantic, preferring to see himself as "pragmatic, realistic and issue-oriented." The decorations in his home, he points out, "are entirely my wife's doing . . . collecting oriental objects interests me very little. Indeed, when she used to go to the *souk*, I, as an ex-athlete, was on the tennis court."

Seelye's family background reads like a history of the worldwide Protestant missionary movement. His paternal great-grandfather was president of Amherst College in the age when Daniel Bliss was a student there. His maternal great-grandfather was one of the early Congregationalist missionaries in Turkey and Iraq. This great-grandfather, William Frederic Williams, born in 1819—the year the first missionaries sailed to the Middle East—had a brother, S. Welles Williams, who became a missionary in China. Fluent in both Chinese and Japanese, Welles Williams was the interpreter for Commodore Perry when the latter opened Japan to commerce in 1852. "My great-great-grandfather pledged that his two sons would serve God, so one went to China and another to the Middle East," Seelye explains.

Seelye and every other Arabist of his generation feels a blood brother relationship with the "China hands," those Protestant missionaries and their diplomatic successors in China, who, like the Arabists, were publicly excoriated in the 1950s. "We're part of the same family tree," Seelye says. In his eyes, at the same time the China hands were falling prey to the McCarthyists, the Arabists were falling prey to the new pro-Israel lobby. While the China hands were accused of having "lost China" to the Communists, the Arabists were tarred with the brush of anti-Semitism. " 'Who lost China? Who opposed the creation of Israel?' It's the same accusation really," complains a friend of Seelye's. "The China hands were merely reporting the truth, which is that Chiang Kai-shek's crowd was corrupt and Mao Zedong was going to take over China. And report the truth was what we always did in the Middle East." (George Bush, who was America's top diplomat in China in the 1970s, might be considered a latter-day China hand. Though, because Bush never learned Chinese, he would be more accurately labeled a China type. This may partly explain Bush's indulgence of the Communist regime during his presidency.)

William Frederic Williams, Seelye's great-grandfather, arrived in Syria in 1849 at the age of thirty. In 1851 he moved to Mosul, where two years later he helped save the life of the head of the local Jewish community, Rabbi Sholoem, whom Ottoman officials had arrested on trumped-up charges. (Whether it is missionaries like Williams or scholar-adventurers like Coon, Sr., when it came to Oriental Jews *in situ*, Americans in the Middle East were generally sympathetic.) Williams later moved to Mardin, near the present-day Turkish-Syrian border, where he was able to acquire some of the priceless Assyrian antiquities then being unearthed at the site of ancient Nineveh. Williams died in southern Turkey in 1871. He had out-lived his four wives, who all fell to disease in the Middle East. A daughter returned to New England where she married a Presbyterian minister, William Nesbitt Chambers—Seelye's grandfather. Chambers, at the be-hest of his wife, converted to Congregationalism and, after graduating from Princeton, went out to eastern Turkey as a missionary, following in the footsteps of his father-in-law, Williams. (It was Chambers, the reader may recall, who had been an eyewitness to the mass murder of Armenians and who, as a result, had written an emotional plea to Woodrow Wilson, ar-guing for a more aggressive U.S. policy in the region. Chambers was also a close acquaintance of the British officer Charles Doughty-Wylie—the nephew and namesake of Charles Doughty and the lover of Gertrude Bell.)

Seelye's mother was born in Erzurum in northeastern Turkey, where Chambers was stationed. While doing graduate work in Islamic studies at Columbia University in New York, she met Seelye's father, Laurens Seelye, himself the son of a Congregationalist minister. The couple moved to Beirut in 1919 when Seelye's father obtained a position as professor of psychology and philosophy at AUB.

Seelye grew up in 1920s and 1930s Beirut, with Stoltzfus, Close, and the children of Bayard Dodge: Grace, David, and Bayard, Jr. "My boyhood in Lebanon was 2,000 percent American," he hastens to note. "I vehemently resisted learning Arabic as a child and had to learn it like any other Foreign Service officer." Otherwise, his memories of "sleepy and peaceful" Beirut, surrounded by Armenian servants—refugees from the Turkish holo-caust—are quite pleasant. "Things changed though. Israel was one of the factors that politicized Lebanon."

When Seelye returned to the New England of his ancestors to attend Deerfield Academy and Amherst College, the idea of going back to the Middle East for his life's work, as his father, grandfather, and great-grandfather had done, had not entered his mind. In World War II, however, Seelye wound up serving in Iran just prior to Stalin's thrust into the region (which Loy Henderson helped to counter). Then, after he entered the Foreign Service, Seelye was dispatched to occupied Germany where John McCloy was high commissioner. Seelye certainly feels an affinity with Henderson, McCloy, and the other "wise men." He intimates that whereas Henderson, George Kennan, and Charles Bohlen were targeted for daring to report the negative aspects of the Russian reality, Arabists of his generation were targeted for daring to report the positive aspects of the Arab one.

Seelye says he "had mixed feelings about serving in Germany after the war, on account of what the Nazis did to the Jews. I went into Arab affairs only because there were too many German-speaking officers and the Middle East was opening up as a career. But given my family history, I suppose my relationship with the Arabs is atavistic. In America we've lost the attribute of the extended family, while the Arabs have this in spades."

Seelye is not the only Arabist of his generation to have served as a young Foreign Service officer in Germany immediately after World War II, where much of the consular work involved the processing of visa applications for Jewish refugees. Parker Hart and Alfred Leroy Atherton, both future assistant secretaries of state for Near Eastern affairs, as well as other Arabists, had this experience. All claim it sensitized them to the Jews' plight, and encouraged their interest in the Arab-Israeli dispute. "It became clear in Germany that the Middle East was where the action would be in the future, and so I wanted to go there," explains one Arabist. The fact that all asked for assignments in the Arab world, rather than in Israel, might have a legitimate explanation: careerwise, Israel was from its birth seen as a dead end for Foreign Service officers. Why learn a different language like Hebrew, which would be useful in only one country, when you could learn Arabic and have the doors of over twenty countries opened to you? Still, it is noteworthy that Seelye and his colleagues, after a living experience in post-Hitler Germany when the ashes of the Holocaust were still warm, requested postings in the Arab world during the first years of the Arab-Israel conflict. It is impossible to know their inner motivations—they themselves might not know.

In 1952 Seelye left Germany to return to the Middle East of his boyhood, which he had not seen since the 1930s prior to his entering Deerfield. What he found was intimate familiarity. His first posting was Amman, Jordan, where as a junior diplomat he had a special relationship with the Jordanian cabinet because "half of its members were ex-students of my father at the AUB." Seelye never looked back. After studying Arabic with a Palestinian teacher, he was to spend the next thirty years as an American diplomat in the Arab world, here and there interrupted by stints at the State Department, where he worked exclusively on American-Arab relations.

Along the way Seelye developed what might be considered traditional Arabist views. He learned a deep respect for the British Arabists of yore, and felt that the Israelis' displacement of the Palestinian Arabs was the core problem of the Middle East, responsible in large part for the region's violence and instability. Seelye talks easily about the time in October 1973 when, as ambassador to Tunisia, he sent Secretary of State Henry Kissinger a cable, advising Kissinger not to send arms for Israel's defense after the surprise attack by Egypt and Syria. Though Kissinger reprimanded him, Kissinger was well enough aware of Seelye's skills as a hands-on Arab specialist to trust him to go to Lebanon as a special emissary in 1976 after the assassination of Ambassador Francis Meloy, Jr. In Beirut Seelye managed the low-key evacuation of U.S. diplomats and their families in the midst of a civil war. Still, Seelye was criticized for employing security men from the Palestine Liberation Organization (PLO) in the operation. "I used the PLO simply because they controlled the area we had to pass through," he explains.

As ambassador to Syria in 1981, Seelye's diplomatic cables—supportive, in the eyes of some, of Syria's actions—would cause Francis Fukuyama, then on the State Department's policy planning staff, to scrawl in the margins: "Talcott Seelye is the Syrian ambassador to Washington, not the American ambassador to Syria." But from Seelye's point of view, "I was bending over backwards to prove that I wasn't ipso facto biased."

By the summer of 1981, Seelye had had it with the strongly pro-Israel policy of the newly installed Reagan Administration and its secretary of state, Alexander Haig. He was not offered a promotion, and on August 31 Seelye called reporters of the *Washington Post* and the Associated Press into the ambassador's office in Damascus to announce his retirement from the Foreign Service. Leaning back in his chair, Seelye went on to disparage the Camp David effort and to call on the United States to immediately recognize the PLO. Seelye also blasted Israeli prime minister Menachem Begin and the "plantation settlements" on the West Bank. Samuel W. Lewis, the U.S. ambassador to Israel then, calls Seelye's action "despicable."

In May 1982, now a private citizen, Seelye addressed the National Association of Arab Americans, saying, "We will have to convince Israel that the Holy City of Jerusalem cannot be forever controlled exclusively by the smallest and least powerful of the religions for which it is holy." Using words that might well have been spoken by Loy Henderson, Seelye added that "a strong American president can override a domestic lobby in the pursuit of U.S. national interests." Later that year, speaking before the Amherst alumni association, Seelye criticized Israeli defense minister Ariel Sharon. Through Seelye's eyes, Sharon was "indistinguishable from a Nazi stormtrooper."

As you might guess, Seelye did not have an easy relationship with American Jews. He recalls an occasion when he and a group of Arabists from the State Department were invited to a Jewish fund-raising dinner. "At the end of the evening, though, we [the Arabists] were all back at the same table alone together. I guess they felt uncomfortable with us and perhaps we with them. It was sort of a shame."

"You might say that I overspecialized in the Middle East," Seelye admits. One of his daughters, however, has continued the family tradition. After studying Arabic at Amherst and the American University of Cairo (AUC), she moved to Jordan to teach. She works as a staff aide to Queen Noor.

The bird-watcher's "love" for the Arabs, as Crossman puts it, need not translate into a difficult relationship with Israel. As there are all kinds of people, there are all kinds of bird-watchers.

Richard Undeland gives you the same remote and penetrating stare as do Seelye and Coon. He was born in Omaha in 1930, but upon entering Harvard, he left the Midwest behind him. A degree from Harvard led to postgraduate studies at Stanford and then to a seminar about Egypt that affected him so deeply that he arranged to spend a year in Cairo on a scholarship. "The moment I arrived in Egypt [in the mid-1950s] the Arabs and their world immediately appealed to me. I just knew it was a place where I would always be welcome. We Americans brought education and medicine to Syria and the Arabian Gulf, and I felt we were bringing similar things to Egypt."

In Egypt Undeland became interested in the United States Information Service (USIS), an adjunct to the State Department that deals exclusively with media and cultural relations. He joined USIS in 1957 and was sent to Beirut to learn Arabic. By this time the State Department had established a field school for Arabic training in Beirut, which, while not officially connected with the AUB, was part and parcel of the same expatriate world. "The AUB offered us lectures and concerts. Its students used our library. We used theirs. We had a lot to do with each other." A year in that hot-house atmosphere of American Arabism convinced Undeland that his first instincts about the Arabs were right: they were for him. From 1958, when he became a press and culture officer at the U.S. embassy in Tunis, to 1992, when he retired from the Foreign Service, he served exclusively in Arab affairs with the sole exception of eighteen months in Saigon during the Vietnam War. "I have more years of living experience in the Arab world than any Arabist in the U.S. Foreign Service." That is a fact. Undeland rattles off his life story in a breezy monotone:

"Nineteen sixty-two to '64, Alexandria; '66 to '67, Algiers, though four months of that time I spent in Rabat; '67 to '69, Washington; '70, back to Beirut; '71, Kuwait; '72 to '75, Jordan; '76 to '77, Kuwait, Bahrein, and Qatar; '79 to '83, Damascus. Yeah, I was on the board of the American School in Syria. The school was near an army barracks that had been blown up by fundamentalists. Walking through the school afterwards, I found a foot by the door . . . But we had an active cultural program. We sent five thousand Syrians to study in the U.S. Our library in Damascus did a big business. . . ."

Undeland and his wife, Joan, were married in Cairo. Their first child was born in Beirut, their second in Tunis, and their third in Alexandria. Undeland's last posting was Tunis, the place where he began his Foreign Service career three decades before. Over that period he made several visits to Israel. "Israelis have a mania with security that I'll never understand." That is as strong as his displeasure gets. "Sure, I disagreed with this and that element of our pro-Israel policy. But I've always felt completely comfortable defending it to my Arab contacts. If you believe, as I do, that the basic things America stands for can lead to the sort of world we all want, then it is never a problem compromising on the details. The key is to know *who* you are, and that what you are is an American, not an Arab, not an Israeli."

Undeland, a tall and thin man like Seelye, became an avid trekker in his later years. Before retiring to Washington, he spent every weekend walking to villages and Bedouin encampments in the Tunisian countryside, enjoying the people and the flora and fauna. "As you can guess, I like the Arab world. I've had a good life here," he shrugs.

And it's just as simple and as complex as that.

Not all the old Arab hands in the Foreign Service are bird-watchers. Some are more the analytical type, like Loy Henderson. Richard Bordeaux Parker was this kind of Arabist.

"Talcott Seelye and Dick Parker were your typical Arabists," a State Department colleague of theirs recollects, not altogether fondly. "They even looked alike." Their physical resemblance to the contrary, Seelye and Parker are quite different. Whereas Seelye was born and brought up in the Arab world in a family steeped in missionary work, Dick Parker was born an army brat in the Philippines in 1923. Three months later his father was transferred stateside, and the family settled in Kansas. Parker's family, unlike those of Seelye and other Arabists, were not New England Brahmins. They did not have the money or social connections to send him to a prestige school. So Parker went to Kansas State University, where he studied engineering. In 1943 Parker entered the army infantry, serving as a platoon commander in World War II. At the Battle of the Bulge, in the Ardennes forest in late 1944, Parker was taken prisoner by the Nazis. They transported him and other captured Americans, in sealed, freezing box cars and with no food, to a prisoner of war camp in western Poland. As the war moved toward its conclusion, in another stroke of lousy luck, he was liberated by the Red Army. The Soviets transported him, in conditions little better than those of the Germans, to Odessa, on the Black Sea. Not until 1946, a year after the war had ended, was Parker released from the Soviet Union.

It was spring. Although the weather was still cold on the north shore of the Black Sea, as Parker's boat sailed southward the air began to warm slightly. And then, suddenly, after three years of grim destruction and desolation, he saw "the walls of Constantinople, the domes and minarets, things that I had never seen before. I never knew things that old existed." For the first time in three years, he saw city lights. But what he remembers most about Constantinople (Istanbul) is the warmth, since the three previous years had been almost a nonstop bout of shivering. But the boat sailed on, ever southward. In Port Said, at the entrance to the Suez Canal, in the delicious spring heat of the southern Mediterranean, Dick Parker experienced freedom for the first time since World War II. "Each of us was given two hundred dollars and allowed off the ship to enjoy the town."

Discharged from the army in 1947, Parker returned to Kansas only to finish college. Then in 1949 he joined the Foreign Service.

At that moment, the State Department was beginning to respond to the new, post–World War II reality of a complex and variegated world of different peoples and language groups, where the United States was a military and economic power competing with the Soviet Union for influence. Such a reality required a truly professional Foreign Service. It was no longer enough, in the words of one Foreign Service official, "to have a WASP club of gong-and-trinket men and blue-blooded, born-to-the-fold amateurs, who had learned schoolboy French and German but knew nothing of languages like Urdu or Arabic. We needed real area specialists."

This realization had one intended and one unintended result. The unintended result was that it provided an opening for the most blue-blooded of WASPs, the "missionary children of Lebanon" like Seelye and Stoltzfus, who, regardless of their actual knowledge of Arabic, boasted a store of inherited knowledge and experience concerning the Middle East that formed an obvious foundation for area expertise. The intended result was that it gave lesser-born but deserving types like Dick Parker an opportunity also.

Parker had picked up German in the POW camp, displaying a natural aptitude for languages that he never knew he had. After a mandatory tour of duty as a junior FSO in Australia, Parker was assigned to the divided city of Jerusalem in 1951. "My wife and I lived by the Mandelbaum Gate [the crossing point between the Israeli and Jordanian halves of Jerusalem]. There I paid a tutor to teach me Arabic."

Formal Arabic training for FSOs was then in its infancy. Until 1950 the State Department had made few provisions for teaching exotic eastern languages, now vital in an era of global competition with the Soviets. William Hodgson in the 1820s and Raymond Hare in the 1920s both had to go abroad to learn Arabic. In 1947, when a young Hermann Eilts entered the Foreign Service, the only place in America where he could study Arabic was at the Harvard Divinity School. "I was taught the basics by a Scotch Presbyterian missionary-type. Afterwards, the Foreign Service gave me a language test, which consisted of asking me to count to ten in Arabic. Having counted correctly, I was pronounced an Arabist." But within a few short years the situation dramatically changed. The Foreign Service established a field school for Arabic language training in Beirut, influenced no doubt by the proximity of the AUB. That's where Parker headed after two years in Jerusalem.

By the time he got to Beirut from Jerusalem, Parker's opinions on the Arab-Israeli dispute were well on their way to crystallization. Unlike Seelye, Parker's family background had no Middle East component. However, his war experience allowed him to empathize with Jews to a degree that Seelye perhaps could not. "Though I was spared the horrors of the Holocaust, being a prisoner of the Germans in a boxcar in midwinter made me much more sensitive than the average American to what the Jews had experienced. When I learned in Australia that the State Department was sending me to the Middle East, I excitedly told the Israeli consul. He provided me with my first reading lists and lessons on Middle East politics. I went out to Jerusalem being pro-Israeli."

Then his ideas changed, as they often do when one is exposed to the reality of living in a place as opposed to just reading about it or visiting it briefly. Let Parker himself explain:

"Gradually, without my being aware, the Arabs ceased being abstractions to me and became real people, some of whom became our friends. Though I don't think I had illusions about them, I did understand their political justifications, and they were more personable than the Israelis. I don't think this was because I was learning Arabic rather than Hebrew. Language is merely a tool for detailed communications. Living in a place is more important for insight than knowing the language." Parker should know. He went on to become NEA's first modern area specialist: the first State Department Arabist to achieve a 4 rating on a scale of 5 in the Foreign Service testing system instituted in the 1950s.

Parker is also right when he alludes to the Arabs being more personable than the Israelis. Crossman in *Palestine Mission* mentions how "tense, bourgeois, central European or even German" the Jews of Palestine seemed. But it went deeper than that. As a British official in post–World War I Transjordan put it, "Years of Arab courtesy spoil us for the rough and tumble of the Western world." The Jews of Palestine—a brash and dynamic settler society that included not a few angst-ridden and intellectual eccentrics—represented that Western world with a vengeance. Crossman describes a conversation in Jerusalem about why "Englishmen can't help being pro-Arab."

The colonel said it was anti-Semitism, but an older officer said that this was true long before Hitler and before any Englishmen knew what anti-Semitism was. Someone else suggested that we always backed the underdog. . . . But this wouldn't work, as another officer pointed out. All through the Arab Revolt, when our men were being shot in the back and protecting the Jews, most of them liked the Arabs: "The old Arab will take a pot at you in the night, but he'll offer you coffee next day when you come to investigate. The Jew doesn't offer you coffee even when you're protecting him." They finally concluded that what made a policeman pro-Arab was Arab courtesy. . . . Then a young officer said: "But it's also because the Arab is somehow below your level. If he was educated and your equal [like the Jew] you mightn't like him so much.

As Parker was able to go back and forth to Israel through the Mandelbaum Gate, he increasingly took for granted the stark difference between Israeli society and the rest of the Middle East. But this was not true of his State Department colleagues based in Damascus and other Arab capitals.

Alfred Leroy Atherton saw Israel for the first time in the summer of 1955, after he had been in Syria for three straight years. "My God, what intense, emotional people the Israelis are!" he thought. "You can't have a discussion with them without feeling physically drained." Michael Sterner, another Arabist of this generation, first saw Israel in 1959, after nearly a decade in the Arab world, working for the Arabian American Oil Company (ARAMCO) and then the State Department. His impressions:

"In contrast to the Arab world, there was an intellectual tone and vibrancy to Israeli life. Suddenly, after unscrewing our Arab license plates on our Morris Minor convertible in the no-man's-land between Lebanon and Israel, I was plunged into a society where everybody seemed to be arguing about the future of socialism. This was a time of idealistic fervor in Israel, before cynicism began to prevail. Oh, but was the food terrible! A succession of overcooked Wiener schnitzels."

Sterner, like Atherton, like Parker, like Talcott Seelye—who made nine short trips to Israel during his three decades in the Arab world—was able to relax upon returning to Araby. Israelis were easy people to respect but difficult people to be around. The problem was they treated you like just another member of their immediate family, without the decorum and comfortable distance normally provided to strangers. Moreover, they were just as smart as you, and what was worse, they never let you forget it.

After Arabic language training in Beirut, Dick Parker's career began to resemble Richard Undeland's and Talcott Seelye's: Amman, the Israel-Jordan desk at the State Department, the Libyan desk, back to Beirut, then Cairo, the Egypt desk in Washington, Rabat . . . In 1960, after finishing his assignment in Washington as the Libyan desk officer, the opportunity arose for Parker to learn Hebrew. "I refused, because it might have had an adverse effect on my career as an Arabist. . . . I admit, there really was lots of localitis back then."

"Localitis," also known as "clientitis," began in World War I, when British political agents adopted the cause of the particular Arab tribal leader to whom he or she was assigned. In the post–World War II State Department, it meant sympathy for one side of an issue and the people associated with it, because of lack of exposure to the other side. This happened in many parts of the globe. For instance, diplomats in New Delhi sometimes became pro-Indian and anti-Pakistani, while those in Islamabad might become pro-Pakistani and anti-Indian. This syndrome became particularly prevalent in the Middle East because of sheer mathematics. Arabic, along with Chinese, Japanese, and Korean is classified by the Foreign Service as a "super-hard" language; more difficult than Russian and Persian even, which are merely "hard" languages.* Learning proper Arabic, therefore, takes years. Having made that investment in an individual, the Foreign Service demands that those linguistic skills be used. While Chinese is useful in only a few foreign countries, Korean in only North and South Korea, and Japanese only in Japan, there are more than two dozen U.S. embassies and consulates in the Arab world, enough to last a diplomatic lifetime. Thus, while a China hand might spend only part of his career in Chinese-related affairs, an Arabist could spend his adult life in the Arab world, and such a circumstance would naturally affect his views on the Arab-Israeli question.

By the late 1960s Parker got a reputation as someone afflicted with localitis. "After the Six-Day War in 1967 [which Egypt lost], I fought a lonely battle in the State Department to get Egypt and [Egypt's President, Gamal Abdel] Nasser to be taken seriously." Parker became one of Nasser's only friends in Washington. So when Joseph Sisco became assistant secre-

---

* Though Persian also employs the Arabic script, it is a member of the Indo-European language group rather than the Afro-Semitic group, making Persian closer to English and therefore somewhat easier to learn.

tary of state of NEA in 1969 and initiated a partial cleaning-out of the Arabist "old boys' network," Dick Parker was among the casualties. He was shifted from Egyptian affairs—in the heart of the Arab-Israeli action—to Morocco, on the periphery of the Arab world and Middle East politics. "I had a personal dislike of Sisco," says Parker, adding that he found his four years in Morocco as the U.S. embassy's deputy chief of mission (DCM) "boring and dull politically."

Parker went on to become the U.S. ambassador to Algeria and then the ambassador to Lebanon in 1977, a year after Talcott Seelye had evacuated the embassy (the security situation for Americans in Beirut had improved somewhat). "I got pretty pissed off with Israeli arrogance and disregard of Lebanese sovereignty. Between the Israelis and the Syrians, there was not much to choose from." By repudiating an agreement on troop movements in south Lebanon, Parker indicates that Israeli prime minister Menachem Begin "embarrassed" him. In Parker's Georgetown home, the walls of his study are adorned not only with Arabic calligraphy but with ugly caricatures of Begin done by Arab artists.

Parker ended his career as ambassador to Morocco, from where he was declared persona non grata by King Hassan in 1979 for reporting on political opposition to the king. Parker calls himself a member of "an elite club, the *Awhab Shubak*—'Arabists Who Have Been Shit Upon by Arab Kings.'" Another reason King Hassan disliked Parker was because it was Parker who had to tell Hassan's friend, the exiled Shah of Iran—then in Morocco—that he could not come to America. "I was instructed to offer the Shah a home in Paraguay or South Africa. I must say he took it like a man."

Parker is sharply critical of President Jimmy Carter for not "closing the U.S. embassy in Iran in 1978 and honoring our friend," the same Shah whom Loy Henderson had put back on the throne a quarter century earlier. Parker, like Henderson, has a tough and unsentimental view of U.S. interests. Parker thinks the United States should have been much harder on the Israelis throughout the decades but also much harder on Saddam Hussein. In this way he can be quite critical of his Arabist friends and colleagues who served in Iraq in the 1980s. "Parker is hard to explain," says a colleague. "There's a curmudgeon side to him that antagonizes both his friends and the Israelis."

Parker, now in retirement, is doing what he refused to do in 1960: study

Hebrew. Engaged in a review of the Six-Day War, he "became frustrated at my inability to read Yitzhak Rabin's memoirs in the original." Anyway, that is the reason he gives for his latest endeavor.

Joseph Sisco, who in 1969 became the first non-Arabist to head NEA, claims he "can identify two dozen different kinds of Arabists. Okay, I'm exaggerating," bearing down on his visitor in a pugnacious way. "But believe me, there is no stereotypical Arabist." As proof Sisco cites his former NEA sidekick, Alfred Leroy Atherton, Jr., who is neither a bird-watcher nor a Loy Henderson clone.

Roy Atherton is a truly rare species of NEA type cum Arabist: an old hand who grew into a modern. He proved to be the most successful and influential of his generation of Middle East specialists, a man whose personal growth regarding the Arab-Israeli question would quietly affect history. Atherton started out in Syria in the 1950s, forming the same impressions about Arabs and Israelis as the other U.S. diplomats there. But Atherton's views kept evolving, though it is difficult to say precisely why. While Atherton spent a significant part of his career outside the Arab orbit, so did other diplomats whose opinions did not approximate his. The answer to this question may have more to do with the mysteries of personality than with any particular experience.

Roy Atherton creates the same impression as Bill Stoltzfus, Carleton Coon, Talcott Seelye, Richard Undeland, and Dick Parker. He is courtly and distinguished, young in the eyes, and full of fond memories of salad days in Araby. But rather than Oriental carpets, Arabic calligraphy, and old lithographs of the Holy Land in his office, Atherton has signed photographs of Menachem Begin, Anwar Sadat, and Henry Kissinger, thanking him for his efforts and his friendship. The day after Begin died in 1992, Atherton sat in his office in a reflective mood. He had known Begin well and negotiated with him. "History will do right by him," observed Atherton. "In giving up Sinai and making peace with Egypt, Begin made some hard, wise choices, that meant repudiating things he had been fighting for all his life."

Born in 1921 in Pittsburgh, Roy Atherton grew up in Springfield, Massachusetts, where his father was an engineer. "We were a solid, middle-class family," he says. "You want to know about anti-Semitism? Well, when a

Jewish family moved into our neighborhood—this was Christian America of the 1930s, remember—you saw real, virulent anti-Semitism; something far worse than the anti-Israel attitudes of some American diplomats I knew."

In Springfield Atherton attended the public schools. Upon his high school graduation, his father made a decision—the kind of decision that the best of parents make—that changed his son's life. "Dad thought I was, well, not prepared emotionally to enter college at that point. I was immature. I lacked confidence. So he sent me for an additional year of secondary school to Phillips Exeter Academy." Founded in 1781 in Exeter, New Hampshire, Phillips Exeter was part of the same elite, prep school world as Phillips-Andover and Deerfield. Because his parents' resources were limited, Atherton waited on tables to help pay the tuition. Ten months at Exeter enabled him to get into Harvard. It also widened his horizons by exposing him to a more worldly set of young people. In 1938 Atherton even made a summer bicycle tour of Germany, staying at youth hostels. "As long as I live I'll never forget the signs, 'Hitler Youth, *Juden Verboten* (Jews Forbidden).' It was the kind of experience that matured me and personalized the abstract." After war broke out, Atherton interrupted his studies to serve in a field artillery unit. Like Parker, he fought at the Battle of the Bulge. The GI Bill made it possible for him to return to Harvard after the war, to get his degree, and to study German. Germany and world politics by now fascinated him.

In those days the Ivy League still functioned as a sort of farm system for the Foreign Service. In the spring of 1947, Atherton passed the Foreign Service exam and was posted to the U.S. consulate in Stuttgart, Germany. Atherton's job consisted of interviewing concentration camp survivors and other displaced persons cast up by the maelstrom of war who had applied for visas to the United States. At this time, a Jewish colleague of Atherton's in the Foreign Service, Seymour (Max) Finger, went to America to attend a ceremony celebrating the creation of Israel. "Max came back to Germany choked up by the experience. I never remember him so emotional. It stuck in my memory." After three years in Stuttgart, Atherton and his wife, Betty, were moved to Bonn, where John McCloy had recently arrived as the American high commissioner to organize occupied West Germany's transition to full independence. In Bonn it seemed that everywhere the junior diplomat looked he saw the Middle East. The Joint Distribution Committee, a Jewish organization, was helping to send concentration camp survivors to Israel. Atherton had made a close friend at the British embassy, Peter Male, who had just been transferred to Bonn from Damascus. Male told Atherton that the Middle East was a coming issue where diplomatic careers could be made.

So on April 1, 1952, near the end of five years in Germany, Atherton filled out what a Foreign Service officer called his April Fool's card: you listed the three posts you most wanted and usually got none of them. Atherton was fortunate. He asked for Damascus, Beirut, or Amman. He got Damascus.

Before going there, Atherton took a Middle East area studies course provided by the Foreign Service Institute, taught by Edward Wright. "Wright was a missionary," recalls Atherton. "He was pro-Arab and anti–Israel." In the face of Wright's indoctrination, Atherton's pro-Israeli tendencies went into hibernation. Atherton then spent the next four years of his life, until 1956, in Damascus. "The mindset of my colleagues in Syria, and myself at the time, was this: mass disillusionment as it became clear that our government was taking the side of this interloper in the Middle East—Israel. I was indoctrinated to believe that the Arabs were innocent victims of Europe's problem with the Jews. Due to the political situation in Syria in the fifties, a latent Arab anti-Semitism had arisen. And American diplomats had sympathy for it. But my colleagues were more pro-Arab than they were closet anti-Semites. This was certainly not the anti-Semitism of Springfield, Massachusetts, when a Jewish family moved in."

The U.S. ambassador of Syria at the time was James Moose, an Arabist with a scholar's grasp of the language and culture, but also someone who was rapidly becoming disenchanted not only with the U.S. policy but with the Arabs, too. One day Atherton nervously entered the ambassador's office to ask Moose for some career advice. Atherton thought it was about time that he studied Arabic in order to become a real Arabist. Moose replied, "Young man, I have studied and learned Arabic and have served in the Arab world. And I have concluded that Arabic is a language that opens the door to an empty room. Take my advice, study French instead."

That's what Atherton did. He says he "regrets" that he never learned Arabic. But Atherton is merely being gracious to his Arabist friends. He knows that had he learned Arabic, his career might not have advanced as far as it did. Atherton, without being aware of it, was starting to acquire the perfect résumé for the Kissinger era: that of someone with solid experience in the Middle East but without the stigma and set of beliefs that went with being a real Arabist, that is, the kind of Arabist Seelye or Stoltzfus or Parker appeared to be.

In 1956 Atherton was transferred from Damascus to the northern Syrian city of Aleppo, where he and Carleton Coon set up a temporary consulate in a room of the old Barron's Hotel. The poor conditions in Aleppo forced Atherton's wife to remain in Damascus. (Their daughter was at the American Community School in Beirut.) It was at a café in Homs in October 1956, while en route from Aleppo to Damascus to visit his wife, that Atherton learned about Israel's attack on Egypt. The simmering crisis over Nasser's nationalization of the Suez Canal and Palestinian guerrilla attacks on Israel from Egyptian territory had culminated in a major war. Great Britain and France, angered over the canal's nationalization, joined Israel in a three-pronged attack across Egypt's Sinai Peninsula. "I was extremely critical of Israel at that moment," says Atherton, "and happily for me, so was Eisenhower." Because President Dwight Eisenhower had suspended economic aid to Israel and was about to force the Jewish State to withdraw from the Sinai territory it had just captured, "we Americans were in good standing with our Arab friends in Syria."*

Thus on January 1, 1957, Atherton was able to raise the Stars and Stripes on the new U.S. consulate building in Aleppo and begin hiring a local Syrian staff. (Coon had just left by car for his new posting in India.) But this brief second honeymoon between Americans and Syrians collapsed the following year when Eisenhower sent U.S. Marines ashore in Lebanon to prop up the Maronite Christian government of Camille Chamoun. The Marine landing led to anti-American demonstrations outside the Aleppo consulate. Also in 1958, the U.S. president—with critical help from Loy Henderson—forged the Baghdad Pact, an anti-Soviet alliance that included Turkey, Iran, Pakistan, and the pro-Western Hashemite regime in Iraq. A military coup then followed in Iraq which overthrew the monarchy established by Gertrude Bell and her British colleagues after World War I. Suddenly, Arab populations in Iraq, Syria, and Egypt were being radicalized, causing Atherton and his diplomatic colleagues to become extremely critical of their own government's policy. "We felt that Israel's existence now made it impossible for the Arabs to be anti-Soviet." Atherton remem-

---

* "This psychological bonding between local Arabs and Americans was not limited to Syria. In Egypt, during the 1956 war, the wife of an American diplomat said in a reference to the Egyptian soldiers fighting the Israelis, "We're so proud of them."

bers a visit from Colonel William and Mary Eddy, his house guests in Damascus. Eddy, of missionary background, was Arthur Close's uncle and the ambassador to Saudi Arabia. Atherton says Eddy was opposed to using the Marines to bail out a Maronite Christian government, even though it was pro-American.

Eddy, according to the scholar Phillip Baram, "was the great and personal friend of the Arabs and expressed their point of view, especially Ibn Saud's, with unceasing advocacy. . . ." In 1947 Eddy resigned from the State Department in protest against Truman's pro-Jewish policy in Palestine. He died in 1962. At his own request Eddy was buried in Lebanon, with the words "U.S. Marines" emblazoned on his tombstone.

But Atherton was never completely comfortable with this partisan environment, which was an outgrowth of the insular and corporate culture of the Beirut missionary establishment. As the control officer responsible for organizing a regional ambassadors' conference in Damascus, Atherton witnessed how the U.S. ambassador to Israel, Edward B. Lawson, was treated by his fellow American ambassadors. "Lawson was the enemy, pure and simple. That he was indeed an *American* ambassador seemed less relevant than the fact that he was assigned to Israel." After the conference Atherton asked Moose to approve a holiday he and his wife wanted to take in Israel. "Moose warned that if I went, the Syrians might declare me persona non grata." Atherton went anyway. "When we returned there were no repercussions from the Syrians. I found them intensely curious about my impressions of Israel."

Atherton concludes his memory of Syria with this statement: "There are two things I don't remember: Arabists serving in Israel and Jewish Foreign Service officers serving anywhere in the Middle East. That's when I began to wonder whether we Americans weren't becoming part of the battle."

In 1959, after twelve years abroad—the last seven in Syria—Roy Atherton returned to Washington to work on the Iraq-Jordan desk at the State Department. He worked under William Lakeland, "an old Arabist who was very much a supporter of Arab nationalism, Nasser, and Sunni majority rule." Because Atherton still had not learned Arabic, it was clear that "I was not quite a member of the club." So after a brief spell with Lakeland, Atherton was moved out of Arab affairs and assigned to the Greek-Turkish division.

"I went from being a big fish in little Aleppo to the doggie work of a bureaucrat in the State Department. It was a lesson in readjusting your self-image. I quickly learned that just as Washington didn't understand what it was like overseas, from overseas you couldn't understand Washington." It was a readjustment that not every FSO was able to make. While many Arabists could deal with Arabs from the rarefied heights of an embassy chancellery, they could not deal with fellow Americans in the grueling and competitive environment of the State Department. But it was in those claustrophobic corridors where reputations were made.

Following two years in Washington, Atherton took a sabbatical to study economics at the University of California at Berkeley. Then he became an economics officer at the U.S. consulate in Calcutta, India. Careerwise, this was a sidestep. But along with the work on the Greek-Turkish desk, it added a healthy balance to the Arabist side of his résumé.

In 1965 Atherton again returned to Washington and the NEA bureau. Raymond Hare, the junior diplomat in Cairo during World War II, was now the assistant secretary of state for NEA. Hare's top deputy was Harrison Symmes, for whom Atherton worked. NEA in this period was a well-greased Arabist machine, functioning as a bureaucratic counterweight to an increasingly sophisticated Jewish lobbying apparatus. NEA, its loyalists would say, was the one place in Washington where the Arabs could get a fair hearing. It was also a place where the Israelis and their supporters could not get a foot in the door. One of Atherton's responsibilities was to deal with relief agencies operating in the Middle East. He noticed that whereas CARE and other groups working with the Arabs were being given all sorts of diplomatic and logistical support by NEA, the various Jewish relief groups working in Israel "were being treated as second-class citizens, not even recognized by the bureau. It was outrageous." So Atherton, in the cool and quiet way for which he was to become known, set about changing the rules. His ability to do this without alienating others in the bureau showed considerable bureaucratic skill that did not go unnoticed by his superiors or by the Jewish lobby, with whom Atherton—again, quietly—began to develop contacts. Atherton's pro-Jewish sympathies, dormant during the Syrian part of his life, were now resurfacing to balance out his pro-Arab sympathies. A colleague of Atherton's remarked, "Roy was as genuinely evenhanded as you could be. He never revealed his opinions. To this day, I couldn't tell you what they are."

As it happened, following Atherton's little coup with the relief agencies came a bureaucratic reorganization of the State Department that landed Atherton in the job of director of Arab-Israeli affairs. Then in June 1967 came the Six-Day War, the bolt that would shoot Atherton out of obscurity.

It should be noted that while all these men—Coon, Seelye, Parker, Undeland, and Atherton—certainly bear similarities, they are also distinct individuals. Coon and Atherton never properly learned Arabic, Parker never went to an Ivy League School, and so on. Generalizations about Arabists are easy, provided one has never met any.

Chapter 7

Never a Dull Moment

"There was never a dull moment in the U.S. Foreign Service," says a smiling and supremely satisfied man with a trimmed goatee, glasses, and silvery hair, sipping a cappuccino in a café along Rome's Via Veneto. Wat T. Cluverius IV, a former ambassador to Bahrein and now the director general of the Rome-headquartered Sinai Observer Force, seems to have done everything in his diplomatic career. In Jidda, Saudi Arabia, he learned how to embalm bodies. "There was no embalming in Saudi because the Moslems buried their dead within twenty-four hours. So a Lebanese doctor did it on the Q.T. I assisted once. I remember we put a dead American in the commissary freezer atop the bacon and ham." Then there was the time when Cluverius investigated a murder. An American woman and her Saudi boyfriend had been accused of murdering her husband. Cluverius, who believed she was guilty, managed to get the woman out of the country before she was beheaded.

These were not the only adventures Cluverius had.

The descendant and namesake of a Dutch geographer, Wat Cluverius was born in Boston in 1934 into a family of career naval officers. Because of bad eyesight he was unable to gain admission to the U.S. Naval Academy at Annapolis, where other men in his family had gone. After graduating from Northwestern University, however, he got into officer candidate school. That led to Naval Intelligence in Washington, where he had to choose among several exotic languages to study. "I got out the almanac and saw that there were twenty-or-so countries where Arabic was spoken, so I listed Arabic as a third choice after Russian and Chinese."

The Navy assigned him Arabic and sent Cluverius to Monterey, California for a year of instruction. Next came two years at a Naval Intelligence listening post in Cyprus, interspersed with trips to Lebanon, Syria, and Egypt.

Cluverius left the Navy in 1962. For over a year he tinkered with the idea of going into business or journalism. Finally, he got a National Defense fellowship to study the Middle East at Indiana University. Not long afterwards, Vietnam became a hot issue on campus.

"It was a nasty time for those of us associated with the military on campus." Wanting to get away from the university world of left-wing intellectuals and back into government work, he joined the Foreign Service in 1967. On June 1 he sailed on the U.S.S. Independence, bound for Saudi Arabia.

In Lisbon harbor, Cluverius received news of the lightning Israeli attack on Egypt that heralded the Six-Day War. By the time the ship reached Naples, U.S. embassies were closing throughout the Arab world. But the embassy in Jidda was somehow remaining open for business. Cluverius flew from Naples to Istanbul, then from Istanbul to Jidda, where he met Talcott Seelye, who was the embassy's deputy chief of mission (DCM), and the man responsible for keeping the embassy open, Ambassador Hermann Eilts.

Along with Roy Atherton, Hermann Eilts was destined to become the only Arabist allowed into Kissinger's inner circle. Like Atherton, Eilts was considered a "nonbaggage" Arabist, an Arabist who did not appear to hold pro-Arab views. Tall, professorial, and avuncular, a pipe ever in hand, Eilts's subordinates fondly referred to him as "Hermann the German," a reflection of his German ancestry and old-world manner. Through every pore Eilts exuded wisdom and experience: a "wise man" direct from central casting, who according to David Long—another U.S. diplomat in Jidda at the time—"labored eighteen hours a day, seven days a week." "One of the great cable writers of the State Department, the result of an extremely disciplined mind," observes a member of the National Security Council staff about Eilts.

Hermann Frederick Eilts was born in 1922 in Weissenfels, a town in Lower Saxony, to a father who had been the German consul general in Jerusalem and Constantinople. In 1926, with depression beginning to tear apart the social and economic fabric of Germany, Friedrich Eilts took his family to Scranton, Pennsylvania, where relatives got him a job on the local railroad. A lump forms in Hermann Eilts's throat when he talks about his father, whom he remembers as a tired railway worker who inspired his son with bedtime stories about an adventurous and privileged life in the diplomatic corps. "My father sacrificed everything in order to give me an opportunity in America. He died while I was at Verdun, fighting in World War II."

From the time Eilts graduated from Ursinus College in Pennsylvania, he knew he wanted to be a diplomat. He headed for the Fletcher School of Law and Diplomacy but needed a job to pay his tuition. As it happened, a Middle Eastern scholar, Halford Hoskins, offered Eilts a job studying the legal status of the Anglo-Egyptian Sudan. Eilts tried to refuse, saying his interest was in European affairs. Hoskins answered, "Young man, if you want a job here, you better take this one." By the time Eilts entered the army in 1942, his interest in the Middle East had been kindled.

Eilts found himself at Normandy in 1944. After sustaining a combat wound in the knee, young Lieutenant Eilts's knowledge of German landed him an army intelligence job, tracking down Nazi documents before the fleeing Nazis could destroy them or before the other Allies could get their hands on them. After the war Eilts picked up where he had left off, entering the Foreign Service in 1947.

"I became a Arabist by accident. Language training was not developed the way it soon became, and there were so few people in the field that despite my limited knowledge of Arabic and the region, I became an 'expert' and was posted to one Middle Eastern capital after another: Teheran, Jidda, Aden, Baghdad. . . ."

In 1964 the job of deputy chief of mission (DCM) at the U.S. embassy in Tel Aviv became available and Eilts maneuvered to get it. Eilts had never given up his original goal of becoming an American diplomat in Europe, something he felt would close the circle begun by his European diplomat father. A posting in Israel, Eilts thought, would force a successful conclusion to his Arabist career and serve as an intermediate step in the direction of Europe. Moreover, Eilts was a bit uncomfortable with the "Arabist" label and with "the cultural types [of Foreign Service officers] prone to localitis" with whom he often had to work. Unfortunately, the under secretary of state for political affairs, Averell Harriman, had other ideas about Eilts's future.

The lease for the U.S. air base in Libya was up for renewal, and because Harriman did not trust the U.S. ambassador in Libya, he wanted a strong DCM at the embassy in Tripoli to watch over the negotiations with King Idriss's government. "I explained to Harriman why it was important for an Arabist to serve in Israel, in order to be exposed to the other side. But the old crocodile pretended not to listen. Harriman just lowered his head and said, 'Eilts, you're going to Tripoli.' "

In 1965 Eilts was rewarded for a job well done in Libya by being made the ambassador to Saudi Arabia at the relatively young age of forty-three. Harriman again delivered a stern lecture to him: "You see, Eilts, had I let you go off to Israel as you wanted, you would not now be an ambassador."

John Kenneth Galbraith, the Harvard economist who once served as ambassador to India, says that "being an ambassador is like being an airline pilot: long periods of boredom followed by short periods of crisis." In early June 1967, a few days before Wat Cluverius arrived in Jidda and two years into his job as ambassador to Saudi Arabia, Hermann Eilts faced such a defining crisis.

Fighting raged across Sinai and the Golan Heights. The Palestinians, who for months had been running Saudi radio, had conditioned the population for great Arab victories. Now news of great Arab defeats were landing like so many bombshells. The Saudi military felt betrayed and informed Eilts that it would have nothing further to do with the United States. Meanwhile ARAMCO was evacuating its employees from the Saudi Arabian oil fields, and Eilts received a cable from Washington recommending that he too evacuate his staff. But Eilts refused Washington's request to close the embassy.

Cluverius, who arrived in Jidda just as this crisis was at the boiling point, says "the French were whispering in the King's ear, telling King Feisal to kick the Americans out since we'll run ARAMCO for you. For the French, the Middle East crisis was just another commercial opportunity." Eilts recalls that ARAMCO wasn't actually the problem. "The real issue was military assistance. The French were ready to sign a big contract with the

Saudis for armored personnel carriers, which, had we departed, would have opened the door for them to take over the military relationship."

The issue of quitting Saudi Arabia went much deeper than fears over losing business to the French. Just as Syria had been the focal point of the American-Arab partnership prior to World War II, Saudi Arabia was the focal point in the postwar era. The Saudis saw us as oil and commercial partners the way that the Syrians had once seen us as partners in education. The relationship had officially begun at the February 1945 meeting between Ibn Saud and Franklin Roosevelt, in which Colonel William Eddy was the translator. In the 1950s ARAMCO moved alongside AUB as the secret driver of the American-Arab relationship, with profane, tobacco-chewing roughnecks from Texas and Oklahoma displacing the missionaries as the most important Americans in the Middle East.

Nothing dramatically symbolized this relationship so much as the "TAP line"—the Trans-Arabian pipeline, a massive, suspended cylinder of cement, with a paved road beside it, that carried oil westward from the Dhahran fields on the Persian Gulf across the northern width of Saudi Arabia to the Mediterranean and Red seas. Ernest Latham, a member of Eilts's diplomatic staff in Jidda calls TAP line "one of the great arteries of Empire, the American Empire in the Middle East I mean, because that's in fact what it was."

Those days of Empire, which extended into the early 1970s—when the Saudis initiated an oil price explosion that sent its former Western masters reeling—contained their fair share of romance. "Saudi Arabia was great back then," recalls David Long. "It was the real thing: an unadorned traditional society without the civilizing layers that the Arabs put on in Egypt and Syria."

Cluverius, along with Ernest Latham and another FSO on Eilts's staff, Graham Fuller, got a firsthand look at this unadorned traditional society when the three of them set out from Jidda with a Wahabi bodyguard—armed with a .38-caliber revolver and a gold-hilted sword—on a tour of the northern part of the kingdom.

"This was raw Arabia," Latham remembers, "the Arabia of Charles Doughty, where men had henna in their beards and fiery looks in their eyes and you could tell a malarial oasis by the black skins of the inhabitants. The blacks had apparently built up an immunity to malaria. So if you drove into an oasis that was populated solely by blacks, you got out of there quick before the mosquitoes came at dusk." Latham and Cluverius recall running into a group of Palestinian schoolteachers at such an oasis. "We were the first civilized people they had seen in months. We sat down over tea and a huge jar filled with quinine tablets and talked for hours with them before it got dark," says Latham. "We and these particular Palestinians discovered how much we had in common."*

Another day, Latham, Cluverius, and Fuller missed a by-pass road and found themselves driving into downtown Medina near the grave of the prophet Mohammed—a holy city, like Mecca, where non-Moslems were barred upon the penalty of death. The Landrover made a 180-degree turn by a petrol station and got out of the city fast.

The three Foreign Service officers were, in fact, savoring not just a high point in their youth but the tail end of an epoch, when U.S. diplomats in Saudi Arabia were just a handful of pioneers working out of a small embassy on Palestine Street in Jidda rather than bureaucrats working out of a large complex in Riyadh. "While ARAMCO was there in the hundreds, we diplomats were there in the tens. We were just the frosting on the cake for their oil empire," Latham explains. "ARAMCO even had its own Middle East library and intelligence bureau, which we went to for information."

Cynthia Barnum, an international business consultant in New York, grew up in Saudi Arabia, the daughter of a TWA representative working with Saudi Arabian Airlines. She says there was no love lost between the American oil and business community in Jidda and the "Dippy Corps," as they referred to the U.S. embassy staff. Each of the two communities was itself divided into "two distinct camps . . . those who had too many Arab friends, and those who sat at home and drank their illegal alcohol and bitched about those damn sand niggers and ragheads." She says that the wide gap between the American and Arab cultures "made it hard to be a human bridge, since you risked slipping into the chasm between the two and being discredited by your side and theirs. So many opted for the comfort of absolutism," hating the Arabs, or "going over completely to their side."

---

*The aftermath of the 1967 war, which caused U.S. embassies throughout the Arab world to close, cut short Ernest Latham's career in the Middle East, as it did those of other Arabists. He went on to become one of the Foreign Service's premier Balkan hands.

The local Arab reaction to the Americans in Saudi Arabia, especially to the scholars and other experts, was mixed. Years later, in 1980, David Long, who by then was running a custom-designed master's degree program for Prince Bandar ibn Sultan, remembers being introduced as a leading Arabist in a "flowery and exaggerated way" to Crown Prince Fahd. The crown prince, a twinkle in his eyes, responded with a quote from the Koran, about "those with much learning and no wisdom, who are like donkeys carrying learned tomes on their backs."

Eilts held this entire American-Saudi relationship together during a critical period when, had he followed Washington's inclinations, it might have disintegrated, the way the American-Syrian relationship had. Eilts was motivated not by clientitis but by a pure American interest of not wanting to lose a hard-won commercial advantage in a burgeoning market to a rival Western power. Significantly Eilts, aided by his DCM, Talcott Seelye, and other staffers, kept the embassy in Jidda open without the need to make political concessions to the Saudis.

The last half of 1967, immediately after the Six-Day War, was an especially tense time, when U.S.-Saudi relations could have ruptured at any moment. Cluverius spent these months as the only official American in Riyadh, doing everything from normal consular work to negotiating leases on houses, preparing for the day when the embassy would move from the Red Sea port of Jidda to the desert capital of the Wahabis, where foreign diplomats had not previously been allowed to live.

Eilts, impressed with Cluverius's work, told the thirty-three-year-old diplomat, "Don't worry, I'll find you a good job after you finish this posting." Eilts had a habit of fostering the careers of younger officers he respected. William Rugh, an Eilts protégé who opened the first U.S. press and culture office in Riyadh, was eventually made ambassador to Yemen, and, later, ambassador to the United Arab Emirates, an unusual achievement for a USIS officer who was not an employee of the State Department.* Another Eilts protégé was Daniel Kurtzer, an Orthodox Jew and

---

*USIS, the United States Information Service, ran the press and culture wings of U.S. embassies. As it was a separate bureaucracy, it was very hard for even its most talented officers to become DCMs or ambassadors.

associate dean at Yeshiva University in New York, whom Eilts recommended to be a political officer at the U.S. embassy in Cairo in 1979, upon the signing of the Camp David peace accords. "The Egyptians might have still been uncomfortable with the idea of a Jewish diplomat. But hell, it was our embassy and thus none of their business." Kurtzer thereby became the first American Jew to serve in a U.S. embassy in a major Arab country. He even had kosher food specially delivered to his quarters. "There were two types of American Jews who worked in Middle East affairs in the U.S. government," says one Arabist. "Those we trusted not to leak to the Israelis, and those we didn't trust. Kurtzer was the first kind."

Eilts did, in fact, find Cluverius a good job for his next posting, in the place where Eilts himself had wanted to serve but couldn't on account of Harriman: Israel. "Eilts told me I had to see both sides and that I should pay no heed to the anti-Semitic bullshit that I had heard from some others in the embassy."

"The conventional wisdom," Cluverius goes on, "was that you could never go back to the Arab world after serving in Israel. Therefore, I received the news with misgivings, but also with a lot of curiosity."

Cluverius was breaking new ground. Never before had an Arabist served in Israel, and it required unusual precautions. Cluverius had to tell his Saudi friends and contacts white lies about his next destination. When the Saudi moving men came to pack up his things, they were told to label all the boxes "Destination: Cyprus." From Cyprus all of his belongings were repacked and sent to Israel.

On July 4, 1969, a few days after leaving his life as an Arabist in Saudi Arabia, Cluverius arrived in Tel Aviv and immediately began to study Hebrew. "Israelis were more curious than suspicious of me. I made a lot of friends in the local archaeological community on account of my photos of Nabatean sites in Jordan, where Israelis couldn't go. My initial reaction to Israel was positive. Israel functioned a lot better then than it does now. I was married with a child by 1969, and Tel Aviv offered excellent housing and school facilities. This was still in the euphoric aftermath of the Six-Day War victory, and Israelis were waiting for the phone call from King Hussein to make peace."

Later on, other American diplomats would trod in Cluverius's path. Thomas Pickering, for example, would go from being ambassador to Jordan to ambassador to Israel. And both Richard Viets and Nicholas Veliotes would travel in the opposite direction: from DCM at the embassy in Tel

Aviv to ambassador to Jordan. But the higher up one goes, the more one is cushioned from the local reality, and the less intensely one travels; thus, the experience of being an American ambassador in an Arab country like Jordan is not all that much different from being an American ambassador in Israel. The techniques of diplomacy are similar and so are the limousines. But Cluverius at the time was still a relatively junior diplomat, who went from the nitty-gritty of Saudi Arabian life to the nitty-gritty of Israeli life.

His first job in Israel was as an economic officer, dealing with U.S. charities that, after Israel's capture of the West Bank in the Six-Day War, had moved from the Jordanian capital of Amman to Tel Aviv in order to continue their humanitarian services to the Palestinians. They included CARE, Catholic Relief, and Lutheran World Service. For the charities it was a traumatic experience to be working with Israelis, who tended to be more efficient and less polite and solicitous than their Arab contacts in Jordan had been. For Cluverius it provided an insight not only into the Israeli occupation authorities but into the reaction of these American Christian relief workers to religious Jews, since the point of contact for both the charities and Cluverius was the Israeli Ministry of Social Welfare, then in the hands of the National Religious party.

"At this time, Israel was putting its best people in the West Bank military government in an attempt to win the hearts and minds of the Arabs. In the early stages of the occupation, the IDF [Israel Defense Forces, the Israeli military, that is] might have won a popular election in the West Bank. But then colonialism, and the corruption that goes with it, gradually set in:

"By the time I left Israel in 1972, I had begun to witness enormous corruption on the part of the Israeli civil-military establishment on the West Bank, in the form of humiliations, physical intimidation, and petty bribes that Arabs had to pay Israeli officials. Old Arab men were made to kiss the asses of donkeys in front of their families. Once the Likud came to power in 1977, they really promoted the head crunchers. They put the toughest and poorest Iraqi Jews and other Sephardim [Oriental Jews] in the West Bank, in order to really beat up the Arabs. One of the untold reasons why [Yitzhak] Rabin stayed on as defense minister in the late 1980s was that he wanted to restore integrity to the IDF in the West Bank."

Cluverius talks about Israel the way the best Arabists talk about Arab countries: not as a promoter, but as an insider who knows the vocabulary, the nuances, the contradictions, the positive aspects, and the self-destructive stupidities. Listening to him, one realizes the basic Arabist-missionary flaw concerning Israel—their failure to intuit the *other* reality: that just as Syria and Saudi Arabia constitute much subtler universes than their black-and-white media images suggest, so too does Israel. And that just as the Arabists have lifelong friends and acquaintances in the Arab world who constitute a sensitive, human element that the rigors of real-politik often don't take into account, diplomats in Tel Aviv have the same experience with their Israeli friends and acquaintances. Arabists are like traveler-explorers: they are the ultimate empiricists. They do not accept that something exists unless they can see it, hear it, and, in sum, personally experience it.

"Arabists are, in most cases, not biased against Israel out of deep emotion, but simply because they didn't take the course," by which Cluverius means that they never lived in Israel. Samuel Lewis, the U.S. ambassador to Israel from 1977 to 1985, says "Arabists and Israel-based American diplomats come out of two entirely different personal-experience systems. The Arabists had their friends and experiences from the Arab world, while the diplomats in Tel Aviv tended to be Soviet or Asian or Latin American specialists looking for an out-of-area tour. That is why Roy Atherton and myself constantly pushed for cross-fertilization in the late 1970s, trying to get Arabists to Israel and vice versa."

As the pioneer in this field, Cluverius used the diplomatic pouch to send copies of Amos Elon's *The Israelis: Founders and Sons* to his Foreign Service friends throughout the Arab world. Elon's book, first published in 1971, is an eloquent psychological study of the first two generations of Israelis. The book is also a testimonial to the liberal, Labor party establishment and has a tendency to sneer at the Oriental Jewish reality of the country that, as the 1970s wore on, bubbled closer and closer to the surface. *Founders and Sons* is therefore a kind of guidebook to what has been called "the beautiful Israel." Menachem Begin, the future prime minister of Israel and former Irgun underground leader, does not even appear in the index. Elon writes about an Israel sans Likud, right-wing settlers, and Sephardim. It is therefore an Israel that many Arabists could at least stomach. To wit, W. Nathaniel Howell, an Arabist who was the U.S. ambassador to Kuwait at the time of the Iraqi invasion of that country, found Israel "vibrant and alive" the first time he visited it in 1971, "with a sensitivity and cosmopolitan leadership that I did not detect in later years."

In the 1970s many Arabists were, in a very real sense, finally on the verge of becoming psychologically comfortable with the reality of a Jewish state when Begin's election to the premiership in May 1977 pushed them back into their 1950s mode of resentment against the partition of Palestine. Talcott Seelye genuinely felt Likud's policies to be "antithetical to Israel's long-term interests." Begin's politics were hard-line. Though he inspired a degree of respect, diplomats found him difficult to deal with on a personal basis. And in the eyes of many, he represented the negative stereotype of the pushy European Jew. Cluverius, having personally watched the deterioration of Israeli society under the Likud, speaks with the vehemence of a true friend of "the beautiful Israel," when he says:

"Begin gets too much credit for Camp David. There would have been no Egyptian-Israeli peace treaty without Labor party types like Moshe Dayan, Ezer Weizman, and Aharon Barak advising Begin. They were the ones who pushed him toward the agreement. Begin was at least wise enough to realize that the Likud had no talent in its ranks, so he went to the Labor party for help. . . . And [Ariel] Sharon just lied to everyone. There was practically no U.S. official Sharon didn't lie to."

Amos Elon, the writer-intellectual, and General "Arik" Sharon, the war hero–turned–right-wing politician, are like the two ends of a pendulum movement for Arabists to record their emotional swings regarding Israeli politics. "Amos Elon, *oh* what a wonderful man!" exclaimed April Glaspie to this writer, in her office at the U.S. embassy in Damascus in 1983, where she was political counselor and DCM. Indeed, mention Amos Elon, and Arabists have a tendency to go overboard with praise. As for Sharon, Seelye is not the only NEA hand who finds the former Israeli defense minister repugnant. Carleton Coon says that "when Sharon talks and smiles, he looks like Goering." Lucius D. Battle, a former ambassador to Egypt, assistant secretary of state for NEA, and president of the Middle East Institute in Washington, says, "Sharon is one of the most sinister and evil figures of this century."

Grossly overweight, with the demeanor of a classic bully, General Sharon is guilty of considerable sins, some better known than others. In the mid-1950s he led a number of overly zealous reprisal raids against Palestinian civilians in the Gaza Strip. In 1982 his policies had the effect of allowing Maronite Christian militia units into the Palestinian refugee camps of Sabra and Chatilla in Beirut, where the militiamen perpetrated a massacre. Throughout his reign as Israel's defense minister in the early 1980s, his treatment of the local Bedouin population was insensitive. One FSO remembers a session with Sharon in Israel. Sharon stood over him and lambasted American policy, forgetting to mention the fact that America was transferring billions of dollars of cash to the country to keep its neo-Stalinist economy afloat. "It was a hot day and Sharon's shirt was open at the bottom because he was so fat. You could see the sweat dripping off his belly button and forming a puddle on the ground."

Sharon absolutely hated American FSOs. Why shouldn't he have? Since he hated Israeli diplomats too? He thought of them as a bunch of naive jerks who would give back Israeli territory just to establish diplomatic relations with more countries.

But considering the villains who have stalked the world in recent years— Nicolae and Elena Ceauşescu in Romania, Saddam Hussein in Iraq, the Ayatollah Khomeini in Iran, Pol Pot in Cambodia, Mengistu Haile Mariam in Ethiopia (responsible for the brutal relocation of millions of people from their ancestral homes, not to mention his culpability in the deaths of more millions from famine), and the Somali and Serbian warlords who starved millions and ran veritable concentration camps—it is extremely doubtful that by any stretch of the imagination, Sharon could even be considered "one of the most sinister and evil figures" of the last decade, let alone the century. These exaggerations, repeated constantly by Arabists about one deceitful, tactically brilliant, rude fat slob of an Israeli general, raise an unavoidable question: is it Sharon they hate, or is Sharon merely a convenient mechanism for discharging bile against Israel?

Is Israel acceptable to them only when it is morally perfect? Cluverius would answer that his colleagues must acknowledge the varying shades of gray between Elon's beautiful Israel and Sharon's unbeautiful one. But it is quite apparent, especially among older Arabists, that while they can lecture a visitor for hours about the awesome complexities of interpreting the Arab reality, they appear blissfully unperturbed about seeing Israel in only the simplest stereotypes.

Cluverius says the highlight of his diplomatic tour of Israel came when Prime Minister Golda Meir invited him into her study to ask what he thought of how Israel viewed the Arab world outside its borders. "I told her Israelis were naive and wrong about many individual Arab trees but that they had a pretty good idea of the Arab forest they were dealing with. I also said Israel was naive about the true feelings of Israeli Arabs and those in the West Bank."

Rather than end his career as an Arabist, the posting in Israel following the one in Saudi Arabia accelerated his career to an unusual degree. Just as Roy Atherton found himself on the Arab-Israel desk during the 1967 Middle East war, Wat Cluverius found himself on the same desk during the 1973 war. When Secretary of State Henry Kissinger began his peace shuttle at the end of that year, Cluverius began to emerge as a principal drafting officer for the various agreements being hammered out, since he was seen by his colleagues as representing both sides in the conflict. In 1976, less than a decade after joining the Foreign Service, Cluverius was named ambassador to the Arab sheikhdom of Bahrein. Rarely in U.S. diplomatic history has someone gone from being a junior officer to an ambassador in such a short time.

Meanwhile Hermann Eilts's decision to resist Washington's suggestion to evacuate the Jidda embassy staff during the 1967 war served to boost his own career—in the long-run, at least. "Rocking the boat occasionally," Eilts says, "helps; it doesn't hurt."

It was the second time in only a few weeks that Eilts had challenged the conventional wisdom. Before the outbreak of the 1967 war, he, along with the new ambassador to Libya, David Newsom, had recommended sending U.S. destroyers through the Straits of Tiran, "guns forward—Corfu style,"* as a show of force to Egypt against closing the Gulf of Aqaba to Israeli shipping and as a way of reassuring the Israelis that the United States was intent on honoring the security commitments made to them after the 1956 Sinai war. "The other Arabists were all against it. They were afraid of Egypt's reaction. It was the same old localitis again," says Eilts. "But Nasser's best troops were bogged down in Yemen, so the Egyptians wouldn't have fired on our ships.† And the Israelis, seeing that we were serious about protecting them, might not have felt the need to launch a preemptive attack on Egypt, as they soon did."

Initially such independent thinking might have played a role in Eilts's next posting: in Carlisle, Pennsylvania, as the deputy commander of the

---

*The British Royal Navy once sent its ships between the Greek Island of Corfu and Albania, as a show of force to keep the sea passage secure from communist Albanian aggression. The British ships' guns were pointed forward, in order to show the Albanian shore patrols that there was no hostile intent.

†The Egyptian army was supporting revolutionary nationalists in Yemen, aligned with Nasser, against the Saudi-backed Yemeni imam. The civil war lasted from 1962 through 1969.

Army War College, a sort of diplomatic exile. Here Eilts languished until one night in the fall of 1973, in the immediate aftermath of the 1973 war, when Joseph Sisco, the assistant secretary of state for NEA, phoned and ordered Eilts to Washington, because "Kissinger wants to talk to you."

Kissinger was then preparing for his first diplomatic tour of Middle Eastern capitals, and he started the conversation by asking Eilts about Saudi Arabia's King Feisal. "I hear Feisal is anti-Jewish. I'm Jewish. Tell me, how do I deal with him." Eilts told Kissinger to "just let Feisal talk, talk, talk. He'll lecture you about the Zionist conspiracy and all of that. Just listen quietly and politely." There would come a moment, Eilts explained, when Feisal would motion the note taker to leave—that would be the version of the meeting sent to the PLO—and then Feisal and Kissinger could get down to serious business.

Kissinger noted to Eilts that "you were one of the only people" to recommend breaking Nasser's blockade of the Straits of Tiran back in 1967. Eilts nodded yes. Then Kissinger offered him the ambassadorship to Egypt, which in a few days was expected to resume diplomatic relations, broken in 1967. Eilts went back to Carlisle that night to pack his bags, since Kissinger had also dropped the news that Eilts would accompany him on the plane to the Middle East and would then remain in Cairo to take up his new duties. Eilts's household effects could be shipped later.

Hermann Eilts was America's ambassador to Egypt from 1974 through 1979. Not only was he, along with Roy Atherton, the only Foreign Service Arabist in Kissinger's inner circle on Middle East policy, but he was the only one in President Jimmy Carter's too. Eilts witnessed and participated in a number of historic events: the two Sinai troop disengagement accords that the United States brokered between Egypt and Israel after the 1973 war, Egyptian president Anwar Sadat's surprise visit to Jerusalem in 1977, and the Camp David peace agreement.

Eilts certainly proved his mettle. "Eilts was the one who interpreted Sadat to Carter, [Secretary of State Cyrus] Vance, and [National Security Adviser Zbigniew] Brzezinski. Since none of them knew what to make of Sadat, Eilts was able to tell them when Sadat was being serious and when he was just engaging in flamboyant theatrics," says a participant in the Camp David negotiations, who goes on:

"Eilts was always careful to treat Prime Minister Begin with deference whenever he met him. He knew that as an Arabist ambassador to Egypt, he might have been suspect in Israeli eyes. But he won their trust. He was always sending polite notes to Begin. When Begin's wife died, Eilts wrote him a long, personal note; All this despite the fact that on a policy level, Eilts hated Begin."

Eilts's place in history has to do mainly with his years as ambassador in Egypt, a job opportunity he owes to Sisco's and Kissinger's intuitions about him. His ability to keep the embassy in Saudi Arabia open and his willingness to go against his colleagues in recommending a show of force in the Straits of Tiran obviously were critical in Kissinger's assessment of Eilts. "Henry and I immediately saw that Eilts was the best of the lot. Eilts was more balanced than the other Arabists, and Henry saw that he couldn't crap all over him like Henry did with other people," recalls Sisco.

But one also senses something else, something that neither Kissinger nor Eilts may admit to. Though not Jewish, Eilts, like Kissinger, was a refugee boy who fled political uncertainty in Germany. Both men had the German immigrant experience in America at roughly the same time. More interesting is that both seem to have lodged deep in their genes an almost nineteenth-century historical framework for interpreting the unfolding reality of the present day. "I have great admiration for Kissinger," says Eilts. "Working with Kissinger was intellectual fun. He had a quick mind. He would come up with ideas. He was a conceptualizer, which was very important. He looked down the road in terms of where we should be going. . . . What Arabists and other area specialists don't always realize is that their part of the world is not all that important compared to the larger picture. They didn't always grasp that Kissinger operated on a much higher level, working with all the pieces of the globe at the same time."

But Eilts had his "encounters" with Kissinger. "Henry is a master of half the story, of half the truth. I twice resigned on him. . . . I guess I'm one of the few ambassadors who did stand up to him, and somehow he did not resent my doing so. He seemed to respect it, and I was one of the few ambassadors whom he never criticized."*

---

*On May 1, 1992, Eilts was awarded the Foreign Service Cup, one of the highest honors a U.S. diplomat can receive. The citation read: "Soldier, diplomat and educator, Hermann Frederick Eilts began a long and distinguished career as an officer in military intelligence in World War II, spent 32 years in the Foreign Service, culminating . . . as ambassador to Saudi Arabia and to Egypt. He was the quintessential Arabist in the Department and, as such, an inspiration to his fellow specialists. . . . Upon retirement in 1979, he became a distinguished professor of international relations at Boston University, where he established the Center for International Relations, and, later, a separate Department of International Relations."

The decisions to send an orthodox Arabist like Cluverius to serve in Israel and to recall an unorthodox Arabist like Eilts from exile were made against the background of a pivotal shift in the history of the Bureau of Near Eastern Affairs—and therefore in the history of America's Arabists. Because the shift constituted a wide arc rather than a sharp turn, it involved several contradictory currents that for many years masked what was actually happening, while to this day making the meaning of this important transition a matter of controversy among those it affected.

Up until 1969 it is easy to make comfortable generalizations about NEA and the larger community of American Arabists. However, from that point onwards, rather than a few bold colors comprising missionary, bird-watcher, and Loy Henderson types, the Arabist canvas becomes a forest of subtler shades. As we shall see, the AUB community remained a diehard exception to this political-cultural modernization. But the State Department did evolve, as a result of two developments that chain-reacted. The first, the less interesting one, concerned the reforms inside the Foreign Service—ongoing since the 1950s—that were increasingly bringing more minorities, ethnics, and middle-class types into the State Department. The second, the more interesting one, was the political philosophy of President Richard Nixon, elected in November 1968, and how it translated into a revolution of sorts within NEA.

Chapter 8

Aggrieved Area Experts

In the Middle East the Six-Day War of June 1967 was a seismic event that changed the region's borders. "Indeed," writes the policy historian William B. Quandt, "the peace process of recent years has been designed largely to deal with the aftermath of that conflict." In the world of Washington bureaucratic maneuvering, however, the Six-Day War was a mixed bag: a mishmash of details that didn't add up to a compelling plot. For the Arabists in the State Department, the buildup to the war as well as the war's immediate aftershocks were fraught with ambiguity.

As Egypt's leader, Gamal Abdel Nasser, ratcheted up the tension in the weeks preceding the outbreak of hostilities, there was a lot of discussion within NEA and other branches of the administration about what to do, but no real vicious policy battles erupted. As Quandt notes, both Arabists and Israelis were essentially on the same side, saying the same thing: that Washington should stay out of the looming conflict. The Arabists were driven by the notion that a war was likely to weaken Israel's position. The Israelis were driven by the opposite notion: that they could win a war if nobody interfered to help the Arabs.

President Lyndon Johnson, like Presidents Dwight Eisenhower and John Kennedy before him, favored the status quo in the Middle East: a combination of emotional sympathy toward Israel—albeit in varying degrees—friendship toward the Arabs, and, most important of all, a desire to avoid conflict. Because Johnson was a president with little expertise and no fixed opinions on the Middle East, he took advice on this subject readily, and the advice he got was often contradictory.

The Arabists (except for Hermann Eilts and David Newsom) were against sending ships to break Nasser's blockade of the Tiran Straits, but other officials in the State Department close to Secretary of State Dean Rusk were in favor of the idea. Yet the U.S. military was cool about it. The result of this and other policy discussions was drift, giving the Israelis the narrow opening they needed to launch a lightning attack on Egypt without having to worry about Washington's reaction. After just six days of fighting, not only the Sinai peninsula but the Syrian Golan Heights, Jordan's West Bank, and the entire Holy City of Jerusalem were in Israeli hands.

For Arabists this was bad news. Israel was strengthened. Arab states were humiliated, and U.S. embassies in Arab countries were closed, forcing many an Arabist to switch careers. (One Arabist, Andrew Killgore, called the war a "disaster" for the Foreign Service.) But in a larger sense, Israel's victory constituted a victory for the West over the Soviet Union, its inferior weaponry, and its client Nasser. As the saying goes, while defeat is an orphan, victory has many fathers. So rather than an atmosphere of repercussions, there was a sense in the administration of things having gone well. Also, for those who remained Arabists, the Middle East was now at center stage, posing a new challenge: how to get Israel to exchange territory for peace. All this tended to mitigate the depression that many Arabists felt over Israel's victory.

In retrospect the Six-Day War can be seen to have set the stage for the personalities who would come to dominate Middle East policy-making into the 1980s. As a result, it changed the face of American Arabism.

There was Roy Atherton, who by virtue of heading NEA's Arab-Israel desk, got to run the State Department's operations task force during the Six-Day War. This meant sleeping on couches and handling many minor details of the war, from evacuating Americans in the affected countries to writing situation reports based on the latest intelligence cables. Also deeply involved was a Middle East expert at the National Security Council, Harold H. ("Hal") Saunders. At last but certainly not least was the assistant secretary of state for international organizations, Dr. Joseph J. Sisco. International Organizations was the State Department bureau handling the

United Nations and the U.S. delegation there. As the Six-Day War produced much UN debate and resolutions, Sisco got to sit in on many of the
Johnson administration's crisis meetings.

Sisco's profile during the crisis, as well as that of others in the administration, was raised by the paucity of NEA types present. The lone NEA
voice in the discussions was often just the NEA assistant secretary himself,
Lucius D. Battle, whose power was undermined by the under secretary of
state, Eugene Rostow. The reason for NEA's weakness in the war crisis,
explains a source, was the belief harbored by key members of the Johnson
administration that NEA was just too pro-Arab.

Luke Battle disputes this claim. Indeed, Battle calls himself the first
non-Arabist assistant secretary of NEA; he had succeeded the Arabist Ray
Hare in the job a few months prior to the Six-Day War. The one prejudice
Battle proudly admits to is that of "being a Democrat." He was a personal
friend and supporter of Jack Kennedy, Lyndon Johnson, and Hubert
Humphrey. Defining Battle, therefore, is crucial for an understanding of
just what constituted a State Department Arabist in this period.

Battle speaks French but never learned Arabic. He had been appointed
the assistant secretary of state for education and culture by Jack Kennedy.
With trouble in Cuba and elsewhere, the next job Kennedy had for his
friend Luke Battle was that of assistant secretary of state for Latin America.
"But I can't even fill in the names of all the Latin American countries on
the map," Battle protested. "I know," Kennedy responded. "But you're
the one I want." In those days the focus was on clientitis south of the
border rather than in Araby, and Kennedy wanted to seed the "banana
circuit" with nonexperts. Fate intervened, however: Kennedy was killed,
and the next year, 1964, the relationship between the United States and
Egypt started to worsen. President Johnson sent Battle to Egypt as ambassador in order to soften up Nasser. Battle got along famously with Nasser.
"Nasser was bright without being educated," Battle remarks. "He completely lacked a political-economic philosophy. Arab socialism for Nasser
was whatever he wanted to do on any given day."

When Johnson brought Battle back to Washington three years later to
be the NEA assistant secretary, Battle did in fact have a more sympathetic
attitude toward the Egyptian regime than other members of the administration. As a close colleague of his says, "Luke's sympathies against Israel
were well-known." Soon after the 1967 war Battle fought the sale of F-4
Phantoms to the Israelis because "they didn't need the planes. The Israeli
position was so strong without them." (The subject happened to crop up

in the 1968 presidential campaign between Hubert Humphrey and Richard Nixon, marking the first time that a Middle East arms sale became an electoral issue.)

By 1968 Battle was advising his friend, presidential candidate Hubert Humphrey. Parker Hart was named the new NEA assistant secretary. "Pete" Hart was definitely of the old school: kind, well-mannered, and courteous to a fault, with a B.A. from Dartmouth and an M.A. from Harvard. He had been the ambassador to Saudi Arabia in the early 1960s, replaced by Hermann Eilts. He spoke German and Arabic well and, like others of the Arabist profession, had worked with Jewish refugees from Europe trying to get into the United States. Though in Pete Hart's case, the experience with Jews was in Austria, not Germany, and it was immediately before the outbreak of war rather than immediately after. Hart saw Nazism raw in Austria and would never forget the experience. Hart, like Battle, had no antipathy toward Jews. Their sympathy toward the Arabs was mainly passive. It amounted to making sure that the Arab position was properly explained and understood in Washington.

Muddling matters further was the fact that Battle was openly supporting the more avowedly pro-Israel candidate in the November election, Hubert Humphrey, whose feelings toward the Jewish historical predicament were, like all of Humphrey's emotions, oversized.

None of this mattered much, though. Seen from the vantage point of what was to come next, both Luke Battle and Pete Hart must be considered the last of the old-school Arabists to run NEA. Because they both saw NEA as Loy Henderson had: an airtight unit of elite professionals, operating entirely outside the framework of the domestic political debate and dedicated to a cold calculation of American interests in the Arab world. Richard Nixon, elected president over Humphrey in 1968, and his new national security adviser cum foreign policy czar, Henry Kissinger, were to change that definition of NEA. And the second rung of officials below Battle and Hart—Sisco and Atherton, in particular—were to become the vehicles of that change.

Richard M. Nixon was not a fan of the State Department. In *Secrets of State: The State Department and the Struggle over U.S. Foreign Policy,* Barry Rubin writes that Nixon "had become famous as the nemesis of Alger Hiss, a symbol to many of State's effeteness and disloyalty. Nixon told Eisenhower that while he had met some fine FSOs on trips abroad, an 'astonishing number of them have no obvious dedication to America' . . . and evinced 'an expatriate attitude.' " Even worse, in Nixon's eyes, FSOs were the kind of people likely to be Democrats. Nixon was also a cold warrior, who saw the Middle East, not on its own terms, but in terms of the worldwide struggle against the Soviets. So too, for that matter, had Loy Henderson. But the Six-Day War that preceded Nixon's election had given Israel more territory and thus a larger strategic value than it had ever had in Henderson's day. Moreover, the Soviets were now irrevocably in bed with the Arabs, making Israel a valuable Cold War asset. And while both Nixon and Henderson obviously had a tortured relationship with Jews, Henderson's first loyalty was always to the Foreign Service, an institution bureaucratically sympathetic to the Arabs because of the large number of embassies in the Arab world. Yet it was also an institution of which Nixon was deeply suspicious.

Nixon's choice for secretary of state was William P. Rogers, a former attorney general under Eisenhower, who lacked both experience in foreign policy and an aggressive personality. Nixon's choice was deliberate: he intended to run foreign policy himself, with the help of an enhanced National Security Council headed by Henry Kissinger, a German Jewish refugee who, perhaps ironically, had been a protégé of John McCloy, the man who had prevented the U.S. military from bombing the railway lines to Auschwitz and who had urged Truman not to recognize Israel. In 1956 McCloy tapped Kissinger, then a little-known Harvard professor, to do a study of Soviet-American relations and afterwards got him a job with Nelson Rockefeller, who would later introduce Kissinger to Nixon's people.

While previous administrations sought to avoid conflict in the Middle East, Nixon and Kissinger saw the imminent threat of confrontation as a series of opportunities for rearranging the pieces of the Arab-Israeli puzzle more to America's liking. As one Middle East analyst puts it: "Kissinger hated the very notion of helping the parties out of a fix. Kissinger basically said, 'Don't help them out. Make them desperate. That way they'll need us.' " However, the aftermath of the 1967 fighting had produced a cold war of sorts between the Arab states and Israel, with Israel arrogantly basking in the glory of its Six-Day War victory and the Arab states still refusing to accept its existence. The regional situation thus appeared frozen. Nixon and Kissinger, therefore, at first treated the Middle East with benign neglect. Besides, with American Jews proud and energized as a result of Is-rael's war victory, Nixon saw Middle East negotiations as a loser in domestic political terms. At some point there might be an upheaval in the region, which would provide the leverage the two men needed to "work" the local reality.

But Secretary of State William Rogers was not going to wait for any upheaval. Because he had two aces in the hole regarding the Middle East, he was determined to try to do something. His first ace was the fact that Nixon and Kissinger were initially ignoring the Middle East, making it an area where the State Department's traditional foreign policy preeminence had not been subverted by Kissinger's National Security Council (NSC).

The other ace was Joseph Sisco. Rogers knew Sisco from the latter's work as assistant secretary of state dealing with the United Nations. Rog-ers, twice a member of the American delegation to the UN General As-sembly, had relied on Sisco for advice. It was Joe Sisco who had written UN resolution 242 following the 1967 war, which basically called for Israel to exchange territory for peace. Sisco was Rogers's first appointment, taking Sisco from the relative obscurity of assistant secretary of state for interna-tional organizations to the higher profile job of assistant secretary of state for NEA, in place of Pete Hart. It would turn out to be a master stroke. Joe Sisco was to be the most bureaucratically effective NEA assistant secretary in U.S. history, with the possible exception of Loy Henderson. Rogers's tenure as secretary of State was well-meaning but ineffectual. If he did anything of lasting importance, it was to appoint Joe Sisco NEA assistant secretary, with Roy Atherton as deputy assistant secretary.

Nevertheless, this wasn't so much Rogers as it was history acting. "Sisco was selected because of the specific need to get an outsider to run NEA in the wake of the 1967 war, when the Middle East suddenly became a global issue," explains William Quandt. Atherton states unequivocally that "the transformation of NEA happened when Sisco came in." In Hermann Eilts's view, "Sisco, certainly, brought to NEA a great sense of balance, which was badly needed."

Sisco was the best proof for that totalitarian cliché, "You have to break eggs in order to make an omelet." He was effective even as he was some-times hated, because he destroyed men's careers. It is interesting that FSOs reserve their harshest criticism—blood lust almost—for Sisco, Kissinger, and James Baker III. Kissinger and Baker were effective secretaries of state who also mistreated the Foreign Service establishment. Sisco, like Kissinger and Baker, intuitively understood that the Foreign Service bureaucracy, however talented, was just a tool that required a taskmaster to pick it up and use it to a specific purpose: his purpose.

In interviews, FSOs complained about Sisco:

"I took a dim view of how Sisco operated," says Luke Battle. "I had a personal dislike of Sisco," says Dick Parker. "Sisco didn't know shit from Shinola about the Middle East," says James Akins, an ambassador to Saudi Arabia in the 1970s. Sisco "didn't know anything about the area. . . . So far as I know, he never read a book about it. Never served abroad at all. He was a special buddy of Kissinger, of course. We [the Arabists] reckoned that their basic tie was a deep affection for the State of Israel and looking to do what Israel wanted done," says Andrew Killgore, an ambassador to the Arab sheikhdom of Qatar.* "Sisco and Atherton were just two little flunkies running around for Kissinger," says another Arabist FSO. "If you go supping at the Siscos, you better have your food taster with you," says still another. "Sisco," says a third Arabist, "was ornery, cantankerous, an arm-twister, and a bullshitter."

But Sisco had his admirers, too, albeit reluctant ones. "It's true. Sisco was not particularly knowledgeable, but he was able to get things done," says a Middle East historian. "He was scrappy, with a resonant voice, and— most importantly—an instant recall of documents and events," says Hume Horan, an ambassador to Sudan and to Saudi Arabia in the 1980s. "Joe Sisco," intones Eilts, puffing on a pipe, lifting his eyebrows, waiting for the precise words to form, "was a bureaucratic *operator*. He was the only department head at State who was able to keep Kissinger and Kissinger's NSC out of his bureau's business. That won Kissinger's respect."

Indeed, Sisco *was* an operator, with a gravelly, Howard Cosell kind of voice and a bullying manner, who got to the top of the Foreign Service without ever serving overseas. He may not have known as much about the Arabs or the Jews as his colleagues who had lived in the Middle East and spoke Middle Eastern languages, but this never stopped Sisco from having all the answers, or seeming to have. Sisco was the master of the sound bite before the term was invented: a deal-making politician much more than a typical FSO. Indeed, Sisco was planning to run for office in Montgomery

---

*Ambassador Killgore's quotes are taken from his oral history interview conducted by Charles Stuart Kennedy on June 15, 1988, under the auspices of the Association for Diplomatic Studies. He was the only retired ambassador contacted who refused to meet with this author.

County, adjacent to Washington, when Rogers selected him to be assistant secretary. Sisco never equivocated. His ideas and opinions were sharp, clear, and absent of nuances. What Sisco lacked in intellect, he made up for with raw energy. "Joe would produce a policy paper and have it in the secretary's hands before others in the bureau had even finished studying the issue," recalls Roy Atherton. "Joe was an aggressive and effective bureaucrat, a take-charge kind of guy. Nixon and his advisers knew this, and that's why they picked Joe, because they wanted someone to shake up NEA." Nixon had enormous respect for Sisco. He would phone him at home often to complain whenever "Henry's nose got out of joint." Nixon twice offered Sisco the job of ambassador to the Soviet Union. Sisco turned him down. He didn't want to be stuck in Moscow while "you and Henry" are making deals "over my head."

Joe Sisco was born in 1919 in Chicago, a first-generation Italian-American from a Depression-era family of five kids whose father made seven dollars a week in the clothing business. In World War II he was an infantry lieutenant in New Guinea, where he contracted a severe and recurring case of malaria. This left him partially disabled for a few years. "I was a guy who didn't get his first job until he was thirty. I was not from the striped-trousers set like the Arabists. I went to the wrong schools and came from the wrong side of the tracks. But I didn't care. I just worked like hell, that's all."

Sisco graduated from Knox College in Galesburg, Illinois, and got an M.A. and Ph.D. in Soviet relations from the University of Chicago. He entered the Foreign Service in the 1950s and impressed his superiors so much that each time he was to go abroad—to Belgrade in the late 1950s and to Vietnam in the early 1960s—the assignment was canceled in order to keep him stateside to spur the bureaucracy, especially at the UN. Only a decade after entering the Foreign Service, Secretary of State Dean Rusk elevated Sisco to the rank of career minister.

The Arabists, as one might imagine, were no match for Joe Sisco. Bill Stoltzfus, Dick Parker, James Akins, Andrew Killgore, and others do not remember him fondly. It was a cultural clash: an ethnic streetfighter versus a courtly and Waspy elite.

But there was something more, as Hume Horan explains: "With Sisco, the foreign and domestic politics of the Middle East fused for the first time. He had a grounding in the American domestic political scene that was unmatched in the history of the State Department." Adds Roy Atherton: "I learned from Joe that you can't put Middle East policy-making in a hermetically sealed tube, isolated from domestic politics and realities."

In other words and put crudely, the relationship between the American president and the American Jewish community now loomed larger than the relationship between Arabists and their personal connections in the Levant.

"Once in office, Sisco made a point of breaking up the Arabist concentration in the Bureau," wrote the columnist Joseph Kraft in a November 7, 1971, article about Arabists in the *New York Times Magazine*. Take Rodger Davies, for instance, "the guru of all the Arabists at the time," according to a colleague.

Rodger Davies was kicked upstairs by Sisco, given a fancy title but with responsibility only for Greece, Turkey, and Cyprus. In Davies's place as deputy assistant secretary for NEA, Sisco got Roy Atherton, who, in Kraft's words, "while versed in the area, had no Arabic language."

"What Sisco did to Rodger Davies was bad. Davies knew more than Sisco and I put together about the Middle East," complains Luke Battle. Even Atherton, who got Davies's job, recalls that "Rodger Davies was one of the finest and fairest-minded people I knew. He was the senior deputy to Pete Hart, and when Pete was going to be replaced by Joe Sisco, Davies effected a smooth transition, telling the troops to be loyal to Sisco. Nevertheless, as soon as he arrived at NEA, Sisco shunted Davies aside." According to Sisco, his motive for off-loading Davies was the following: "I needed people who could write policy papers fast—in a matter of hours. Davies couldn't do that, Roy Atherton could."

Sisco's transfer of Davies to Greek-Turkish affairs resulted in Davies being named the ambassador to Cyprus, where in the summer of 1974 he was assassinated during the violence that accompanied the overthrow of Archbishop Makarios's government and the subsequent Turkish invasion of the island. Rodger Davies, beloved by his Arabist colleagues, might be alive today if Sisco hadn't pushed him out of Arab affairs. Some of the Arabists' hostility toward Sisco might be explained by that fact.

Davies wasn't the only Arabist that Sisco pushed aside. Wrote Kraft in the *New York Times Magazine:* "The most pro-Arabic of the Arabists, Richard Parker, went from the Egyptian desk to Morocco. The Arabist reputed to be the most hostile to Israel, Robert Munn, went from the Israel desk to Turkey. Embassies that came open in Libya, Kuwait, Lebanon, and Jordan went to non-Arabists."

It wasn't quite as simple as that, which is why twenty years later some Arabists still go livid when "the Kraft article" is mentioned. For example, Dick Parker had "fought a lonely battle in Washington to get people to take Egypt seriously" despite its defeat in the 1967 war. This made Parker "sick of the subject" by the time Sisco arrived at NEA in 1969. Parker and Sisco also didn't get along, a dislike that Parker claims was unconnected to policy differences. Nor did the transfer to Morocco as DCM hurt Parker's career. In a few years he would be named ambassador to Algeria, to be followed by ambassadorships to Lebanon—a significant country in Arab-Israeli terms—as well as to Morocco.

Yet there is no doubt that Sisco's arrival signaled a changing of the guard within NEA. Luke Battle admits, "Yes, definitely, there was a dramatic demotion of career people." This demotion helped turn the post–World War II generation of Arabists into what has been called "aggrieved area experts": men whose devotion to U.S.-Arab relations was systematically being stymied by the need, partially generated by American domestic politics, to provide for Israel's well-being.

Certainly there was no Arabist more embittered by Sisco's personnel changes than Andrew I. Killgore. Tall, with a pleasant southern drawl, Andy Killgore was born in 1919—the same year as Sisco—in a small town in western Alabama, where he grew up on a farm, listening to the old men talk about Shiloh, Chickamauga, and the other battles of the Civil War in which they had fought. Killgore's origins, like Sisco's, were humble. In an interview for the Foreign Affairs Oral History program, he referred to his background as "Protestant redneck." He went to a small teacher's college, not to an Ivy League school, and fought in the Pacific in World War II. Like other Arabists, Killgore's diplomatic career began with refugee work in Germany after the war under the direction of John McCloy, the U.S. high commissioner. Like McCloy and Sisco, Killgore had a keen sense of having come from the wrong side of the tracks. "People who come in from the outside, who are not sort of establishment families, they are ambitious to join the establishment," Killgore remarks.

Again just like Sisco, Killgore's formal entry into the Foreign Service came in the 1950s as part of an early reform program that sought to bring people from diversified backgrounds into the diplomatic corps. In 1955 Killgore volunteered for formal Arabic-language training, and for the next quarter-century until retirement, he served in Arab countries and in Arab affairs posts at the State Department. He says that "most of the Arabists, we felt like we were a very special bunch. We were overwhelmingly veterans of World War II. That was a camaraderie. It's difficult to learn Arabic. You have to work like hell at it. We were both amused and a bit put out by the term *Arabist,* which is actually a euphemism employed by the Zionists to signal, 'Watch out for this guy.' " In Killgore's view "to describe a complex, brilliant officer [perhaps someone like himself] in the Foreign Service, in terms of him being anti or pro a particular foreign country, is terribly demeaning. . . ."

In the late 1950s and early 1960s Killgore traveled "to every single part of the West Bank," then in Jordanian hands. "There's hardly a village I didn't go to." He found the Palestinians "very attractive. They are a bit like the southerners, very much family oriented . . . absolutely enjoined to be generous . . . all the things that I learned as a boy down on the farm in Alabama. I found them very, very attractive, on the whole. A tremendous emphasis on food. By God, you think we eat in this country? You should go out there!"

In 1961, after four years in Jordan, Killgore was transferred to the Iraq-Iran affairs desk at the State Department. Then in 1965 he was dispatched to the U.S. embassy in Baghdad. Israel's victory in the 1967 war spelled disaster for him, though. Because of the closure of many embassies in the Arab world, Killgore was transferred to the far-off Bangladeshi capital of Dacca for three years before coming back to the State Department to work under Talcott Seelye at NEA's Arabian North division. To this day Killgore blames Secretary of State Dean Rusk and the Israel lobby for preparing the ground for the 1967 war "as early as 1963/64."

In 1972, after Sisco came to NEA, Killgore was sent as a political counselor to Iran. In 1974 Killgore thought he was going to be named ambassador to Bahrein when all of a sudden he found out he was to be the DCM in New Zealand, an exile if ever there was one. "I thought that as long as

Sisco was there, I'd never get a good job [in the Arab world], because the Zionists, in my view, had it in for me at that time." Killgore considered Sisco a Zionist sympathizer, charging that "Sisco was playing heavy footsy with the Israeli embassy." Sisco is perplexed by these charges. "What's he got against me? I barely had anything to do with Andy. Those decisions were made by personnel committees."

As for Kissinger, Killgore states, "Henry, of course, was just a fifth columnist, as far as I'm concerned. He was working for the Israelis. . . . Henry's real objective was to get out of the Middle East the Arabists that the Zionists didn't like. Because Henry was not so crypto—he just was Zionist."

It wasn't only Sisco who had grave doubts about the advisability of promoting Andy Killgore. Says another former NEA assistant secretary, "Andy gets mixed up with anti-Israel attitudes and anti-Semitism." And still another former NEA assistant secretary: "Killgore did come across as having blind spots toward Israel."

In 1977 Killgore was brought back from his New Zealand exile to become the ambassador to Qatar, the Arab state with the smallest population (it has fewer people than Charlotte, North Carolina, and a land area smaller than Connecticut). "Qatar was the perfect place for him. No critical reporting was required. Killgore was no conceptualizer," says Hermann Eilts, shaking his head.

In 1980, only weeks after retiring from the Foreign Service with the rank of ambassador, Killgore became an active lobbyist and public speaker for Arab causes. At a 1982 meeting in Washington of the Holy Land State Committee, a group aligned with the extremist Liberty Lobby and dedicated to "liberating the United States from the domination of Zionism," Killgore stated: "There is one thing I do personally. I let no Zionist statement go unchallenged." At a meeting of the same group a year later, this former U.S. ambassador said: "My status as a Christian and as an American is threatened by Israeli actions."*

Among Killgore's other comments are these:

"It is wrong and perverse for fanatical elements within the two and a half per cent of our population who are Jewish to hold Congress hostage."†

". . . America must regard the Israeli progression from penetration to direction of U.S. foreign policy as the work of a master criminal."‡

---

*See Steven Emerson's *The American House of Saud* in the bibliography.
† *The Washington Report on Middle East Affairs,* July 1988.
‡ *The Washington Report on Middle East Affairs,* February 1987.

Killgore became best known in Washington in the 1980s and 1990s as the publisher of *The Washington Report on Middle East Affairs,* a monthly magazine that by all accounts provides some of the most obsessively pro-Arab and anti-Israel reading in America. In its April–May 1992 issue, Killgore's publication suggested that the Mossad, Israel's secret service, may have shot JFK:

". . . we find it remarkable that Americans are so quick to suspect the CIA . . . but seldom allude to the possibility of Mossad involvement. Yet the result was the death of a president about whom the government of Israel was deeply uneasy, and his replacement by the most pro-Israel president in history."

In the same issue Killgore writes that had the Jews not come to Palestine, Hitler would not have had to murder them: "Without the Balfour Declaration of 1917, would defeated Germany have turned on Europe's Jews for revenge in 1933? . . . Israel's founders exploited the myth of Jewish power to give birth to the Balfour Declaration. Now, seventy-five years later . . . Israel lives with the legacy of the myth: a Holocaust in Europe."

Andy Killgore is the exception that proves the rule: which is that the overwhelming majority of Arabists are not extreme anti-Zionists. While Killgore appears to meet almost every criterion of a Jewish lobbyist's worst-case caricature of an Arabist, other Arabists don't, and only a few even come close. Nearly all of those are now retired. Given the circumstances of their professional lives, Arabists have certainly been antagonists of Israeli foreign policy, but they were motivated by what they honestly saw as America's best interests in the Middle East, which did not always coincide with Israel's best interests, especially as these interests came to be defined by successive Likud governments. In the long list of historical adversaries of the Jews, the Arabists could easily claim to be the least noxious. The best of enemies, in other words.

Not all the Arabists were as aggrieved by Sisco's new order as was Killgore. Joe Sisco, after all, did make NEA *matter.* He gave it a clout and a media prominence it had not previously enjoyed. Sisco met with Nixon a lot more times than Luke Battle or Pete Hart ever met with Johnson. "Sisco," wrote William Quandt in *Decade of Decisions: American Policy Toward the Arab-Israeli Conflict, 1967–1976:*

was a consummate bureaucratic politician; he knew the ins and the outs of the State Department; he was a man of drive, a skillful speaker, and a shrewd tactician. Working closely with him was . . . Atherton, first as office director for Israel and Arab-Israeli affairs and later as deputy assistant secretary for the Near East. Atherton represented continuity, experience, professional expertise. He was cool when Sisco was hot. The two were a formidable pair in Middle East policy-making circles.

Sisco and Atherton divided the old Arab hands into two groups: those whose skills could be useful to the new order in NEA and those who were either too troublesome or not worth saving. Rodger Davies's very prestige among his Arabist colleagues constituted a threat that might have made him a difficult adversary on policy matters, so he had to go. Men like Talcott Seelye, Bill Stoltzfus, Michael Sterner, James Akins, and Dick Parker were considered hot-shots who should be saved while someone like Andy Killgore was not. Seelye, for instance, in the first Sisco years was the office director for Jordan, Lebanon, Syria, and Iraq; by no means an insignificant policy position. In 1972 he was promoted to the rank of ambassador and sent to Tunisia for four years. Shortly after concluding that assignment, he was named ambassador to Syria, arguably the key Arab country in Middle East politics. Seelye, notably, has some good memories of working with Sisco and later with Kissinger, after the latter became secretary of state in 1973.

Yet as Atherton admits, while all of these men became ambassadors, "none made NEA assistant secretary or even deputy assistant secretary" or were given any real access to power over Arab-Israeli matters. "Those people were not kept out of power by Sisco and Atherton so much as they were preserved in the bureau for another ten years," says Nicholas Veliotes, a former NEA assistant secretary and an ambassador to both Jordan and Egypt. "For example, Talcott Seelye effected a great evacuation of Americans from Lebanon [in 1976]. Nobody ever doubted his talent and professionalism overseas.* But could you imagine someone like Seelye on Capitol Hill, as an assistant secretary? Dealing with congressmen and the lobbyists? It would have been a tragic misuse of his considerable abilities. Sisco knew that.

"Overseas," Veliotes goes on, "you deal with foreigners—with Arabs.

---

*Kissinger, for one, did not doubt Seelye's field competency, since it was Kissinger who picked Seelye for the sensitive mission in which Seelye, working with the PLO, was able to arrange two discreet evacuations by sea of American diplomats and their families in June and July 1976.

But in Washington, as an assistant secretary or a deputy assistant, you have to deal with other Americans. The State Department is not the British foreign office. It operates within realities of American democracy. Lobbies are not nuisances but legislative players. And as our society became more and more open in the 1970s, there became more and more players. In this climate you could throw on the table your twelve years in Mauritania or Kuwait or Syria, and it had little relevance. Because here in Washington, a new set of skills were required."

Sisco is even more blunt: "Neither Parker, Seelye, Davies, or certainly Andy [Killgore] had the writing capacity or the hard-hitting analytical sense or the knowledge of how to relate to Congress. They were better as ambassadors abroad." That is not to say that Sisco did not respect the troops he inherited. "For the five years that I ran NEA, the Arabists gave me straightforward, solid advice. They never tried to make me a captive of their views. They laid things out objectively. I don't recall a single political appointee in NEA. It was a thoroughly professional staff. Because NEA was always taking initiatives, it was inescapable that it would be vilified. Because pro-Israel groups cannot personalize their differences with the president or his secretary of state, they often find it useful to attack Arabists."

On the other hand, Sisco says: "Among Arabists, there was a stronger propensity for localitis than among other area specialists. They had a disinclination to be direct and confrontational with the Arabs. They felt that the Arab cultural-political-economic component was being given short shrift in U.S. policy. In particular, there was that 1950s group of men who interchanged diplomatic posts in every Arab country but never served in Israel. But I didn't require strategic thinking from them. That was not their job."

The very breadth, depth, and texture of the Arabist's knowledge of the Arab world, he means, had worked to immobilize their analytical thinking about it.

Sisco lacked that deep knowledge. So, too, to a lesser degree, did Atherton. Instead of becoming hooked on the region in a cultural or even a broadly political sense, they became hooked on "the problem." Says Sisco: "When I got involved in NEA, I got this incurable disease, that this thing ought to be resolved." The Arab-Israeli conflict became to them like a chess game, or a crossword puzzle, or a physics question that they couldn't tear themselves away from until they figured out the perfect equation that would fit the parts together. While their NEA colleagues enjoyed Oriental rugs and old British travel books, Sisco and Atherton fell in love with documents and memoranda. Sisco and Atherton, along with Hal Saunders at the NSC, had invented a new Arabist label: they were not so much Arabists as they were "peace processors," precursors to the Washington policy wonks of the 1980s and 1990s.*

Atherton, writes Quandt in *Decade of Decisions,* was the perfect counterpart to the volatile Sisco. As a colleague recalls, "Roy was a nice guy, easy to get along with, not strategically minded, but a lot of good judgment lay behind his affability. Roy was—to a degree—a faceless, careful, at times timid bureaucrat. It is surprising how deeply involved he was in all the great negotiations of the 1970s, yet he left no stamp on policy. Roy was not a man of ideas. His strength lay in his cautionary advice. He contributed to the process by constantly preventing stupid things from happening."

Besides the Sisco-Atherton duet another key relationship that began to evolve at this time was the one between Atherton and Hal Saunders. Though occasionally vocal in recent years on behalf of the plight of the Palestinians, Saunders was back then a lot like Atherton: extremely low-key and easy for everyone to get along with. "The main reason why there was so little friction between the White House and the State Department concerning the Middle East was on account of Atherton at State and Saunders at the NSC. They kept each other informed and thereby cemented the relationship" between the two branches of government, explains a source.

With the support of Secretary of State William Rogers, Sisco aggressively sought to get peace talks started between Israel and Egypt in 1969. While Andy Killgore and other Arabists saw Sisco as pro-Israeli, the fact is that for most of his tenure as the head of NEA, Sisco was pushing peace strategies that the Israelis deeply feared. "The Israelis liked me from the beginning, though," says Sisco, "even when I was urging them to return territory. And do you know why? Because they knew I was not an Arabist, I was just like them [i.e., an ethnic from the wrong side of the tracks]."

---

*The term "peace process" was reportedly first used by Hal Saunders, just as the term "shuttle diplomacy" was first used by Sisco.

Sisco's first attempt at peace processing culminated in the Rogers Plan, which Egypt did not respond to and which Golda Meir's government rejected outright. The Rogers Plan of 1969 asked Israel to withdraw from all the territories it had captured two years earlier in return for a vague recognition of its sovereignty by Egypt and Jordan. The plan's fatal flaw, though, was that it was seen by the Israelis as merely a State Department plan, in which neither Nixon nor Kissinger had invested his prestige.

The year 1970 proved to be a turning point in the Middle East, a year when events occurred that were to inflame the Arabists' hatred of Sisco.

Though the Rogers Plan had failed, Sisco did manage to cobble together a cease-fire between Israel and Egypt, ending a prolonged bout of desultory post-1967 fighting known as the War of Attrition. But when U.S. intelligence confirmed that Egypt was violating the terms of the cease-fire, Nixon, after meeting with Rogers, Kissinger, and Sisco on September 1, 1970, decided to sell Israel eighteen F-4 Phantom jets.

Frightened by the prospect of a separate peace between Nasser's Egypt and Israel, with still more arms going to Israel, the Popular Front for the Liberation of Palestine (PFLP) hijacked three airplanes, flying two of them to Jordan. The hijackings helped ignite a civil war in Jordan, whereby Palestinian guerrillas, helped by invading Syrian tank units, sought to topple King Hussein's pro-Western government. Nixon and Kissinger saw the crisis in classic East-West terms: they suspected a Soviet hand in both the Egyptian cease-fire violations and the move by Syrian tank units into Jordan. Guilty or not, the Soviets would benefit by the overthrow of King Hussein, they knew. But when King Hussein cried for help, the Pentagon told Nixon that the U.S. military lacked the capability for fast intervention on the ground.

Nixon and Kissinger faced a stark realization: only Israel could save the king of Jordan and preserve the balance of power in the region. The threat of Israeli military intervention caused the Syrians to retreat, allowing King Hussein to crush the Palestinian guerrillas in what came to be known as the Black September War.

The U.S.-Israeli strategic relationship was born amid the ashes of the failed fedayeen revolt. In the three years leading up to the 1970 Jordan crisis, annual U.S. military aid to Israel averaged under $47 million. In the three years succeeding the crisis, the annual aid averaged over $384 million. Both AIPAC's power and Arabist rage was to grow proportionally, with Sisco as the Arabists' scapegoat.*

Nasser died just as the Jordan crisis subsided, and he was replaced by his seemingly unimpressive vice president, Anwar Sadat. Bolstered by their success in standing down pro-Soviet elements in Jordan, Nixon and Kissinger assumed it was now safe to ignore the Middle East and seek new foreign policy glories in China. Nevertheless, the irrepressible Sisco, backed by Rogers, made another try at Middle East peace processing. This second, less widely known attempt was more tantalizing and had its roots in the personal experience of a particular Arabist, Michael Sterner.

Mike Sterner was another old hand, one whose diplomatic career would conclude as ambassador to the United Arab Emirates. He was born in New York City in 1928 and graduated from St. George's Episcopal boarding school in Newport, Rhode Island, and Harvard (class of 1951). He had studied French and Arabic and was inspired by Lawrence's *Seven Pillars of Wisdom.* "I also read a good deal of Doughty, Bell, Philby, and Thesiger. The Brits were such good writers. . . . And I remember Antonius's *The Arab Awakening*: a political classic that got into the bloodstream." A family friend got Sterner a job with ARAMCO in Saudi Arabia, from where Sterner got to travel to Egypt, Syria, Iraq, and Lebanon. In Saudi Arabia Sterner also became friendly with many Palestinians. He admits that "a certain sympathy" was born within him for the Palestinian cause. "My experience in Saudi Arabia made a major emotional impact on me in terms of partisanship. There were no Israelis, no Jews around. And I shot the breeze with the Palestinian workers all the time; hearing how they had been evicted from this village and that village where they had grown up."

Sterner later joined the Foreign Service and was posted to Yemen, followed by a year of Arabic-language instruction in Beirut. Then, from 1960 through 1965, Sterner served in Egypt, where his job at the embassy was to report on Egypt's internal politics. In this capacity Sterner spent a lot of time observing the Egyptian National Assembly, which Vice President Sadat "presided over in ham, avuncular fashion. The whole thing was a sham,

---

*AIPAC is the American-Israel Public Affairs Committee, the chief arm of the pro-Israel lobby in the United States.

but it was a good place to practice Arabic, and, as it happened, to get to know this guy Sadat." Sterner goes on:

"You have to understand. I was the only American attending these assembly sessions. So Sadat would invite me to tea, and we would talk at his house in Giza, in spacious but not quite palatial pseudo–Louis XV surroundings."

In February 1966, shortly after Sterner arrived back in Washington, he and the U.S. ambassador to Egypt, Luke Battle, arranged for Vice President Sadat to visit the United States. Because Nasser and his pro-Soviet policies were not especially popular in America, Battle had to pull strings to get Nasser's chief yes-man invited. "We got Sadat twelve dollars per day in expenses and a tourist-class seat on TWA. Then we got TWA to upgrade it to first class," Battle recalls. "Sadat was like a guy holding out his hand in the dark, asking, 'Will you treat me all right?' "

Upon arrival in America, Sterner accompanied Sadat everywhere. "This was Sadat's first-ever visit here, though he had been often to Moscow carrying out missions for Nasser. We wanted to impress him, so we flew him out to California," Sterner explains.

In Sacramento Sadat spent a whole day following around Governor Edmund "Pat" Brown. First, they went to a session of the California state assembly, where Brown was grilled by legislators on various issues, and then to a meeting that the governor had scheduled with high school students, where again Brown had to answer tough questions. Sadat, says Sterner, was goggle-eyed at the easy commingling between Brown and average citizens. "I remember those high school students were really peppy. But Brown subjected himself to the ordeal with humor. Sadat was absolutely bowled over by the experience, deeply impressed with the vitality and openness of American life. Remember, he had known Moscow in the dark days of Stalin. I think that was the key moment, when Sadat was first sold on America."

In New York, prior to returning to Egypt, there was a luncheon scheduled for Sadat at the 21 Club, which Mayor John Lindsay was to attend. "Due to pressure from Jewish groups, Lindsay canceled out only three hours before the lunch. Sadat was momentarily hurt. But he got over it. I asked him if there was anything he wanted to do to kill time. He told me he wanted to buy a complete collection of Zane Grey westerns. When he and other Egyptian nationalist leaders had been imprisoned by the British during World War II, the only thing they had to read in the prison library was

Zane Grey. And especially after California, he was hooked on this cowboy image of America. Being a New Yorker, I knew exactly where to take him: to a bookstore on Fourth Avenue on the East Side. You should have seen the joy on Sadat's face when he found the books. John Lindsay was forgotten. Sadat had this romantic strain in his personality. He was clearly a man of exaggerated gestures. I can still see him in that Edwardian morning coat of his, like a character in a David Niven movie."

In 1970, just as Sadat succeeded Nasser, Mike Sterner became the director of Egyptian affairs at the State Department. "I knew it was a new ball game. I advised my colleagues and superiors 'not to write the new guy off as a facsimile of Nasser. He will take Egypt in a different direction.' "

Few, least of all AIPAC and Golda Meir, would take Sterner seriously. After all, wasn't Sterner just a romantic Arabist who had a crush on this new, lightweight version of Nasser? As it happened, in the early spring of 1971, Sadat startled the senior American diplomat in Cairo, Donald Bergus, with a plan for an Egyptian-Israeli settlement.* Sterner flew out to Cairo from Washington, and on April 23 he and Bergus met with Sadat.

Sterner remembers: "We met north of Cairo, at some kind of Faroukian resthouse where we sat in wicker chairs over cool drinks and coffee. Sadat whistled for maps. It was a U.S. Survey map of Sinai. 'If the Israelis were willing to pull out here, I'd be willing to open the canal. . . .' And so he went on. Having suffered through the Nasser period, we suddenly realized that this guy wanted to negotiate peace. He was serious. This was important stuff. But what we didn't know was whether he was going to be dumped."

Days later Sadat allayed some of those fears, unleashing the first of his many surprises. He arrested the powerful, pro-Soviet head of his own political party, Ali Sabri. By summer Sadat would kick his Soviet military advisers out of Egypt. Yet Sadat's domestic position still appeared somewhat fragile. Though both Israeli defense minister Moshe Dayan and foreign minister Abba Eban were interested in Sadat's initiative, Prime Minister Meir was far more suspicious.

While both Rogers and Sisco came out to the Middle East to push the parties together and while Sadat was making further concessions, "the whole thing just ran into the sand," laments Sterner. "It seemed that all

---

*Egypt officially cut relations with the United States in 1967, so Bergus did not enjoy the rank of ambassador.

the pieces were in place, but it was a conundrum we couldn't quite crack." Atherton, who was deeply involved with Sisco in the initiative, admits, "Even I was skeptical of Sadat's sincerity. We didn't take him seriously enough as an institution until the 1973 war." That and other factors contributed to the failure of this second try at peace proceedings. As Atherton also admits, "The Israelis were right, there was too much emphasis on borders and not enough emphasis in these talks on the *essence* of peace." And even if these flaws had not existed, this initiative, like the Rogers Plan, was seen as a State Department project that both parties could sneak away from at the last minute without incurring Nixon's wrath.

Indeed, the failure of the spring 1971 initiative further undermined Rogers's State Department, allowing Nixon and Kissinger to take control of Middle East policy. Neither the Israelis nor the Egyptians were happy with Rogers and Sisco at this point. NEA was battling with AIPAC over each arms delivery to Israel, while Sadat felt that NEA, in Quandt's words, "had played [him] for a fool." In 1972 Sadat appointed Hafiz Ismail national security adviser, a newly created position that, as Atherton explains, had only one purpose: to "provide Sadat with a back channel to Kissinger," who had the same title in the U.S. bureaucracy.

"The area experts in NEA were aggrieved because Kissinger was obviously not interested in a peace settlement in the 1971–1973 period. And Kissinger lacks the grace to admit his wrongness," Sterner says. Sterner continues to regret that neither the Israelis nor the Nixon administration trusted Sadat's overtures prior to the Yom Kippur War of 1973. Sterner shows his guest a montage from a 1971 edition of the Israeli newspaper *Ha'aretz* ("The Land"), depicting himself, Roy Atherton, and some other State Department Arabists in Lawrence of Arabia costumes. "This is how the Israelis ridiculed us," he laughs. "Had they believed us about Sadat, a large number of their boys wouldn't have been killed in 1973."

Sterner admits that on account of failures with the peace process and increased arms sales to Israel, a bunker mentality prevailed in NEA in the early 1970s. "There was a feeling that we were the only ones in Washington offering a balanced counterpart to the general atmosphere of pro-Israel partisanship." This was when the Arabists began to seriously identify themselves with the China hands persecuted under the McCarthyism of the 1950s.

But the old time Arabists were to get no respite. Kissinger's takeover of NEA predated his September 1973 appointment as secretary of state by about four months. In May 1973, under the cover of the Vietnam Paris peace talks, Kissinger secretly met with his Egyptian counterpart, Hafiz Ismail, after being briefed beforehand by Sisco and Atherton. William Rogers, though nominally secretary of state, was completely out of the picture by then. May 1973 in Paris was the first time that Atherton dealt with Kissinger. "I was impressed what a quick learner he was. He didn't need much of a briefing at all," Atherton recalls.

Kissinger's formal arrival at State completed NEA's transformation. His sense of realpolitik stood on its head the Foreign Service's concept of diplomacy.* In his memoir, *Years of Upheaval,* Kissinger outlines his skeptical view of the service:

> The Foreign Service had developed in the early years of our history when no direct physical threat to America's security was apparent. America's foreign involvement was considered to flow less from a concept of national interest—which was thought morally myopic—than from enlightened notions of freedom of trade and the implementation of moral, or at least legal, principles. . . . The Foreign Service emphasizes negotiability—which is another way of saying consciousness of what the other side will accept.

In a word, Kissinger thought of FSOs as a bunch of missionaries, out to do good and to meet villains halfway, at the expense of the national interest.

Kissinger's brilliance of manipulating the bureaucracy was demonstrated by his decision to keep Sisco as NEA assistant secretary. Sisco was generally seen to be Rogers's man, and Kissinger was known to dislike Rogers. Moreover, Kissinger took a dim view of Sisco's constant attempts at peacemaking, which Kissinger derided as "activity for activity's sake." Obviously, however, Kissinger correctly divined how powerful a tool Sisco would be as "his" man. Although Joe Sisco, like Hermann Eilts, never thought twice about talking back to Kissinger—screaming at him, even— Kissinger tolerated dissent from people he deeply respected.

Mike Sterner is one old hand who takes a reflective view of the change Kissinger and Sisco wrought at the State Department, and particularly at NEA: "Kissinger brought a healthy corrective to foreign policy. He saw how decision making suffered from uncontrolled bilateralism. It's true, there is a built-in institutional bias in favor of bilateral relations at the State Department [relations between the United States and this Arab country, between the United States and that Arab country, etc.]. So Kissinger in-

---

*See the chapter on the Nixon-Ford administrations in Barry Rubin's *Secrets of State,* listed in the bibliography.

troduced a new architecture, whereby institutional checks were put in place to keep matters in perspective, because certain states and ideals were always more important than others."

The 1973 Yom Kippur War, though a partial result of Nixon and Kissinger's neglect of the Middle East after their victory in the 1970 Jordan crisis, provided Kissinger with the perfect opportunity to quickly disprove the classic Arabist notion, most clearly articulated by Loy Henderson, that the United States had to choose friendship with twenty-odd Arab states or with one Jewish state, because it couldn't have both.

Well, yes, it could. Though Israel won the war, it had been badly bloodied by Sadat's surprise attack across the Suez Canal, and Syrian leader Hafez Assad's attack on the Golan Heights. Israel's strategic and psychological advantage over its Arab neighbors had been drastically reduced. This setback allowed Kissinger to pressure Israel into concessions. The Arab states now learned that only the United States precisely on account of its close relationship with Israel, could get back their lost territory. So even as the U.S.-Israeli relations remained close, Syria and Egypt renewed official ties with Washington.

Kissinger, Sisco, and Atherton were the core of the State Department's traveling team for the historic negotiations that followed the October 1973 war, negotiations that involved the reopening of the Suez Canal, the withdrawal of Israeli forces from the western part of Sinai, and the creation of a demilitarized zone in the Golan Heights. Hermann Eilts was the man they chose to reopen the U.S. embassy in Cairo, and Richard Murphy was their man to reopen the U.S. embassy in Damascus.

It was Atherton who had spotted Dick Murphy as sort of "a new breed, nonbaggage, non-Arabist Arabist." But what distinguished Murphy from old hands like Seelye, Parker, Stoltzfus, Killgore, Sterner, and others was much subtler: rather than a new breed, he represented a *lite* version of those men (though Murphy, like some of those gentlemen, would certainly distance himself from the kinds of statements about Israel and Zionists made by Killgore).

Murphy, like Atherton, was a graduate of Exeter Academy, where he first encountered Doughty's *Travels in Arabia Deserta*. After Harvard and a stint in the army, Murphy joined the Foreign Service in 1954. He studied Arabic in the hills above Beirut and the Koran with a theology student at a local mosque. He visited Israel for the first time in 1959 and there discovered "that taking sides was really a stupid thing to do," especially for one's career. In February 1962 he was handing out photos of astronaut John Glenn by the U.S. consulate in Aleppo in an attempt to promote America's image among local Arabs. The next day the Syrian media accused him of handing out photos of Nasser (this was during a breach in relations between Egypt and Syria). Murphy complained to Syrian officials and received an apology. But the next day he read in the paper that it was in fact he who had apologized. "I made the mistake of trying to reason with them. It's that kind of experience, again and again, which immunizes you from becoming emotionally pro-Arab."

After Atherton became deputy assistant secretary, he got Murphy the job as ambassador to Mauritania. Atherton knew from his own experience that the best thing for an Arabist's career was to get out of the mainstream of the Arab world. Besides being on the Arab periphery, Mauritania gave Murphy the chance to join the ranks of ambassadors at a relatively young age, making him eligible for the Syria post when Kissinger reestablished relations. Murphy was deliberately chosen over Stoltzfus, Killgore, and others with more seniority and more Arab experience. Atherton also helped Murphy get the job of ambassador to the Philippines in 1978, after Murphy completed his stint as ambassador to Syria. By the early 1980s Murphy had the perfectly rounded résumé to become the NEA assistant secretary during the Reagan era.

There was never again to be a hard-core Arabist at the head of NEA. In 1974 Atherton replaced Sisco in the job when Kissinger promoted Sisco to under secretary of state. Atherton was succeeded by Hal Saunders, Kissinger's former NSC aide and one of the original peace processors. And after Saunders but before Murphy came Nick Veliotes.

Nick Veliotes was an ethnic Greek from California who had attended the local public schools and had degrees from the University of California at Berkeley. His first Foreign Service posts were in Naples and Rome from 1955 to 1960. "Five beautiful years in Italy, before the pimps, the prostitutes, the garbage, and the pollution destroyed the place. For my wife and I, it was the best years of our lives. It's been downhill ever since," he deadpans in a streetwise, I-know-the-score kind of voice.

Veliotes's next overseas posts were in Vietnam, India, and Laos. In 1973, at the age of forty-five, he was asked to choose between Bangladesh as ambassador or Israel as DCM. The overwhelming majority of FSOs would have chosen Bangladesh. A State Department FSO, whether he or she admits it or not, has only one goal: to become an ambassador before retirement. To be offered an ambassadorship in one's forties—no matter how small the country—puts an FSO in an elite category where other, even bigger doors may suddenly blow open.

Veliotes is a gambler. "I didn't want to go back to Asia. I had gotten every disease in the book out there and I didn't want to invent new ones. I was afraid of becoming intellectually bored. Also, I had kids and Israel was a better family post."

Israel proved to be exactly what Veliotes was looking for. In the wake of the 1973 war, he found, rather than intellectual boredom, "enormous workloads, seven days a week." Veliotes found that "Israelis had a sort of attractive arrogance. There was a frenetic, electrifying, mid-Manhattan feel to Tel Aviv. The American embassy was in the middle of the red-light district. It was a great post."

In 1975 Veliotes returned to Washington to work on Kissinger's policy-planning staff. In 1977 Atherton named him deputy assistant NEA secretary, and in 1978 he became ambassador to Jordan. The gamble of rejecting the Bangladesh ambassadorship had paid dividends. "There were those [i.e., Arabists] who tried to undermine me getting the Jordan job, on account of my time in Israel. What they didn't realize was that the Jordanians wanted me precisely because of my insight on Israel."*

The nudging aside of the old time Arabists in order to make room for those like Murphy and Veliotes did not always go smoothly, however. In late 1975 Kissinger fired the ambassador to Saudi Arabia, James Elmer Akins, for insubordination; for being, allegedly, just too partial to the Arabs. Akins

---

*Veliotes concluded his career as ambassador to Egypt after serving as NEA assistant secretary from 1981 to 1983.

had to learn about his dismissal through a column written by Joseph Kraft. This was Henry Kissinger at his bureaucratic nastiest. What drove him to such lengths? As one might expect, policy differences were only the surface causes.

Jim Akins was not your typical old-boy Arabist. He was not courtly and polite, in the way of an Andy Killgore or a Talcott Seelye or a Bill Stoltzfus, or even a China type such as George Bush. Akins was both abrasive and truly brilliant.

He was born in Akron, Ohio, in 1926; not a rich WASP but a poor Quaker. Instead of Princeton or Amherst or Harvard, he graduated from Akron University. Instead of a degree in literature or political science, he got his degree in physics. That's a clue to Jim Akins: he is a "hard" scientist; everything about his personality and thought processes is severely analytical and not, definitely not, mushy. He is the antithesis of the soft, social-science type of Arabist that neoconservatives, in particular, love to hate.

Akins's hard science personality coupled with his Quaker upbringing also made him a moralist and, some would claim, a self-righteous one. At the beginning of the 1950s, Akins served with the American Friends Service Committee in Poland, Czechoslovakia, and Germany, until the Quaker group was expelled by the Communists. (This service was similar to the relief work that Loy Henderson, who also grew up poor and religious in America's heartland, did with the Red Cross after World War I.) Akins at this time discovered an ability with languages. Physics had introduced him to German, and now he was easily mastering French. He also became a Hellenophile. In 1951 he made a walking tour through Greece and Asia Minor, visiting the remote Orthodox monasteries on Mount Athos. This happened relatively soon after the Greek civil war, and much of the countryside was still brutalized. In Turkey Akins traced the path of Alexander the Great on foot, something, he notes, not even celebrated British travel writers like Freya Stark ever accomplished. "My interest in the Levant came primarily through Greece," he explains.

The youthful Akins pitched up in Beirut in 1952 and survived for a while teaching physics and chemistry. "I grew up extremely poor. I didn't know what the Foreign Service was until I got to Beirut. I figured it was for rich kids. I knew I was smarter than them. I waited to take the annual Foreign Service exam at the U.S. embassy. I had no doubt that I would pass." As it happened, the exam papers never arrived, and the next year, 1953, budget cuts and pressure from the red-baiting Senator Joe McCarthy prevented new admissions. After hanging around Lebanon and Syria for a time—Roy Atherton, then a diplomat in Syria, was the first FSO Akins ever met—Akins returned to Washington, where in 1954 he was finally admitted to the Foreign Service.

In 1956 Akins was posted to Damascus. Here he displayed a brilliance (also an arrogance) that one just had to respect. "This was still before the days of family allowances for schooling and paid home leave," he begins to explain. "In other words, the Service was still, basically, a rich man's institution, where the salaries were not high and you had to pay much of your own way. It was easy to be honest in your cables if you were rich, since if you had to leave the Service there was always another income to go back to. But I didn't have that luxury. That's when I decided that whatever the consequences, I was going to act like a rich boy. I was going to write and say exactly what I really thought." So Akins penned a report citing "sixteen signs" of an impending political union between Syria and Egypt. "I sent it through the dissent channel. The DCM destroyed my analysis. But I turned out to be right. He was wrong."*

Next came a short stint at the U.S. consulate in Madras, India, before going to Beirut to study Arabic. "I easily caught up with people who had been studying the language full-time," he reminds his visitor, lamenting that "the school was closed for a time when Eisenhower invaded Lebanon." In 1959 Akins went to Kuwait, replacing Seelye as vice consul, who in turn had replaced Stoltzfus there. Then in 1961 Akins began a four-year term in Baghdad as the embassy's political counselor. "On account of the Baathist coup [in 1962], we enjoyed better relations with Iraq," he happily notes. (Another tidbit: Akins's predecessor as political counselor in Baghdad was Bill Lakeland, whom Akins considers "the best Foreign Service officer I ever met." This is the same Bill Lakeland whom Atherton described as "very much a supporter of Arab nationalism, Nasser, and Sunni majority rule.")

In 1967 Akins's knowledge of the oil-rich Arab world, combined with his scientific expertise, got him the job of director of the State Department's Fuels and Energy office. Akins proved to be a Cassandra. In 1970, when gas was seventeen cents a gallon, he formally proposed a gasoline tax in order to curb consumption and prepare America for an upcoming oil crunch, which he predicted in the spring of 1973, a few months before the Yom Kippur War and the subsequent Arab oil embargo.

At a meeting with Nixon's domestic policy adviser, John Erlichman,

---

*The union, known as the United Arab Republic, came into being in 1958 and was dissolved in 1961.

Akins argued for an energy-conservation plan. Erlichman responded by saying that "conservation was not a Republican issue." "Erlichman was wrong," says Akins. "America's first great conservationist, Teddy Roosevelt, was a Republican. But of course," laughing, "I didn't think of saying that until after I left the White House."

Akins's appointment as ambassador to Saudi Arabia, just as the Yom Kippur War began, seemed a perfect choice. What better than an Arabist and an energy expert to be the ambassador to the Arab kingdom that was the world's leading oil producer? But Akins caused problems immediately. On October 25, 1973, a few weeks after taking up his duties in Saudi Arabia, Akins told ARAMCO executives there "to use their contacts at highest levels of U.S.G. [United States government] to hammer home the point that oil restrictions are not going to be lifted unless political struggle is settled in a manner satisfactory to Arabs."* The investigative reporter Steven Emerson wrote in *The American House of Saud: The Secret Petro-dollar Connection* that Akins's "action was truly extraordinary. Here he was, the American ambassador to Saudi Arabia, attempting to reinforce the Arabs' blackmail of the United States."

Kissinger and Sisco were, to say the least, not happy. Akins makes no bones about his dislike for them and his preference for the previous secretary of state, William Rogers. Yet Akins denies that this has anything to do with a partiality for the Arab cause. By his lights, he fought for Kissinger and for Israel. "King Feisal was not disposed to see Kissinger. He was a Jew, a Zionist, the king said. I told Feisal that 'you must see Kissinger or I will have to resign. Since I will have no credibility as ambassador if I cannot get my secretary of state in to see the head of state to the country to which I am accredited.'" Akins adds that he "had to spend an awful lot of effort arguing with the Saudis that Kissinger was not involved in the killing of Feisal," who was assassinated by a distraught Saudi prince in March 1975. Furthermore, Akins says, "George Habash [the radical Palestinian leader] called me the most dangerous American in the Middle East, because I allegedly had an unholy influence over Feisal. In fact, I changed Feisal on Israel: from no psychological acceptance of a Jewish state whatsoever to accepting in his own mind the legitimacy of Israel within its pre-1967

---

*This is from an ARAMCO document printed in U.S. Senate Subcommittee on Multinationals's hearings, ("Multinational Corporations and United States Foreign Policy," Part 7, February 20–21, March 27–28, 1974, page 517).

borders. And Akins, a tall, imposing man with a somewhat grating and intimidating manner that appears to hide a more sensitive soul underneath, has another thing to tell his visitor:

"I didn't want the oil prices to go up. I argued with Feisal against raising the prices. I told him that by hurting the Western economics, rising oil prices would only help the Communists, whom the king hated. Feisal said that 'if you convince Iran, then I'll go along' with a price freeze. But Sisco and Kissinger were annoyed at my suggestion that they pressure the Shah to hold down the oil price.* They wanted the Shah to make money so that he could buy our weapons. But I kept pressing them. It was my rich-boy mentality operating again, my hubris. I thought that because I knew so much more about these things than Sisco and Kissinger and because of my close relationship with King Feisal, it would keep me from getting fired."

Hume Horan, Akins's DCM in Saudi Arabia, backs up a part of this story when he says, "Jim definitely fought for U.S. interests. He was tough, bullying Feisal almost; pushing things right to the edge, then pulling back, marshaling his forces, and trying again with the king. Jim's was a cliff-hanging performance, full of bravura."

Hermann Eilts, who had just arrived in Egypt as the ambassador and who was privy to many of these discussions, says that Akins's claim about Kissinger not wanting to pressure the Shah "was an appendix to the main story," which was that Akins sometimes refused to carry out Kissinger's instructions and gave the impression of refusing to pressure Feisal to lift the oil embargo. "Akins," Eilts laments, "was brilliant, but bad in bureaucratic interactions. He was confrontational, though often intellectually right. He had localitis. And he was egotistical. Akins thought himself as pure as Ivory soap."

"Jim," says Hume Horan, "was certainly stiff-necked. This is the guy who once told members of the Fortune 500 to put out their cigars because he was such a militant nonsmoker."

In short, there was no room, or no driver's seat, big enough for both Jim Akins and Henry Kissinger, who may have been more alike than they each are willing to admit. Aggravating the personality clash of two intense, brilliant, and arrogant men was the difficulty of the times; clearly Akins was under a lot of pressure to deliver Feisal on the oil issue, and whatever he

*Andy Killgore suggests in his oral history interview that this was part of a Sisco-Kissinger plot to trap the Arabs between two militarily powerful non-Arab countries: Israel and Iran.

achieved was never quite enough or achieved quite soon enough. So each side claims that the other was the villain. The persons Kissinger tolerated backtalk from on the Middle East—Sisco and Eilts—were men who largely had the same outlook on the Arab-Israeli problem. But Akins didn't think much of Kissinger's power-and-pressure-oriented way of dealing with the Arabs. He explains: "I remember when a large number of reports appeared in the American media about the United States occupying the Arabian oil fields. I gave a TV interview saying that 'anyone who thinks that should happen is a madman, a criminal, and an agent of the Soviet Union.' Well, it turns out that Kissinger was the briefer behind those reports [it was Kissinger's way of making the Arabs nervous]. Had I known that, I obviously would not have chosen the words I did. I may be brazen, but I'm not suicidal."

Sisco, meanwhile, complains: "To this day Akins hates me. I know he does, and I don't know why. I tried to save his job. He's from a poor family. Fine. So am I. We should have been allies."

According to Eilts, Sisco did try to save Akins. "Sisco said to me: what's with Akins, doesn't he know that if he keeps acting like that, Henry will have to fire him?" Eilts recalls an incident involving the foreign affairs columnist of the *New York Times,* C. L. Sulzberger. "Sulzberger asked me if I could help him get into Saudi Arabia. Sulzberger was Jewish and they didn't officially allow Jews in. I said, 'Just send a message to our ambassador, Jim Akins. You're the columnist of the *New York Times,* the Saudis have got to let you in.' But Sulzberger told me that he had already contacted Akins and that Akins wouldn't help. So I got a Saudi contact to get Sulzberger his visa. Then I get an irate message from Akins, saying the visa should not have been issued."

The final straw came after David Rockefeller returned from a trip to Saudi Arabia and had a private chat with Kissinger, a longtime friend, at the State Department. Rockefeller told Kissinger, "You should get rid of your ambassador in Saudi Arabia. For one thing, he's bad-mouthing your policy. And for another, he's more Saudi than the Saudis."

Kissinger acted immediately, and Akins was gone.

But incidents like the Sulzberger one, amplified by numerous statements Akins was to make after leaving the Foreign Service in 1975, unfortunately make for an unsettling impression of this highly talented man. Typical was a speech Akins prepared for an energy conference in London in September 1981. Besides suggesting that Saudi Arabia should use the oil weapon against America if America's policy was not sufficiently pro-Arab, Akins attacked the "enemies" of Saudi Arabia, such as "Jewish writers" Joseph Kraft and William Safire, whom he compared with Nazis. His specific beef with Kraft and Safire was that while they were quick to condemn any manifestation of anti-Semitism, they overtly ridiculed Arabs in the same insensitive way that Nazis ridiculed Jews.

Akins's larger point—that the American media has a hypocritical blind spot in regard to the ethnic stereotyping of Arabs—is, of course, a good one. Ethnic slurs against Arabs, especially in newspaper cartoons, have been so common in America that one barely notices them. Imagine what it must be like for Arab-Americans to see this stuff in the paper on a regular basis. But one wonders whether Akins had to compare Jews with Nazis rather than use a less incendiary comparison. He accuses Safire and company of having an agenda, but what about Akins himself?

Akins shows his visitor a sketch of King Feisal that he keeps in a prominent position in his study. "The Saudis were about to throw it away because for them it constituted a graven image; so I asked if I could have it." Akins worries about Saudi Arabia. Besides being a militant nonsmoker, he is a firm believer in birth control. He explains that if the Saudi population keeps growing as it has been and water depletion in the kingdom continues apace, Saudi Arabia, as well as other parts of the Arab world, could be "like Bangladesh" sometime in the next century: a country with not enough resources to sustain its people. His predictions on oil in the 1960s were on target, and this complicated and not altogether pleasant man will probably again be proven right.

By the time Jimmy Carter took over the White House in 1977, Akins was gone, Stoltzfus had retired, Killgore was in Qatar where he could do no damage, and Atherton was firm in the saddle as NEA assistant secretary. But to assume that NEA was a totally reformed bureau as a result of the Nixon-Ford-Kissinger-Sisco-Atherton era would be wrong. It was a bureau in transition. That same year, 1977, saw Seelye appointed ambassador to Syria and Dick Parker appointed ambassador to Lebanon. Iraq, moreover, as we shall witness later, was still a haunt of old Arab hands.

The state of the transition is best gauged through the experiences of Samuel W. Lewis, who in 1977 became the U.S. ambassador to Israel.

American ambassadors to Israel are members of an odd species. Because Hebrew is spoken in only one country in the world, it is not usually a wise move for an FSO to become a Hebraist. In almost every case the ambassador in Tel Aviv has been an "out of area" man—and never a Jew, for the obvious reason that a Jewish ambassador to Israel would automatically be undermined by the assumption of a pro-Israel emotional bias. Perhaps because American-Israeli relations are so deeply developed, and thus so complex and controversial, successful ambassadors have shown an occasional tendency to stay in their posts a long time. Walworth Barbour, for instance, appointed by President Kennedy, was the U.S. ambassador in Tel Aviv for eleven years in the 1960s and early 1970s. Samuel Lewis remained in his post for eight years, from 1977 until 1985. Lewis worked with two presidents, Carter and Reagan, and four NEA assistant secretaries, Atherton, Hal Saunders, Nick Veliotes, and Dick Murphy.

Sam Lewis, born in 1930 in Houston, is a Texan with an accent similar to James Baker's. Educated at Yale, Lewis is cool and commonsensical, blessed, like Hermann Eilts, with the enviable faculty of seemingly emanating wisdom. Lewis has known Jim Akins most of his life. Nick Veliotes is a close friend, who inherited Lewis's Naples apartment when Lewis moved back to Washington and Veliotes came out to Italy. When you meet Lewis, it's just like meeting another FSO. The fact that he was ambassador to Israel rather than to an Arab country doesn't seem to make much of a difference to an outsider.

Though Lewis was a DCM in Moslem Afghanistan and served in top posts on Kissinger's policy-planning staff and the United Nations delegation, his specialty, if he had any, was as a Latin America hand, with an emphasis on Brazil. Nevertheless, in 1977, when Andrew Young, Carter's new UN ambassador, cleaned out the Nixon-Ford era people from the UN mission staff, Lewis was offered the choice of three ambassadorships as compensation: India, South Africa, or Israel. "Israel had not even entered my mind until that moment. But it clearly was interesting. So I took it," he shrugs.

Lewis's starting point for considering the relationship between Arabists and the American ambassador to Israel is an incident that occurred in 1961 at the Ledra Palace Hotel in Nicosia, Cyprus. Lewis was then an assistant to Chester Bowles, President Kennedy's special representative for Africa, Asia, and Latin America. Bowles had called a chiefs-of-mission conference in Cyprus, where all the ambassadors from the Middle East could get to-gether with Pentagon and CIA area specialists. Each ambassador got to brief his colleagues about the situation in his particular country. But Lewis will "never forget that when Wally Barbour briefed the old-time Arabists about what was going on in Israel, there was a very tangible disdain and skepticism. Barbour was not a part of the club, that was clear."

By the time Lewis was named ambassador sixteen years later, there were fewer old-time Arabists, and peace negotiations between Israel and Egypt quickly became the center of the action—1977 was also the year that Sadat went to Jerusalem—so Lewis had a more pleasant experience with his NEA colleagues than had Barbour. "At NEA I was never made to feel that I was a second-class citizen. If anything, *they* were second-class citizens."

"They" means Dick Parker and Talcott Seelye, who were cut out of the Camp David action because Lebanon had no role and Syria refused to take part. According to Lewis, Parker and Seelye were sort of growling on the sidelines while Eilts in Cairo and Lewis himself in Tel Aviv shared the spotlight with Atherton and Secretary of State Cyrus Vance. Though Jordan and Saudi Arabia also didn't have much of a role in the negotiations, Lewis says he got along just fine with Veliotes, then the ambassador in Amman, and with John C. West and Dick Murphy, the ambassadors in Riyadh. "West even invited me to Saudi Arabia. Dick Murphy was never a problem to deal with. And I got to Jordan on occasion from Tel Aviv. But when I asked Talc Seelye if he could arrange a visit for me to Damascus, he said he really couldn't ask the Syrians for permission. I thought that was ridiculous."

Lewis goes on: "I had my problems with Parker and Seelye. It had to do with the lateral cable traffic. They got to see my reports on the Israeli view of events, and I got to see theirs on Lebanon and Syria. We had spirited arguments, nasty on occasion. Parker seemed to identify deeply with Leb-anon's tragedy and against the Israel–Maronite Christian coalition fighting there. Seelye, meanwhile, was sending cables that to my mind got more and more intemperate, about how the whole region was going to explode and the Arabs were going to burn our embassies down if we didn't do this and this."

Seelye has a different recollection of his own cables: "If I had presented everything in its stark reality, I'd have sounded like I was pleading a case." Seelye must have been a lonely man in Damascus in the aftermath of Camp David. Not only was Lewis criticizing his cables from the vantage point of

Tel Aviv, but at the policy-planning staff in Washington, Reagan political appointee Francis Fukuyama found Seelye's writings pro-Syrian in the extreme. No wonder Seelye blew his top and called in the press to openly criticize the Camp David peace process in August 1981. His perspective, from Damascus and Beirut, was completely unlike that from Tel Aviv and Washington.

The events there provide a cautionary tale about how Arabism had changed, how new qualities—such as an ability to deal effectively with America's domestic realities—had been thrust to the fore, making the AUB-style old hands unsuited for future service.

William Stoltzfus, Jr.

Several generations of the Stoltzfus family served in Araby and Africa, first as missionaries, later as diplomats, and finally as Peace Corps volunteers. Above, Janet and William Stoltzfus, Jr., leave Taiz, Yemen, in 1961, after Bill completed two years as the U.S. chargé d'affaires. Below, newly appointed Ambassador Bill Stoltzfus presents his credentials to Sheikh Sabah al-Salem, ruler of Kuwait, in 1972. Their life in the Arab world did not prevent the Stoltzfuses from developing a compassionate sensibility toward Arabs *and* Jews.

William Stoltzfus, Jr.

Above, in Western dress, patrons of the YWCA founded by missionaries like the Stoltzfus family in turn-of-the-century Smyrna, Turkey. Below, at left, Daniel Bliss, founder of the Syrian Protestant College (later the American University of Beirut); at right, his son, Howard Sweetser Bliss, the college's second president. The Blisses were the "first family" of the American community in the Arab world for over a century.

Beirut harbor (above left), with Mount Lebanon in the background, suggests the tranquil atmosphere of old Beirut in an era dear to Arabists. A typical excursion of those times appears below left, as a group of missionaries prepare to depart for a picnic in Sidon. Above right, former president Teddy Roosevelt enjoys the diversions of a more leisurely time in the Sudan. Below right, the AUB's first graduating class, in 1870, foreshadows the school's importance in the Arab intellectual awakening.

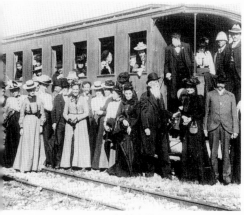

American Arabists greatly admired their British colleagues, in particular explorer Richard Burton (above right), whose mastery of native languages and dress enabled him to pass as a native, earning him the nickname "the White Nigger." Thomas Edward Lawrence ("of Arabia") (above left) led the Arabs to victory against the Turks in World War I. Below, Gertrude Bell, one of Lawrence's British colleagues, picnicked with King Feisal of Iraq in 1922.

The Bettmann Archive

Above, delegates to the 1919 Paris Peace Conference, where Lawrence (middle row, second from right) tried to win independence for the Arabs. King Feisal is in the foreground. Below, the gallows in Damascus, then under French rule, after Lawrence's attempts failed.

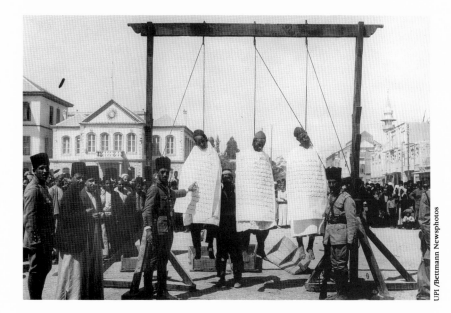

UPI /Bettmann Newsphotos

In the 1940s, America entered the Middle East as a great power. Above, Saudi King Abdul Azziz ibn Saud holds court with American military authorities. At right is American Minister James Moose, Jr., who would later remark to Roy Atherton that knowledge of Arabic "opens the door to an empty room." Below, King Farouk of Egypt confers with President Franklin D. Roosevelt on an American ship near Cairo in February 1945.

Loy Henderson (above left) became the prototype for many State Department Arabists. His career is brilliantly critiqued in H. W. Brands's *Inside the Cold War*. Above right, Henderson arrives in Persia as the new U.S. envoy in 1951. Rear Admiral Wat T. Cluverius (below right), who survived the explosion aboard the battleship *Maine* in Havana in 1898, was the namesake of Wat Cluverius IV, the first Arabist posted to Israel. Below left, Carleton Coon, Sr., the great American ethnologist and travel writer, in 1942.

Loy Henderson inspired a generation of Arabists, including U.S. envoy Talcott Seelye, shown above in 1976 with Lebanese Druze warlord Kemal Jumblatt, who was killed shortly after this meeting. Below, U.S. Embassy staff in Beirut are evacuated to Athens in 1976 at the height of the Lebanese civil war, in a successful and low-key operation personally planned by Seelye.

Above, Ambassador to Lebanon Richard Parker listens as Secretary of State Cyrus Vance talks with Lebanese President Elias Sarkis in 1977. Below, Alfred Leroy (Roy) Atherton, who led the way to a more contemporary attitude toward Arabs and Jews in the State Department, with Israeli General Moshe Dayan.

Ambassador to Egypt Hermann Eilts, above at left, one of the greatest Arabists, at Cairo Airport in 1977 upon the arrival of Assistant Secretary of State Roy Atherton and his wife Betty. Below, Egyptian Minister of State for Foreign Affairs (later UN Secretary General) Butros Butros-Ghali lectures Atherton (at right).

Above left, Eilts greets Egyptian President Anwar Sadat. Above right, Donald Bergus, Chief of the U.S. Interests Section in Cairo (left), and Michael Sterner, Director of Egyptian Affairs, with Sadat in 1971. Below, an Israeli newspaper montage pokes fun at State Department Arabists. Sterner is on the left, Atherton to the right of T. E. Lawrence.

Above, Israeli Ambassador to the U.S. Yitzhak Rabin seated with Assistant Secretary of State Joseph Sisco (right) in 1971. Sisco was Secretary of State Henry Kissinger's right-hand man in the days of the Middle East "shuttle diplomacy." Below, Kissinger, who modernized the State Department's handling of Middle East affairs, conducts high diplomacy. Eilts is in the foreground on Kissinger's right, and Sisco is on Kissinger's left. The Nile River flows behind them.

Above, James E. Akins is sworn in as Ambassador to Saudi Arabia in 1973. Mrs. Akins holds the Bible. Henry Kissinger would later force this prescient and controversial diplomat out of his job. Below, Hume Horan (in tie at right) and Ambassador L. Dean Brown in Amman, Jordan, during "Black September," 1970.

Hume Horan (photo by Dave Valdez, The White House)

Above, Hume and Nancy Horan with Vice-President and Mrs. Bush in Khartoum in 1985, after Ambassador Horan completed the airlift of Falasha Jews from Sudan to Israel. Below, Jerry Weaver shown with a lion he had shot in southern Sudan; Weaver carried out the secret rescue operation under Horan's direction.

Jerry Weaver

In the 1980s, Americans became targets of religious extremists in the Middle East. Above left, Ambassdor to Syria William Eagleton (left) with freed hostage Lawrence Jenco in 1986. David Dodge (above right), the great-grandson of AUB founder Daniel Bliss, was the first American taken hostage in Lebanon. Below, Ambassador to Lebanon John Kelly (in suit and tie) protected by bodyguards in 1988.

April Glaspie, Ambassador to Iraq and an Arabist of the old school, appears before the Senate Foreign Relations Committee in March 1991. Glaspie's failure to confront Iraqi President Saddam Hussein helped bring a tragic end to a long chapter in Arabist history. However, another chapter awaits this group of heretofore mysterious and distinguished American diplomats.

Chapter 9

Mugged by Reality

From the rustic, idyllic backwater of its early-century golden age, Beirut had become a bustling city of Levantine glitz and glamor, replete with nightclubs, intelligence activities, and combustible politics. There were now two American Arabist communities in Beirut: a "culture" and "goodwill" community based around the AUB and an embassy community based on realpolitik. Terry Prothro was a witness to the metamorphosis.

A professor of psychology for most of his life, E. Terry Prothro has the wonderful ability to see himself and his lifelong friends and colleagues from a cool, objective distance. In his self-depreciating southern style, he provides the last word on the AUB.

"I'm a native of Louisiana, which, as you may know, is the westernmost of Arab states—from the point of view of multicultural cuisine and political corruption. After World War II I taught at LSU [Louisiana State University]. Maybe because I come from a world of Bible-Belt Protestantism, I became one of those antiracist, liberal idealist types. That's what caused me to go to Lebanon and AUB.

"I arrived at AUB in 1951 and stayed on staff all the way until 1984. When I came, Bayard Dodge had just left and Steve Penrose was settling in as the new president." As Prothro explains, the pre–World War II years saw the AUB community slowly realize "what rough beast was slouching toward Bethlehem to be born." By which he means not just a Jewish state in a part of Palestine but the whole sorry phenomenon of pan-Arab nationalism, as it came to be defined through the Palestine issue.

In 1948, Prothro says, "the AUB faculty became infused with Palestinian teachers who had fled" their homes in the wake of the creation of Israel. In the 1950s the university "became a place where the Arab student body tried out all their political responses" to the challenge posed by the Jews in Palestine. Yet the political atmosphere was still, on one level at least, ecumenical. Prothro remembers that the president of the psychology association was a radical Palestinian, the vice president a Shiite, and the treasurer a Jew.

Liberal idealism reigned supreme in the AUB of the 1950s. There in the sunny Levant a dedicated faculty educated those less fortunate others who upon graduation were assuming leadership roles in their own new nations, carved out of a dead European imperialist order of which their teachers were entirely innocent. On account of the profusion of new Arab states, the charter meeting of the UN in 1945 had boasted more AUB graduates among the representatives than graduates of any other university.

In an essay recalling those heady days, Malcolm Hooper Kerr, a graduate student and teacher who would later become the AUB's president, states how he and other members of the American faculty openly sympathized with the political aspirations of their Arab friends. " 'Arab-Western relations' was *our* subject. It consisted, if not exactly of our own private relationship, then of our awareness of the thoughts and deeds of a stable of familiar figures on whom our minds could take a firm grip, heroes of the past hundred years . . . Faisal I of Iraq and Nasser. We also had our villains," among whom Kerr includes Israel's founding father, David Ben-Gurion, along with the British imperialists. "We had our revered texts, such as George Antonius's *The Arab Awakening. . . .*" Kerr also writes of "the problems of the Arab-Western relationship," including "the usurpation of Palestine by Zionists."

Kerr's essay, written in honor of a late Jordanian prime minister, Abd al-Hamid Sharaf, goes on to champion Western liberalism, Arab nationalism, and the universalism uniting Islam with Christianity. He argues against the very notion of Western political and moral superiority to the Arabs. Kerr, a Princeton graduate who was born on the AUB campus in 1931 and died on the campus in 1984—assassinated by a Moslem extremist—traveled throughout the Arab world but, in the tradition of Bayard Dodge, preferred not to visit Israel, except as a base for touring the occupied West Bank. He once remarked to a colleague that visits to Israel "would stigmatize me in the Arab world."

The bulk of Kerr's career was spent at the University of California at Los Angeles (UCLA), where he initiated joint research projects between American and Arab scholars. In some Middle Eastern circles UCLA's Near East center under Kerr's influence became known as LAFLOP—the Los Angeles Front for the Liberation of Palestine.

Malcolm Kerr was a quintessential child of the AUB. The 1950s, report Elizabeth Warnock Fernea and Robert A. Fernea in *The Arab World: Personal Encounters,* was a decade when "American social scientists with Middle Eastern interests . . . waxed enthusiastic" over just about everything they found in Lebanon. For them Lebanon constituted proof that Islam and Christianity could coexist in peace and "harmony" in "a free, capitalist, and pluralist society." Many of these same American social scientists of the era would also wax enthusiastic over Nasserism and Syrian and Iraqi Baathism. Such people, who practically became secular missionaries, had been aptly described by Richard Burton a century earlier, when he spoke of "the delusions in which even honest men can live." Burton said that what missionaries and missionary types could not realize was that "religion is the mental expression of a race, and it cannot advance without a corresponding intellectual improvement on the part of its votaries."*

Back to Terry Prothro: "I remember the argument over taking AID [Agency for International Development] money. This led to tension among the American faculty, which didn't want the university compromised. The AUB faculty wanted education, democracy, liberalism, the Arab point of view, and all those things. It wasn't comfortable with the politics [and therefore the money] of the U.S. government."

But the money came anyway, not just from AID but from the Ford Foundation. This further encouraged AUB's status as the "Oriental queen," able to finance scholarships for students from the entirety of the Arab-Islamic world, from Morocco to Afghanistan. "Then in the 1960s," says Prothro, "on account of the Peace Corps, you had a new flood of idealist liberal types to campus. In AUB terms, it was a glorious period."

The glory days for AUB ended in June 1967, when Israeli soldiers— calling Nasser's bluff—took Sinai, the Golan Heights, and the rest of Palestine, precipitating a massive and temporary evacuation of Americans

*See Rice's biography of Burton in the bibliography.

from Beirut. As Prothro and others tell it, the Six-Day War was the first stage of a three-stage rocket that was to radicalize the AUB faculty and lead to identifiable fissures within the American community in Lebanon. The second stage was the PLO's failed Black September uprising—foiled by King Hussein, with help from Israel, Nixon, and Kissinger—which sent fresh waves of Palestinians into West Beirut, where the AUB was located. The third stage, which in a sense paralleled the first two stages, was the campus's reaction to the Vietnam War.

Prothro says these events put the political process at AUB in fast-forward. Everything became "more exaggerated" than on the campuses in America during this period. "The faculty was anti-Nixon, antiwar. It interpreted the actions of the American government in the Middle East through its mistakes in Southeast Asia. Israel was viewed as the arm of American imperialism in the area, the same way the South Vietnamese government was. Washington didn't try to understand the Arabs enough—so the faculty suggested." Prothro even recalls the creation of a "pro-Arab, pro-Palestinian group made up largely of AUB people," called Americans for Justice in the Middle East. Protests against tuition rises also fed the atmosphere of radicalism.

"In the late 1960s all you heard on campus was *Fatah**—we'll liberate our land ourselves like the Vietnamese," explains another on-scene observer. This person remembers telling a bunch of Palestinian students that their cause would be better served by studying than by striking. "Don't get logical with me," one of the Palestinians shot back, rejecting, in effect, a century of Western thought that the missionaries had tried to instill in the people of the region.

"The faculty, including the Americans, were pro-Palestinian because they were Arab nationalists, and Arab nationalists defined themselves through the Palestinian issue," says yet another observer. "But the AUB administration," Prothro reports, "was pro-Nixon, pro–U.S. government." After all, the administration, unlike the faculty, was more keenly aware of who was paying many of the bills.

The Arabists at the U.S. embassy in downtown Beirut were also pro–U.S. government. "The AUB," recalls the Arabist diplomat, Hume Horan, "stood for the Wilsonian vision of America in all its purity, which was

---

Fatah is the main wing of the PLO.

a position that the embassy—having to deal in the real world—was not able to take."

This three-way split between faculty, administration, and embassy personnel should not be overstated, however. Seen from any vantage point except that of the Arab-Arabist community itself, these were three different aspects of what was essentially the same mind-set. Bill and Janet Stoltzfus, in their estimable candor, clarify the situation perfectly with their comment about how the American community in Lebanon *was almost, to a man, psychologically opposed to the State of Israel. But very few went over the line into anti-Semitism.*

The AUB administrators, especially, were torn by the politics of Vietnam and the Six-Day War. But, in a way, they had it coming to them. By openly encouraging Arab nationalism and seeking a student body not just from Greater Syria but from all over the Arab world, they had over the decades unwittingly made the AUB a battleground for Arab politics, which had turned out to be far less uplifting and far more bloody than the missionary fathers of the school had ever imagined.*

In early 1975 came the bloody culmination of post-1948 inter-Arab politics: the Lebanese civil war. Beirut became a writhing nest of rival militia gangs as a coalition of Palestinians, Sunni Moslems, and Druze—who basically represented the AUB's version of Lebanon—fought the Maronite Christians—who represented the nearby University of St. Joseph's version of Lebanon. AUB, located in Moslem West Beirut, was physically as well as psychologically on the Palestinian side. But surprise of surprises, the ruler of Damascus—that "throbbing heart of Sunni Arabism"—Hafez Assad, was at the time supporting the hated Maronites. *No damn Palestinian was going to drag him into a war with Israel that he wasn't prepared for.* The missionary fathers of AUB must have been rolling in their graves.

A State Department official admits that the American community in Beirut was so friendly with the Palestinians that when the civil war broke out, "most of our sources were Palestinians because those were the people we had mainly been dealing with."

The deterioration of campus life after 1975 was, in Prothro's words,

---

*As a comparison, the American University of Cairo always limited the number of students who could attend from outside Egypt. By keeping the student body primarily Egyptian, AUC was able to avoid internecine Arab politics and thus maintain the atmosphere of a normal campus.

"grave and heartrending." No campus radicals in the United States were ever mugged by reality the way those at the AUB were: the civil war made the faculty and student complaints of the 1960s seem "laughable." In the end, as the war dragged on and Western hostages were taken and after Malcolm Kerr himself was murdered, "there was no politics among the Americans anymore on campus," Prothro says. "Staying alive was the only thing that mattered."

Graeme Bannerman, a former student and faculty member at AUB, describes the university's problem: "The atmosphere at AUB was dynamic and Western. Ideological battles raged over socialism, Communism, liberalism, etc. These arguments were deep and articulate. There was nothing superficial about the intellectual climate. But the problem was that this atmosphere *was not Lebanese*—there were few Maronites and few Shiites. AUB became dominated by three elements: Sunnis, the Greek Orthodox, and the Palestinians."

In political terms, AUB was thus dominated by an Arab nationalist coalition, because the Greek Orthodox—like other Christian groups in the Middle East, with the notable exception of the Maronites—had since World War II been among the most ardent of Arab nationalists. George Antonius, author of *The Arab Awakening,* was a Christian Arab, as were Michel Aflak, a founder of Syrian Baathism, and the two radical Palestinian leaders, George Habash and Nayef Hawatmah. Arab nationalism, on account of its emphasis on Arab nation building, constituted a secular alternative to the Moslem fundamentalism threatening non-Moslems. Arab Christians, therefore, tended to support the Arab nationalist movement with special fervor in order to protect themselves against the politics of Islam and to establish their bona fides in the larger Arab community. An unflinching stand against Zionism was often the most effective way for a Christian to show his Moslem neighbors that he, indeed, was an Arab. Other forces driving the Greek churches toward anti-Zionism were the traditional anti-Semitism of elements of the Greek Orthodox clergy and the commercial competition that prevailed between Greeks and Jews in the Middle East prior to World War II. The animus of Arab Christians toward Israeli Jews was most pointedly emblemized by Hilarion Capucci, a Jerusalem cleric who was imprisoned by the Israelis for using his office to smuggle explosives to Palestinian terrorists.

Arab nationalism, as defined by anti-Zionism, had by the early 1970s become an undeniable AUB cause, notwithstanding the official disclaimers of the school's administration and board of trustees about taking "no political positions." The Lebanese civil war—by exploding Maronite–Sunni Moslem tensions like dynamite in a dry barn—put the political attitudes of the missionary-AUB community into stark relief, especially after the June 6, 1982, Israeli invasion of Lebanon, which had the effect of helping the Maronites.

By furthering the disintegration of Lebanon and threatening its Moslem population, the Israeli invasion had an unintended consequence: it sparked an influx of fundamentalists from the Ayatollah Khomeini's Iran to help the Lebanese Shiite community. Lebanon's Shiites were poor and politically invisible until the civil war. But a rising birthrate and deepening poverty had led to increased power and a radicalism that reached critical mass with the arrival of the Iranians.

The Shiites were not subtle. They didn't distinguish between Israelis and Americans. It didn't matter to them that the American expatriates in Lebanon were pro-Moslem, anti-Israeli, and alienated from their own country's foreign policy. To the Shiites the Americans in Lebanon were all just a bunch of Zionist imperialists. They thus became fair game for kidnapping: an age-old Moslem occupation for extracting political concessions from a rival clan was now extended to foreigners.

It is both symbolic and highly ironic that the very first American taken hostage in Lebanon was David Stuart Dodge—the son of Bayard Dodge and the great-grandson of Daniel Bliss—who was born in 1938 in Beirut and educated there at the American Community School and later at Deerfield Academy and Princeton; who worked for ARAMCO and the Trans-Arabian Pipeline Company for twenty-seven years; who at the time of his abduction was acting president of the AUB; and who was proud that "AUB had fostered an atmosphere from which Arab nationalism could be born and develop."

Dodge draws a parallel between his abduction and the assassination of Malcolm Kerr in 1984. "The people who kidnapped me and who killed Kerr were Iranians using Lebanese gunmen." The Iranians, he reminds this writer, were in Lebanon because the Israelis were there. "I was taken in July

1982, just when the Israelis took control of Beirut. I was released a year later, in July 1983. I was traded for Shiite hostages being held by the pro-Israeli Falangists (Maronite Christians)."

The Syrians conspired with the Iranians to kidnap Dodge. U.S. ambassador to Syria Robert Paganelli and his staff, including April Glaspie and Eilts's protégé, William Rugh, negotiated with the Syrians for Dodge's release. "April and Bob were the first Americans I saw after I was freed."

Bob Paganelli, who had replaced Talcott Seelye as ambassador to Syria after Seelye had quit on account of the Camp David process, was one of the most refreshingly unorthodox and undiplomatic of U.S. diplomats. "Paganelli alienated everyone except his close friends," says Nick Veliotes with a laugh. "I always felt like a wimp compared to Bob," says Hume Horan. Horan remembers Paganelli insulting Zbigniew Brzezinski over the appointment of John West, a former governor of South Carolina, as ambassador to Saudi Arabia (Paganelli likened West to a reckless Kentucky colonel). Paganelli also insulted Secretary of State George Shultz over a 1983 accord between Israel and Lebanon, which Paganelli correctly predicted the Syrians would repudiate. "I hope you know the agreement is going to fall apart in your face," Paganelli reportedly yelled at Shultz. "Shultz was ready to fire him," remembers Veliotes, the NEA assistant secretary at the time. "But I told Shultz that this is exactly the son of a bitch we need to deal with the Baathis in Damascus." Veliotes was right. Paganelli blew his top with the Syrians, as he had with Brzezinski and Shultz. "You assholes," Paganelli reportedly screamed at top Syrian officials. "You let the Iranians trick you into transferring David Dodge at Damascus airport onto a plane for Iran." Paganelli, like Jim Akins, was a militant nonsmoker and wouldn't allow Syrian officials to smoke in his office. A short time later Dodge was released, and Shultz was glad that he hadn't fired Paganelli.

No American hostage, not even Terry Anderson, received the loving attention from NEA that David Dodge received. The reason was simply that Dodge was the living embodiment of American Arabist aristocracy. Dodge spent part of his captivity in Iran and has spread the word among his friends that it is an experience he prefers not to talk about or be asked about. So rather than ask Dodge about the details of his imprisonment, a visitor asked him about what he had learned politically from the experience, whether it had affected his views on the Middle East in any way.

Dodge thought for a moment and said: "Because of being held hostage,

I felt we should be more evenhanded. We condoned Israel's invasion of Lebanon, and my kidnapping was in part due to the actions of Israel and U.S. support of Israel. Yes, I feel more strongly than ever that American policies in the Middle East are not evenhanded enough."

Dodge, of course, was not alone among the hostages in this belief. In fact, his patrician upbringing caused him to be far more circumspect in his thinking than were other American expatriates in Lebanon held captive by radical Moslems.

David Edwin Long, the son of a Presbyterian preacher, was a State Department Arabist born in Washington, Georgia, in 1937 and educated at Davidson College in North Carolina, Dean Rusk's alma mater. Long became fascinated with Araby while serving under Hermann Eilts in Saudi Arabia. Long was part of the same gang in late-sixties Jidda that included Wat Cluverius and Ernest Latham. But it was while working on the State Department's policy-planning staff and counterterrorism unit in the early 1980s that Long developed a healthy skepticism about the missionary community in Lebanon. It had to do with one hostage, Ben Weir, a teacher at the Near East School of Theology in Beirut, who was kidnapped on April 8, 1984.

Though Weir and his wife, Carol, are Presbyterians, the Near East School of Theology is an interdenominational Protestant seminary, training men and women for service in the Protestant community in the Arab world. The Weirs represented the extreme evolutionary offshoot of the American missionary adventure in Lebanon. The AUB, because of its Ivy League ties and political connections and the money it received from such institutions as AID and the Ford Foundation, was still a part of the East Coast Establishment. Nor, because of its prestige, was it completely at the mercy of the local environment, at least not to the extent that a small institution like the Near East School of Theology was. With no links to the U.S. government or to internationally known institutions, the Near East School and its staff—people like the Weirs—were totally dependent upon the good will of the Arab governments that had come to power in the post–World War II era. As you might expect, the Weirs were far more integrated into the local Moslem Arab culture than were even people at AUB.

"The Weirs treated me and the State Department as the enemies, even though we were their government, trying to help get Ben Weir released," David Long complains. "Carol Weir and her church group had this holier-than-thou attitude toward the U.S. government. They didn't even want the CIA to debrief him when he was released, even though the debriefing could have helped other hostages. To them, the CIA and the Israelis—not the kidnappers—were the enemy." Long describes people like the Weirs as "sui generis expatriates," who "knew the Arab world intimately but were incredibly politically naive at the same time."

After Ben was released, Ben and Carol Weir wrote a book for a small press in Philadelphia, *Hostage Bound Hostage Free.* They portray themselves as a couple more at home politically, spiritually, and morally in the Arab world than in America. In fact, the allegation of dual-loyalty made against American-Jewish supporters of Israel by pro-Arab types in America seems especially ironic after reading this book.

Ben Weir had been living in Lebanon for thirty-one years prior to his capture. His youngest daughter was about to accept a teaching position in Egypt, and his oldest daughter was working in Saudi Arabia after having worked in Beirut. Carol Weir admits that she had "so little contact with the embassy" that she didn't even know the name of the U.S. ambassador.* Having little contact with the embassy is quite common for Americans abroad. But given that the ambassador is usually the best-known American in the local community and that ambassadorial changes are accompanied by gossipy speculation, it indicates an extraordinary degree of estrangement not to know the ambassador's name. When an embassy official pointed out that it couldn't protect its own personnel from kidnappings and that it had urged all nonessential Americans to leave Lebanon long ago—this was after Dodge had been kidnapped and after Kerr had been killed—Mrs. Weir replied that the problem was not the kidnappers but "our foreign policy." This is why, as she admits, she "didn't want to talk with anyone in [State's office of] counterterrorism." According to Mrs. Weir, Jesse Jackson and Syrian ruler Hafez Assad had a more rational approach to the Middle East than the U.S. government. Her ideological journey reached a kind of climax in March 1985 during a surreal meeting with Secretary of State Shultz in Washington, in which Shultz criticized the Shiites holding her husband and she and her group seemed to defend the

---

*The ambassador was Reginald Bartholomew, a non-Arabist.

Shiite kidnappers as people sincere in their beliefs, who "had some legitimate grievances against the United States." As Mrs. Weir's description of the meeting makes clear, there was a total disconnect between her Beirut missionary version of reality and the State Department's version.

From the perspective of Mrs. Weir and that of David Dodge and Talcott Seelye—who was also born in Beirut and who had resigned from the Foreign Service in demonstrated disquiet at his own country's policies in 1981—America's toleration of Israeli actions was at the root of the whole tragedy in Lebanon. For them, owing to their friendships, their family histories, and their years in Araby replete with memories of a peaceful and sleepy Lebanon that was no more, it was a very personal tragedy. In their minds they were the ones who were concerned purely with American interests and American values, while it was their Jewish adversaries in America who suffered from a more complicated and sullied form of patriotism. The fact that their patriotism was also complicated—though in a different way—was something these people apparently never considered.

Seelye's blast from the U.S. embassy in Damascus and Mrs. Weir's encounter with Secretary Shultz might be considered the last gasps of the Arabist old guard before they drowned under the weight of an America and a State Department that was rapidly changing. Foreign policy in every country, not just in America, is a reflection of how the society at home looks out at the world. As that society changes, so will its foreign policy. The historic relationship between a group of privileged Americans and the educated stratum of Arabs in Greater Syria was just not something that an increasingly ethnic and middle-class society in the United States was even aware of or to which it could easily relate. Regarding Israel, while those like Dodge, Seelye, and Mrs. Weir were in a unique position to witness the very worst aspects of the Israeli national character, Americans at home could identify with positive aspects of Israeli life more easily than they could with anything going on in the Arab world, especially in blood-spattered Lebanon. For all its faults and crude tactics, even AIPAC was psychologically closer to mainstream America than the AUB crowd was.

But AUB continued to exert influence, if not on mainstream America, then on the Foreign Service. The change in attitudes at NEA that began in the Sisco-Atherton era was a gradual evolution. For two decades afterward,

NEA continued to harbor old-guard elements. The AUB presence was felt through the field school in Beirut, where FSOs went to learn Arabic until 1975, when, on account of the Lebanese Civil War, the school was relocated to Tunis. Almost all the Arabists mentioned in this book learned their Arabic at the Beirut field school. Explains one former State Department official: "There was a Moslem West Beirut intellectual attitude on the world which was anti-Israeli and which generations of Arabists were processed into. This was intensified by the fact that the field school for learning Arabic was usually located near the PLO headquarters. Both the field school and the PLO moved to Tunis from Beirut. This was ironic and accidental, but it happened."

Bernard Johns, who studied at the Beirut field school in the early 1970s with April Glaspie and other Arabist FSOs, puts it this way: "Look, you sit for twenty-one months in a classroom learning Arabic. Your teacher is a Lebanese or a Palestinian. At night or on weekends you socialize with Americans from the AUB. You are psychologically processed as an Arabist—you are, to an extent, brainwashed. It's subtle, it's unconscious. People deny it. But it happened to all of us. . . . You even learned, if you hadn't inherited it along the way, a certain bias against American Jews which translated into a moral pro-Arab stand. Because prejudice, as prejudice, could not be openly expressed, since it is no longer socially acceptable in [white-collar] American society."

Johns should know about these things. He was the State Department's first African-American Arabist.

Bernard Johns was born in 1939 in the Crown Heights section of Brooklyn, at a time when blacks and Jews got along much better there than they do now. (In the early 1990s Crown Heights was the scene of intercommunal violence between blacks and ultra-Orthodox Jews.) He graduated from Howard University in Washington, D.C., the nation's elite black college. He served in the Marine Corps and was an exchange student on a kibbutz in Israel. "When you're raised in Brooklyn and go to public schools you learn about the Middle East early. It's a local issue for New Yorkers. I remember a joke when I was a kid: 'What's a Nasser sandwich?—A chicken squeezed between two slices of Jewish rye.' "

Johns joined the Foreign Service and NEA in 1971, when the Sisco-

Atherton reign was moving into high gear. After finishing Arabic training in Beirut, he went on to serve in Libya, Morocco, and Saudi Arabia. But his most memorable posting was at the U.S. consulate in East Jerusalem from 1973 until 1976.

The Jerusalem consulate is the most controversial U.S. diplomatic mission in the Middle East, if not in the world. It represents the Arabist front line against the pro-Israel section of the State Department, as represented by the U.S. embassy in Tel Aviv, forty-five minutes away with no crossing points in between.

The consulate building in Arab East Jerusalem was a rebuke to the State of Israel. It was, to all intents and purposes, an American embassy located on territory controlled by the Israeli government. But the consulate did not recognize the Israeli government in Jerusalem, nor did it primarily deal with Israelis: its main purpose was to deal with the Arabs in Jerusalem and the West Bank under Israeli military rule. Because the United States did not recognize Jerusalem as Israel's capital, the consulate tried to insist that when the U.S. ambassador to Israel visited Jerusalem from Tel Aviv he should not fly the American flag on the hood of his limousine. Jerusalem was the consulate's turf, not the embassy's. The consulate in East Jerusalem, a graceful old stone building near the medieval Arab souk, was Araby, while the embassy, situated on a noisy and garish street in the heart of Jewish Tel Aviv, clearly was not. A war raged between the two installations.

Johns made friends on both sides of the diplomatic and ethnic divide, because he genuinely liked dealing with both Arabs and Jews. This was unusual, since most U.S. diplomats stationed in Jerusalem or Tel Aviv tended to prefer one group to the other. All diplomats would claim to have Arab and Jewish friends, but it was always clear by their behavior and their schedules with whom they felt most comfortable. When it came to the Israelis, you have to feel a bit sorry for the Arabists at the consulate. "The Israelis were, personality-wise, without hypocrisy," explains Johns. "If they didn't like you, they showed it. They gave new dimensions to rudeness." And the Israelis, for obvious reasons, didn't like the consulate Arabists. Johns didn't care. For one thing, he was a bachelor, and as he delicately puts it, the options in the more Westernized Jewish side of town were numerically greater. For another, "I had an advantage that other Arabists didn't: I had *lived* the other side." By which he means that, because he was African-American, he knew what it was like to have lots of chips on your shoulder, as the Israelis had. So he could forgive their boorish behavior.

Johns is critical, not just of his Arabist colleagues in Jerusalem, but of the non-Arabist diplomats at the embassy in Tel Aviv.

Although the embassy staff, because it had volunteered to serve in Israel and got to see things from the Israeli side, was more pro-Israel than the rest of the State Department, it did not necessarily feel close to the Israelis. As Johns explains, "I remember once there was talk of a 'morale problem' at the Embassy. The staff felt lonely because they were Gentiles in the midst of a city where everyone else was Jewish. They felt isolated. Sunday in Tel Aviv was not the sabbath but the first day of the workweek. Some people even complained about being restricted with regard to whom they could date. In a subtle way Tel Aviv was a culturally hostile environment for them. *Hell,*" raising his voice, "I had been a minority all my life—you learn to work with what you've got. But for the diplomats, it was a new experience for them." In Third World capitals hostility didn't matter much because the population was so obviously different. But Tel Aviv, Johns explains, spooked some diplomats, because it was a city of "white people who somehow weren't Christian."

Johns's ability to resist the "brainwashing" that occurred in the politically charged environment of Moslem Beirut was clearly a consequence of his unique background and experience prior to joining the Foreign Service. But sometimes there are no easy explanations as to why some people turn out differently than expected. Matters of class and political-cultural conditioning have a tendency to pale when set against that mysterious and unquantifiable factor called *character,* especially when that *character* is interwoven with an intellectual depth that has a way of overcoming the environment into which it is cast. Some people are just stars, not supporting actors.

Now it's time to meet another graduate of the Beirut Field School.

Chapter 10

Horan of Arabia

It was at an Oxford soiree where Robert Graves, the British poet and classicist, first met T. E. Lawrence. The year was 1920, and Lawrence had won a fellowship to All Souls' College to complete *Seven Pillars of Wisdom*. Graves vividly describes the scene in his own memoir, *Good-bye to All That*:

"Lawrence's eyes immediately held me. . . . [They] flickered up and down as though making an inventory of clothes and limbs. . . . Lawrence, talking to the Regius Professor of Divinity about the influence of the Syrian Greek philosophers on early Christianity, and especially of the importance of the University of Gadara close to the Lake of Galilee, mentioned that St. James had quoted one of the Gadarene philosophers (I think, Mnasalcas) in his *Epistle*." Lawrence then "went on to speak of Meleager, and the other Syrian-Greek contributors to the Greek Anthology, whose poems he intended to publish in English translation. I joined in the conversation and mentioned a morning-star image which Meleager once used in rather an un-Greek way. Lawrence turned to me. 'You must be Graves the poet? I read a book of yours in Egypt in 1917, and thought it pretty good.' "

Graves and Lawrence became fast friends. Initially Graves did not speak to Lawrence about Arabia. After all, they had so much else to talk about. Besides Greek poetry Lawrence was deeply interested in the "moderns": Siegfried Sassoon, John Masefield, and Thomas Hardy. And there were

Graves's own poetic works, which Lawrence helped to edit. Graves's book on Lawrence, *Lawrence and the Arabs,* was more hagiography than biography. But clearly Graves was on to something about Lawrence.

As a close reading of *Seven Pillars of Wisdom* would reveal—Lawrence's use of Greek algebraic concepts to devise a guerrilla strategy, for instance— what is essential about this icon of British imperialism is not his military daring, his physical endurance, his conflicted sexual life, his going native with the Arabs, or any of that. As with Richard Burton, it is the breadth and texture of Lawrence's intellect that sets him apart from his contemporaries. Lawrence's knowledge of Arabic and Arabia is merely one facet of an intensely curious mind. That is why Graves, who would go on to write *I, Claudius; The White Goddess;* the greatest rendition ever of *The Greek Myths;* and more than thirty other books on the most erudite of subjects, was able to appreciate Lawrence better than could Lawrence's own colleagues in the British Arab bureau.

Lawrence, of course, had his flaws. Like other British Arabists of his day, he was an inspired amateur rather than a professional. The nature of the British class system and of the boys' schools in particular, led to various behavioral eccentricities—like romanticism and homosexuality—to which Lawrence was prone.

But imagine, if you can, a more normal, middle-class Lawrence, an American of the Cold War era rather than a Briton of Empire days; someone with both an intellectual and an operational brilliance, who suffered from no identity crises, whether national or sexual; someone with a suburban house and a family, too self-reflecting to take sides; a thoroughly modern, post-industrial Lawrence, in other words.

Up until now Hume Horan has lurked at the periphery of this story. Like the other Arabists he was at the Beirut field school. If you ask anyone at NEA who was the bureau's greatest Arabist in terms of actually speaking the language, you get an instant, three-syllable reply: Hume Horan. Horan is the only Arabist ever to complete the field school's twenty-one-month course in twelve months. He emerged with the highest rating ever awarded by the Foreign Service's scientific linguists, who considered him more than fluent and almost bilingual. In Beirut Horan spent the evenings translating a popular Arab novel into English, Mahmoud Teymour's *The Call of the*

Unknown. Later, in Libya, he would audit courses in *shari'a* law at an Islamic university. And in Washington he would study biblical Hebrew in order "to read Amos, my favorite prophet, in the original" and to "understand Israelis as Israelis, to know them through their own language, a language of boulders tumbling down mountains—*wow,* no wonder they can be so tough. Hebrew is a parallel line traveling with Arabic. . . ." Horan races on, his eyes swimming in enthusiasm and sensitivity. If only he had one more life.

Yet Horan is also fluent in Spanish, French, and German. He can sing the Argentinean national anthem, quote whole sections of Goethe (in German) and Edgar Allan Poe, hold forth on West African novels, Mayan exploration, and children's literature. He talks in stirring detail about such subjects as the history of Haiti and the early settlement of Quebec. Deeply steeped in Americana, Horan gives a blow-by-blow description of John Wesley Powell's journey down the Colorado River in 1869 and can rattle off the lesser known stanzas of "The Star-Spangled Banner." His is the kind of intellect that has largely gone extinct in the electronic media age, when even the brightest of minds spend less time reading than in former eras.

In Jordan, during Black September 1970, when Nixon, Kissinger, and Sisco were masterminding developments on a strategic level from Washington, Horan was the DCM in Amman, where during the fighting he rescued one of the U.S. embassy's secretaries from a bombed-out building; making his way back to the diplomatic compound through a series of checkpoints manned by Palestinian fedayeen, he convinced them in Arabic that he represented the Red Cross. The new ambassador, L. Dean Brown, had arrived just as the combat got under way. The only way for Brown to present his credentials was for King Hussein to send an armored convoy at 6 A.M. to fetch him and Horan. The convoy shot its way from the embassy to the palace. Horan was too hungry to worry. *Would the king give us breakfast,* he thought. (The king did.) Holed up for two weeks in the bullet-ridden embassy, Horan was limited to a quart of drinking water a day, of which he denied himself enough to shave and wash the collar and cuffs of his shirt. Horan is nothing if not meticulous.

When the 1973 Yom Kippur War broke out and Saudi Arabia unleashed the oil weapon, Horan was the DCM in Jidda, running the embassy on his own, waiting for the arrival of the new ambassador, James Akins. Horan, keeping his own counsel, saw the whole nasty drama between Akins and

Kissinger unfold. Whenever Kissinger would come to Saudi Arabia, Horan was a coordinator on the ground, dealing with the Saudis about all the multitudinous details. Horan spent five years as DCM in Saudi Arabia in the 1970s, managing the embassy for three successive U.S. ambassadors. His unmatched hands-on knowledge of Saudi Arabia and the Saudis would be a factor in his downfall a decade later.

Hume Horan is so cerebral that, exactly like T. E. Lawrence, the size of his head seems out of proportion to the rest of his body. His eyes flicker about and drink light, focusing on some blank sheet of inner peace, the kind a physicist might look at. It is as though Horan is disembodied: a distilled brain in a jar. He doesn't say, "Come over to the house to talk." He says, "Come over and we'll excogitate."

Hume Horan excogitating: "Here is the dilemma: *God spoke Arabic.* Oh, he may have delivered an earlier, flawed message in Hebrew, in the Old Testament, or in Greek, in the New. But he damn sure got it right the third time. The Koran is not history or biography, like the Bible. It is pure revelation. Arabic is coterminous with God. So, unlike English, which is a compost, a welcoming cathedral, the most catholic of languages, Arabic is a completely closed system, resistant to loanwords, a terrifyingly logical, well-oiled piece of machinery that just clicks, clicks away. Once you've got the infixes and the prefixes in your head, and the three-consonant root verbs, you can construct any word you want. It's like gene-splicing. And the religious etymology is so intense, unlike English, where unless you've studied Greek or Latin, you can't really *feel* the original meaning of the word. Another problem is that Arabic is so beautiful to listen to. So you find yourself putting up with all kinds of crap from these people because of the crystalline way their language lays itself out in space. Just look at the Koran. The English translations are incompetent, I know. The first chapters should really be footnotes at the end: nothing but laundry lists, supplemental legislation—Leviticus. 'The Chapter of the Cow'—bah, how dull! But later on, *bang,* the revelations come at you with a muzzle velocity of three thousand feet per second that just knocks you flat on your can."

Horan races toward his theme, not pausing for breath. Arabic, he intimates, may be no more insulated a language than Chinese or any other non-European tongue. Chinese, one could argue, is even more inimical to

Western thought constructs than Arabic. While Arabic tenses do not have a finely chopped up sense of past, present, and future, Arabic time is at least linear, while time in Chinese is not. But the Arabs are desert monotheists unsoftened by millennia in a Western diaspora, averse to graven images, harboring, in Lawrence's words, a "clearness or hardness of belief, almost mathematical in its limitations. . . ." They thus gravitate toward the abstract. Painting, sculpture, and other plastic arts are not Arab fortes. "The medium in which the aesthetic feeling of the Arabs is mainly expressed," writes Horan's late mentor, the Oxford Orientalist, Sir Hamilton A. R. Gibb, "is that of words and language—the most seductive . . . certainly the most unstable and even dangerous of all the arts." For Arabs, writes Gibb, "speech is the supreme art," and art often deceives.

Horan jumps a few compass points to pick up another strand that will intersect with the one about speech. Islam was revealed in sixth-century Arabia, a world of political anarchy and social degeneracy. "Mohammed— unlike Jesus, whose mission could assume an ongoing classical order—had to propagate not just a religious message but a social and political one. So Mohammed in effect created a supertribe based not on consanguinity, but on a common belief. This social invention proved more practical than Mohammed's political one: his political system broke down with the assassination of the fourth caliph. From then on, Arab regimes lacked legitimacy. They had only expediency to fall back on." Alienated from politics, and linguistically gravitating toward the ideal and the abstract, the intellectual energies of the supertribesmen began focusing exclusively on religion, *shari'a* law, "a universe of splitting hairs and infinite refinements," Horan says. Politics was ignored, so that there are "no legitimizing precedents for political life as it is lived in contemporary nation-states." Socially Mohammed's message "was progressive in the Middle Ages but not now." The existence of a supertribe, stirred by the most idealizing and artistic of languages and employing a medieval social code, yet operating in a complete political vacuum—a real Darwinian universe of survival of the fittest—"makes the Middle East a dangerous place not only for Christians and Jews but for all nondominating minorities, even Moslem ones like Kurds and Palestinians."

Horan, born in 1934, is gangly and boyish, a jumping jack of energy. He jogs, plays tennis, and is a dedicated bike rider. Soon after the Black September war in Amman, he went on a water-skiing vacation in the Gulf of Aqaba, a guest of Jordan's crown prince Hassan. Finishing a jump badly, he hit a sandbank and broke two ribs and several vertebrae. He spent a month on his back in an Amman hospital. Now Horan is again on his back, after not one, but two bicycle accidents. (Lawrence killed himself on a motorbike.)

Horan, of course, would be embarrassed by these comparisons with Lawrence. Asked by an unknowing magazine photo editor if he had any pictures of himself in Arab regalia, Horan replied, "If I did, you can be sure I would have burned them by now." He distrusts "the cultural remittance men and international groupies who fill out their personalities in exotic backgrounds, pretending to be what they are not." Rather than as a Lawrence, Horan would like to be seen "as a Bruno Bettelheim, peering through a magnifying glass, making notes on autistic children." Gesturing with his right hand and left crutch, he provides his observations on Libya, where he and his wife, Nancy, lived for several years:

"We're dealing with the traumatization of the disadvantaged, the ultimate vacuity, settled at the last moment by the loser tribes kicked out of Egypt and Tunisia, who were then colonized by the Italians—rulers as nasty as they come. In World War II, battles waged back and forth across the desert, and the rape is complete. Afterward it is the poorest country in the world, its biggest export, scrap metal from the war. Then, *bang*, instant wealth and a coup that brings a true believer to the fore. The wealth goes to their heads, and of course, they hate everybody. Libyans are passive, suspicious, dour, and troubled. . . . But you go out of your way to get to know them. Why, for instance, does this particular undersecretary in the Libyan foreign ministry debauch someone's eleven-year-old daughter? So you invite the man over for dinner, to try to understand what makes him tick. . . ."

Horan is the Foreign Service's equivalent of a Talmudist. "He's the real thing, a scholar-Arabist in the classic Bernard Lewis* mold," says a former White House official who has rarely had a good word for FSOs. "When we do our job perfectly," says John Collier, of the Foreign Service Institute's School of Area Studies, "the result is a Hume Horan."

Horan's story begins in the 1920s, when well-born Mary Robinson Hume of Washington, D.C., met a handsome Persian diplomat, Abdollah En-

---

* Bernard Lewis is a renowned British-born orientalist and the Cleveland Dodge Professor of Near Eastern Studies Emeritus at Princeton.

tenzan. Mary Hume was a free and outgoing spirit, a dancer and an athlete whose father was the mayor of Georgetown and whose grandfather was a U.S. diplomat in the administration of Abraham Lincoln. (Horan has a picture of his maternal great-grandfather with Lincoln's secretary of state, William H. Seward.) She was also the cousin of the poet Stephen Vincent Benét. Entenzan took his beautiful bride to Persia for a long visit. Mary Hume fell in love with the country and its people at a time when there were only two other American women in Teheran. The marriage lasted over a decade, which, considering the cultural differences as well as the self-styled independence and impulsiveness of the bride, was quite an achievement.

Their son was born in Washington not long before they divorced. Abdollah Entenzan went back by himself to Persia where he rose to become a foreign minister under the late Shah and afterwards the head of the national Iranian Oil Company. When Entenzan died in 1985, the former British ambassador to Iran, Sir Dennis Wright, wrote in the *London Times* that Entenzan had a reputation for "quirkiness, brilliance, and absolute integrity."

Mary Hume remarried. Her new husband was a journalist and businessman, Harold Horan. Harold Horan, who spoke French, Italian, and Spanish, took her and her son by Entenzan to Argentina, where Hume grew up in a multilingual environment during World War II.

Again there is an interesting parallel with Lawrence, though one must be very careful about it. Lawrence was born illegitimate. To be so born in Victorian England was considered a scandal and was obviously something that Lawrence preferred to keep hidden, something of incalculable importance in his emotional development. Abdollah Entenzan and Mary Hume were still married when their son was born, so there is no scandal that way. But due to the Waspy nature of the older Arabist community in the United States, being half Iranian was quite unusual and undeniably controversial. The Persians have been age-old adversaries of the Arabs. If Horan were dark-skinned or in any way looked as Iranians are popularly supposed to look, his descent would all matter less because the whole issue would have been out in the open. But Hume Horan, with his fair complexion, his straight, iron-gray hair clipped in Marine style, his gray wash-and-wear suits, and his clear and welcoming eyes full of studied benevolence that loudly proclaim Protestant America, looks and talks like the Hollywood caricature of an American diplomat.

It's not that Horan ever tried to hide his background. He talks easily about it when asked. He visited his father twice in Iran prior to the Islamic revolution, when Entenzan was living in a two-room flat on a modest government pension. (Entenzan died quietly, left alone by the Khomeini regime.) But neither did Horan advertise it. Many though not all of his colleagues in NEA knew about it, and those that knew, rarely knew the details. This gave rise to a certain amount of mystery and misinformation. One colleague, leaning over a Washington restaurant table, whispered to this writer, "Don't you know, Horan is the short form of Horani. That's his real Iranian name."

Hume Horan is someone who knows on a unique and extremely subtle level what it means to be different. (He was, after all, the DCM for five long years in Saudi Arabia, a country where Iranians are especially disliked.) Horan's ability to empathize with and to intuit the other side's reality without having actually experienced it might understandably be tied to the facts of his birth.

As a teenager Horan returned to the United States from Argentina to attend Portsmouth Priory in Rhode Island, a boarding school run by Benedictine monks, where the atmosphere was, in his words, "chilling and life-denying. There were no girls." Horan was thrown out. His parents then sent him to St. Andrews, an Episcopalian school in Delaware, "where there were girls and the teachers were married." He liked it. From St. Andrews Horan went to Harvard, where he majored in American history, which he calls "a great background for the Middle East." Horan has a sermon about how "important it is to know who you are, where you come from. To know that you are an American, so that you can be protected from the danger of identifying too closely with the disease agent of the local environment"— going native, that is. It may be worth noting that Horan is "not a particular fan of the AUB school of Arabists."

After service in the army, Horan returned to Harvard, where at the Center for Middle East Studies, he took all the Arabic language and literature courses available. "I can't say what drove me, I just had a feeling I would enjoy the Middle East." Horan's personal tutor was the great British orientalist Sir Hamilton A. R. Gibb, the Laudian Professor of Arabic at Oxford, who was periodically at Harvard. "It was a modern Arabic reading course. I would sit there and ploddingly translate a book, and Sir Hamilton would correct my grammatical mistakes. It was slow work. The book we were reading was by Munifal Razzaz, a Baathist. I remember being so disappointed. Finally I was beginning to be able to penetrate this difficult language, and all I found was, well, half-baked philosophy and pseudointellectualism. Sir Hamilton told me, 'It's an Arab book, Horan, this is as good as it gets.' "

If there is anyone Horan idolizes and tries consciously to model himself after, it is Gibb. "I always felt throughout life that I had to work especially hard so as not to let Sir Hamilton down. I'll never forget his briefcase. When he opened it, it was always filled with literature, real literature, in different languages. What he knew about the Middle East was in context with what he knew about the rest of world culture." Gibb's writings are replete with exquisitely subtle criticisms of Arab Islamic civilization. Yet he is nevertheless loathed by a number of Zionist and Jewish scholars, such as the late Elie Kedourie, because of his fundamental toleration of the benign character of Arab nationalism. Kedourie, in a June 1991 issue of *Commentary,* makes a scathing reference to "the old-established and far-flung firm of Sir Hamilton Gibb and Sons, principal purveyors of this kind of mental baggage." Yet at the other extreme is the Palestinian Arab scholar Edward Said, who writes in his book *Orientalism,* that "Gibb's inaugural biases remain a formidable obstacle for anyone hoping to understand modern Islam." Horan, who knew Gibb personally, sees himself in the lonely middle between the pro-Zionist and pro-Palestinian intellectual subcultures that Kedourie and Said represent. It is a loneliness that Horan shares with other Arabists.

Despite a multilingual childhood, boarding school, a B.A. and an M.A. from Harvard, and private tutoring from Gibb, it would be a mistake to dismiss Hume Horan as the product of an interesting background and a good education. His fluency in French and German is self-taught. Hopping around his library, he pulls a German novel off the shelf with his crutch, turning the pages with it, proudly showing his visitor his old vocabulary lists. In Horan's case, being an Arabist is merely one facet of being a humanist. He thus constitutes an instant rebuke to any pro-Israel lobbyist who wants to take the easy way out by pointing to Andy Killgore as an example of State Department Arabism. Horan insists that as an ambassador "you're not just supposed to represent the State Department, but also the U.S. Congress, the White House, Washington, and the whole idea of America."

Horan's view of America can be pretty down to earth, evidenced by an article he wrote on an inspiration for the March 1992 issue of the *Foreign Service Journal,* describing a Washington Redskins' victory celebration. Instead of an international snob, he reveals himself as a true populist:

> For an hour and a half on January 29, the country's greatest display of Americana was not in the Mall's museums, but on the Mall itself. One hundred thousand Redskin fans, half white, half black, rocked at the "Mall Ball," cheering their XXVI Super Bowl Champions. . . . But you should have seen the outfits: A young woman with a field jacket she must have stolen from General Noriega . . . dramatic emblem-whorls and red/gold enamel . . . Norman Rockwell should have been with us. It was one of the few contemporary Washington scenes he'd have understood. For a morning there was no Jew nor Gentile. Only 100,000 cheering fans, stomping in the "Hog Mud" while the only raised finger to be seen was the index.

Horan joined the Foreign Service following his graduate studies at Harvard. After Beirut he served in Baghdad from 1962 to 1963. From 1964 until 1966, he was in Baida, a town in eastern Libya. He returned to Washington for a few years before going to Amman, and then to Jidda, as DCM. His stellar performances in Jordan during Black September and in Saudi Arabia during the Yom Kippur War got him promoted to the rank of ambassador in his early forties. His first ambassadorial assignments were to Equatorial Guinea and Cameroon. Then, in the summer of 1983, he was given his first ambassadorial post in the Arab world: Khartoum, Sudan.

Before observing Hume Horan on post in Khartoum, we should take note of a book that helped fire his enthusiasm for his job as an Arabist. Tellingly, it is not a book by an Englishman, but by an American, John Lloyd Stephens.

John Lloyd Stephens was born in 1805 in New Jersey. He grew up in New York City—still close to its "overgrown Dutch village" roots—where he graduated from Columbia. Later he traveled in the Ohio and Mississippi valleys and abroad in Russia, Poland, and Asia Minor. In 1835, needing a "mild tour" to recover from a throat infection, he set out to explore the Middle East at a time when the only other Americans in the region were a handful of missionaries. The result was *Incidents of Travel in Egypt, Arabia Petraea, and the Holy Land,* a work that Edgar Allan Poe honored with a twelve-page tribute written for the *New York Review.*

Dressed in native garb and armed with guns, pistols, a few dozen bottles of claret, a personal library, a servant, and a "star-spangled banner" that Stephens had an Arab tailor stitch for him and that he flew over his boat, the author set sail down the Nile. After Egypt he explored the desert in what is today Israel and Jordan, the Dead Sea region, and Jerusalem. "Stephens was [a] true Jacksonian," Horan exults. "Early America's spirit breathes throughout his narrative." Horan cites the author's populist enthusiasms for both Arab and Jew in the Holy Land, his hatred of Turkish despotism and recognition of the suffering of African slaves, his contemplation of the practical "improvements" made in plague-ridden Alexandria, and his complete lack of paternalism and condescension. Horan is particularly taken with Stephens's determination to confront a desert sheikh who tried to cheat him:

> I assured him [the sheikh] that . . . I did not believe there was a worse Arab in all his tribe than himself; and finally, throwing open my trunk, I told him that I did not fear him or all his tribe . . . turning my pistols in my belt, that they should not get it while I could defend it.
>
> Keep cool is a good maxim, generally, in a man's walk through life, and it is particularly useful with the Bedouins in the desert; but there are times when it is good to be in a passion, and this was one of them.

Horan, like Stephens, has found that when dealing with Middle Easterners there are times when "it is good to be in a passion." Khartoum in the mid-1980s was one of those occasions. But what Horan accomplished in Khartoum would not have been possible without the help of another Arabist, an individual who was in many respects the polar opposite of Horan.

Chapter 11

Indiana Jones

O n account of geography the Arabic-speaking states of North Africa have always been peripheral to the Arab-Israeli conflict and therefore peripheral to the drama of American Arabism. Egypt, of course, has always been an exception, and Sudan, being a southward extension of Egypt, has to a degree been another exception. Because of its size and its position adjoining both Egypt and Libya—and across the Red Sea from Saudi Arabia—Sudan did not lack for Arabist drama, as this story makes clear.

The Midwest starts in Newark, Ohio, where the hardscrabble hills of Appalachia flatten out finally into the lonely interior of America. High school football is king in these parts, the central organizing factor of community life. Here Woody Hayes found the beefy linemen that would give his Ohio State Buckeyes one Big Ten championship after another. In 1957 Newark High School had two star offensive tackles. One was Jim Tyrer, who went on to become an all-American at Ohio State and played a dozen years as an all-pro lineman for the Kansas City Chiefs. Then late one night in 1983, Tyrer, who had recently retired from the National Football League and was having trouble in his new business ventures, ripped out a gun from his closet and killed his wife and himself in bed.

The other tackle at Newark High that year was Jerry Weaver. Jerry Weaver would go on to do even more exceptional things than Jim Tyrer, though very few people would know about it.

Jerry Weaver, born in 1939, was, back then, crazier than Jim Tyrer. Weaver, who, as long as he can remember, has had a fascination with guns, lied about his age and joined the National Guard at sixteen. While in the Guard, he had to quickly marry his girlfriend. After high school he spent a year in the U.S. Army rather than play for Hayes's Buckeyes. Then Weaver managed to get a football scholarship to Ohio University. By the time he was twenty-one, Weaver and his wife had three kids. "Jerry, you know that there is such a thing as birth control," his family doctor advised him. "Well," Weaver acknowledges, "that's sort of when I began to discover a very scary thing: how much I didn't know—I mean, how little common sense I had." Over the coming years Weaver's knowledge about his lack of knowledge would keep growing.

About the same time that his marriage was breaking up, Weaver was also learning that he wasn't stupid: he got a B.A., then an M.A., in political science. For someone from his background, even majoring in a subject like poly sci in 1960 was like putting on airs. City boys studied poly sci. Weaver's type took business administration, accounting, and phys ed courses mainly. Newark, Ohio, didn't need political scientists. By the time Weaver left Ohio University to pursue a Ph.D. at the University of Pittsburgh, he was a man completely on his own. While everyone from Newark understood and approved of what Jim Tyrer was doing in the NFL, nobody had a notion of what Jerry Weaver was up to.

After getting his Ph.D., Weaver got a job teaching at UCLA. During one seminar Weaver told an off-color joke, a legacy, perhaps, of his plebian roots. "I apologize to the ladies present," Weaver said, when he had finished.

"And to the men too, I should hope," came a huffy, disapproving voice in the audience. It was the noted Middle East scholar Malcolm Kerr, who took an instant dislike to Weaver, which Weaver in turn reciprocated. Weaver, of course, secretly envied Kerr. "The most awful thing in the world," says Weaver, "is not only when you realize just how much it is that you don't know, but when you become aware how far behind you are in sophistication and background compared to those around you." Weaver says that it wasn't until he was in his thirties that he even knew what the

Foreign Service was, and that while a Ph.D. in poly sci from Pitt was a big deal for someone from Newark, Ohio, it was less impressive in the larger world that included Ivy League scholars.

Throughout the early and mid-seventies Weaver published monograph after monograph on social policy subjects, stuff like health care in the developing world. He married and divorced again, though this time without children. And he got to know and to sympathize with Palestinian students at UCLA. He was on his way, in other words, to becoming another liberal, social science also-ran. In 1977, though, he grabbed an offer to take a one-year leave to be a policy analyst at the State Department–affiliated Agency For International Development (AID) in Washington as part of AID's lateral-entry program for people already in mid career. Weaver never did go back to academia. Like a lot of late bloomers making up for wasted time in their youth, he knew much better than the well-born how to squeeze one precious opportunity for all it was worth.

In 1978 the U.S. embassy in godforsaken Khartoum needed a "refugee coordinator" to monitor the human havoc wreaked by a civil war in neighboring Ethiopia. Weaver volunteered. Just before his fortieth birthday Jerry Weaver had achieved his dream: he had become a member of the U.S. Foreign Service.

Weaver did what Hume Horan sternly cautions against. In dusty, dirty, sun-drenched Arab Khartoum, an oversized sandpaper village of dark, chocolate-colored people at the confluence of the Blue and White Niles, cratered and disease-ridden and "exotic," Jerry Weaver filled out the missing parts of his personality. "I'm really a misfit who found my niche in a wide open desert space among the Arabs," he admits.

The niche he found was certainly not among his fellow FSOs at the U.S. embassy. For one thing, Weaver wasn't Ivy League or even an Ivy League type. For another—much more significant—he wasn't married, and the handful of single women in the American diplomatic community didn't inspire him. So he wasn't comfortable at embassy social functions. Weaver, unlike other diplomats, didn't drink. "I had more sophisticated ways of getting high," he said. Also, while the other FSOs were familiar with living in places like Khartoum from previous postings, Weaver was genuinely star-struck by Sudan. Owing to his rural boyhood he was an accomplished hunter and outdoorsman, the perfect attributes for enjoying this wild and sprawling Arab African country.

But there was one more thing: Jerry Weaver, despite all his years on college campuses, was never quite comfortable with other academic-policy types. Put him in, though, with a group of truck drivers, peasants, sleazy wheeler-dealers, or just about anyone other than upper-middle class Westerners, and Weaver—a big, tough ex-football player—showed unmatched social gifts. Weaver never formally studied Arabic, but he picked it up, nevertheless. However imperfect it was, he could, to a significant degree, communicate with Arabs as well as a Malcolm Kerr could—and not just with the Arabs: Weaver's social web soon began to include Greek ivory traders, Pakistani oil merchants, and all forms of smugglers. Weaver would just begin to talk about how to fix rifle barrels or how to reload magnum shot in a spent cartridge shell or what kind of fertilizer to use, and the Arabs would just sit there and listen: here was one *khawaja* (white foreigner) with whom they could really communicate.

Weaver became a big-game hunter. His Arab and Greek friends took him into the jungles of southern Sudan, where he shot lion and leopard; not from a safe distance either, but from up close. With his huge physique, trimmed beard, and devouring expression Jerry Weaver even began to look like Ernest Hemingway. He had a German girlfriend for awhile but also had a stableful of Eritrean and Tigrean beauties half his age. He was clearly living a myth, but neither was he a wannabee. As he stayed in Sudan year after year, improving his Arabic and making undercover forays over the Sudanese-Ethiopian border into the rebel territories of Eritrea and Tigre to monitor the refugee traffic, Weaver became the embassy's most knowledgeable hands-on expert on the Horn of Africa.

But he went too far. In his office he displayed a framed picture of himself standing over a lion he had just shot. Instead of a suit and tie, he wore a safari suit to work: sometimes even a bush hat. And like his Arab friends he fasted during the Moslem holy month of Ramadan. Jerry Weaver had gone native. Sudan had truly become his home, and the embassy was just the place where he happened to work. The striped-pants FSOs at the embassy were appalled.

In Foreign Service jargon, Sudan is a "hardship" post. Most tours there last three years. Four years in Khartoum stretches the limit of endurance. By 1983 Weaver had been in Khartoum for five years and had no desire to leave. In July of that year, however, he had a bout of nerves. The ambassador, Bill Kontos, was departing. It was partly Weaver's good relationship with Kontos and his wife that had kept him from being booted out. What would the new ambassador be like? Weaver worried. The first impressions spelled trouble.

Hume Horan was Foreign Service to a T: boarding school, Harvard, Arabist, looked like an airline pilot, had an elegant wife and kids. When Horan called him into his office, Weaver figured it was the end. Then it got worse: Horan started speaking to Weaver nonchalantly in Spanish. Weaver was disoriented. "Oh I'm sorry," said the new ambassador. "It says here on your résumé that you know Spanish." Red with embarrassment, Weaver explained that it had been years since he had spoken Spanish in California. Horan smiled and asked Weaver for a briefing on the refugee situation.

Weaver told Horan about the Eritreans and Tigreans who were continuing to filter into eastern Sudan, escaping war and drought. Soon there would be Chadian refugees in the west. And there was an ongoing civil war between the Moslem Arabs of northern Sudan and the African animists of southern Sudan. (Horan would later describe Sudan as "the place where the Four Horsemen of the Apocalypse stable their steeds.") The ambassador next asked Weaver about the black Ethiopian Jews, known as Falashas, whom Horan had been charged in Washington to "discreetly keep an eye on." Since 1980 Falashas had been trickling in and out of Sudan on their way to Israel as part of a low-key Israeli Mossad operation. When Weaver first met Horan in mid-1983, about one hundred Falashas a month were being smuggled out of the country. Weaver hoped that by early the following year the Falashas, a "political hot potato," would be all gone and with them the loudmouthed American-Jewish and Canadian-Jewish amateurs, who kept turning up in town to try their hand at Falasha rescue work, getting caught by the Sudanese security forces in the process. Horan raised his eyebrows and nodded. The meeting ended.

A few days later at a reception, Weaver got to see the new ambassador in action. Horan bantered in perfect Arabic to the Sudanese, in perfect French to the French ambassador, in perfect German to the German ambassador, and so on. This guy, thought Weaver, was not just résumé-fluent, he actually knew languages. Also at the reception a military attaché—a green-beret type from Vietnam, who had once given Weaver a lesson in his office on how to kill someone with your bare hands—told this great joke about "niggers" disemboweling each other in West Africa. Everybody laughed, except the new ambassador. Weaver noticed that Horan, without making a scene, had quietly slipped away. A few days later the attaché was ordered home: Weaver thought Horan had something to do with it.

Months went by. Weaver eased into a relationship with Horan. Not only did Weaver find the ambassador "both intellectual and operational-minded," Weaver also found him "trusting." Unlike other higher-ups, Horan chose not to edit Weaver's cables to Washington, except to make fine grammatical points and an occasional abstruse reference to a poem that this or that cable had reminded him of. Jerry Weaver, looked down upon by the other diplomats, felt complimented.

Weaver's nemesis, however, was the new DCM, David Shinn. There is no harder job at an embassy than that of DCM. As the second-in-command the DCM must be the ambassador's bastard, the chief administrator who makes sure all the desks are clean, that security regulations are adhered to, and that, so to speak, the trains run on time and those who are not on board get shafted. Weaver, a born slob who couldn't keep his desk clean and who kept strange hours and wore strange clothes, had a hard time with Shinn.

In early 1984 Weaver's prediction to Horan that the Falashas would be all gone proved terribly wrong. A famine of biblical proportions was beginning to engulf Ethiopia. Tens of thousands of refugees, including Falashas, were flooding eastern Sudan. An American, Peter Parr, who ran a suboffice for the UN High Commissioner for Refugees (UNHCR), informed Weaver that "the people of special interest are now dying at Um Raquba," a refugee camp near the Ethiopian border. Weaver cabled Washington about it. Nothing happened. Weeks went by. With the famine gathering force, Weaver had a refugee circus to contend with, and the Falashas were not uppermost in his mind.

Summer came. One day, a Swedish relief worker and evangelical Christian named Peter burst into Weaver's office and began to cry. "They're dying; it's terrible; you've got to do something about Um Raquba." What came to be known as Operation Moses might be said to have been born that moment.

When, in the first week of January 1985, the story broke in the world press about the dramatic rescue of thousands of Ethiopian Jews, credit immediately went to the Mossad, Israel's secret service. Indeed, the handful of books and magazine articles that followed on the subject tended to high-light Israel's role in the evacuation of Jews from this Arab country and to downplay the role of America's diplomats. Though Jerry Weaver's and Hume Horan's names popped up in many of these accounts, they are mere footnotes. The journalists were not lying; it was just that while Israeli and Jewish-American sources were willing to blab about everything, taking credit for what they did (also for what they did not do), the American diplomats involved in the rescue had been ordered to shut up. Hume Horan spoke to no one. When British author Tudor Parfitt wrote to Weaver, requesting an interview for his book, Weaver did not even answer the letter. Parfitt's book, *Operation Moses,* mentions Weaver only twice yet, at the same time, makes it clear that Weaver was the key man in the operation. Here is the untold story of Operation Moses.

When Weaver visited Um Raquba, about eight Falashas a day were dying of starvation. On one June day a few weeks before he came, fifty had died. Weaver had seen "shit holes" all over Sudan, especially in the jungly south. But Um Raquba ("Mother of Shelter" in Sudanese Arabic) was the worst, a squishy sea of mud where twenty thousand people crowded into grass huts designed for one tenth that number. There wasn't enough water, let alone enough food. There were few blankets, almost no medical equipment, and the Sudan Council of Churches refused even to assign a doctor to the camp. Like others involved in the issue, Weaver immediately noted two things about the Falashas that distinguished them from other Ethiopian refugees: unlike the Christians and Moslems, the Ethiopian Jews, paradoxically, had somewhere to go, a country that was willing to take them, Israel; and precisely because they were Jews, the Falashas were worse off than the other refugees. They were being beaten and persecuted by the Christians and Moslems. In *Operation Moses,* Tudor Parfitt reports an Ethiopian Christian pointing to a group of Falashas at Um Raquba and saying, "Those people are Jews. They killed Christ." The aid workers at Um Raquba reported hearing constant rumors about how the Falashas ate Christians and caused women to have miscarriages.

Weaver had already talked to Nicholas Morris, the head of UNHCR for Sudan, about the Falashas' plight. According to Weaver, Morris replied gruffly that "we aren't going to give them any special treatment." So

Weaver went to Horan, who told him to cable Washington about "everything you've seen and heard." Horan was aware how important this issue was in Washington. At roughly the same time that Weaver was traveling back and forth to Um Raquba to report on the situation, Israel's deputy prime minister, Yitzhak Shamir, was in Washington, meeting with Secretary of State George Shultz. With half a million Ethiopian refugees in eastern Sudan on account of the famine, it should be an easy thing, Shamir argued, to arrange for a few thousand of them to be flown out. Shamir spoke from experience: he had been imprisoned by the British in Eritrea and knew the area well. Concomitantly, Horan's immediate superior, the deputy assistant secretary of state for Africa, Princeton Lyman, was feeling the heat from American Jewish groups, who were berating the State Department for not doing anything to help the Falashas.* After consultations between Horan, Lyman, and the State Department's bureau of refugee programs, it was decided that Lyman and Weaver would meet in Geneva in October with representatives of the Israeli government and secret service.

Sudan's commissioner for refugees, Ahmad Abdul Rahman, would also travel to Geneva, as Sudan had an interest in "solving its Falasha problem," though, obviously, Ahmad would not attend the meeting and would not—officially, at least—know or want to know of the Israeli involvement.

When the ex-football player and also-ran political scientist, Jerry Weaver, walked into the room in Geneva with Deputy Assistant Secretary of State Princeton Lyman and three Israeli officials, it would seem that Weaver was out of his depth. In fact, it was they who were out of theirs. By October 1984 Weaver had been living for six years in Sudan. The area of eastern Sudan under discussion was where he often went hunting for gazelles. When Weaver heard one of the Israelis talk about rescuing the Falashas from Um Raquba Entebbe-style, Weaver, for the first time in his life, found his voice, as it were:

"If you try it, the Sudanese are just going to shoot you down. My friends in Sudan state security told me so. That's exactly what they're expecting you to try to do. There's only one way to do this thing. You move these people from Um Raquba to Gedaref and from Gedaref to Khartoum air-

---

*Sudan, unlike other Arab countries, came under the domain of State's bureau of African affairs rather than NEA. Princeton Lyman, the deputy assistant secretary for Africa, was an unsung hero of the Falasha story. He held the fort in Washington, assaulted by American Jewish groups, even as he knew that a secret rescue operation was in progress that he couldn't tell them about.

port. You do it seemingly openly, with the full cooperation of Sudan security. You need a few vehicles, planes, and state security escorts."

The Israelis were silent. Here was an American cowboy who appeared to know what he was talking about. One of them asked Weaver: "Would the Sudanese agree to this?"

"I'll ask 'em," Weaver shot back.

Weaver went downstairs to the lobby where the Sudanese commissioner for refugees, Ahmad Abdul Rahman, was waiting. "It was surrealistic," Weaver recalls. "I was wearing my jungle khaki (the others at the meeting were wearing suits) and Ahmad was in his national dress," a flowing white robe and headdress. "We held hands—the way Sudanese men like to do— and walked up and down the marble corridors. All these Swiss were staring at us. Ahmad never asked me with whom I was dealing in the meeting, but of course he could figure it out. I told Ahmad, 'We have found a way to get these people off your hands.' " Weaver then explained to his Sudanese buddy what he and the Israelis had in mind. He knew that Ahmad was a professional politician: this was a Sudanese who could quote John Keats to Americans and who at Khartoum University was connected with both the right-wing Moslem Brotherhood and the left-wing Communists. Ahmad's answer was noncommittal, but he indicated that it would be a token of goodwill if the Americans could arrange for him to get a nice job with the UN in Geneva. (As it turned out, poor Ahmad was to become Sudan's ambassador to Libya.)

The Geneva conclave ended with an understanding that Weaver would pursue the matter in Khartoum and then report back to the Israelis. In Khartoum Weaver went again to see Ahmad, who told him that Sudanese state security would have to issue internal travel permits for the Falashas to travel from Um Raquba to the airport. Weaver already knew that. He replied to Ahmad—not believing what he was saying—"I want you to arrange a *fetur* between me and Omar."

A *fetur* is a traditional Sudanese breakfast of kidney beans, sesame seed paste, and tea that is taken leisurely at nine-thirty in the morning. "Omar" was General Omar el Tayeb, the number-two man in the country and the head of Sudan's state security service. Though Weaver had dealings with lower-level security types, he did not personally know Omar, and he did not really expect that such a meeting could be arranged. Weaver also knew that any dealings between the U.S. embassy and Omar el Tayeb were handled through the CIA's Khartoum station chief.

The next day Ahmad told Weaver that "Omar will meet you for *fetur.*"

Weaver marched into the ambassador's office to tell him the news. "We better get the station chief in here," Horan said. Like many CIA station chiefs around the world, the one in Khartoum was "declared," meaning that Sudanese state security and a few others who needed to know knew who he was. He was more like the CIA's official ambassador to Sudan's secret service than he was an actual spy. A former "lurp" (long-range recon patroller) in Vietnam who wore cowboy boots, this particular station chief fit the popular image of one. The station chief told Horan, "I think it's better if you and I see Omar for *fetur* instead of Jerry." Horan said, "Fine, no problem."

Weaver studied Horan closely. The ambassador seemed so relaxed, as if this decision—that is, agreeing to go with the CIA station chief to meet with Sudan's chief security heavy about the smuggling of thousands of Jews out of an Arab League country the survival of whose government the United States had a big stake in at that moment and with which a number of military-strategic deals were on the negotiating table—was as easy a decision to make as going to this or that cocktail party. *He doesn't chicken out,* Weaver noticed. *He's not saying to me and the station chief that he's got to cable back to Washington five times over for instructions and reconfirmations like other ambassadors would do. This guy's a star, they're talking about him as a potential future NEA assistant secretary and he's risking it. He's willing to put his dick in the cracker over this—now here's a guy with balls.*

At the breakfast meeting Omar el Tayeb told Horan and the station chief that he would only agree to the operation if "the CIA ran everything from start to finish." Omar said he wanted "no leaks." And to him the CIA "meant good security." As it turned out, the CIA was distinctly cool about the whole operation. Political pressures in Washington, however, plus Weaver's own cables home, encouraged the State Department's bureau of refugee programs to volunteer for the assignment. This action led to a compromise that the CIA was rightfully uneasy about: Weaver would carry out the rescue, deputized by the CIA. In other words, as one participant in the deliberations explains, "the CIA would have no control, but all the blame" if things went wrong.

Before the deal with the Sudanese could be struck, Omar el Tayeb needed to meet with and take stock of Jerry Weaver. "Omar and I got on," says Weaver. Of course, this was exactly what Weaver excelled at: shooting the breeze about guns and animal hunting with Arab military types. Weaver gave Omar advice about weapons maintenance, and Omar confided to Weaver his deep admiration for CIA Director William Casey and how he wanted to remodel the state security building in Khartoum along the lines of the CIA's headquarters in Langley, Virginia.

Six months later, after a coup that would depose Sudan's President, Jaafar Nimeiri, the media in Sudan and abroad would heap abuse upon Omar el Tayeb, painting the picture of a thuggish state security chief who sold Sudan out to foreign powers. Hume Horan, however, insists on putting Omar el Tayeb into perspective. "Omar el Tayeb was one of the few security chiefs in the Arab world who was not a sociopath, perhaps the only one who did not have real blood on his hands. And I can say he did not have a scintilla of animus toward Jews. Now what's so bad about that?" Horan's larger point is that the very openness of Sudanese society and the relative lack of fear in which Sudanese had lived, both before and after the April 1985 coup, allowed for the criticism and the leaked information about Omar that would have been inconceivable in far more brutal Arab states, where this kind of material would never have seen the light of day.*

Despite Omar's cooperation Horan also had to sell the idea to Sudan's president, Jaafar Nimeiri. "Nimeiri may not have had the IQ of a five-year-old, but, boy, he was tough. He had the will to power which is so important in that part of the world. I told him about all his admirers in America and how here was a chance not to disappoint them: to show the world how human and kindhearted the Arabs were." The other argument Horan used, a much more potent one, was that the Americans were actually doing Nimeiri a favor: they were off-loading this political football for him, to protect him from having to deal with a possible military rescue attempt by a certain unfriendly state. "Nimeiri didn't respond to what I was saying, but neither did he voice an objection," Horan says.

Nimeiri's regime contained, in Horan's words, "a lot of sleaze but no real violence." For example, Nimeiri's chief adviser at this time was Dr. Baha Eddin Idris—called Mr. Ten Percent on account of the commissions he was allegedly reaping on state contracts. A former zoology professor at Khartoum University, Dr. Baha had been discharged for divulging exam papers to a young girl student with whom he had fallen in love. Horan describes him as a fellow "with a Lolita complex." As it would later

---

*A truly brutal regime did not come to power in Sudan until the summer of 1989, when a group of fundamentalist junior officers toppled a weak parliamentary government elected in the wake of Nimeiri's overthrow.

turn out, the Falasha rescue would become, in Sudanese terms, just another scandal involving an alleged payoff.

Everything was set to roll.

The CIA station chief told Weaver "to come over to my house tonight and you'll meet your Sudanese counterparts" from state security. Weaver met Musa and Fathi, "yin and yang." Musa, Weaver says, "was laconic and light-skinned. Fathi was dark-skinned and jumped around holding a .45-caliber, single-action revolver. He was Omar's assistant, his operations man." Weaver immediately began talking to them about hunting. "We got on." He invited the pair to his place the next night.

What Musa and Fathi found when they entered Weaver's house was an arsenal: many different kinds of assault rifles, pistols, and sawed-off shot guns; scopes for long-range killing; a device for melting lead in order to cast bullets; hundreds of pounds of magnum shot in cloth sacks; and a desk stacked with mechanical reloaders. A true gun aficionado, Weaver insisted on loading the powder himself into each individual bullet shell. There were also the usual ivory tusks, swords, crossed spears, and other gongs and trinkets. And there was Leo, one of the lions Weaver had killed, completely skinned with a reconstructed skull, covering one of the beds.

Musa and Fathi were perplexed. *Who, exactly, was Weaver?* they thought. *Here was this American who had been living in Sudan for six years, who knew all the generals in the army, who fasted during Ramadan, who liked feturs, and who was—what?—a refugee coordinator? No, he must be CIA.* But Weaver was not like any CIA station chief they ever met or any diplomat they ever met, either. They finally settled on the assumption that Weaver was part of a supersecret spy organization run by the State Department, separate from the CIA. After all, Arab countries like Sudan often had several intelligence agencies that competed with and spied upon each other.

Weaver began to get together often with Musa and Fathi. Occasionally, the three of them even enjoyed a toke of marijuana at Weaver's house. For Sudanese who were not religious, this action was no different from Westerners talking over a glass of wine. Weaver was doing what Arabists are supposed to do: deal, one on one, with Arabs.

Then Weaver took Musa and Fathi with him to Um Raquba and to nearby Gedaref to talk to the local state security officer. "An operational plan was forming in my mind. I told the state security officer in Gedaref that we'd need safe houses, communications radios, vehicles, and escorts who would be paid top salaries. But this guy worried me. He was a big mother of a Dinka [a Nilotic tribesman from southern Sudan]. He must have been six feet seven. He was wary. He basically said, 'What's in it for me?' I knew that was a question I'd have to solve."

Weaver's mind was now operating in overdrive. *There were so many details to think about. Blankets were needed for waiting in the cold, food in case the planes were late, potable water at the transfer points, a sideband five-hundred-mile radio operating on its own frequency, at least fifty metric tons of fuel for the buses, lubricants, auto mechanics, and a garage for the buses, the buses themselves, the drivers, Nissan patrol vehicles, etc., and none of this could be bought on the open market in Khartoum. Or else everyone would find out what was going on.* Weaver's plan was to transfer all the approximately ten thousand Falashas over a dirt track from Um Raquba fifty miles north to Tewawa, a place near to Gedaref, which would be designated Falashaville. From Falashaville they could be brought to the airport each night. "I figured a 707, stripped bare to its fuselage, could handle four busloads of Falashas, about 240 people."

He goes on: "I cabled Washington with the full plan. Horan signed off on everything. He didn't even change a comma this time." Washington instructed Weaver that "it was go." He flew back to Geneva to meet the Israelis. They were going to provide him with money, donated by American Jews, to set up everything on the ground in Sudan. The first installment was for $250,000 in hundred-dollar bills in a Samsonite suitcase given to Weaver by a man with a limp at Geneva airport in late October 1984. But the Israelis were already making trouble. "Could you believe it, they wanted me to exchange the money at the official rate in Sudan and Saudi Arabia [where chassis for the buses were going to be purchased— Weaver had thought of that, too]. And they wanted receipts to prove it. Nobody exchanges that kind of money at the official rate in Sudan and Saudi Arabia. I told them what rate I could get on the black market. They said no. God knows what kind of petty bureaucrats they had at the Mossad in Tel Aviv. I did it anyway and I told them so. At the official rate it would have been like throwing away thousands of dollars."

So as to avoid a customs inspection, Fathi met Weaver at Khartoum airport. The next morning Weaver marched into Horan's office and said, "Mr. Ambassador, I've got the money. It's in a suitcase in my office."

Horan swung around in his chair, his hands clasped behind his head. There was no expression on his face. Horan replied in a very measured tone: "Jerry, I don't need to know every detail. But my office is always open to you. You don't need an appointment. If there is ever anything I can do to help on this matter, don't hesitate to walk in here and ask."

Weaver read that two ways. Horan was going out on a long limb for this project. But on the other hand, in case it failed, the less the ambassador knew about such things as Israeli bagmen the better for his own career. *Jerry, this is your baby,* he seemed to be saying.

It so happened that Weaver had a hunting buddy, an Italian expatriate named Luigi, who promised Weaver three Sudanese pounds to the dollar—the official rate was 1.5 pounds to the dollar. Weaver held out for 3.4, telling Luigi that the $250,000 was only the first installment on what would be a million-dollar bonanza. Next, Weaver flew with a suitcase full of black market Sudanese pounds to Jidda, where a state security colonel from the Sudanese embassy met him at the airport. Accompanying Weaver on many of his forays was a locally hired assistant, a Sudanese Greek named Nikola Mandrides, whose Arabic was perfect and who, like Weaver, had a penchant for young women and adventure. Weaver, Mandrides, and the Sudanese colonel attacked the money souk in Jidda, going from stall to stall, bargaining for the best rate for Saudi Arabian riyals. When they got it, they ordered the Toyota bus chassis, the tires, and plenty of spare parts, all to be shipped immediately across the Red Sea to Port Sudan by the Sudanese embassy. That night, when they got back to Khartoum, Weaver and Mandrides went out to eat with Musa and Fathi. A waiter told them that, an hour before, the Sudanese pound had been devalued by 25 percent vis-à-vis the Saudi riyal. They all burst out laughing. They had really stuck it to the rich and haughty Saudis!

Once the chassis arrived, the actual frames for the buses could be built locally by a Greek friend of Weaver's and Mandrides's. But they needed fuel for the buses, Weaver realized. And they couldn't buy such large amounts of fuel on the open market without declaring its purpose. Again, Weaver had another hunting buddy, the director of the Sudan office of the World Health Organization, a Pakistani, who introduced Weaver to another wealthy Pakistani who was a fuel importer. Weaver needed fifty tons of diesel and five tons of petrol for the escort vehicles. After a price was agreed upon, Weaver said he would hold on to the fuel drums. The Pakistani didn't understand, telling Weaver that he could get rid of the drums and save Weaver the trouble. Weaver insisted, however.

Next, Weaver went back to Gedaref to see the big Dinka who was the local security officer. Weaver told him that as the buses used up their fuel, there would be a growing mountain of fuel drums at the garage that would have to be gotten rid of fast, so that no one would notice them and get suspicious. "I don't care how you do it, just do it," Weaver told the Dinka, who now seemed more pleased with the whole arrangement. Weaver knew that the drums could be sold for five Sudanese pounds each; that money would constitute part of the Dinka's payoff. Weaver was now buying and renting safe houses in the Gedaref area for the drivers, mechanics, and security officers. It was understood that after all the Falashas had gone, the houses, vehicles, and other equipment would all become the bounty of the Dinka and other state security people.

By now Weaver had collected more money shipments from the Israelis, and cables were flying back and forth between Khartoum and Washington and between Washington and Tel Aviv. State security started making new demands: they claimed they needed a plane to fly between Gedaref and Khartoum, which they would presumably get to keep after the operation was completed. Weaver and others argued them out of it. Horan had no choice but to become increasingly involved. "There always seemed to be a detail to worry about. Somebody who was not cooperating, somebody who hadn't got the word, or the money," Horan recollected. "I had unlimited access to the ambassador, even at his home," Weaver says. "If he had a meeting going on in his office, he'd break it to see me."

Not everyone was so enthusiastic, however. Although Secretary of State Shultz, the White House, and Vice President George Bush, in particular, were behind Operation Moses, the State Department was worried. And more than a few of the Africanists, who handled Sudan, hated the whole thing (until it succeeded, that is; then they claimed credit for it). Sudan, the geographically largest country in Africa, was, in their view, highly strategic. It reached deep into Black Africa and had a long coastline on the Red Sea facing Saudi Arabia. Were Nimeiri's already shaky pro-Western regime to collapse; not only would Egypt be undermined but Sudan could then join Marxist Ethiopia and radical Libya in an arc of Soviet influence. In the view of State's area specialists, pressuring Nimeiri to cooperate in the exfiltration of Jews was incendiary.

It was mid-November 1984. The first night of Operation Moses was approaching. An Israeli Falasha, whom Weaver dubs James the Falasha Finder, arrived from Geneva. "Since one Ethiopian refugee looks like another, James's job was to make sure that only Falashas got on the planes. Our client [the Israelis] wanted the right merchandise."

Another arrival in town was Georges Gutelman, a fifty-one-year-old

Belgian Orthodox Jew, who ran a Belgian charter company called Trans European Airways. Gutelman had close links with the Mossad and for years had been flying Sudanese Moslem pilgrims on the Haj pilgrimage to Mecca in Saudi Arabia: in short, the perfect man for the job. Weaver bought Gutelman a Suzuki minivan for shuttling his air crews from Khartoum airport to the Friendship Palace Hotel, an isolated luxury establishment far from the city center where the crews would attract little attention. At the airport Fathi and Musa introduced Gutelman to the other security officials, some of whom Gutelman already knew from the Haj flights. "This man was a real pro," Weaver says. "He was stocky, with dark hair. He spoke French, English, and Arabic and seemed of indeterminate nationality. The Sudanese weren't sure who or what he was. He quickly bribed the people in the control tower. And when the whole operation blew up in a publicity storm, he was gone without a trace." Gutelman reminded Weaver of Kurtz—not the Kurtz of Joseph Conrad's *Heart of Darkness,* but the Kurtz of John le Carré's *The Little Drummer Girl,* the Mossad agent who was a "bustling veteran of every battle since Thermopylae," with wrinkles "made by centuries of water flowing down the same rock paths." Kurtz "wheeled and dealed and lied even in his prayers, but he forced more good luck than the Jews had had for two thousand years."

Horan also met with Gutelman. They spoke in French. "There was a sympathetic, practical idealism about the man," Horan recalls. "He was neither a mercenary nor a visionary. He said he had a lot of experience in the 'extraction' business and that he could not guarantee that there wouldn't be any leaks. 'Nothing is a secret forever,' he remarked. But he told me not to worry, since when the information inevitably did come out, by then it would likely be overtaken by other events that none of us could predict. I felt comfortable with him. I felt that he knew what he was doing."

A few days before Thanksgiving, on November 21, 1984, Operation Moses began. There were four buses, two escort vehicles, Weaver, Musa and Fathi, and James the Falasha Finder. It was a dark and cold desert night, and Weaver wore a down-filled L. L. Bean field jacket that made him look even bigger than he was. He was armed with a Walther pistol and a long cane. Sudanese security forces, helped by James, had by now taken all of the Falashas out of Um Raquba and had isolated them at Falashaville in

Tewawa. A riot erupted as every Falasha in Tewawa tried to squeeze onto the buses. Weaver had to use his cane. The four buses drove in a convoy at a moderate speed for five hours to a designated holding area that Weaver had equipped with extra blankets and water, where they waited for a radio signal to enter the airport through a back gate. Gutelman's Boeing 707 was hours late arriving from Brussels. Weaver, Musa, Fathi, James, and the 240-plus Falashas huddled in the dark. "They were like sheep, absolutely quiet. The kids weren't even crying. The only sounds were of vomiting and defecating. These people were starving and sick. And we were bringing out the frailest and oldest and youngest ones first," Weaver explains. At 4 A.M., November 22, the four buses drove up to the door of the 707. Three Israeli doctors and nurses were on the plane. When everyone was packed in, Weaver had an altercation with the pilot over the number of people on board. They had miscounted, and there were more people than the pilot said the plane could handle. Weaver pointed to his Walther and threatened the pilot. The plane took off. But with the riot, the late plane, and the dispute with the pilot, the first night had not gone well.

Early the following morning the station chief marched into Weaver's office. "We've got trouble," he announced. "Fathi says no to the rest of the operation unless you can guarantee that everything will be more efficient than last night."

Gutelman assured Weaver that no more planes would be late. As for the riot that caused an extra few people to squeeze on board, Weaver had an idea. He and Mandrides went to the souk in Khartoum and bought large quantities of cloth in different colors. They cut the cloth into ribbons. Before each flight James the Falasha Finder would distribute ribbons to the 240 people chosen. One night he would distribute red ribbons, another night green, another blue, and so on. The color for each flight would be kept secret until the last moment, so there was no way the Falashas could obtain the correct ribbons on their own.

From November 21, 1984, until January 5, 1985, Gutelman's airline flew thirty-five flights from Khartoum to Tel Aviv by way of Brussels. The morning after each flight had gone out, Weaver notified Horan in his office and then cabled Washington. Sometime in December, though, "things began slowing up," according to Horan. "Omar was okay, but the lower levels of [Sudanese] security officers may have had misgivings. Convoys started being postponed. That sort of thing. I was worried." Partly to help and partly because he was just plain curious to see the operation in the flesh, Horan told Weaver that he would like to come out one night and watch the plane load up. "It wouldn't hurt for the lower-level Sudanese to see that this thing has high-level backing," said Horan. "Yeah, no problem, Mr. Ambassador. Come on over to my place around 1:30 A.M., and we'll go to the airport together."

At Weaver's house Horan's eyes took in all the guns, scopes, magnum shot, mec reloaders, and other paraphernalia of Weaver's strange life. Horan knew that Weaver "was somewhat of a wildman," but he hadn't expected such a "pirate's den." Opening his eyes wide at the mec reloaders, Horan said to Weaver, "You've really got a factory here, Jerry." Weaver laughed. "Yes, Mr. Ambassador, I guess I do."

Years later, Horan explains his forbearance of Weaver this way: "I knew Weaver had his problems. He was living in the wrong century, a gun-in-pants-type fellow. His personal life was messy, sure. Stories went around the embassy about his bimbos, and whatever else he did at night. But if I had transferred responsibility for the operation to your conventional, cover-your-ass FSO—the kind who dots his *i*'s and fills in his travel vouchers the first morning back from a trip—the Falashas would never have left Sudan. But Weaver had enough swash and buckle in him to break through any barrier. Boy," jabbing the air with his finger, "they'll carve on Jerry Weaver's tombstone that here was a man who got the job done and who handled large amounts of cash doing it, without any of it sticking to his fingers. That's more than you can say for a lot of people."

From Weaver's house Weaver, Horan, and Mandrides drove to the airport. Weaver and Mandrides got out to direct things, but the ambassador lingered for a few moments alone in the car, watching through the window as the four buses pulled up in the night to planeside and a dark, moving sea of humanity, straight out of a biblical time warp, began climbing up the ramp and into the twentieth century, headed for the Promised Land; their faces, according to Horan, registering "relief, exhaustion, terror, and anticipation all at once."

The ambassador got out and made the rounds of Sudanese security officers, showing the flag as it were. Then he entered the plane, eyeing the three Israeli doctors and nurses going up and down the aisle, ministering to people who had never seen a car or a plane before. "They were all so silent," says Horan. "They had no suitcases, just the clothes on their backs. We went on for weeks, just pumping them out of Sudan."

Weaver recalls that Horan too was silent. "The ambassador's eyes were lit up in shock and amazement, as if the whole thing was a revelation to him. He seemed to be saying with his eyes, *hey, this is neat, we're really doing something here."*

Horan says this: "I felt that at that moment we were really behaving like Americans should. That this was what the Foreign Service was all about. You know, you spend so many years working on this policy and that policy whose effects wither away, and it's rare that you get the opportunity to do a good deed, a sheer *mitzvah.* No matter what was going to happen to these people, you knew they were going to be better off where they were going than where they were."

It is almost as though there were a spiritual line connecting the likes of Asahel Grant and Justin Perkins in 1830s Persia and Samuel Zwemer and James Cantine in turn-of-the-century Arabia to Jerry Weaver and Hume Horan in 1980s Sudan, a line that zigzagged from one good and adventurous deed to another, circumventing in the process the whole sorry history of the relationship between Arabists and Zionists.

Weaver remembers that the next morning Horan called him into his office and asked him, in a reflective tone, what he was going to do when "all of this is over"—as if, no matter what each of them did from then on, Operation Moses would have to be the high point in their professional lives. (Weaver honestly hadn't thought much about life beyond Sudan.) "I always called Horan 'Mr. Ambassador,' " Weaver mentions. "It was always very formal with him. But I kind of got the feeling that, in his own way, of course, Horan was a loner like me."

It was early January and only a few flights remained before all the Falashas would be gone. Weaver took a few days off to fly to Austria to have an elephant gun made. It was there that he heard the news that a massive evacuation of Ethiopian Jews from Sudan to Israel was underway. The news leak had originated with the Jewish Agency, the Zionist organization in Jerusalem responsible for immigrant absorption. Weaver flew back to Khartoum. The Sudanese, terrified by the media reports, immediately shut down Operation Moses with roughly five hundred Falashas still on the ground waiting to leave.

Cables started flying between Khartoum and Washington and Washington and Tel Aviv: *what to do?* In the first week of March 1985, Vice President George Bush flew to Khartoum. Though there were a number of outstanding issues between the U.S. and the Sudanese governments, in-

volving famine aid mainly, it was the remaining Falashas that brought
Bush to Khartoum. A White House official at the time says, "When it came
to the Falashas, Bush was really supportive. It was something he felt very
deeply about and which he never tried to capitalize on politically afterwards, though he certainly could have. I guess it went back to his World
War II experience of waiting in the sea to be rescued. *You get your people out
who've been left behind,* that sort of thing."

Bush and Horan met with Nimeiri in the garden of Nimeiri's dilapi-
dated presidential mansion by the Nile. The United States was willing to
release fifteen million dollars in suspended aid in return for another rescue
operation that had President Ronald Reagan's personal blessing. Nimeiri
insisted that this time there be no Israelis involved. Horan then met with
the station chief: Weaver would plan Operation Sheba, but unlike Operation Moses, it would be carried out entirely by the CIA.

That night there was a reception for Bush at Horan's residence. Pictures
were taken of the Horans and Weaver with the vice president, and Bush
awarded Weaver a citation for masterminding Operation Moses. Weaver
then went back to his house, where he and Mandrides passed a wild night
with a couple of Ethiopian girls on a lion's skin. Weaver came into the
embassy the next morning at seven-thirty, sat down at his electric type-
writer, and banged away. By ten the plan for Operation Sheba was completed. It was devastatingly simple. The remaining Falashas would be
trucked to an airstrip a few miles north of Gedaref, where six CIA-operated
C-130 transport planes, circling overhead, would land at twenty-minute
intervals to collect passengers. The planes would then fly straight to Israel.
It all happened on the night of March 28, 1985.

But there was still the issue of the payoffs to be settled. Being a pro, Gutelman didn't wait to be asked. As his planes were flying into Khartoum
empty, he started by bringing in fruits and expensive chocolates as gifts for
the security officers and the control tower operators; these items were a rare
delicacy in a miserably poor country like Sudan. When Gutelman learned
that Musa's daughter needed a bicycle, he brought in an expensive brand-
name model on one of the planes. When state security mentioned that it
was badly in need of "comm gear" (high-tech communications equip-

ment), Gutelman flew in a planeload of the stuff. And then there were the six-hundred-dollar Rolex watches for some of the Sudanese officers and an engraved Smith & Wesson .44 magnum pistol—the Dirty Harry gun—that was meant for a particular Sudanese general but which Weaver got to keep, claiming he never had a chance to deliver the gift.

Finally, one of Omar's assistants casually mentioned to Weaver, "We think the Jews ought to make a contribution to the building fund," by which he meant Omar's plans for new state security headquarters, with a helipad on the roof to impress Arab dignitaries. The amount mentioned was three million dollars.

Following consultations with Horan and the station chief, Weaver met with a Mossad representative, who thought $1.5 million would be an appropriate sum, provided that more business could be done with Sudanese state security. The Israelis were actually quite impressed with the Sudanese. Despite the country's poverty and lack of education and consequent reputation for inefficiency, the Sudanese had *delivered.* The Israelis now queried Weaver about overflight rights for El Al planes in Sudan. Weaver went back to the Sudanese with the request. Omar told him to open a bank account in London for the transfer. But soon after Weaver had done that, a coup in Sudan topped Nimeiri's regime in early April 1985.

Nimeiri was out of the country at the time of the coup, but Omar el Tayeb was caught and sent to prison. Sudanese newspapers publicized the U.S. embassy's role in the Falasha operation. There was hell to pay. Local media accused Ambassador Horan of being an enemy agent. Anti-American sentiment rose in intensity. Horan found himself living with several Sudanese bodyguards in his ambassadorial residence. But like John Lloyd Stephens facing the sheikh in *Incidents of Travel in Egypt, Arabia Petraea, and the Holy Land,* Horan decided not to keep cool.

"At every reception I attended in Khartoum I told people I was proud of what we had done and that they should be proud, too. I told the [new] Sudanese government that the departure of a few thousand hungry people was not going to alter the correlation of forces between the Arab world and Israel. I had found an issue to meet people head on with—so they knew that the United States stood for something."

While Horan's life had not been specifically threatened, Weaver's had. After seven years in Sudan, Weaver had to leave in a hurry, with no time for good-bye parties or even to pack more than an overnight bag. Embassy security officers had to pack his personal effects and ship them home. And that turned out to be Jerry Weaver's downfall.

The square-faced, crew-cut boys from security were less amused by Weaver's weaponry and ammunition-making devices than Horan and Weaver's other visitors had been. They didn't like the dirty dishes and the rest of the mess in the house, or the crossed spears or ivory tusks, either. FSOs, as a rule, collected exotic bric-a-brac, but this was simply too much. So they took the place apart. First they found the marijuana, and then the gold bullion.

Back in Washington an inch-thick security file was slammed on the table as security officers worked Weaver over for hours. Weaver was his usual self:

What was the marijuana doing there?

"Why," Weaver answered, "I had it for my Sudanese friends. If we could drink alcohol in their presence, why couldn't they smoke a little dope in ours." *Do you think one of the tight-assed FSOs in the embassy who never smoked dope and didn't know any Arabs could have saved the Falashas?* he was thinking.

And what about the gold bars?

"It was a small investment."

Horan was interviewed by security about Weaver, and so were others who knew him. "Weaver became a real Typhoid Mary," Horan laments. "People knew it wasn't good for their careers to be seen with him."

In 1987, after almost two years on a desk assignment in an annex of the State Department that was heading toward Nowheresville, Weaver resigned from the Foreign Service. They don't fire you in bureaucracies, they let you rot.

Jerry Weaver is sitting on the back porch of his farmhouse in Licking County, Ohio, east of Newark in the first gentle foothills that mark the western slope of the Appalachians. This is not the Ohio of car plants or the Cleveland ghetto: the Rust Belt, in other words. This is pure Sherwood Anderson country, the idyllic heartland of apple orchards and deer bucks and cow manure, where people wear leather boots instead of Reeboks and still don't need to lock their doors at night; a vanishing myth of America, just like Weaver himself.

A thunderstorm is in progress, and the awesome show of nature brings a tranquillity to Weaver's voice. "I had my innings," he says, a bit dejected about what happened. Not only was he shafted by the Foreign Service, but the Israelis didn't even have the good manners to formally thank him or to invite him to Israel to see the folks he saved.

Instead of a bush hat and a safari suit, Weaver now wears a gas station hat and chews Red Man tobacco as he drives around in his pickup truck. The farm Weaver refurbished himself, putting up the fifteen miles of fence, buying the tractors and the other equipment, all of which he repairs with the help of a farm girl he lives with. In the house are the guns, the mec reloaders, the spears, the African head masks, and everything else, making it look like a Hollywood set for the private hideaway of Indiana Jones. Leo is upstairs covering a guest bed. And on the wall, by the double bed supporting a leopard skin in the main bedroom, hangs a photo of Weaver standing alone beside George Bush. "To Jerry Weaver, a great humanitarian," Bush has written at the bottom.

In the history of American Arabism, Jerry Weaver was like a bolt out of the blue. He came and went fast and was not even rated by the State Department establishment. But he made a difference.

And his neighbors in Newark, what do they think of him?

"They don't know much about Sudan or the places I've been. They hear my stories and see the photo of me with Bush and say, 'Jerry must have been some kind of a hit man for the CIA.' "

Weaver exemplifies the ultimate irony of the Arabist experience: he became so steeped in the culture surrounding him that he became virtually unanswerable to the State Department. As a consequence, the State Department squeezed him out. But this affinity for Arabic culture in no way implied a hostility toward Jews. In fact, the Arabist who did the most for Jews was also the one who had, to a greater degree than any other, gone native.

But what about Hume Horan?

Parker Hart, a peppy and impeccably mannered octogenarian, leans back in his chair amid the white pilasters, cream-colored walls, and gold leaf of Washington's Cosmos Club and remembers the swearing-in of Hume Horan as the U.S. ambassador to Saudi Arabia in 1987. Pete Hart had himself been an ambassador to Saudi Arabia prior to becoming NEA assistant secretary in 1968. Saudi Arabia is more than America's principal strategic and financial ally in the Arab world. Its uncompromising desert is where the foundation stones of Bedouin culture and Islam were laid. For a State Department Arabist, therefore, no position is more exalted than the ambassador's post in Riyadh. And to Pete Hart's mind no one's credentials for the job were quite of the standard of Hume Horan's.

"Hume Horan speaks such fine Arabic," says Hart wistfully, in the accent of a Boston Brahmin. "Upon taking the oath as ambassador, Hume recited an Arabic poem by heart. I don't know what it was, but it was beautiful to listen to."

It was part of a poem, really, written by Sami al-Barudi, a late nineteenth-century Egyptian politician, who had been exiled by the British to the Seychelles for two years. Horan compares Barudi's exile with that of Yitzhak Shamir, who had been sent by the British to Eritrea. The recitation, translated into English, began with the line

By my life, the period of separation has grown long . . .

And ended with

yet maybe every expatriate returns to his dwelling place.

Horan had actually taken two separate parts of Barudi's poem and stitched them together, hoping no one would notice his use of poetic license. He needn't have worried. No one at the swearing-in ceremony had ever heard of the poem or the poet, and most could not even understand the Arabic. Yet the quotes he had chosen were apt. Horan, in a sense, was returning if not to his "dwelling place," then at least to the Arab country he knew best, Saudi Arabia.

There seemed to be no individual in the American gene pool better qualified at that moment to be ambassador to Saudi Arabia than Hume Horan. Not only was his Arabic fluent, but he had just completed his third ambassadorial assignment, to Sudan, with flying colors. In Khartoum Horan had given a textbook illustration of the precise role of an ambassador. When Horan left Khartoum, a Sudanese official, referring in part to the ambassador's complicity in the smuggling-out of the Falashas, remarked to Horan that "you weren't exactly popular here." Horan, smiling, replied: "Being popular was not my job. My job was to represent the values and interests of the United States." And by the United States Horan meant "not just the State Department but the U.S. Congress and the White House, too."

Moreover, Horan's appointment to Riyadh was also a sign, intended or otherwise, that the United States had learned the lesson of Iran in the 1970s, when the Shah fell: don't let a military and economic relationship with a regime keep you from knowing its domestic opposition. Horan's five years in Saudi Arabia, when he virtually ran the embassy for three ambassadors, combined with his fluency in Arabic and his outgoing personality, made him an expert on the local scene there. "You know Hume," laughs former NEA assistant secretary Nick Veliotes, "he's the kind of guy who is so friendly and makes lots of local contacts. In five years in a place like Saudi, he would know everyone, without the interference of a translator, either." Horan himself says, "In the seventies I ate fried chicken at simple restaurants with a lot of people who went far in the Saudi government." Horan's contacts were not only with government types but with the ulema (Islamic scholars), and that made the Saudis nervous.

For while Washington was pleased with the appointment of Horan as ambassador, the Saudi rulers were less so. To an extent Horan was their worst nightmare. Horan's Falasha escapade may have been water off a duck's back to the Saudis, but the last thing King Fahd and his cronies wanted was a hands-on type of American in Riyadh, one who knew Arabic, who was streetwise, and who consequently would be able to challenge the rosy-eyed vision of Saudi Arabian life being peddled in Washington by the Saudis' all-powerful ambassador, Prince Bandar Ibn Sultan. The Saudis, obviously, had experience with U.S. ambassadors who were good Arabic speakers. The very first ambassador to the kingdom, Colonel William Eddy, was a prime example. So were Pete Hart, Hermann Eilts, Jim Akins, and Dick Murphy. But with the possible exception of Colonel Eddy, Horan's Arabic was distinctly better than that of those other men. And unlike Horan, Eddy was a missionary child with well-known pro-Arab political sympathies. More significantly Horan had a reputation as not being "a limousine ambassador": the kind whose friendships were limited to the foreign community and whose Arab contacts were restricted to formal settings and to those of his own station. Horan liked getting out on the streets and talking to people.

There was also the matter of Horan's Iranian paternity, which he neither advertised nor kept secret. There may have been no reasoning with the Saudis on this matter. It was the kind of issue, like their aversion to Jews, that highlighted the worst aspect of the Saudi national character: its tendency for the nastiest and most infantile sort of conspiracy mongering, something to which the most sophisticated of Saudis were prone. Precisely for this reason the issue was never discussed. Washington, having chosen the man it wanted, rightly did not consider the subject legitimate. The Saudis agreed silently.

But all of these factors might not have amounted to anything if bad luck had not intervened.

In late 1987 Horan was just settling in to his new job when he and his embassy staff, assisted by "national intelligence findings"—satellite photographs—began to solve the latest riddle of the sands. Why, for instance, was the Chinese food disappearing so fast from local markets? As the embassy staff later learned, it was because Chinese technicians were eating it. They were in the desert south of Riyadh, installing medium-range ballistic missiles, Silkworms, easily capable of reaching Israel, which, as Horan says, put the Saudis "in a new strategic ballgame." The Saudis had given a secret promise to Washington not to deploy such weapons, but it was a sensitive topic. Prince Bandar, the Saudi ambassador in Washington, had reportedly closed the deal on the Silkworms himself during visits to China. Bandar was more than just the most powerful foreign ambassador on the Potomac, he was affable, ingratiating, full of dollars and influence, and had excellent ties with the National Security Council and President and Mrs. Reagan.

Nevertheless, the State Department in March 1988 instructed Horan to make it clear to King Fahd just how distressed the United States was by the deployment of the missiles. When Horan received the instructions, he understood the Saudis well enough to know that "this was big-time stuff," which could easily get him removed as ambassador. So the morning after receiving the instructions, he phoned Washington for a reconfirmation, asking NEA, "Are you sure you want me to deliver this message?" The answer was affirmative. Horan was aware that in such a situation, being a fluent Arabic speaker was a distinct disadvantage. As his friend Nick Veliotes explains, "This is when you don't want to know Arabic, when you want a translator to say the difficult words for you, so that in the king's mind you're less personally identified with what's being said." Thus, rather than ask to see the king, Horan put the protest in writing and personally delivered it to the palace.

Such tact might have worked. True, the letter shamed King Fahd, who even before its delivery had never received Horan in a private audience, as he had done with previous and subsequent U.S. ambassadors. But what really put the knife in Horan's back was the action of the Reagan White House. Within hours of delivering the letter, Horan received a cable from Washington telling him "to cease efforts" on the Silkworms because "a different communication" had gone out direct from Washington to Riyadh. Bandar reportedly "backchanneled" through his White House contacts to get Horan's orders rescinded after they had been carried out. King Fahd thus had two letters in his hand, one from Washington, saying that the missile deployment was an issue requiring discussion but perhaps nothing more, and another letter from this inquisitive, Arabic-speaking ambassador who was half Persian, saying that the deployment was unacceptable. What was unacceptable, in the king's eyes, was this kind of ambassador. The king made it clear that Horan, in Riyadh only a few months, could no longer be a viable interlocutor.

Washington recalled Horan and quickly dispatched Walter Cutler, a highly rated generalist, as the new ambassador. Cutler, though he spoke no Arabic, was to have a hassle-free tour and enjoy good access to King Fahd.

A feeling persisted within the Foreign Service community that Horan was done in not just by the Saudis and their powerful friends in Washington, but also by senior bureaucrats within the State Department for being too perfect an area specialist, that is to say, for understanding the Saudis better than they wanted to be understood. Horan brushes these suspicions aside: "There is a Kleenex quality to ambassadors. We're policy instruments, not policymakers, there to take the blame, to be wiped away so the process can continue."

Referring to Washington's conduct, Horan will say only this: "After the facts of the Falasha rescue became known and the new Sudanese government wanted me removed, Chet Crocker [the assistant secretary of state for Africa] bluntly informed Khartoum that if 'Sudan wanted to continue to deal with Washington it would have to do so through Hume Horan.' I'll always be grateful to Crocker for that support. As for how the Department reacted when the Saudis applied similar pressure, let's just say that it was not a Corregidor performance," a reference to the brave resistance of U.S. troops on Corregidor Island prior to surrendering the Philippines to the Japanese in May 1942.

After his recall from Saudi Arabia, Horan served on a number of high-level commissions and was then elected by his fellow FSOs as the president of the American Foreign Service Association. Following that, he was appointed the ambassador to the Ivory Coast, the most important Francophone country in West Africa, where his French-language skills could be put to use.* Nevertheless, for a former ambassador to Saudi Arabia and the best Arabic speaker in NEA history, it was not, in conventional terms, a successful end to a career. But Horan was never conventional. Again there is an analogy with a British Arabist, Sir Richard Burton. Burton, despite his having penetrated the holy city of Mecca in what is today Saudi Arabia and his role in the discovery of the source of the Nile not far from Sudan, was relegated by the British foreign office to West Africa, where he was named ambassador to Dahomey, close to the Ivory Coast, in 1861.

Horan, in a whimsical, self-mocking tone, once described Arabists like himself as "the Pekinese orchids begot by an American superpower. I suppose only a rich and powerful nation has a justification for us." Like Lawrence and Burton in the service of imperial Britain, Horan was the orchid of orchids. He represents the most advanced form of the Arabist species before it began going extinct. And as with Lawrence and Burton, the bureaucracy didn't know quite what to do with him.

Not long after Ambassador Horan left Riyadh, a not-so-humble second secretary, Ray Anthony Custis arrived. Custis, born in the Midwest in 1961, was another Jerry Weaver: a fellow who came and went fast but left more of a mark than other diplomats who spent entire lifetimes in Araby. Custis, like Weaver, was a talented rebel, the sort all bureaucracies sooner or later expel as though it were some disease germ. But in the 1990s Custis's story is particularly relevant because it highlights the real problem now facing NEA and the State Department, which is not so much clientitis as it is the bureaucratic regimentation of embassy life.

Ray Anthony Custis is a fictitious name. His exact identity must remain hidden. "I don't want to end up like Salman Rushdie," Custis explains.

---

*The Ivory Coast is now officially known by its French equivalent, Côte d'Ivoire.

What Custis did would in fact enrage Moslems to no lesser degree than what Rushdie did.

Ray Custis is a descendant of a Civil War general and slaver. Custis mastered Arabic at an Ivy League university, and after graduation in 1982, he volunteered to work on an archaeological dig at Tel Elan, an ancient site in northern Syria, not far from the Carchemish dig site over the border in southern Turkey, where T. E. Lawrence had gotten his start in the Middle East in 1910. Tel Elan, a second millennium B.C. capital of the Assyrian king Shamshi-Adad I, was being excavated by Yale professor Harvey Weiss. Weiss, though Jewish, was one of the few American archaeologists whom the Syrian Baathist authorities had ever allowed to work in their country.

Weiss, Custis, and the other Americans were followed everywhere by Syrian secret police. Custis lived in a mud hut without electricity. The nearest town was Kamishli, "a filthy, scummy, dusty place with little food in the stores." But Custis loved the atmosphere of intrigue—you were close to both the Turkish and Iraqi borders, and the ground rumbled with weapons convoys due to the Iraq-Iran War.

Custis returned to Syria in 1983, this time with a Fulbright Scholarship to study at Damascus University. Though drunk on the writings of Lawrence, Charles Doughty, Abdullah Philby, and Freya Stark, Custis was too bright and far too arrogant not to notice the negatives of Syrian university life:

"Syrians and Iraqis are like people on steroids. You never know when the veneer of politeness and hospitality is going to crack and reveal the pent-up violence and rage underneath. . . . Damascus University was one disorganized mess. Classes were always being canceled, everybody was cheating, and the Syrian professors were pedantic idiots regurgitating nonsense from quaint books written by English lords. The campus was full of peasants on scholarships who were neither qualified nor serious. One of the school's directors was running a prostitution ring with Polish female students. . . ."

But Custis, who looks like the picture of perfect innocence, is no easier on the American diplomats he encountered in Syria in the early 1980s:

"They were a bunch of imbeciles. They didn't know what was going on. I lived in a dorm at Damascus University, speaking Arabic all the time, fending for toilet paper and food items, which were often in short supply, and the dips were in their airlock called Little America with their own electricity generator and Rice Krispies."

The American diplomat whom Custis particularly disliked was April Glaspie, the political counselor and later DCM. "Imperious April. She just thought she totally knew everything through her contacts with the vapid, politically emasculated Syrian upper class who showed up at embassy cocktail parties with their Paris suits and gold lamé dresses."

Custis claims he told Glaspie when the notorious Defense Companies, a praetorian guard run by Rifaat Assad, the brother of Syrian president Hafez Assad, were being disbanded. "I knew because the brother of a friend of mine at Damascus University—one of Rifaat's soldiers—informed me that everyone in his unit was being discharged from the military. 'Nope,' said April. We have our sources, our precious intelligence data. April didn't want to listen to some unofficial American who spoke Arabic, even if I was one of the few in the whole country. I was glad to see April get her comeuppance over Iraq."

Bernard Johns, a friend of Glaspie's who studied Arabic with her in Beirut and also knows Custis, provides an explanation: "Every embassy political officer, when he or she arrives on post, inherits his predecessor's contact list—the names of locals whom you can contact socially and who know about the local political scene. April's list obviously did not include this one itinerant American student who thought he knew everything and who in this case just happened to be right. Ray [Custis] is brilliant and thrives on intellectual combat. But he has the arrogance of the young, and it turns many people off."

Custis's reading of Abdullah Philby and Freya Stark fueled his desire to visit Yemen, the last bastion of unspoilt Arabia. But flying direct from Syria was too expensive. It would be cheaper to fly via Saudi Arabia with a *haj umr* visa. So Custis converted to Islam in order to get the reduced-fare ticket. "It was just a matter of going to the courthouse at the entrance to the souk in Damascus, filling in a form, answering a few questions from a judge, and testifying that 'there is no God but God and Mohammed is his Prophet.' I'm from a family of religious Methodists. We don't drink or dance, so what's the difference? There is this idea that the only people who convert to Islam are fanatics like Cat Stevens. Why can't you convert and be a bad Moslem, like so many of those who are born into the faith?"

Following his visit to Yemen, Custis returned to the United States to attend law school. In 1985 he went on the television game show *Jeopardy* and won $72,000. In 1986 he went back on the show and won $100,000. "With that much money I thought, *who needed to become a lawyer?*" So he joined the Foreign Service, thinking that with a little effort on his part he could easily rise through the ranks of the mediocrities he had observed at the U.S. embassy in Damascus.

Custis arrived in Riyadh in January 1989; like Jerry Weaver in Sudan, he fell in love with Saudi Arabia but instantly hated embassy life.

By 1989 the U.S. embassy in Riyadh was a far cry from the quaint building in Jidda where Wat Cluverius, Ernest Latham, and David Long had learned to love the Foreign Service. The new diplomatic compound, built of glass and reinforced concrete, comprised both the embassy itself and some of the living quarters. It had more the aura of a corporate base than of an embassy. Twenty minutes outside town, the compound had "security" written all over it, with apartments that faced inward on each other. There was a courtyard with trees, a patio-bar, a swimming pool, and tennis courts. Everyone had VCRs. The whole place was enough to make Ray Custis want to puke. He had come to Saudi Arabia to be among Arabs and instead found a sterilized Peyton Place, full of catty cliques and bureaucratic back-stabbing. "It immediately became clear to me that the people who were getting ahead were those who never left the office but who answered every cable from Washington. The kind of guys who crammed for their Arabic exam in order to get a high point-rating, but who couldn't utter a phrase in the street. Washington already had a policy on everything in Saudi Arabia and these guys sat there all day and parroted it back in cablese."

Custis's contempt for the whole atmosphere knew no bounds: "It came to me in Riyadh that people who have never been in the military develop this passion for military phrases. Like 'How long have you been in-country?' What bullshit! The people talking like this rarely left the embassy compound."

Custis used every opportunity he could find to leave the embassy. On weekends he traveled in the desert with a four-wheel-drive vehicle, a copy of Doughty's *Travels in Arabia Deserta* beside him. At night he hung out until all hours of the morning at cheap chicken-and-kebab stalls with young Saudis. He appreciated the surreal mix of modernism and medievalism that Saudi towns had to offer: "You go to a shopping mall, to Wendy's for a hamburger, then you take in a beheading at the central square. The crowd at the beheadings was always 90 percent foreign: Indians, Paks, and embassy Marines who liked that stuff. I remember once three Saudi highway robbers got the chop from a black slave who was a traveling executioner. The heads popped off to light applause, like at a golf match. Then they tied the heads back on the body and hung them on gibbets. In the local context it seemed so ordinary, as though it wasn't happening."

After six months of this routine, Custis was bored. Given that he was still nominally a Moslem with identity papers to prove it and that the U.S. intelligence community was always desperate for information from the holy cities of Mecca and Medina, where non-Moslems could not go, Custis volunteered to go to Mecca on a reporting assignment. He made the pilgrimage in late June 1989 with an Arab-American friend.

"We signed up for a package pilgrimage tour for the equivalent of $150, available only to Moslems, that included an air-conditioned bus from Riyadh and an air-conditioned tent in Mecca. We left in the evening. The bus was six hours late. We were nervous about the prayer times. Though both of us spoke Arabic, not being religious, we weren't really conversant with the prayers.

"The bus traveled all night. It had no air-conditioning. The first shock was a few hours out of Riyadh when we stopped. I was dying of thirst and grabbed a Pepsi with my left hand. These pedantic little religious guys who had been watching us all night like hawks, intensely suspicious of us, started lecturing us in Arabic about the sin of eating and drinking with your left hand [the hand with which you wipe yourself after a bowel movement]. And then there was the urinating. I had to do it squatting down like everyone else, remembering to recite the relevant prayer. You know, 'the Prophet, peace be upon him . . .' Had they seen the toilet paper I was hiding I would have been dead in that crowd. These were religious Arabs in a real pious and self-righteous mood.

"The bus stopped at Taif. We all went into a mosque and changed into our haj clothes: two seamless pieces of white cloth to cover your body, plastic sandals, a money belt, and a sun umbrella. A bunch of guys were hawking plastic sandals and souvenirs. Someone selling haj T-shirts could have made a fortune.

"It was a couple of more hours to Mecca through a volcanic landscape of barren hills. The Jidda-Mecca highway is full of billboards advertising watches and this awful Formica furniture."

Custis was now in an area that only a handful of Christian Westerners, most notably Sir Richard Burton, had ever seen. This is how he describes the holy city of Mecca:

"It is not in any sense pretty or mysterious or picturesque. There is a grim souk built around an old Turkish fort. But the city is buried under modern, antiseptic construction. The atmosphere is heavy, sterile, lifeless, depressing, and pious. Concrete and dust. It's hot and uptight and crowded. They took us to our tents in the holy plain of Arafat outside Mecca. The air-conditioning consisted of a small fan blowing the hot air around.

"You have to realize, we were with thousands of other pilgrims in a tent city, one tent on top of the other. And all of these people were extremely religious and unsophisticated peasant types. There were Africans, Iranians, all suspicious of each other. There were unbelievable masses of people, frenzied and hysterical and running around. All I could think about was the crowding and the elbowing. You always seemed to be waiting on line—for bedding, to use the toilets, to get water. Everybody was always arguing over what to do, where to go for this prayer, where to wait for the bus that would take us into Mecca, where to wait for this thing. . . . And there were these jabbering, aggressive, know-it-all types, the guys who lectured me about how to drink the Pepsi, who drove you crazy. The possibilities for unrest, for riots over the smallest problem, were constant.

"The Grand Mosque was simply one huge construction project of concrete dust and scaffolding. Everyone knows about the crowds circumventing the Kaaba. What is not noticed is all the activities going on in the courtyard. There are religious classes, lectures, and all these kids running around. I don't want to sound racist, but the intellectual caliber of the discussions was not exactly high.

"The final activity was stoning the pillars at Mina [the stones represent devils]. But again it was all confusion. You gathered your stones, and in a huge elbowing crowd of people, you all threw them in the direction of the pillars. As soon as it was over, my friend and I took a taxi back to Jidda and splurged on a meal at the Holiday Inn.

"Soon after I got back to the embassy and filed my cable, I was told that I couldn't attend some meeting. 'You don't have the proper ORLOP-DEFCOM clearance,' or whatever ridiculous acronyms they use. I had been in the Grand Mosque in Mecca. I could have been torn limb from limb if those people had known I was a U.S. embassy political officer on assignment. But it didn't matter to these military types who had never been in the military. Real diplomacy and reporting is a dying profession."

If that is true, then Custis's account of his trip constituted one of the last great reporting cables. It went to U.S. embassies around the world, and diplomats as far away as Pakistan raved about it.

In May 1990 Custis completed his assignment in Riyadh and was transferred to the consulate section of the U.S. embassy in Dubai on the Persian
Gulf. The dull consular work was the last straw. After little more than a
month in Dubai, he quit the Foreign Service, unable to realize that diplomacy means relating to your own colleagues as well as to the "natives."

What he couldn't have known then, however, was that only a few weeks
after handing in his resignation letter, the very insulated embassy existence
he had been ridiculing and the diplomatic "mediocrities" he so despised
were to be major factors in the greatest debacle in the history of America's
Arabists: Iraq.

Part III
Debacle

Chapter 12

The Icy Eyes That Had Contemplated Nineveh

First impressions are often the most penetrating. When D. H. Lawrence arrived in Florence for the first time, it was late at night, and he walked directly from the train station to the hotel. The next morning a friend found him typing deliriously. Asked what he was doing, Lawrence said, "I am writing an essay on the Florentine mentality." The essay, it has been said, is a masterwork that Lawrence's subsequent writings on Italy did not improve upon. Here are a traveler's first impressions of Iraq in the mid-1980s:

Saddam International Airport: sweeping steel arcs, ceilings of colored glass and copper beams forming traditional Islamic semidomes. The line at passport control snakes slowly through one vast marble hallway and into the next: blank-faced contract workers from Europe, America, South Korea, Pakistan, the Philippines, Egypt, and other countries have come to work tax-free, building up the Iraqi military state. The arrivals' hall is filled with "Hollywood uglies": men with bulging suits that conceal a weapon, speaking into walkie-talkies, their dark eyes reminding one of insects' feelers; icy and black voids that contain only the most chilling of abstractions. On each vertical surface there is a picture of Saddam. His eyes achieve a watchful, monolithic poise that the West is familiar with on account of Stalin. Thus, for the first few days in Iraq, a visitor sees Saddam as the Arab

243

Stalin. But that comparison—like the one with Hitler that would become fashionable in 1990—revealed less about Saddam than about the West's own experience with evil.

The Palestine Meridien Hotel had an airport coach service run by Filipinos and Pakistanis. Through the coach window one notices new multi-lane highways and poured-concrete overpasses lit up like prison yards in the airless night heat. You almost feel the hum of the high-wattage lamps against the coach window. Despite a war with Iran that is several years old and that has taken the lives of hundreds of thousands of men, the atmosphere is dominated by the prosperity of the oil boom. You push open the window. The night air in March is dense, suffocating: a few wispy palms and the smell of dung and dried sulphur mud from the Tigris. Mud-caked streets next to modern highways begin to form and converge, then come cinder-block storefronts with crudely painted sheet metal signs in Arabic script: the aura of an endless construction site. One sees a few tall buildings and strange steel forms like dragon's teeth breaking into the night sky. Mud is always thick in the air, refined by the breeze off the river and breathed into your nostrils as dust. The Tigris meanders like slow-moving sewage, blacker than the night. The Palestine Meridien and Ishtar Sheraton form one complex under round-the-clock surveillance, grafted onto the pancake-flat Mesopotamian landscape like launchpads on the cratered surface of the moon.

In the Meridien lobby Hollywood uglies occupy all the sofa space. Western and Asian businessmen prowl the floor with stir-crazy looks in their eyes, like prisoners in an exercise yard. For journalists Iraq is a place where one rarely gets a visa. But as soon as you arrive, you find the hotels packed to capacity with foreign visitors, all of them businessmen.

These are the days before CNN International. You turn on the state television channel. A haunting dirge blares in your eardrums; the guttural stops are like a man choking. The screen shows bullet-ridden and badly bloodied corpses, nothing but dead bodies on the screen, one after the other. No commentary, just dead Iranian bodies and chanting Arabic music. The camera zooms in for a long, meditative close-up of one corpse. The music builds toward a slow, powerful, rhythmic ejaculation. You turn to the next state channel: same thing. In the lobby the rental videos are all pornographic.

In the morning you drive by the long, machine-gun-guarded walls of the president's palace, then past a severe and modernistic dome with a kind of shield collapsing on top of it—one of several public memorials to the war dead from which the public is barred at the point of a gun. There is no humanity in any of this architecture, just the chilling aggression of bronze and copper sheets, like the monuments to the gods of Sumer and Akkad in old Babylonia. Only officially are these monuments meant to honor fallen soldiers; in truth, they deify Saddam. In *Ancient Iraq* the French archaeologist and Orientalist Georges Roux writes of Amar-Sin—the "bull calf of the god Sin"—who reigned four thousand years ago in Sumer, south of Baghdad, who, like his father, Shulgi, and like Saddam, divided his time between the building of monuments and the conduct of wars in Iran and Kurdistan. Amar-Sin "was deified and, with complete lack of modesty, referred to himself as 'the god who gives life to the country.'" Saddam, referring to himself in the third person, says "he is to be found in every quantity of milk provided to the children."*

All regimes, even Communist ones, reach into the past to define their present. Usually this is restricted to such spheres as art, poetry, and architecture. In Iraq it is more. These fierce and jagged cubistic shapes on raised platforms are true temple precincts. Few dare wander over to them, unless in organized school or military groups. To do so could be taken as a sign of disrespect, the same as if you were caught staring in the middle of the street at a photo of Saddam. So you keep moving, head turned aside, unless you want to risk being shot—or worse. Mondays and Thursdays are hanging days at the prisons, the diplomats say.

In a 1960 article for the *New York Times Magazine*, Lawrence Durrell wrote that national groups, whatever changes may occur in their racial characteristics, "bear the unmistakable signature of place . . . you could exterminate the French at a blow and resettle the country with Tartars, and within two generations discover, to your astonishment, that the [French] national characteristics were back at norm . . . even though their noses were now flat."† Durrell is exaggerating less than one might think. Just look, for example, at how the Middle Eastern landscape of Israel transformed the

---

* For this and other interesting quotes from Saddam, see Daniel Pipes's "Will Saddam Back Down—or Fight?" in the *Wall Street Journal*'s European edition, December 28–29, 1990.

† "Landscape and Character," *New York Times Magazine,* June 12, 1960.

personalities and physical appearances of European Jews in just one generation. And of all the landscapes and geographical situations across the earth, according to Georges Roux, Iraq's is among the least changed throughout history.

Roux's book neatly bridges the gap between the romantic vision of Mesopotamia, based on the first chapters of Genesis, and the grim landscape outside one's hotel window in Baghdad.

Adam and Eve, it turns out, did not live in a garden paradise, but in a turgid mud swamp. The Tigris and the Euphrates "flow with such a low gradient that they meander considerably and throw numerous side-branches," creating many "lakes and swamps," interspersed with "dreary wastes strewn with dry wadis and salt lakes." The ancient Mesopotamian towns, writes Roux, "were built of nothing but mud." And there is Robert Byron's description of Iraq, thousands of years later, in 1933, in *The Road to Oxiana:* "It is a mud plain. . . . From this plain rise villages of mud and cities of mud. The rivers flow with liquid mud." But keep in mind that this swamp has the bone-dry climate of a desert, which is constantly cracking the mud and blowing it into fine dust. Roux notes that temperatures in Mesopotamia, from prehistory onwards, reach 120 degrees in summer, and the average annual rainfall is under ten inches, most of which comes in the early spring, causing floods.

However, since all the land to the west until the Mediterranean Sea coast and all the land to the east until the Indian subcontinent is riverless, rainless desert, this dreary artery of mud was where ancient civilization could at least develop.

But it did not exactly prosper. Contrary to popular belief, fed by biblical clichés adopted by some media pundits during the Gulf War, the valley of the Tigris and the Euphrates does not make Iraq an old and unified land in the way that the valley of the Nile makes Egypt an old and unified land. Both river valleys may have been the mothers of history and of civilization, narrow lines of life amidst desert nothingness, but that is where the similarities end.

Roux explains that since antiquity the Nile had an "annual flood of almost constant volume," with "the great lakes of East Africa acting as regulators." Because the Nile "freely inundates the valley for a time and then withdraws," it required only the "cheap and easy 'basin type' of irrigation," where canal slits were dug and men simply waited for them to fill up. But the Tigris and the Euphrates have no great lakes at their source to regulate their floods. They are two rivers instead of one, with the Tigris born in the snows of Kurdistan and the Euphrates flowing down from the mountains of Armenia. Moreover, their annual flooding occurs too late for the winter crops and too soon for the summer ones. Irrigation in Mesopotamia, therefore, has always been a never-ending drudgery that involves reservoirs, dikes, and regulator sluices. Even then, unlike Egypt, nothing is guaranteed. Low waters over a few years mean drought and consequently famine, while high waters can sweep away the mud houses as if they never were. Roux states that "this double threat and the uncertainty" about the future it created, bred a "fundamental pessimism" among the inhabitants of Mesopotamia.

This pessimism grew not only out of the perennial struggle against nature but also out of the struggle of men against other men—another thing that did not exist in Egypt. In an appendix to *East Is West*, Freya Stark, in a rare display of political insight, expands on this point:* "While Egypt lies parallel and peaceful to the routes of human traffic, Iraq is from earliest times a frontier province, right-angled and obnoxious to the predestined paths of man."

In other words, the Nile has always been a natural migration route. People didn't need to cross it, but to go up or down it. The Nile brought ivory and spices from Africa. The Tigris and the Euphrates brought nothing except their waters. The times that foreign invaders violated Egypt by sea, or by land across the Sinai peninsula, are few enough to be well known—the aggressions of Alexander the Great and Napoleon, for example, which brought learning and economic progress. For most of its history, however, Egypt was a stable entity left alone unto itself.

Iraq was never left alone.

The valley of the Tigris and the Euphrates, as Freya Stark indicates, runs at a right angle to one of history's bloodiest routes of migration. From the Syrian desert in the west came the Amorites, the Hittites, and the medieval Arab armies of the Umayyad caliphs in Damascus: a threat that in modern times has been represented by the rival Baathist regime in Syria. In the east was the high plateau of Elam, "the mountain of terror," from where invaders, including Aryan Kassites, Persians under Darius and Xerxes, Mongols, and Ayatollah Khomeini's Iranians, have marched down into Mesopotamia since time immemorial.

---

* The appendix is entitled "Islam To-day" (Faber and Faber, 1943).

Yet the most important difference between the Nile valley and Mesopotamia was that while the former was always a demographically cohesive unit, the latter was always a nebulous border region where various groups clashed and overlapped. Outsiders have been inclined to interpret Iraq as a modern outgrowth of an age-old polity known variously by such names as Sumer, Akkad, Assyria, Babylonia, the Baghdad Caliphate, or most recently Iraq. In truth, as Roux painstakingly documents, each of these civilizations encompassed only a part of present-day Iraq and was often at war with all the other parts. The Sumerians, who lived in southern Mesopotamia, fought the Akkadians of central Mesopotamia, and both of them fought the Assyrians, who inhabited northern Mesopotamia. The Assyrians, in turn, fought the Babylonians, who occupied the border region between what had been, in a previous millennium, Sumer and Akkad. All of this is to say nothing of the many islands of Persians who lived in the midst of the native Mesopotamians, thus forming another source of strife. Though the ancient Greek historians called the region Mesopotamia, meaning "the land between the (two) rivers," Roux points out that the inhabitants of Mesopotamia themselves "had no name covering the totality of the country in which they lived, and the terms they used were either too vague ('the Land') or too precise ('Sumer,' 'Akkad,' . . .). So deeply embedded in their minds were the . . . narrow politico-religious divisions."

Throughout antiquity three basic splits predominated: between the mountain people, usually Kurds, of the north; the people of central Mesopotamia around today's Baghdad; and those of southern Mesopotamia near the Persian Gulf. In the medieval and modern eras these splits were to become far worse.

The birth of Islam in the seventh century A.D. and its subsequent division into Sunni and Shiite parts transformed the gulf between central and southern Mesopotamia from a vaguely historical one into a specific religious one, since the Shiites, until today, predominate in the south by the Persian Gulf while the region around Baghdad is overwhelmingly Sunni.

The split between Sunnis and Shiites was followed in the eighth century A.D. by the rise of a new city, Baghdad, built by the Abbasid caliphs, descendants of al-Abbas, an uncle of the Prophet Mohammed. The golden age of Baghdad, associated with the caliph Haroun al-Rashid and the tales of *A Thousand Nights and a Night*, lasted five hundred years. But in many respects the age was not so golden. It was more like all the previous periods in Mesopotamian history. A ninth-century chronicler, Wazir Ziad, called

Baghdad's inhabitants a "people of plots and turbulence." The first Abbasid caliph was called *Al-Saffah* (The Bloodshedder): at the feet of his generals were once the bodies of eighty Syrians he had invited to a diplomatic banquet and then had murdered before continuing his repast. For the first time in history, a leathern was regularly laid beside the ruler's seat to serve as a carpet to catch the blood during the daily executions. The Abbasids were at first Shiite, then Sunni, and most of the cultural and artistic influences were Persian; thus, by inference, Shiite. *A Thousand Nights and a Night* was essentially a Persian work, written by Al-Jahshiyari in the tenth century. The bloody wounds of these medieval divisions never healed. When reference was made to "the golden age of Baghdad" during an interview with Hassan Tawalba at the Iraqi Ministry of Information, Tawalba responded: "But you know there was the bad Persian influence during that period because the Abbasid caliphs had Iranian blood on their mothers' side."

The Mongols under Hulagu, a grandson of Genghis Khan, overran Baghdad in early February 1258, reducing the Abbasid capital to ashes and exterminating most of the population. The Mongols destroyed Mesopotamia's irrigation system, leaving a corpse-strewn, malarial swamp in their wake. Baghdad was later rebuilt, only to be captured by Persian Shiites in 1623. The Shiites killed thousands of Sunnis and destroyed all the Sunni mosques. Fifteen years later the Ottoman Turkish sultan, Murad IV, a Sunni, captured the city and slaughtered thousands of Shiites. After a 280-year uneasy Ottoman sleep the British defeated the Turks in World War I, and Mesopotamia fell under the control of the likes of Gertrude Bell. What came about next would turn out to be the creation of another Lebanon; only a Lebanon untempered by the fresh and liberating western breezes of the Mediterranean.

The new nation was called Iraq, an Arabic term meaning "well-rooted," though Iraq was anything but. Rather, it was a cobbled-together colonial Frankenstein of three forlorn Ottoman provinces: Kurdish Mosul, Sunni Baghdad, and Shiite Basra.

The Kurds never really got the local autonomy that the British and the League of Nations had promised them. What emerged in the years between World War I and World War II was a tense and unstable polity of conflicting national interests. Each of these nationalisms—Kurdish, Sunni, and Shiite—because it clashed with the others on a heavily populated and fast-developing frontier region, became that much more extreme. Britain poured money, schoolteachers, and technical know-how into Iraq, which helped to make it more economically and politically dynamic. The dynamism, however, was always pulling in different directions, making it dangerous and volatile.

For a time, King Feisal II's talented prime minister, Nuri Said, held these passions in check by appeasing one group, then another. The balancing act came to a halt on July 14, 1958, when a group of army plotters led by Colonel Abdul Karim Kassem killed the Hashemite king and his prime minister, handing over the bodies to the mob for public mutilation. Then it was as if all the ghosts of Iraq's grim and brutal past came forward to make it, in the words of the scholar and Arab specialist Michael C. Hudson, "the least governable of the Arab countries."

Colonel Kassem immediately turned his attention to the Kurds in the north. When negotiations with them failed, his air force destroyed no less than 1,270 Kurdish villages in 1961. But the Iraqi Kurds continued their guerrilla raids. Sensing Kassem's weakness, a group of Baathist military officers led by Abdul Salem Aref toppled and executed Colonel Kassem in 1963. Young Baathists, including twenty-six-year-old Saddam Hussein, "roamed the major cities of Iraq unleashing orgies of vengeance."* In 1964 Aref murdered many of the Baathists who had brought him to power. In 1968 Baathists ostensibly led by Hassan al-Bakr overthrew and murdered Aref. Al-Bakr's internal security chief was Saddam Hussein, an educated and urbanized peasant from the Sunni town of Tikrit, north of Baghdad. One of Saddam's first actions was to uncover a "CIA-Zionist plot," which led to the public executions of about two dozen people, among them ten Iraqi Jews. Saddam made Iraqi militiamen march past the victims' bodies in a public ceremony.

But despite this instability and political barbarism, Iraq had achieved a much higher level of social development than Egypt, Syria, or any other Arab military heavy. Michael Hudson writes: "Paradoxically it is the

---

* See Pelletiere entry in the bibliography.

higher level of social development and political consciousness in Iraq that makes the loads on system legitimacy so great and so complex" (on account of all the historical and tribal hatreds crammed into one state), thus making Iraq "the archetypical overloaded political system," an academic phrase that perfectly intuits the overbearing air of oppression and paranoia that grips a visitor in Baghdad.

Saddam, in other words, was the ultimate Hobbesian nemesis. Mesopotamia had seen his like many times before: Ennatum, Sargon, Shulgi, Amar-Sin, Ashurnasirpal, to name just a few. "Ashurnasirpal," Roux writes, "possessed to the extreme all the qualities and defects of" the other rulers. "There is no smile, no piety, almost no humanity in the statute of him found at Nimrud," only "the rigid attitude of a conceited despot, . . . the straight-looking eyes of a chief who demands absolute obedience, and in his hands the mace and the spear . . . the colossus of stone whose icy eyes had contemplated Nineveh."

Though totalitarianism, as defined by Hitler and Stalin, is a product of the twentieth century, megalomania and its attendant personality cult first broke ground in the mud swamps of Mesopotamia in antiquity. The Egyptian pharaohs, as part of a pagan pantheon, were worshiped as god-kings. But the empire builders of ancient Assyria—Ashurnasirpal, Tiglathpileser, and Sennacherib—demanded worship as earthly rulers competing alongside the gods. Their behavior, moreover, is characterized by a methodical and mechanized chill that appears almost modern. Tiglathpileser, who ruled Assyria in the middle of the eighth century B.C., is the father of mass deportations, having deported 30,000 from the deserts of Syria to the high mountains of Iran, 18,000 from Mesopotamia to Syria, 65,000 during another military campaign, and 154,000 during still another. Sennacherib, who ruled Assyria in the late seventh century B.C., describes his own similar deeds against Babylon: "I devastated, I destroyed, by fire I overthrew." In 1990 such phrases from Saddam would become familiar: "I will consume half of Israel by fire . . . the earth will burn beneath their [the Americans'] feet . . . no military leader can become master of the world unless he controls Babylon."

In Iraq one came face to face with the living past. There were modern hotels, new highways and supermarkets, air-conditioning systems everywhere, marble palaces, and commercial offices full of Arabs busy at computer terminals. But the Iraqis working at these modern keyboards, unlike their counterparts in Bahrein and Kuwait, did not seem pleased about the experience. Their expressions were like those of slaves carrying buckets of mud up the steps of ancient ziggurats. As in the praetorian states of old Mesopotamia, the efficiency all seemed to have a singular and evil purpose. When Taha Yassin Ramadan became minister of industry in 1972, he made a speech to his ministry officials, saying: "I don't know anything about industry. All I know is, anyone who doesn't work hard will be executed."

This was a society being kept at peace through the rigors demanded of it by a war of conquest against Iran. Later Saddam would make war against Kuwait: another perverse result of Iraq's own legitimacy crisis. Saddam had found the answer to the question that had baffled Nuri Said, Colonel Kassem, Aref, and al-Bakr: *how to rule this fiery and unstable monster of the British?* By doing what Tiglathpileser and Sennacherib did, by embarking on ceaseless wars of plunder and conquest. "The Iraqis are prone to violence and extraordinary bestiality that is not fully explained by the artificiality of their state," notes Talcott Seelye. He and another Arabist, W. Nathaniel Howell, the U.S. ambassador to Kuwait during Saddam's invasion, said in separate interviews that the Iraqis are not purely Arab but probably have Mongol blood in them stemming from Hulagu Khan's thirteenth-century invasion.

Such were the historical and ground-level realities of Iraq in the 1980s. But there were other realities—literary, intellectual, and political—that American diplomats brought with them to Baghdad.

Though the American public, particularly the pro-Israel lobby, viewed Iraq, and Syria, too, with mere disgust, for Arabists these two ancient lands represent the historical, literary, and linguistic core area of their lives' work. "Syria is the apogee of Arabism," explains Hume Horan, "because the Syrians have everybody else's number and nobody has theirs. If the Syrians say it's okay for the other Arabs to do something, then it's okay. I always regret that I never got to serve in Syria. Syrian Arabic is the Arabic I most enjoy listening to. Iraqi Arabic, on the other hand, is less aesthetically pleasing, because it has a heavy admixture of Kurdish, Persian, and Turkish." Yet this linguistic fact is evidence of a different allure: Iraq, in addition to being an Arab urban center second only to Egypt in importance, is home to the Fertile Crescent, the richest overlay of Near Eastern civilizations. There are those picturesque marsh Arabs, for instance: Arab Shiites who have lived for thousands of years on floating islands near the Tigris in huts made out of reeds. This unchanged way of life captivated such British writers as Freya Stark, Wilfred Thesiger, and Gavin Young and not a few American Arabists. For these and other reasons, Horan observes, Arabists exhibit "a certain weakness, a *faiblesse*," for Syria, and for Iraq, too.

This *faiblesse* merges with the Arabists' grasp of the modern histories of the two states, a result of prodigious reading, often in Arabic, and of actually living in Baghdad and Damascus. For living in Baghdad, as we shall see, lays bare a somewhat more complicated reality than the first impressions just described.

There was also the political baggage thrust upon U.S. diplomats in Iraq, baggage that, because of the traditions and psychology of their profession, Arabists were more than willing to bear.

It is late fall 1991. At the prestigious Cosmos Club in Washington, Marshall W. Wiley is having lunch with two of his ambassadorial buddies, Andy Killgore and Jim Akins. The atmosphere is both poignant and congenial. These men go back a long way.

It is a leisurely lunch. Each man, tall and athletic-looking with a full crop of white or gray hair, leans forward over the table, sharing quiet talk about the Middle East. There is whispering and occasional laughter. Andy Killgore, former ambassador to the Arab sheikhdom of Qatar, is publisher of the *Washington Report on Middle East Affairs,* the fulfillment of Killgore's singular vow: "There is one thing I do personally. I let no Zionist statement go unchallenged."* Jim Akins, a former ambassador to Saudi Arabia fired by Henry Kissinger, contributed one thousand dollars to Killgore's *Washington Report* in 1991. And Marshall Wiley, a former ambassador to the Arab sultanate of Oman, is well worth talking to at length.

A few months later Marshall Wiley greets a visitor, again at the Cosmos Club, where he is a member. Though he was born in Rockford, Illinois, in

---

* Quoted from the *Saudi Report,* September 6, 1982.

1925, a date that puts him in his late sixties at the time he was interviewed, Marshall Wiley appears younger. He exudes vigor and good cheer, like a jogger. There is a likable Midwestern openness about him. As a man completely at peace with himself, Marshall Wiley is only too willing to tell his life story.

"I went to the Illinois public schools and served in the navy in World War II. I was a carrier pilot like George Bush. I flew dive bombers. He flew torpedo bombers. . . . I got my degree from the University of Chicago and studied under the great teacher Mortimer Adler. I just loved philosophy and focused heavily on the great books.

"Throughout life I have loved learning and being a student. I went on to get a law degree and a business degree from the University of Chicago. Then I did further graduate work in philosophy at Columbia University."

Wiley went to work at the State University of New York at Albany with money from the Ford Foundation, which was involved in joint projects with the U.S. Agency for International Development (AID). In the early 1950s Israel was still a relatively poor country and entitled to help from AID. Thus, Wiley became the deputy head of AID's Israel program.

From 1954 through 1957, Wiley lived in Israel, not far from the sea in Herzliya. It was at the U.S. embassy in Tel Aviv where Wiley took the Foreign Service examination. In those years Wiley had a tennis partner, another American, by the name of Leon Uris. Uris, the author of a book about the Greek civil war, was at the time researching his second novel, to be called *Exodus*. *Exodus* would become not only one of the all-time best-sellers but also, perhaps, the greatest public relations triumph ever on Israel's behalf, responsible for creating the noble sabra myth of Israel as a nation of handsome, morally upright warriors and dark-haired, lusty beauties. Wiley, however, did not see Israel in quite the heroic terms that his friend Leon Uris did: "Among the things I remember are the old Arab villages from the pre-1948 era that the Israelis had bulldozed."

Wiley wanted to see "the other side," and he did. His first Foreign Service posting was to Yemen—the epitome of exotic Arabia—in 1959, where he served with Bill Stoltzfus. Wiley's memories are similar to Stoltzfus's: "They closed the medieval city walls of Taiz at night. Westerners were not permitted in San'a [the royal capital]. The only currency was the Maria Theresa thaler. I was the mission's dispensing officer. I'd go down to Aden, fording rivers, and buy the heavy coins in sackfuls. Then I'd drop each coin on a table to see if it rang, that way I knew if it was real. Of course, there were no banks in Yemen then," smiling fondly at the recollection.

Wiley did not study Hebrew during his three years in Israel, but in 1960 he left Yemen for Beirut in order to formally learn Arabic at the Foreign Service field school. "We had professors from the AUB who gave us the political background of the area. The previous conquerors didn't displace the population the way the Israelis displaced the Palestinians. There was some resentment on my part toward Israel, because the viewpoint I had gotten in Israel was exposed as false when seen from the Arab side. The Palestinians lived in miserable conditions. Israeli colonialism is, in my view, worse than that of the [Ottoman] Turks."

From Beirut Wiley's career trajectory was standard-issue Arabist. He was the economic officer at the U.S. embassy in Jordan, where he "came up against the real Palestinian refugee problem." During the 1967 war he was an Arab desk officer. "The experience was frustrating and disillusioning for me because [President] Johnson was in league with the Israel lobby. After the war there was no effort to get Israel out of the West Bank." In 1968 Wiley spent a year as a scholar at the Rand Corporation in California. Then, from 1969 through 1973, he served in Egypt at the U.S. interests section of the Spanish embassy. "There were only eight or ten of us of what used to be 120 before the [1967] war," when Egypt officially broke relations with the United States on account of Israel's victory. Wiley also mentions that during the war of attrition which followed the Six-Day War, "Israeli bombs hit an army camp near Cairo American College where my three kids were at school."

Wiley was back at the State Department, on the operations' desk, during the 1973 war. From 1973 until 1975, he worked on the North African desk, dealing with countries that were all Arab. And in 1975 Wiley was appointed the head of the U.S. interests section in Baghdad, Iraq.

In the mid- and late-1970s, when Wiley lived in Iraq, Saddam Hussein was still officially the number-two man in the regime of President Ahmad Hassan al-Bakr. (Saddam assumed the presidency in 1979.) "But Saddam was a legendary figure among the Iraqis then, because of how he had dug a bullet out of his leg with a pocket knife after he had tried to kill [Iraqi leader Abdul Karim] Kassem" in 1958. There was always a high degree of violence in Iraq. It was necessary for the regime's survival. Iraq never should have been one country."

But Wiley did have a pleasant few years in Iraq: "I traveled among the marsh Arabs of southern Iraq, having read the book about them written by Wilfred Thesiger. Iraq was totalitarian yet dynamic. There was an idealistic element to Baathism that is not appreciated in the West. Baathism is modeled after East European Communism rather than Soviet Communism."

Wiley defends Saddam Hussein's attack on Iran in 1980, which led to an eight-year war between the two countries: "I remember Saddam coming to the Iranian national day celebration at Iran's embassy in Baghdad in 1976. It was the first time Saddam had ever come to a foreign embassy's national day. He was clearly reaching out. But Iran responded with an attempt on [Foreign Minister Tariq] Aziz's life, the redrawing of the border, the bloodcurdling anti-Iraq propaganda on [state] television. So Saddam struck first. He figured that war was inevitable and that he might as well attack before Iran reorganized" following its revolution. "If Saddam had attacked Iran more vigorously in 1980," Wiley believes, "he might have won the war. The Iraqi population also saw the war as inevitable, so they didn't blame Saddam for it."

Wiley also provides some justification for Saddam Hussein's invasion of Kuwait in 1990. "The invasion of Kuwait was not like any other invasion in history, since it was an invasion of some people rather than of another country. Iraq and Kuwait are not really two separate countries."

After finishing his tour in Iraq, Wiley became the DCM at the U.S. embassy in Saudi Arabia for a year. Then in 1978 he became the ambassador to Oman, a job he enjoyed. As he explains, the Omani capital of Muscat had been the capital of an Arabian empire until the Portuguese built their forts there in the late fifteenth century while developing the sea route around the Cape of Good Hope to India.

In 1981, upon concluding his tour in Oman, Wiley resigned from the Foreign Service. "I had to work for succeeding American administrations that I fundamentally disagreed with. It came to a head, and I retired." Wiley implies that while previous U.S. administrations had lacked balance in their strong support for Israel, the incoming Reagan administration's support for the aggressive actions of the Jewish state was of a degree that he just could not abide. Wiley lauds the "honorable esprit de corps of Arabists who are up against the Israel lobby." He considers Killgore's *Washington Report on Middle East Affairs* a "well-done" magazine and "quite objective." And while Hume Horan describes the State Department, the U.S. Congress, and the White House as all representing "America's interests," Wiley says that "only the State Department is interested in U.S. interests. The White House and Congress are only interested in elections." In an interview for the Foreign Affairs Oral History program, Wiley explained his attitude toward Israel:*

"Israel is only about 2 percent of the [Middle East] population, and because of our support for that 2 percent, we're willing to alienate the goodwill of the other 98 percent, which have most of the land area and most of the resources, which, I think, in terms of our national interest, is a mistake."

Loy Henderson couldn't have put it any better. But Henderson, unlike Wiley, was dealing with the reality of 1948, not of 1989 when Wiley gave the interview.

Having quit the Foreign Service, this ex-ambassador armed with a law degree from the University of Chicago joined the prestigious law firm of Sidley & Austin in Washington to organize its Middle East activities. Wiley said in his oral history interview that another reason he resigned from the Foreign Service was financial: he had three children to put through college, and he could make two to three times as much money in a law firm than he could as an ambassador.

In 1984 Iraq resumed full diplomatic relations with the U.S. (they had been broken during the 1967 war). Marshall Wiley now had the opening he needed; he was about to truly come into his own.

"In 1985 I organized the United States–Iraq Business Forum with the blessing of Nizar Hamdoon," Iraq's ambassador to the United States. The Wiley-Hamdoon alliance was a natural fit. Marshall Wiley, an Arabist, a lawyer, and a man with a business degree, had zeroed in on what, prior to the collapse of the Soviet empire, was one of the world's few unexploited but potentially lucrative markets: Iraq, the one Middle East nation that had it all—vast reserves of oil, sufficient water, grandiose development plans, and a large population that was neither miserably poor like Egypt's nor radicalized by religious fundamentalism like Iran's. Nizar Hamdoon, for

---

* See Georgetown University entry in bibliography.

his part, was a smooth-talking, ever so sophisticated, and oh so civilized ambassador, whose mission was to sell Saddam Hussein to the American media and business community. Hamdoon's success became legendary. He was all over Washington and all over the United States in the second half of the 1980s, winning over scores of journalists and businessmen to the gospel of Iraq's moderation. *Washington Post* columnist Jim Hoagland, who won a Pulitzer Prize for his coverage of Iraq, compared Hamdoon to Nazi propaganda chief Josef Goebbels. Hoagland further described the Iraqi ambassador as an "intelligence operative . . . and as good a snake-oil merchant as there is."* Hamdoon, the product of an education by American missionaries in Iraq, was labeled by *U.S. News & World Report* as Saddam's "chief influence peddler."† Wiley needed Hamdoon to do business, and Hamdoon used Wiley to sell Iraq to top U.S. corporations.

As described by *U.S. News & World Report*, Wiley's Business Forum "proved lucrative. More than seventy companies paid annual dues of between $2,500 and $5,000, and the list included corporate giants such as General Motors, Amoco, AT&T, Mobil and Westinghouse." A report in the journal *Covert Action*, "Trading with the Enemy" by Jack Calhoun, depicts how the U.S.-Iraq Business Forum, which worked closely with the State Department and the newly opened U.S. embassy in Baghdad, became a "revolving door" for retired Arabists like Wiley.‡

In an interview with the *New York Times*, Wiley denied that the Business Forum was a lobbying organization in the strict sense.§ But "we did consider it part of our mission to find out what was happening on Capitol Hill in the way of new legislation that might impinge on U.S.-Iraqi commerce and to inform our companies," who could then, Wiley indicated, lobby Congress directly. In the same interview Wiley described the Business Forum "as a mediating factor" between the American private sector and the Iraqi government.

In a public-policy sense, though, Wiley was very much a promoter of Iraqi interests. After the gassing of thousands of Kurds by Saddam Hussein's regime in mid-1988, Wiley published a letter in the *Washington Post*,

---

* Jim Hoagland, "As Good a Snake-Oil Merchant As There Is," *Washington Post*, November 13, 1990.

†Gloria Borger and Stephen J. Hedges with Douglas Stanglin, "When the Enemy Is Us," *U.S. News & World Report*, February 18, 1991.

‡*Covert Action*, 37 (Summer 1991).

§Robert D. Hershey, Jr., "Group That Promotes Ties with Iraq Feels Glum," *New York Times*, August 20, 1990.

arguing against the imposition of economic sanctions on Iraq.* The sanctions, Wiley argued, "would reduce, rather than increase, our ability to influence Iraqi behavior. Our experience with economic sanctions has clearly demonstrated that this practice has . . . increased our balance-of-payments deficits, deprived us of employment opportunities and depressed our economy . . . morality detached from reality is stupidity. The president should veto the sanctions legislation. . . ." Wiley got his wish, of course. Sanctions were never imposed. Business with Iraq flourished, and so, presumably did the Business Forum. By 1989 U.S. trade with Iraq reached $3.6 billion, a rise of 600 percent in six years, according to *U.S. News & World Report.* Iraq invaded Kuwait the following year.

In June 1989 having successfully helped clear the sanctions hurdle that had arisen after the extermination of troublesome Kurds, Wiley led a delegation of twenty-five key forum members to Baghdad. They included representatives of General Motors, Westinghouse, Hunt Oil, and Kissinger Associates, a New York–based consulting group set up by former secretary of state Henry Kissinger. This is Wiley's description of the visit:

"The Iraqi government gave the forum its official seal of approval. We had our pictures taken with [Taha Yassin] Ramadan," the minister who had decreed that anyone who did not work hard would be executed. "We also met with Saddam. He was charming, personable, with an infectious grin."

Saddam told the group, "No matter what happens with political issues between the United States and Iraq, your business interests will always be welcome."

Immediately upon his return from Baghdad, Wiley wrote a "special report" for Andy Killgore's *Washington Report on Middle East Affairs* entitled "Iraq Seeks to Expand U.S. Trade."† Wiley told the readers of Killgore's publication that the Business Forum's delegation "was received by the Iraqi president in an extended and friendly two-hour session, as part of a crowded itinerary. . . ." The forum "suggested [to the Iraqi leadership] that a restructuring of Iraq's short-term debt to a longer time frame would make its current debt-servicing problem more manageable and improve Iraq's credit standing in the eyes of U.S. leading institutions. . . . The proclivity of the U.S. Congress to impose trade sanctions for political purposes was not brought up in the course of the discussions. . . ."

---

* Marshall W. Wiley, "Sanctions Against Iraq: Let's Not Be Stupid," Letters to the Editor, *Washington Post,* August 20, 1988.

† August 1989.

Following Saddam's invasion of Kuwait in August 1990, Wiley hit the ground running. He became a periodic guest on CNN and on PBS's *Mac-Neil/Lehrer Newshour*, where he argued not only against the use of force but against a trade embargo of Iraq. "There has been too much focus on moral issues," he told CNN. On these talk shows Wiley was usually identified as a Middle East expert and a former ambassador to Oman, not by his leadership of the U.S.–Iraq Business Forum.

Wiley feels that UN inspections of Iraq's nuclear facilities were "intrusive. A lot of countries are going to have nuclear bombs anyway." He suggests that it is somewhat hypocritical to prevent Iraq from acquiring weapons that Israel already possesses. As for the now-defunct Business Forum, Wiley explains that for "five years, I argued Iraq's societal potential as the coming country in the Middle East. And it *is* the coming country, only the realization will take much longer than I originally assumed." Wiley sees himself in this regard as an idealist who was tripped up by an unfortunate military adventure by Saddam that no one could have predicted.

He is not in the least bitter, however. "I can't complain," he says. "I've had no problem getting my point of view across in the media." Wiley is trying to put all of this behind him by going back to his first and foremost love, that of pure learning. "I'm now a graduate student at Johns Hopkins University, studying for a master's in liberal arts. I'm looking into the French Enlightenment, the history of ideas—the history of history, in other words," he says, his voice full of enthusiasm.

As is well known, financial interests, the distraction provided by upheavals in Eastern Europe, and plain inertia are what propelled the Bush administration's appeasement of Iraq after the Iran-Iraq War ended and Iraq's strategic value against Shiite fundamentalism diminished. Arabists were not the only architects of this pro-Saddam policy. Moreover, as we shall see later, the analytical challenge posed by Saddam's behavior in the late 1980s caught NEA at its weakest moment in history, when bad management by non-Arabists made the give-and-take of ideas within the bureau—necessary for accurate analysis—that much more difficult. Nonetheless, the Arabists' proclivity to hide behind the actions of President George Bush, Secretary of State James Baker, and pecuniary circles like the wheat lobby, the rice lobby, and those of their own colleague Marshall Wiley, is too convenient. *We were only following orders* or *We were only small fish in a big policy-making pond* are excuses that sidestep a crucial point:

While NEA was only one player in crafting a policy of wooing Iraq, perhaps never was there a policy handed down from above with which Arabists felt so psychologically and politically comfortable. NEA, as we have seen, has a history of whining about pro-Israel policies it is forced to implement, but maintaining good relations with Saddam Hussein was one directive from the White House that not only NEA didn't whine about, but that it worked diligently to carry out and win converts to. Though Arabists like to point out how much they hated Saddam, there is no paper trail or any other tangible proof indicating that they ever directly challenged, or even questioned, the Bush administration's approach toward Saddam. Indeed, NEA promoted it. Wiley at least is honest and open about his role in helping Iraq. His opinions, moreover, are consistent. He sang the same tune both before and after the war.

Such deductions by themselves may no longer be interesting, given the amount of space and time the media has devoted to this subject. What *is* really interesting—precisely because the arguments of Arabist true believers are not totally without merit—is the psychological reasoning process by which Arabists adapted to Saddam's Iraq. Marshall Wiley was no fool; he was just unlucky. His remark about the "societal potential" of Iraq is very astute. That observation, together with Wiley's animus toward Iran and toward Israel, are important clues in a psychological reasoning process that we are now about to penetrate.

Chapter 13

Cowering in a Dark Alley

The United States never really had an Iraq policy. It had an Iran policy, and our official attitude toward Iraq through August 1990 was a product of that framework. In 1980, when William Eagleton became the head of the U.S. interests section in Baghdad, the American public was consumed with fear and loathing of the Ayatollah Khomeini's Iran, which had recently swept away the pro-American Shah and taken American diplomats in Teheran hostage.* Eagleton arrived in Baghdad just as Saddam Hussein launched a war against Iran. Think of it. Here was an FSO whose fellow FSOs were being held captive just over the border in a Persian state; a state, moreover, that the Arab country to which Eagleton had just relocated was now at war. How could Eagleton, an Arabist of the old school, not feel at least some measure of sympathy for Iraq at this moment? And such sympathy would certainly have been in keeping with U.S. interests. Saddam's frontal military assault on America's worst enemy was like an answer to our prayers. The fascist, totalitarian nature of Saddam's regime was unfortunate, and his radical posture against Israel was inconvenient, but the old adage *the enemy of my enemy is my friend* was something that could just not be ignored.

---

* Eagleton replaced Ed Peck as head of the interests section; Peck in turn had replaced Marshall Wiley when the latter left in 1977.

William Eagleton is called by his former colleague Dick Murphy "the last of the great pashas" in the State Department. "Bill always had time for another trip to the souk or into the Kurdish mountains, which he thoroughly enjoyed. He loved getting away from Washington and into the field, which is not a bad thing." Marisa Lino, a U.S. consul general in Florence, who served with Eagleton in both Iraq and Syria, explains that there are two kinds of State Department Arabists, the Washington policy type and the overseas cultural type, and that Eagleton was definitely the overseas type. Eagleton ran the U.S. mission in Baghdad from 1980 through 1984. He helped pave the way for the resumption of diplomatic relations between Iraq and the United States that occurred after his tenure. He later became the U.S. ambassador to Syria and then left the Foreign Service to work for the United Nations in Vienna on behalf of Palestinian refugees. More significant is that Eagleton is the only American diplomat with a working knowledge of both Arabic and Kurdish to have served in Iraq. If ever someone in the State Department had the mental tools to understand Iraq and where it was headed, it was—or should have been—Bill Eagleton.

Eagleton was born in 1926 in Peoria, Illinois. He attended local public schools before going to Yale, where he began to master Spanish and French. His first Foreign Service job was in Madrid. "It was through southern Spain, with its Moorish element, that I became romantically interested in the Arab world," he explains. "I requested a Middle East posting and got Damascus in 1951," a period when he befriended Carleton Coon, Jr., and attended the Beirut field school for Arabic training. From that point onward, Eagleton's overseas addresses appear more akin to those of an adventurer than to those of a diplomat: Kirkuk, in Iraqi Kurdistan; Tabriz, in northwestern Iran; Tangiers; Noukchott, Mauritania; Aden, South Yemen; Algiers; and finally Tripoli, Libya, before going to live in Baghdad.

"Read, travel, read, travel, that's the way to go," Eagleton says. "Certainly the old Victorian travel books, but also some of the modern political stuff. An Arabist is someone interested in getting deep into the culture and people of the region. Those who aren't interested in the culture don't deserve the title of Arabist." Concerning Gertrude Bell, Eagleton says, "I read all of her books. I rate her very high." Eagleton himself has authored a political history of the short-lived Kurdish Republic of Mahabad (in post–World War II Iran) and a celebrated book on Kurdish carpets.

In all of the places where Eagleton served, he was his own boss, without even the need for ambassadorial protocol—running a lonely consulate in a provincial backwater or an interests section in a radical Arab capital with which the United States did not have full diplomatic relations. When Eagleton was nominated to be ambassador to Syria in 1984, his long stints in radical countries raised eyebrows in Congress. "I had gotten into trouble because I was the messenger from bad regimes. The State Department didn't help me out much. I had to get Jewish friends from Cleveland and elsewhere to call [Senators Rudy] Boschwitz and [Howard] Metzenbaum to tell them—well, you know—that I was okay." Eagleton felt compelled to tell his visitor about his confirmation troubles, even though he hadn't been asked. Actually Eagleton's motives for passing his life in places like South Yemen, Libya, and Iraq are quite easy to fathom. At sixty-five his eyes still appeared young and full of enthusiasm: these are the eyes of a traveler who has retained a youthful disposition through a diet of constant adventure, challenge, and cultural stimulation. Eagleton, who crossed the Sahara Desert in Algeria six times, is another spiritual descendant of the early missionary-explorers.

His critics on the State Department's policy-planning staff and on the National Security Council in the early 1980s—Reagan administration appointees, for the most part—were never impressed, however. "Eagleton was a classic case," one of them says. "He didn't know how to apply his cultural and ethnographic background knowledge to political analysis. We'd laugh at his cables." Another member of the policy-planning staff, the political philosopher Francis Fukuyama, says, "I remember Eagleton as the one who always fed us horseshit about how Saddam was a potential moderate."

"Iraq is the only Arab country that has oil, water, and a sizable population," says Eagleton. "It had tremendous potential, and one good thing about these terrible regimes is that they provide education to their people. . . . I got to see Foreign Minister Tariq Aziz very often and other officials, too, but not Saddam. . . . I was always cynical about Saddam's regime. In the early eighties, though, his wider ambitions were not expressed."

In June 1981 Eagleton had to suffer the Israeli air strike against Iraq's nuclear facility near Baghdad. Such an attack, given the Iraqi belief in American-Israeli "plots," did not exactly make his job easier. Yet the Iraqis did not demand that Eagleton leave. From the Arabist point of view, Baghdad's reaction to this direct assault on its sovereignty was, by Iraq's standards, quite restrained. Even if Saddam was in an increasingly desperate military situation vis-à-vis Iran, and it was no time for him to alienate a superpower.

The very danger of Khomeini's forces overrunning Iraqi defenses, thereby threatening pro-American regimes throughout the Arab world, was what drew the United States, and the Arabists, closer to Saddam. In 1982, partly as a result of Eagleton's reporting, the Reagan administration took Iraq off the list of nations charged with sponsoring terrorism. As a result, Iraq was now considered like any other Free World nation and became eligible for high-technology items suitable for military purposes. While the facts for Saddam's supposed commitment to stop helping terrorists rested on extremely shaky ground, moderate Arab nations, including Egypt and Kuwait, urged the United States to help the Iraqi leader. By 1983 U.S. trade with Iraq was beginning to boom, and the United States was beginning to put into place a covert policy to aid the Iraqi military at the highest levels, with intelligence data garnered from spy satellites.

Even a brief visit to Iraq in this period revealed, however, that this was a nation enjoying both guns *and* butter. The overpowering physical reality was the oil-fueled construction boom, not the war. It was plain for anyone to see how Saddam was fighting only a limited war while shaking down the Gulf Arabs to pay for it. Though Khomeini's teenage troops broke through Iraqi positions here and there, they still had many miles of marshland, barbed wire, and mine fields to cross before seriously threatening Iraq. And their supply lines were nonexistent: plastic keys to paradise may a brave army make, but not the kind that pays attention to details like food and ammunition. Iranian soldiers were being found wandering around areas without bullets in their magazines. Moreover, the Iranian Shiites had no demonstrable support among the Shiites in Iraq, Kuwait, and Bahrein, who were all Arabs.

Nevertheless, Washington had groped its way toward a well-defined policy construct of helping one thuggish regime against another thuggish regime that was openly and viciously anti-American. That policy may have been ill-based and cynical, but it could be defended as making some sort of sense. And at least it *was* a policy. Besides it perfectly dovetailed with the Arabist assumption that Iraq had displaced Syria as the big player and potential spoiler in the Arab world, meaning the United States was now forced to "engage" it. This belief rested on three facts: Iraq's economic potential; Syria's recent estrangement from the Arab mainstream because of its alliance with Iran; and Iraq's leadership of the Arab rejection front as evidenced by the 1978 Baghdad conference, which had assailed Egypt's peace venture with Israel.

This was the political background music when a horrific incident occurred in Baghdad that the media, for all intents and purposes, failed to report.

In June 1983 Robert Spurling, an American engineer from Illinois who was overseeing the construction of the Novohotel in Baghdad, had arrived at Saddam International Airport with his wife and three daughters in order to fly home to the Midwest. At passport control an Iraqi official informed Spurling that there was a "small problem" with his exit visa and asked him to wait while the rest of his family proceeded to the departure lounge. After his wife and daughters passed through the barrier, Spurling was arrested as a spy for Israel and America. Iraqi officials then ordered Spurling's wife and children onto the plane without him. Somehow his wife managed to phone the U.S. interests section from the airport.

For three months the Iraqi authorities denied any knowledge of Spurling. Then in August, after persistent appeals by Eagleton and his top assistant at the embassy, Arabist Barbara K. Bodine, Iraq admitted that it was holding such-and-such a man. Eagleton's and Bodine's checks into Spurling's background revealed that the Iraqi allegations of espionage were nonsense. In October the Iraqis delivered Spurling to Eagleton's doorstep in Baghdad. "Our investigation is complete, we are releasing him," they said. Spurling had been subjected to electric-shock torture with alligator clips attached to his genitals and other sensitive points of his body. He had been beaten with weighted fists and wooden bludgeons. His fingers and toenails had been ripped out and his fingers and toes crushed. He had been kept in solitary confinement on a starvation diet. One of his torturers had told him, "If you don't confess to being a spy for Israel and America, tomorrow we're going to start cutting pieces off you." Spurling refused to confess, figuring once the Iraqis had a signed confession, that would be the end. When he didn't confess and they didn't amputate any of his limbs, he dared for the first time to hope that he might be released.

A Canadian diplomat related the whole story, all of which Eagleton confirmed, in Baghdad in March 1984, adding that Spurling had spent a week recovering at his official residence before flying back to America.

"This is a completely arbitrary system," Eagleton said then. "There are no laws, no charges filed; anything can happen. I wish I could recommend one Iraqi official who would be worth talking to, who might say something to you meaningful about his country. Unfortunately, there is no one I can think of. They're simply too scared." Eagleton said that the Iraqi security apparatus responsible for Spurling's arrest and torture was headed by Saddam's half brother, Barzan Ibrahim al-Takriti. (Barzan later became Iraq's human rights delegate in Geneva.) In this vein, Eagleton mentioned a group of Australians who were heard singing one night, "Saddam in the sky with Allah" to the tune of "Lucy in the Sky with Diamonds." "I wouldn't say they were tortured, but they were arrested and treated very severely."

Eagleton also spoke about the Kurdish mountains he often visited. He indicated that one could not comprehend the puzzle of Iraq by knowing the Arab pieces alone—an insight that was less ordinary in 1984, when he expressed it, than it is now. Yet Eagleton was enthusiastic about Arab Mesopotamia. "You should read what the British had to say about Iraq. They loved this place." Though Eagleton dutifully noted the Spurling incident in his annual human rights report, he urged his visitor to see the matter in perspective. Never before had something like that happened to a U.S. citizen here, and Eagleton implied that he had obtained a commitment from the Iraqi authorities that it never would again. "Saddam is at the tough end of the moderate Arab world," Eagleton assured his visitor in 1984. "Even when the Iran-Iraq war ends, Saddam could not return to his radical policies, because Iran will continue to be a threat, and Iraq will need help from the Gulf Arabs."

Seven years later in Washington, after the Iran-Iraq war and the war between the United States and Iraq that followed, Eagleton defended that statement. "I don't think I did anything wrong. Saddam was at the time moving precisely in the direction we wanted him to go—toward moderation. There was a period of a year back then when we had no documented evidence of Iraqi involvement in terrorism. So our policy, encouraged by [King] Fahd and [Hosni] Mubarak, reflected this. But I despised Saddam. I knew Iraq in the good old days [before the 1958 coup, which ended the monarchy]. Now I couldn't even invite my friends from the bazaar to come to my house and look at my rugs. They would have been arrested. . . .

"Saddam's megalomania just got worse and worse. We all fell into the same syndrome that the Israelis fell into prior to the 1973 war: no one could bring himself to believe that Saddam would do what he did, invade Kuwait. It was a faulty assumption."

But Eagleton, who was held in suspicion by some of Saddam Hussein's clique because of his demonstrated concern for the Kurds, and who deserves credit for Spurling's release in 1983, did not feel then that the impending resumption of relations between the United States and Iraq was worth disrupting over a single incident, however unfortunate. He needn't have worried: with Iran then cast as the demon, the Spurling affair had no obvious theme to interest the media.

An innocent American had been torn from his wife and children and tortured in the manner of a dreary, bureaucratic procedure, unconnected to any war or invasion with which the United States was involved. If appeasement was a force gathering from a variety of particulars, then the U.S. government's ability to overlook the troubling implications of what Saddam's half brother had done to this one American seems indeed seminal. *

After seventeen years during which relations were officially suspended because of the Israeli victory in the Six-Day War, the Stars and Stripes were finally raised over the banks of the Tigris in November 1984. The embassy building in Baghdad was—even more so than American embassies in other countries—like a walled fortress fitted with the latest security equipment. It was a metaphor for the life of the diplomats who worked inside. An Arab official in Iraq who was close to the American community says, "The U.S. diplomats were good and able, but they were in a sea where they couldn't swim. They were *so* limited in their contacts with Iraqis. They had no access to anyone except to flaks in the Ministry of Information and in the Foreign Ministry and to the embassy drivers, who all spied for the secret police. They were confined to the diplomatic rumor mill. A big break for them was whenever the Japanese embassy held a reception and real Iraqis came, whom the U.S. diplomats could then talk to, maybe. But because the

---

* In 1984, a year after Spurling was tortured, another American, Scott J. Nelson, was arrested and tortured so badly by Saudi officials that his knee joints snapped. Nelson, a safety monitor at a Riyadh hospital, says his offense was to have embarrassed the Saudi government by reporting safety hazards at the hospital. After lobbying from the Saudi ambassador to the United States, Prince Bandar ibn Sultan, the State Department sided with the Saudi government on this matter.

Iraqis had allowed the U.S. embassy to reopen in 1984, mentally there was a feeling among the Americans that *they had to make it work.* By providing for their physical safety, and by not getting nasty with the diplomats whenever the United States did something that Iraq didn't like, the Iraqis sort of pampered them. So the diplomats basically bought the line that Saddam was moderating."

Archie Roosevelt, the grandson of President Theodore Roosevelt and a pioneer Arabist at the Central Intelligence Agency, wrote in his memoir, *For Lust of Knowing:* "Baghdad held so many fascinations it was difficult to tear myself away, but an entire country had yet to be explored and understood. In the task I had set for myself of making a definitive study of the tribes of Iraq, I had tentatively mapped out eleven tribal areas and hoped to make eleven separate expeditions. . . ." Roosevelt goes on in that vein; his enthusiasm is catching. But it is the period of World War II he is writing of, and as he himself points out, Baghdad was then a backwater of a backwater: a supply base for the British in neighboring Iran, who were holding back the Germans and, after a fashion, the Soviets there. His activities were less a function of the need for intelligence on these tribes than of his own fascination with them and with Iraq. David Newton, a protégé of Hermann Eilts and a friend of Hume Horan, as the first U.S. ambassador to Iraq since the 1967 War, brought a similar enthusiasm to his job:

"Einstein was right," Newton tells a visitor. "Time really is the fourth dimension. If you have a strong historical knowledge of a place, you see it through different eyes. And if you really know Baghdad, you can still get a sense of the Ottoman city, but it's hard—sort of like reconstructing *homo erectus.* But I love the souks. I'm a romantic at heart. During my time in Baghdad, I used to give small groups of embassy personnel guided tours around the city. One of the appeals of Iraq is that it's so distinctive. Once you're there, you can't be anywhere else. It's a reality that's not quite Persian or Turkish or even Arabian."

Newton laments that "the world is being deromanticized, many diplomatic staff have no particular interest in the region they cover. In the old days, our people in Iraq would take R and R in northern Syria to see an archaeological site. Nowadays people just go home for their vacations."

Like Eagleton before him, Newton combined a romantic interest in Iraq that, it must be said, in no way blinded him toward its horrors. These two men were quite willing to be sources for the few journalists who happened to show up in Baghdad to write about the regime's brutalities. When I first met Newton in the Iraqi capital in August 1986, another foreigner—Ian Richter, a British businessman—had just been arrested by the Iraqis on trumped-up charges. "This is the most terrified population in the Arab world," Newton had said. "If the security services somehow get it into their heads that you've done something, there's not much any of us can do to help."

It was during that same, second visit to Iraq that I had my own brush with Iraq's regime-induced paranoia. I had been granted a visa to travel with a group of pro-Saddam Kurds in the north who held territory over the border in Iran. But upon introducing me to my Kurdish hosts, Iraqi security men confiscated my passport. I did not see it again until two weeks later when, in a car stuffed with the same morose-looking security men, it was handed back to me en route to the airport. In Iraq you really were on your own in a dark alley. The men with the switchblades were in total control. The rest, including the foreign diplomats and businessmen, were either cowering in the corners or paying some form of protection in order to keep their lucrative enterprises going. Robert Spurling, Ian Richter, and the other foreign nationals in Iraq who were detained, held for a time in the uncharted hell of the Iraqi prison system, and occasionally murdered—like a South Korean and some others from Asian and Third World countries whose governments dare not criticize Iraq—were, in fact, hostages. But because Saddam, unlike the Shiite kidnappers in south Beirut, ruled a member state of the United Nations that was borrowing hundreds of millions of dollars from the West and had billions of dollars in oil and construction contracts to offer, the word *hostage* was never used. A conspiracy of silence surrounded the foreign community in Baghdad in the 1980s. When the name Spurling or Richter was mentioned, people just shrugged their shoulders and raised their eyebrows as if to say, *What can you do? It's one of the risks you take doing business in this creepy country where there is a lot of money to make and very few taxes to pay.* Here even someone with an American passport could be pushed down a hole in time and be ground up by the moving steel teeth of Tiglathpileser or Sennacherib. And who would notice?

But Western diplomats did not have to live with these stomach-churning fears. They inhabited a privileged and airtight security bubble in which the worst thing that could happen to them, even if they were caught spying, was to be detained for a short time by the police in a civilized fashion and then expelled. Saddam made certain that Iraq was the safest place in the Arab world for American FSOs. Unlike FSOs in less repressive regimes—Egypt, for example—FSOs in Iraq didn't have to take different routes to work out of fear of being assassinated by some radical group seeking to embarrass the host government. While fundamentalist Iran was revolutionary and therefore chaotic—a situation that allowed for its own breathing space—Iraq was like a huge prison yard where nobody operated without orders from Saddam. From the standpoint of personal security, this was a godsend for FSOs. "There was unspoken synergy between the regime and the American diplomats. For the diplomats Saddam was the only alternative to chaos," says an Arab observer in Iraq at the time.

The arms-for-hostages affair, in which the Reagan administration sold weapons to Khomeini in return for the release of Western captives in Lebanon (Ben Weir, for one), came to light in November 1986, halfway through Newton's tenure as ambassador. Its result was to move the Arabist community closer to Saddam Hussein. "Scratch an Arabist and you'll find an anti-Iranian," went the saying.

Arabists saw arms-for-hostages and the related Iran-Contra scandal as attempts by pro-Israel elements of the Reagan administration—particularly the former national security adviser, Robert C. McFarlane, and his assistant, Howard R. Teicher—to help non-Arab Iran in its war against Arab Iraq. As anti-Jewish as Khomeini's regime was, in strategic terms its war against the largest standing army in the Arab world was clearly beneficial to Israel. NEA felt that its efforts to engage Iraq had been seriously sabotaged by the likes of McFarlane and Teicher, who, in the Arabists' view, had an anti-Arab agenda.

The arms-for-hostages scandal, together with the heavy battlefield losses inflicted by Iran on Saddam's troops in early 1987, caused FSOs in Baghdad to fear anti-American demonstrations and the expulsion of U.S. diplomats. But it didn't happen. Moreover, when a U.S. military attaché, Colonel Marc B. Powe, was caught taking photographs of an Iraqi arms convoy, though the Iraqis expelled him, they quickly allowed the United

States to send a new attaché to Baghdad.* The U.S. diplomats in Baghdad thus were inclined to see Saddam in the best possible light. So in March 1988, when Saddam gassed five thousand Kurds in the village of Halabja on the Iraq-Iran border, the embassy's reporting sought to put the incident into "perspective."

In the wake of America's own war with Iraq, Ambassador David Newton was asked to discuss what, exactly, he thought he had been accomplishing in Baghdad.

By 1991 Newton had become the international affairs adviser at the National War College in Washington, his spacious office in a domed brick building bordered by a golf green, the Washington Channel, and the Anacostia River. These comfortable surroundings made one realize how ridiculous the notion is that Arabists have fallen on hard times owing to the debacle in Iraq. Newton, born in 1936, is a dapper man with a trim moustache. He has years of firsthand experience in five Arab countries, in addition to fluency in Arabic and German. This kind of man, unlike so many of the policy mavens who crowd Washington, has tangible assets that lose little of their market value because of this or that failure in prognostication. Arabists are like doctors and lawyers: you can be angry with them, but you will always have a need for their skills. During the war with Kuwait, Newton acted as an adviser to the Pentagon.

Like Hume Horan, Dick Murphy, Michael Sterner, Roy Atherton, and the two Carleton Coons, Newton went to Harvard. "But I was a local Irish boy who worked my way through as a commuter," he hastens to add. "I was a bookworm as a kid. By eleven I wanted to be an archaeologist, because of a fascination with ancient Egypt." Like Horan, Newton was hooked permanently on the Near East by Sir Hamilton Gibb, "a wonderful Orientalist," whose lectures Newton attended at Harvard. Newton is another one of those deeply sensitive, scholarly types who has visited Israel often, has met with people like Shimon Peres, and is genuinely troubled by the notion that just because someone is interested in Arabs, he is therefore, at some level, assumed to be anti-Jewish. Among Newton's favorite Arab-

---

* He was Colonel David L. Lemon, who arrived in Iraq in April 1987.

ists is Leopold Weiss, an Orthodox Polish Jew, who went to Arabia as a journalist in the 1920s and converted to Islam, adopting the name of Muhammad Asad. Asad (Weiss) rose to become an adviser to Saudi king Ibn Saud and a deputy foreign minister of Pakistan, whose Islamic constitution he helped write.* Newton extols Asad's spiritual and sensualistic panegyric about life in the open desert, *The Road to Mecca,* as a book by a Westerner that allows you to glimpse "so much of what evaporates when you translate" Arabic and the Arab experience into English. Newton was not the first Arabist this writer met who talked of what is lost in translation, of experience that can't be transmitted.

Prominently displayed in Newton's office are color photos of himself and April Glaspie—his successor as the U.S. ambassador to Iraq—in the presidential palace in Baghdad, both smiling as they introduced Saddam and Iraqi foreign minister Tariq Aziz to a congressional delegation led by Senators Robert Dole and Alan K. Simpson. This was the occasion, a few months before the Iraqi invasion of Kuwait, when Dole and Simpson apologized to Saddam for Voice of America broadcasts critical of his regime. "I keep these photos in the office as a teaching device: they fascinate my students," says Newton. Newton seems to be a man completely at peace with himself, who talks easily and honestly about his mistakes.

"Saddam put a lot of emphasis on nation building and the Westernization of the economy, which was popular. Because he had everybody scared, one would have thought that there was no reason for excess brutality. Obviously, the gassing of the Kurds [in March of 1988] affected my view. We worked on intuition, with very few sources. We never really knew what was going on. There were only the rumors, what we called 'the souk-telegraph.'"

"After the Kurds were gassed, why didn't you just pull out, close the embassy?" he was asked, allusion being made to a conversation some years before with Robert Keeley, an ambassador to Greece who later became president of the Middle East Institute in Washington. Keeley shut the U.S. embassy in Uganda at the time of Idi Amin's reign of terror. Keeley explained, "You maintain a diplomatic presence so long as you're effective. But in Uganda there came a point when we really were no longer able to

---

* Asad was one of a band of eminent Jewish Arabists that included Francis Turner Palgrave and Ignaz Goldziher. Palgrave, whose grandfather was one Meyer Cohen, a London stockbroker, was a rival of Richard Burton's in Arabian exploration of the mid-nineteenth century. Goldziher, of Hungarian Jewish descent, wrote many volumes on Orientalism around the turn of the century.

have an effect. To be true to our own values, the only thing we could do was to leave, and scream about Amin from the outside."

Newton replies, "That made sense for Uganda"—a land-locked country of no strategic or economic importance to the United States. "But it's naive to think you can just pull out of a militarily powerful and oil-rich developing country on the Gulf with which American companies were doing hundreds of millions of dollars of trade." What might have been accomplished in Iraq, according to Newton, was that, over time and with U.S. help, "Iraq's level of repression could have been improved to that of Syria."

Arabist bashers could have a lot of fun with that statement, reeking as it seems to of moral relativism. But it needs explaining. Despite several visits to Syria, I was shocked the first time I arrived in Iraq. In Damascus I could walk into the telex room of the post office and punch out a story unsupervised. In Baghdad plate glass separated me from the telex machines. Copy was handed to an Iraqi on the other side of the window, and that was that. I could travel wherever I wanted to in Syria; trying to do that in Iraq would have landed me in prison. Going to Syria from Iraq was like coming up for air. Making a Syria out of an Iraq would be a minor human rights miracle. "But appreciating this," notes Peter Bechtold, who runs the Middle East area-studies program at the Foreign Service Institute, "requires a frame of reference based on travel experience that not only most Americans lack, but so do people on the National Security Council."*

"Frame of reference" is the clue to understanding the behavior of Newton and his colleagues in Iraq. Not only, as Newton says, does knowledge of local history allow you to see a place differently, but, obviously, so does actually living there. And living in Baghdad lays bare a second reality besides the one of the prison yard and the torture chamber: the reality of an urban, essentially middle-class culture crying out silently to the West. For in no other densely populated zone of the Arab world is Islam so downplayed and literacy so widespread as in Iraq. This urbanization has not come about through the destabilizing migration of peasants into the big cities, as has occurred in Iran and Egypt—although it is true that Iraq *is* unstable: because its relatively efficient and well-educated people live in crowded conditions and are riven by tribal and national feuds, extreme

---

* This was Talcott Seelye's point when he complained of the inability of policy-planning staffers like Francis Fukuyama to understand the complexity of the situation in Syria.

levels of repression have been required to hold the country together. Yet the promise of an Arab state empowered by its middle class, and thus truly modern, has always been there; it is what attracted the British and, afterward, Americans such as Marshall Wiley. As far back as the beginning of this century, David Hogarth, the academic father-figure of Lawrence and Bell, felt that "the force of economic gravity in the great plain-land of South-West Asia" must "inevitably . . . swing round" to Mesopotamia, whose industrial and agricultural potential remains unrivaled in the Middle East.* Even Howard Teicher, no friend of Baathist Iraq, admits: "In the Arab world, Iraq has the biggest abstract potential for social modernization and democratization."

It was this same ever-present pageant of secular urbanism, so much more visible and dynamic than in other Arab countries, that formed the ground upon which American diplomats placed their hopes, theorizing that whatever the gruesome brutalities of the regime, the societal reality would eventually have to overcome that which the regime tried to impose on it. One just needed to be patient and work in the interstices until that day dawned.

Take the story of Jack McCreary, Newton's press and culture officer at the embassy: a self-described child of the sixties, who had spent nearly two decades of his life in the Arab world, Jack McCreary experienced a moment of true satisfaction when in January 1988 he opened the doors of the new American cultural center on Mansour Street in Baghdad for the first time. *At last,* McCreary thought, *there was one place under Saddam Hussein's rule where ordinary Iraqis and Americans could talk to each other in the same room and the Iraqis could encounter our cultural values.* "The great thing about living for long stretches in an awful country," he says, "is that the smallest victory, no matter how pathetic and inconsequential, gives you an incredibly big boost."

Life in Baghdad for McCreary, his wife, Carol, and their daughters, Kate and Joanna, was made up of many such boosts. If anyone could squeeze a little water from an ugly regime's monolithic stone, it was he.

After graduating from the University of California at Berkeley in 1968, McCreary entered the Peace Corps, serving in Marrakech, Morocco, where he and Carol met and were married. At the American University of Cairo, McCreary perfected his Arabic. He then joined the U.S. Foreign Service, working as a political officer at American embassies in Qatar, Saudi Arabia,

---

* See Winstone entry in the bibliography.

and Yemen. McCreary, who plays jazz saxophone and loves slashing across the Arabian desert in his four-wheel drive Isuzu Trooper and chewing *qat* (a mildly stimulating, caffeinelike leaf) with native Yemenis, was becoming frustrated. Doing his job properly meant immersing himself in Arabic with Arabs, he felt. "I still marvel at the physical beauty of Arabic script. I'm shocked at people who come to Arab countries and can't read the signs." But Yemen, like Qatar and Saudi Arabia, was politically closed and sterile. Embassy officers were denied regular contact with official Yemenis. Mc-Creary, who has a 4-plus rating in Arabic out of a Foreign Service test scale of 5—meaning he speaks and reads Arabic fluently—was meeting nobody except other foreign diplomats. So he gave up the job of political officer in order to run the embassy's press and culture division. Careerwise, this was an unorthodox move. But McCreary's life changed. "Suddenly I was with Yemenis all the time."

"It's the embassy cultural officers who get the real internist's-eye view of a difficult country," observes Hume Horan. "They have fewer restrictions placed on their movements. Since Arab writers and artists are in a terrible financial situation and nobody cares about their work, they come cheap: for the price of a meal and a bit of appreciation, they'll pour their souls out to you, providing the kind of psychological clues to the workings of a system that a political officer will never get from his Foreign Ministry contacts."

In the summer of 1987, after finishing his assignment in Yemen, Mc-Creary was posted to Iraq. "On a strictly political level, nothing was happening," McCreary explains. "The embassy people knew nobody at the palace. We had no access to the Baath party. We'd invite Iraqis to receptions, and they were too frightened to show up. For us to claim we knew Baghdad would have been like a Third World diplomat claiming to know Washington because there was one desk officer at the State Department who returned his phone calls. But on the cultural level in Iraq, there was tremendous hope."

Western secular culture was a bone that Saddam tossed to his affluent urban subjects. Baghdad, alone among Arab capitals, offered classical piano and violin recitals and a degree program in European music. McCreary's daughters took ballet lessons at an Iraqi government school. McCreary became involved in a jazz club, *Al-Ghareeb* (The Stranger), in downtown Baghdad, where he played the saxophone and Joseph Wilson, the embassy's DCM, sang, while McCreary's daughter Kate—along with a crowd of Iraqi artists—drew charcoal sketches of the performances. "It was a marvelous place: jazz at night, me playing, Kate and the Iraqis drawing away. From the point of view of my job, the Iraqis' interest in classical music and jazz was certainly to be encouraged."

The jazz club and his daughters' ballet lessons brought McCreary and his wife rare entrée to the homes of numerous Iraqi families. "It was an artsy-fartsy crowd of ancien régime types and politically neutered intellectuals. Carol and I worked constantly to give these people a sense of American values, to demonstrate how free people think and behave: to show them it was *possible*. But they were cowed. The big crisis in one family was the teenage daughter, whose beauty had attracted one of Saddam's Takriti goons. The family had carefully worked out a plan to get her out of the country in case she was compromised."

The U.S. Information Service (USIS) helped arrange for an American singer, Billy Stephens, to give a concert in Baghdad. Stephens sang "We shall Overcome" and John Lennon's "Imagine." But when the singer asked the crowd of English-speaking Iraqis to join in, there was silence. "Nobody dared," Carol McCreary lamented.

"But there was such hope, things really were getting better," Carol pleads to their visitor over dinner in their Washington area home. She heatedly describes the lifting of internal travel restrictions after the Iran-Iraq war ended, the end of bread and butter rationing, and how "a whole nest of little safety valves was opening, one by one." Carol, Jack, and the rest of the American diplomatic community in Baghdad assumed there was a tantalizingly thin wedge of opportunity they could exploit and operate inside of, especially in the wake of the December 1989 revolution in Romania. *Maybe it could happen here.* They all knew it wasn't much of a hope, but it was enough to keep them going.

Jack McCreary falls silent, then says: "Of course, considering all that has happened, this must sound silly to you. I'm embarrassed to talk about it. They were building chemical and nuclear weapons while they let a few diplomats open a library and play in a jazz club. It all seems so stupid and misguided."

The McCrearys, whom a right-wing observer might be tempted to ridicule as liberal, multicultural Peace Corps types, had in fact tested a canon of neoconservative interventionism—the export of democracy—on a deeply personal level under the worst possible conditions, and they have the emotional scars to prove it.

William Rugh, an ambassador to Yemen and to the United Arab Emirates, as well as a protégé of Hermann Eilts in Saudi Arabia, remembers journeying to Iraq in the spring of 1990 to help inaugurate an English program at the new cultural center. "While the very opening of the center was a sign of hope, the terrified atmosphere among the Iraqi students reminded me just how far away Iraq was [psychologically]. And on the next night Saddam gave that shocking and abhorrent speech about burning half of Israel. But at the same time, we were working at a different level"—the cultural level, Rugh means, in a valiant attempt to infuse a few individual Iraqis with the ideal of freedom.

To be sure, for Newton, McCreary, and the others the sheer professional (and in some cases, romantic) excitement of living and working in a core Arabist country provided an incalculable motive for investing one's tour with a high goal. By the time this enthusiasm wore thin, giving way to cynicism, the diplomat's tour had expired, and a replacement arrived bearing a fresh supply of idealism. Competition for a posting in Baghdad was always intense.

Norman Anderson, an Arabist who served in Morocco, Lebanon, and Tunisia and also as ambassador in Sudan after Hume Horan, makes this observation relevant to his colleagues in Iraq: "There is not enough posting continuity in the Middle East, because with so many embassies in Arabic-speaking countries, it is rare for a diplomat to go to the same place twice." Those Soviet experts of yore—Loy Henderson, George Kennan, and Charles Bohlen—"were able to be on target regarding Stalin because they each had several tours of duty in the Soviet Union, the only place where Russian is spoken." But Arabists rarely went back to Baghdad a second time, and even then the tours were too short. Though this situation was ameliorated by "lateral cable traffic," whereby reports from the Baghdad embassy were sent for review and comment to Arabists with earlier experience in Iraq, one was nevertheless reminded of something that had occurred in Vietnam: because every ambitious officer wanted time in a combat zone, they all got twelve-month tours, and in the process little institutional memory was accumulated on the battlefield.

Some Arabists argue that the closed and totalitarian nature of the Saddam thugocracy made assessments of it problematic. Chas Freeman, the ambassador to Saudi Arabia during the Gulf War, disagrees. "Area expertise means sufficient understanding of a language and a local reasoning process in order to put yourself in the position of a decision maker in that society and make a fairly accurate prediction about what he will do. If the number of decision makers is limited, then you actually have a better statistical chance of predicting the future, because all your analytical energies can be focused on one individual: Saddam."

But the succession of embassy staffs in Baghdad, impressed, like the British, by the awesome human and economic potential of Iraq, were not thinking coldly enough about the bloodstained ruler of the country.

At least through the tenures of Bill Eagleton and David Newton in Baghdad, the Arabists were operating within the well-defined policy construct of helping one awful regime against another that was far more anti-American than Iraq's was. Even in March 1988, when Saddam gassed five thousand Kurds at Halabja, there was still a measure of ambiguity, albeit minute, regarding his intentions. After all, the Iraqis had been using poison gas against invading Iranian troops for much of the war. One might still have argued that Halabja was in a border zone where Iranian troops had recently encamped. Thus, it was not completely clear whether the gas attack was deliberately meant for Kurdish civilians or whether the civilians might have been mistaken for Iranians.

On August 20, 1988, however, a cease-fire was declared in the Iran-Iraq war. Saddam Hussein was suddenly less of a weapon against the Iranian ayatollahs. Five days later, Iraq launched gas attacks against Kurds in northern Iraq that drove thousands of Kurdish civilians over the border as refugees into Turkey. Unlike the incident at Halabja a few months before, these outrages did not occur in the maelstrom of war but were unmistakably designed to kill innocents. Now was the time to begin a vigorous reassessment of the U.S. tilt toward Iraq, especially since a new administration was entering the White House and a new ambassador was about to be dispatched to Baghdad.

But an honest policy review was never to take place. It was April Glaspie's fate that she succeeded David Newton as ambassador at a time when there was more drift than actual policy. And so, as in the days of Her Majesty's colonial administration—when British Arabists such as Gertrude Bell were a law unto themselves—the area specialists were left to occupy the vacuum with their own goals and justifications for being in the awful country they were in.

Chapter 14

Hostages to Idealism

Iraq certainly has a way of conferring fame on unmarried female Arabists. But let it be known that April Glaspie is in a league entirely different from that of Gertrude Bell and Freya Stark. They, despite their impressive knowledge, were essentially amateurs whose leisure time, the result of inherited wealth, allowed for the development of their personalities in exotic climes. Glaspie is the polar opposite: the consummate professional and "Washington-type" Arabist, a workaholic upper-echelon bureaucrat rather than a grand lady. In an interview conducted in August 1983 in Damascus, where she was the political counselor, she appeared driven, somewhat cynical, and yet not without hope. "The Syrian economy," she said, "is the typical socialist disaster. If the regime would just let its population alone to make money without the controls . . . There's really nothing dramatic going on here, no grounds for a lot of optimism, but," shaking her head like a remonstrating parent, "we try." Bernard Johns, a retired black FSO, who recalls exhibitions of prejudice by other Arabists, remembers Miss Glaspie as a true friend, free of any such biases. "When you got to know April, you had to like her and respect her. She was that kind of person."

She was also a quirky person: a middle-aged woman who wore pigtails, and little or no makeup and had a high-pitched laugh. Hers was a personality with sharp edges.

April Catherine Glaspie was born in April 1942 in Vancouver, Canada. She graduated from Mills College in California and got an M.A. from Johns Hopkins University in 1965. The following year she joined the Foreign Service and was posted to Amman, Jordan, beginning a life consumed by an interest in the Arab world, where she frequently brought her mother to live with her. From 1967 to 1969, she served in Kuwait. In 1972 she was attending the field school in Beirut, learning Arabic. In 1973 she went off to Cairo as a political officer, where she attracted the attention of Henry Kissinger, then engaged in his first rounds of shuttle diplomacy. This was just before the United States reestablished diplomatic relations with Egypt, and America's diplomatic staff was consequently skeletal. Glaspie did everything from finding a quick-service laundry operation for members of Kissinger's delegation to dealing with consular matters to analyzing Egyptian political trends. Glaspie was a bundle of energy and enthusiasm. "April is fun," explains a colleague of hers. "She's effervescent, bubbly, unlike so many of the dry, New England types of Arabists. So the Arabs liked her, and she became enormously successful [in Egypt and later in Syria] in getting information and concessions out of them." Indeed, Glaspie went on to win the State Department Director General's Award for diplomatic reporting out of Egypt. When Hermann Eilts arrived in Cairo to take up his duties as ambassador at the end of 1973, he too became impressed with Glaspie, who he told a visiting journalist would one day become an ambassador. But fifteen years later, when Glaspie was named ambassador to Iraq, Eilts was less certain. True, in his mind, she had been among the best cable writers and reporters of the Arab street scene he had known. She was also, however, just a bit too enthusiastic and earnest about what she was reporting about. Not only Eilts but Nick Veliotes, among others, draws the picture of a person who, to put it in journalistic terms, while a star wire-service reporter, lacked the shrewd and seasoned skepticism of a good editor.

After four years in Cairo, Glaspie became a staff assistant to NEA assistant secretaries Roy Atherton and Hal Saunders. Then she went to London, where the U.S. embassy always had one political officer working exclusively on Arab affairs. In 1980 came a tour at the United Nations, followed by two years in Tunisia, where she ran the Arabic language field school for FSOs. In 1983, upon completion of that assignment, came her posting to Damascus, where she was political counselor to Bob Paganelli and then DCM to Bill Eagleton, after he had left Baghdad to succeed

Paganelli as ambassador to Syria. From 1985 until she became ambassador to Iraq, Glaspie was the director of the office of Jordanian, Lebanese, and Syrian affairs in the State Department, a job where one's personal views on such litmus-test issues as terrorism and the Arab-Israeli conflict simply could not be hidden.

The above résumé reveals a successful and ambitious career woman, who was effective with Arabs and had the commendations to prove it. Besides the reporting award for work in Egypt, Glaspie was to garner Distinguished Honor and Superior Honor awards for work in Syrian and Lebanese affairs. Secretary of State George Shultz calls Glaspie "a genuine heroine" for getting the Syrians to help release American hostages.

Glaspie was also several other things that seem contradictory but really aren't: she was both a feminist trailblazer and among the last of the old-boy Arabists in NEA. Her posting to Kuwait in 1967 marked the first time a woman was assigned to serve in Araby, and her appointment as ambassador to Iraq in 1988 marked the first time a woman was named ambassador to an Arab country. By 1988, however, she was also one of the few Arabists in NEA still left from before the 1967 war, when embassy closures had ended many a career. One of the ways she proved herself as a woman back then was to be twice as much of an old boy as the real old boys. Though on a human level, as Bernard Johns observes, Glaspie was free of biases, on a political level her opinions were very much of the Arabist old school. While a woman, she was definitely not a "modern." To wit, one of her closest allies was Bill Eagleton, a man unpopular among some Arabists in NEA, who considered him "one of the worst of the apologists" for radical Arabs.

But unlike the bird-watchers, April Glaspie—partly, perhaps, because she was single and ambitious and thus modern at least in a life-style sense—was very much at home in the world of Washington bureaucratic maneuvering. Wandering off into the Kurdish hill country to collect carpets, one of Eagleton's favorite pastimes, was definitely not for her. Glaspie was a "formidable" presence at NEA. "April has never been involved in any issue where she was not a policy driver," says a former colleague who knows her well. "She was dynamic and aggressive and supremely confident. April dominated issues. It was just not in her character to be a passive ambassador implementing a policy she did not fully agree with." Rather just the opposite: in NEA circles you tend to hear stories about how Glaspie "walked all over people."

Glaspie's talents at bureaucratic infighting were most severely tested while she was the office director for Jordan, Syria, and Lebanon in the mid-1980s, when she waged an ongoing struggle against State's counter-terrorism office over how and whether to punish Syria for its links with Palestinian terrorists. In 1986 British and Israeli intelligence officers caught an Arab terrorist, Nizar Hindawi, attempting to smuggle a bomb aboard an El Al jetliner at London's Heathrow Airport, using the suitcase of his un-suspecting pregnant girlfriend. Electronic eavesdropping revealed that Hindawi had been receiving orders through the Syrian embassy, whose ambassador was subsequently expelled. The European Community took the highly unusual step of imposing sanctions on Syria before even the United States did. "April and [Ambassador to Syria] Bill Eagleton were violently opposed to a tough American reaction," says a colleague. "I re-member violent discussions with them. April Glaspie was much more pro-tective of radical Arabs than our policy justified." One source describes the policy dispute between Glaspie's Jordan, Syria, and Lebanon division and State's counterterrorism people as a bureaucratic "guerrilla war." Another source says, "that's putting it mildly. It's more like the two sides were lobbing mortar shells at each other at point-blank range." Not only the counterterrorism people, but also those on the policy-planning staff were absolutely outraged at Glaspie and Eagleton for trying to undermine the European Community's tough stand against Syria just when the Commu-nity was showing some backbone in standing up to Arab terrorism.

This was also when Glaspie's reputation for "shaving" opinions came into its own. As one NEA source explains: "A good staff person is supposed to be the best advocate for each competing side, in order to present his or her superior with the fairest range of options. In other words, a good memo would argue the pro side as effectively as the anti side. But April didn't do that."

In September of 1987, when the State Department had submitted Glaspie's name to the White House and Congress for approval as the next ambassador to Iraq, some members of the Senate Foreign Relations Com-mittee had not been pleased. True, her résumé was impressive. But as one former Senate staff member says, Iraq in 1987 was the only Arab country fighting a major war, and it had the most brutal and difficult regime in the Arab world, and yet the State Department was "pushing hard" a nominee who had never before been tested as an ambassador—for a job where, as another Senate staffer now puts it, "one's reporting skills are less important than one's *representing* skills."

Glaspie's reputation for being too sympathetic to Arab radicals did not help her. Another irritating factor was that at roughly the same time that Glaspie's name was submitted, the State Department had asked Congress to confirm Robert H. Pelletreau, Jr., as ambassador to Tunisia. Pelletreau was extremely popular in Washington. A former Arabist ambassador to Bahrein who had also worked at the Defense Department, Pelletreau had firsthand experience in dealing with Israelis as well as with Arabs and had a reputation for being bold, analytical, and tough as nails. "We felt Glaspie should have gone to Tunisia, a less challenging post, to gain ambassadorial experience," says a Senate source, "and Pelletreau should have gone to Iraq. He was the perfect person for dealing with Saddam."*

There was something else, though, about April Glaspie that bothered not just the Senate staffers but other Arabists besides. This was something so sensitive that people profusely apologized to this writer for what they were about to say, then spoke in whispers on the subject. The whispers always began with a phrase like *of course I'm no Neanderthal or male chauvinist, but . . .* and then would come a comment like *you don't send a woman to a place like Iraq to deal with a fellow like Saddam Hussein.* One Arabist old-timer was more quaint, "Iraq is no place for a gal."

As retrograde as these comments might seem, there is a serious point here. The unofficial but oft-spoken rationale for nominating a woman to represent the United States in Baghdad was that Iraq's secular modernism under Saddam Hussein made it an appropriate place for the first female ambassador in the Arab world. But these Senate staffers and State Department Arabists labeled such logic the epitome of social science *bull,* abstraction and naïveté. The telling fact about Saddam, more so than his "secular modernism," was that he was a Bedouin thug surrounded by other Hollywood uglies who ran a military state the way a mafia gang runs a neighborhood. And however good it made us feel about nominating a woman, Saddam merely saw the appointment as a sign of U.S. weakness. There was a distinct feeling that Glaspie's nomination was being pushed not because she was the best and most appropriate candidate for the job—which she wasn't—but "because of pressure to nominate a woman to a major ambassadorial post." One NEA hand says bluntly, "If you're willing to go beyond political correctness, it's possible to say that the United States fought a war

---

* As it turned out, Pelletreau became the U.S. government's sole interface for conducting talks with the PLO while ambassador to Tunisia. Later he became ambassador to Egypt.

because of affirmative action." Another Arabist says, "I wouldn't have had a problem with a really tough and professional woman like Jane Coon, but I always felt Glaspie was just too—I don't know how else to put this— romantic when it came to dealing with Arabs."*

As it turned out, the Senate committee held up Glaspie's nomination for six months before confirming her. "A few people were uneasy about the choice," a staff member says. "But there was no smoking gun."

By the time April Glaspie was ensconced in Baghdad in early 1989, George Bush had been sworn in as president, James Baker had taken over as secretary of state, and John H. Kelly had replaced Dick Murphy as the NEA assistant secretary.

"John Kelly," snaps Hermann Eilts: "a disgrace, the worst assistant secretary in the living memory of NEA." Eilts has a lot of company in that assessment. Many of the comments made about Kelly to this writer are unprintable. Kelly was the Frankenstein monster unwittingly created by Jim Baker and Baker's powerful director of the policy-planning staff, Dennis Ross, who latched onto Kelly only after learning that several other nominees could not be confirmed on Capitol Hill. (For instance, Frank Wisner, Baker and Ross's first choice, was disliked by Jesse Helms.)

Jim Baker, to an even greater degree than Henry Kissinger, came into the State Department in January 1989 with guns blazing. He and a group of operatives, including Ross, took complete control of State's bureaucratic machinery, forming a narrow, canalized chain of command that made the Kissinger regime at the State Department look positively democratic. Chas Freeman, who worked with Kissinger on his China expeditions and was ambassador to Saudi Arabia when Saddam invaded Kuwait, explains: "Kissinger quickly acquired the talent to dig into the bowels of the bureaucracy while circumventing senior officials, in order to suck out the bank of information the area experts represented." But Baker, Freeman and others imply, had even less interest in the Arabists and other area specialists than did Kissinger. Baker never felt comfortable with them to the degree that

---

* Jane Coon, the wife of Carleton Coon, Jr., was ambassador to Bangladesh and enjoyed a high reputation in the Foreign Service.

even Kissinger could. In particular, Dennis Ross, a superbly gifted policy wonk who traveled in pro-Israel, neoconservative circles, took a dim view of NEA. And having seen NEA assistant secretary Nick Veliotes run bureaucratic rings around other branches of government at the beginning of the Reagan era, Ross and Baker had no intention of permitting someone as formidable as Veliotes or Dick Murphy to run NEA under them. So Baker and Ross fulfilled a Jewish lobbyist's dream, even if the Jewish lobby was never to be grateful to them for it: they emasculated the State Department Arabists by running Arab-Israeli affairs directly through the policy-planning staff—which Ross headed—rather than through NEA.

An explanation is in order: the policy-planning staff, as its name implies, plans policy based on a long-range approach to overseas developments. Because the "line bureaus" (NEA, African affairs, Latin American affairs, etc.) to which diplomats in the field report are concerned with day-to-day matters, the view of NEA on a given issue is often at odds with that of the planning staff. It's like the difference between the rushed dispatches of war correspondents and the more theoretical analysis found in quarterly magazines. The planning staff thus evolved over the decades into an instrument for providing the secretary of state with a second opinion. This was never so much the case as at the start of the Reagan years, when neoconservative intellectuals like Francis Fukuyama and Daniel Pipes sat on the planning staff and old hands like Talcott Seelye and Bill Eagleton were in the field. Because the planning staff draws the political appointees, who usually leave government after a few years, it lacks the bureaucratic staying power of NEA and, therefore, historically has had less influence. Said one former planning staff member, a Reagan political appointee, "I didn't feel that I was part of the State Department so much as I was in some halfway house between government and the university."

Baker and Ross dramatically overturned this arrangement. They did it by appointing John Kelly, a man they could control because he knew little more about the Middle East than they did.

On the surface Kelly might have seemed an inspired choice to them. He wasn't an Arabist: except for a short stint as Ambassador to the Maronite Christian enclave of Lebanon, Kelly had no experience whatsoever in the Middle East. He was a Europeanist, known to be an intellectual and a quick study, someone with whom Ross, a Soviet expert, could identify. Moreover, nothing in Kelly's background indicated the kind of bureaucratic talent that, say, a Joe Sisco, another nonexpert, was able to muster; meaning Kelly could be relied on to be a weak adversary to the planning staff.

As a former ambassador to the Maronite enclave in Lebanon (the only part of Lebanon where in the late-1980s it was safe for U.S. diplomats to operate), Kelly came into the bureau with one strike against him. Traditional Arabist hatred of the Maronites had roots going back over a century to the early missionaries. While criticism of Jews was highly unacceptable in NEA circles by the late 1980s, vocal dislike of the Maronites knew no bounds and carried no such penalties. Moreover, in East Beirut Kelly was tangentially involved in the arms-for-hostages affair. (He had used a CIA backchannel to communicate over the head of Secretary of State George Shultz directly to the Reagan White House about hostage releases.) But these were minor matters, easily forgotten, had Kelly demonstrated the slightest ability to rally the troops when he assumed command of NEA. Instead, he exhibited a terrible temper and an unbridled paranoia that nobody, not even those who appointed him, ever quite knew he had. Kelly's reign at NEA began with the "Friday Afternoon Massacre." He axed a deputy assistant NEA secretary, Ned Walker, a first-rate Arabist with experience in both Israel and the Arab world, and brought in David Macke, another well-regarded Arabist, but someone who had a reputation for not standing his ground and arguing policy positions. And as his top deputy, Kelly brought in James "Jock" Covey, whose experience cast him as an "Arab-Israeli *wallah*" with no serious background in inter-Arab or Gulf affairs. Covey, whose reputation was as a "political operator" rather than an area specialist, was to become an ally of Kelly against the rest of the bureau. The only truly positive change that Kelly made was the one on which Ross insisted. Kelly brought in Daniel Kurtzer as a deputy assistant secretary to deal exclusively with Arab-Israeli matters. Kurtzer, an Orthodox Jew and former dean at Yeshiva University in New York, was a protégé of Hermann Eilts and former ambassador to Israel Samuel Lewis, who in 1979 was sent to Cairo as the first Jewish-American to serve in an important embassy in the Arab world. Kurtzer's rise was not mere tokenism. Unlike Jock Covey, Kurtzer is an Arab-Israeli *wallah* who is universally described as brilliant and likable. "Dan's a latter-day Hal Saunders, the very best of the peace-process wonks," says one Arabist. But Kurtzer was clearly Ross's man, a vehicle to keep the policy-planning staff in control of NEA on the crucial Arab-Israeli issue, a man who consequently did not involve himself in Gulf Arab affairs. When it came to inter-Arab affairs, the fact is that Kelly brought in no one of real intellectual ability, although he desperately needed such a person to compensate for his own lack of area expertise.

Unlike Joe Sisco's dramatic personnel changes of 20 years before, the changes Kelly made weakened NEA's interdepartmental bureaucratic maneuvering ability rather than strengthened it. And not only did Kelly dismiss people, but he was rude while doing it. Arabists were devastated by Kelly's behavior. NEA had constituted a tight-knit, collegial group that had worked long hours together under intense public scrutiny and was not used to being divided against itself by an outsider, whom they all knew was a weak "internal political appointee" of Baker's and Ross's. "This was a bureau where in 1989 and 1990 nobody was talking to each other, where psychological walls divided people," says one NEA staffer. "NEA had always been known as 'the mother bureau,' a bureau where everyone watched out for each other. Under Kelly it became known as 'the motherfucker bureau.' " It is noteworthy that some of the best Arabists in NEA fled to overseas posts, or to other bureaus at State, rather than work with Kelly.

According to Eilts, it's very important for a senior officer to demonstrate a willingness to listen to his junior officers in the field. Not only does this build the confidence of junior officers, but it gives the senior officer a feel for what's going on out in the street. However, what everyone mentions about Kelly was his unwillingness to listen to advice. Charles Forrest, an officer in Saudi Arabia, remembers a visit by Kelly where the NEA assistant secretary gave the embassy staff an "arrogant monologue about Saudi politics without even bothering to ask our opinions over what was going on in the country." Thus, as the countdown to Saddam's August 1990 surprise attack began, NEA was saddled with terrible morale in the field and the mediocre analysis of Kelly and his lieutenants in Washington.

John Kelly and April Glaspie were not exactly fond of each other, mainly because each had the other's number. They had worked badly together when Kelly was the ambassador to Lebanon and Glaspie ran the NEA subbureau in which Lebanon was included. Kelly saw Glaspie for what she was, an old-guard Arabist who preferred the Sunni Moslem Syrians to the Maronite Christians: the kind of person with which he and Ross felt uncomfortable. (They didn't even want to deal with Dick Murphy, who in every sense was a lot more solid, even-handed, and smoother in interpersonal relations than was Glaspie.) And Glaspie saw Kelly for what he was, a politically imposed outsider running a bureau that had rarely known political appointees, and worse—whatever his reputation in European affairs—an insecure bureaucrat who hated listening to advice. She could admire someone like Kissinger, whose views were often different from hers, because Kissinger had obvious brilliance. Kelly brought nothing like that to NEA, she knew. He was destroying a bureau to which she had dedicated her professional life.

Here is where Glaspie is deserving of compassion, though only a little. There could have been few lonelier diplomats in Baghdad than she. Whatever her old-guard Arabist tendencies, she was no camel-riding, gong-and-trinket woman like Gertrude Bell. She thought purely in policy terms. And she was sharp enough to deduce that, in a policy sense, she was in an impossible situation. Though the war with Iran was over, she saw no signs of the demilitarization of Iraqi society or the moderation she continued to hope for. Rather, she saw Iraq as run by a goon who, if you rattled his cage, might use the fourth largest army in the world to wreak havoc on his neighbors, some of whom were America's friends. Moreover, the U.S. embassy had no influence and few meaningful contacts in this police state. She was prohibited from moving around freely. And being a woman didn't make her job any easier. Back in Washington, meanwhile, her boss at NEA was someone who had no grasp of the Gulf region, who was bureaucratically weak, and who had reason not to like her. For their part, the secretary of state and the planning staff were preoccupied with the collapse of the Soviet empire and the reunification of Germany. The Arab-Israel dispute was the only Middle East issue that registered on their radar screen, and in 1989 and 1990 even that registration was only intermittent on account of the momentous events in Europe.

Yet the Bush administration policy was to keep the door open to Iraq. At an October 27, 1989, address to the Middle East Institute in Washington, John Kelly said that "Iraq is an important state with great potential. We want to deepen and broaden our relationship." And as an FSO married to her career as well as the first woman American ambassador to the Arab world, April Glaspie was determined to succeed at that task, no matter what!

As she told H. Norman Schwarzkopf, the new head of the Pentagon's

Central Command, whose responsibility was the Middle East, Iraq was "too powerful a nation for the United States to ignore: 'it would be like denying cancer.' "* She therefore suggested to Schwarzkopf that since Iraq was a military state, perhaps he could establish military-to-military contacts with Iraqi generals as a way to get some kind of a handle on this dangerous and unstable regime. Around the same time, according to Richard Straus of the *Middle East Policy Survey*, Glaspie went over Kelly's head directly to the deputy secretary of state, Lawrence Eagleburger, to recommend limited sales of nonlethal military equipment to Saddam as another way of establishing a rapport with the Iraqi leader. Eagleburger told her it was an interesting idea, but she would have to "staff it out," meaning put the proposal on paper and submit it to the relevant bureaus. She did. Policy-planning rejected it. The staff's Middle East experts were starting to become leery of U.S. attempts to woo Saddam and didn't want the policy to go any further than it already had. The political-military and human rights bureaus also rejected the proposal. When it landed on the desk of Laurence Pope, an Arabist who handled northern Gulf affairs at NEA, Pope buried it, aware that several bureaus had already turned down the idea. But Kelly, rather than thank Pope for protecting him from dealing with a proposal that nobody liked, accused Pope of hiding documents from him and then sent Glaspie's proposal back up to Eagleburger, having formally rejected it and making sure that Eagleburger knew that everyone else in the department had rejected it too, thereby humiliating Glaspie.

The significance of this story is twofold: it illustrates how Kelly went out of his way to antagonize his own bureau people even when there was no policy dispute, since Glaspie's idea was already killed by the time Pope got it; and it illustrates how, whatever Kelly's faults, it was April Glaspie the Arabist, not Kelly the Europeanist, who was leading the charge at State in trying to woo Saddam.

Also around this time, November 1989, was the Baghdad international trade fair, where, partly thanks to the efforts of Marshall Wiley, Ambassador Glaspie was able to announce, "We are pleased . . . that a record number of companies are participating, representing a wide range of America's most advanced technologies and demonstrating American confidence in Iraq's bright future. The American embassy places the highest priority on promoting commerce and friendship between our two nations."

---

* See Schwarzkopf entry in the bibliography.

By January of 1990, Rick Herrmann and Steve Grummon, two members of the policy-planning staff, had decided that this friendly policy toward Iraq was fundamentally wrong, and they began circulating numerous memos within the State Department to that effect.* What is interesting about this is that the two staffers reached their conclusions on their own, without any input from NEA or from the Arabists at U.S. embassies abroad.

(Ross, who headed the planning staff, had become extremely skeptical of the policy of coddling Saddam. But Ross's problem was this: he was already operating a three-ring circus—nuclear arms reduction talks, the "two-plus-four" German reunification talks, and Arab-Israeli issues. He simply had not the time or the excess bureaucratic clout to go to the mat over Iraq. Moreover, by so formally and completely taking Arab-Israeli matters out of NEA's hands, his relations with NEA's rank and file were strained enough without his taking even more responsibility away from the bureau. Ross, in effect, whether aware of it or not, gave NEA enough rope to hang itself.)

The next month, February 1990, the Iraqi government shocked the world by executing a British journalist as a spy and dumping his body in front of the British embassy in Baghdad. Though the journalist, Farzad Bazoft, was Iranian-born, he carried British papers and worked for a British newspaper, and an exhaustive investigation involving several Western intelligence services cleared him of any suspicion of espionage. Bazoft was basically an unlucky version of Robert Spurling. The State Department's reaction, which offended the British, was low key. NEA sought to downplay the affair. On April 1, however, John Kelly finally had had enough. After hearing Saddam's famous speech where he threatened to burn half of Israel, Kelly, with the help of planning staff director Dennis Ross and Under Secretary for Political Affairs Robert Kimmet, "made a run" at putting the U.S. relationship with Iraq "on ice."† As it turned out, their effort foundered at a White House meeting when it encountered opposition from Bush's national security adviser Brent Scowcroft. Then Ross got involved with a trip by Baker to the Soviet Union, and the whole issue was dropped. Again, what stands out is that Ross and the other members of Baker's

---

* See Don Oberdorfer, "Missed Signals in the Middle East," *Washington Post Magazine,* March 17, 1991.

†See *Middle East Policy Survey,* Washington, D.C., April 27, 1990.

narrow cabal were too preoccupied with history-making events in Europe to make a long and serious attempt to change what was by now a policy being driven primarily by the White House, NEA, and the U.S. embassy in Baghdad. Nevertheless, Kelly is on the record as trying to draw a line in the sand on April 1, 1990, rather than take appeasement down to the wire on August 2, when Saddam invaded Kuwait. For this Kelly deserves credit.

Two weeks later, in mid-April, a delegation of five U.S. senators led by the Republican minority leader, Bob Dole, met with Saddam Hussein in Mosul, a city in northern Iraq. That meeting became infamous because of the apology delivered by the senators to Saddam for Voice of America broadcasts calling for democracy in Iraq. What is less well known, however, is that the apology was the result of a briefing given by Glaspie, which "conditioned the senators for the cave-in." As one congressional source says, "I am 100 percent sure that the apology was the result of Ambassador Glaspie's briefing." The source continues, "If Jerry Brown were ever elected president of the United States, expect April Glaspie to be his secretary of state."

The degree of Glaspie's increasing isolation is even more poignantly evinced by something Saddam said. Accompanying the senators on that trip to Iraq was the previous ambassador, David Newton. Due to a jam-up with the elevators, Newton and the senators arrived in the room to meet Saddam a few minutes before Glaspie did. When someone suggested that they wait for the present ambassador to Iraq before starting the meeting, Saddam bluntly interjected, "No, you are better represented by this ambassador anyway," pointing to Newton.

Yet as the countdown to August 2 continued, Glaspie continued on her course to engage the Iraqi dictator. Neither the White House nor the State Department encouraged her otherwise. Not only was the Bush administration preoccupied with other issues, but by indicating its intention to withdraw from the Gulf those ships that remained from the 1988 Kuwait reflagging operation, the administration was giving diplomats in Baghdad signs of further withdrawal, not involvement. Moreover, despite his behind-the-scenes attempt in April to freeze U.S.-Iraq relations, Kelly, as an internal political appointee whose hot temper had destroyed whatever power base he might have had within NEA, now had little choice but to continue to do the administration's bidding on Capitol Hill by fighting efforts to impose sanctions on Iraq.

What the media failed to clarify about all this was that the White House's own appeasement of Saddam was largely due to the advice it was getting from NEA. For example, the fabled security memorandum, NSDD 26, that Bush approved in late 1989, which allowed for increased economic assistance to Iraq, was in fact crafted by the NEA staff with significant input from deputy assistant secretary of state Jock Covey, whose own ideas had obviously been influenced by cables from the Baghdad embassy. (Richard Haas, who worked for Brent Scowcroft on the National Security Council, also played a role in drafting this infamous memorandum.) Bush signed this document—along with many others—in the same period that the Berlin Wall collapsed; obviously he had other things on his mind. When it came to matters concerning Iraq, the White House was being terribly served by the Foreign Service establishment—this is the ultimate heart of Iraqgate. For the fact is that, whatever the faults of Bush and Scowcroft, who were not Middle East experts and had never lived in the region, those who did consider themselves "experts" and had lived in the region and had studied the language were, to a man, in favor of this policy—until after Saddam's invasion of Kuwait, that is, when some of them tried to claim otherwise.

April Glaspie met with Saddam Hussein on July 25, 1990, in Baghdad, one week before Iraq invaded Kuwait. Glaspie saw Saddam without a note taker, because she had been summoned to the Iraqi Foreign Ministry on short notice and did not know she was about to meet the Iraqi president, with whom she had never had a private, one-on-one meeting during her two years in Baghdad. To confront a powerful and volatile dictator, an ambassador needs specific instructions from Washington. Otherwise—as the Foreign Service drills into the heads of its career officers—an ambassador is supposed to ferret out the ruler's intentions and report immediately to the State Department. In fact, the instructions Glaspie got, in addition to the other signals she was getting vis-à-vis Kelly's statements on Capitol Hill, were to definitely not rattle the goon's cage: to calm him down; to appease him, in other words, But Glaspie compounded these bad instructions:

As a single woman who traveled around the Arab world with her mother, Glaspie was more than just a loyal FSO: she was married to the Foreign Service as though to some religious order. In terms of procedure, she was a

Foreign Service professional like no other. And this situation was made to order for the Foreign Service rulebook, or so it seemed.

At the first meeting with a head of state, an ambassador is supposed *to establish a relationship.* If an ambassador can't do that with a ruler, as Hume Horan found out in Saudi Arabia, he or she is useless and might as well go home. The way to establish a relationship with a hostile head-of-state is *to work the issues,* that is, *to blur differences and to seek out areas of common agreement in order to avoid confrontation.* Doing this was particularly important in this situation because Glaspie knew that Saddam didn't like her and that he would have preferred to deal with Newton. Perhaps she could flatter him. After all, hadn't that worked so well for her in dealing with other Arabs throughout the years and decades in Egypt and Syria? It was worth a try, since this was the first real opportunity she had had in two years in Baghdad to create a rapport with the leader: the ultimate personal goal of every ambassador, which usually, but does not always, dovetails with the official goal of "representing the best interests of the United States."

Glaspie's remark to Saddam about the United States having "no opinion on the Arab-Arab conflicts, like your border disagreement with Kuwait," might have been dictated to her by the State Department instructions. But these instructions represented a policy line with which Glaspie not only completely identified, but for which she had consistently been the State Department's leading cheerleader. Moreover, her remarks to Saddam that ABC News reporter Diane Sawyer "was cheap and unjust" to him and that she, Glaspie, counted herself among those "diplomats who stand up to the media" were certainly not dictated to her by Jim Baker. Nobody would ever put such a thing in instructions. This was pure April Glaspie, improvising in an attempt to flatter, and thus to calm down, the goon. "Glaspie's easy contempt for a free press was the diplomatic currency paid to the dictator. On this point, at least, she [and Saddam] had achieved . . . mutual understanding," writes the *New Republic*'s senior editor, Sidney Blumenthal.*

But Saddam didn't flatter as easily as the Arabs of Egypt and Syria she had known and with whom she had been so successful in the past. He was of an altogether different sort. Two years of living in the absolutely terrifying, torture-filled prison yard of Iraq should have taught her at least that.

Glaspie was no pushover, though. For example, when Saddam greeted

---

* "April's Bluff: The Secrets of Ms. Glaspie's Cable," *New Republic,* August 5, 1991.

her with a pistol strapped to his waist, she pointedly told him that wearing a gun in her presence did not exactly indicate a conciliatory approach. So he took it off, and they sat down to talk. She could be tough and nervy. As Kelly and her other bureaucratic enemies knew, that was never her problem.

Her actual problem was twofold: first, what was required in this situation was not so much tough talk as straight talk. She was not straight with Saddam. Whatever may have been Washington's official position at the time, an Iraqi invasion of Kuwait was going to result in some sort of a strong U.S. response—common sense would tell you that—and she failed to point this out to him. Second, here was an area specialist who completely misjudged the overall situation, as Gertrude Bell had misjudged it with King Feisal and as the missionaries had repeatedly misjudged it with the Sunni Arab nationalists, all misjudgments that stemmed from the hubris that allowed Westerners to think they could modify the behavior of another culture and shape it in their own perfected image. *Saddam could be moderated if only he had the right incentives, like nonlethal military equipment. . . .*

After Saddam told her that he had just spoken on the phone with Egyptian president Hosni Mubarak and had consequently agreed to settle his differences with Kuwait through negotiations, Glaspie congratulated him for his open-mindedness and sent a telegram to Washington emphasizing Saddam's message of friendship to President Bush. She then left Iraq for a vacation. She seemed utterly clueless as to his real intentions, as David Newton, Bill Eagleton, and Marshall Wiley had been.

Glaspie's performance was emblematic not only of the policy vacuum in the Bush administration but also of the pathetic labors of the U.S. embassy in Baghdad in the six years since relations had been reestablished. Glaspie, in the opinion of many observers who know her, was the ultimate "staff" personality—obsessed with the diplomatic process to the point where she couldn't accept that sometimes it was better for the process to collapse than to continue pointlessly. Glaspie later told the Senate Foreign Relations Committee that "by staying [in Iraq] we could undertake diplomatic activity," such as extracting a promise from the Iraqis after the Kurds were gassed "that they wouldn't do it again." Listen again to the embassy's press and culture officer, Jack McCreary: "In an awful country the smallest victory, no matter how inconsequential, gives you an incredibly big boost." These are not unlike the rationalizations of hostages, who try to occupy the endless stream of days with uplifting activity. Just as the American captives in Lebanon and Robert Spurling in Iraq were hostages, so too were the Arabists. Rather than appeasers, the Arabist FSOs in Baghdad—in the absence of responsible guidance from Washington—became hostages to a professional idealism that blinded them to the obvious: by the late 1980s having diplomatic relations with Iraq was not an achievement but a concession. Throughout that decade the Baghdad embassy was, in the words of one Arabist FSO, "little more than a glorified concierge service" for business and congressional delegations paying homage to the Iraqi ruler. Another Arabist adds, "we had absolutely no influence there." And a third, Dick Parker, the former ambassador to Lebanon, to Algeria, and to Morocco as well as an old-guard contemporary of Talcott Seelye and Bill Eagleton, says, "We certainly should have lowered relations in 1988. We shouldn't even have reestablished them in 1984. All it did was help massage Saddam's ego."

Yet sustained by only vague hopes, April Glaspie and the other Americans in Iraq, like Freya Stark and the British a half century before, were destined to watch in disbelief as another *farhoud* (looting) unleashed its fury, though this time Kuwaitis, not the inhabitants of Baghdad's Jewish quarter, paid the price.

On March 20, 1991, April Glaspie appeared in public for the first time since she had gone back to Washington on vacation prior to Saddam's invasion of Kuwait, eight months earlier. She was testifying before the Senate Foreign Relations Committee. Sidney Blumenthal of the *New Republic* notes that she appeared "without makeup or jewelry; her long gray hair was pulled back and her dress absolutely plain. Her puritan austerity suggested virtue." Indeed, she looked every inch the missionary.

Glaspie told the senators that the Iraqi transcript of the meeting, which depicts her as acting in a fawning manner toward Saddam and as appearing to indicate that the United States did not care how Iraq settled its border dispute with Kuwait, was doctored; that in fact she had been much tougher with Saddam than the transcript suggested. But a few months after this testimony, when the senators finally got hold of the cables Glaspie had sent to her own superiors in the State Department about the meeting with Saddam, it turned out that her own account of the meeting and the Iraqi transcript tracked "almost perfectly." Not only that, the cables revealed that, following the meeting with Saddam, she urged Washington to mute its criticism of him. Senate staffers were enraged by her attempt to mislead the Foreign Relations Committee, which in their opinion signified her "contempt" of Congress.

Some of her fellow Arabists suggest that Glaspie may have been set up by Kelly and the Baker cabal in the State Department. According to this theory, Glaspie was told to tell the senators she was tough with Saddam, believing that the cables would never be made public. Afterward the Kelly-Baker crowd leaked the cables. True or not, the Arabist defense of Glaspie as a victim of the Bush administration policy toward Iraq has little merit since there is a mountain of evidence showing that she was a driver and a hard-core believer in this policy down to the very end. And while Kelly's machinations weakened the bureau, there were still quite a number of Arabists both in Washington and in the embassies in the Arab world who might have sounded an alarm at the Iraq policy, though almost none did. The fact that the White House, the secretary of state, and the policy-planning staff director were preoccupied with historic issues in Europe gave Arabists like Glaspie even more freedom in policy matters than they normally would have enjoyed. None of them used that freedom to argue for a tougher policy toward Iraq. Not only Kelly's lieutenants but all of NEA and the wider Arabist community in Washington were caught blind by the invasion. Admits one U.S. ambassador in the Gulf at the time of Iraq's invasion: "Yes, Arabists were, to an extent, victims [of how Kelly weakened the bureau]. But there is an old Afghan proverb, *he who would be buggered supplies his own grease.*"

Dick Murphy, the NEA assistant secretary prior to Kelly as well as the Middle East specialist at the Council on Foreign Relations, says: "I feel solace knowing that not just us, everyone—the Egyptians, the Jordanians, the Saudis—all screwed up on Iraq. But I'm willing to be stripped of the title of area expert. We're just specialists, first or second class. Let's stay modest."

The failure of the Arabists looks especially striking when seen against the behavior of the Sovietologists of an earlier era. These men, including Loy Henderson, George Kennan, and Charles Bohlen, whose professional lives, like those of the Arabists, were wrapped up in the study of a particular foreign language and a culture—in this case, Russian—and moreover enjoyed collecting such trinkets as icons and samovars, were nevertheless consistent in their opposition to U.S. recognition of the Soviet Union, even though such recognition would have opened up further career opportunities for them. And after the United States did recognize the Kremlin, these experts never stopped emphasizing in their cables the brutal iniquities of the regime, emphasis that ran counter to the more positive image of Soviet Communism then prevalent in Washington. Rather than urge their superiors in Washington to put the human rights violations of a dictator "into perspective," as a string of U.S. mission chiefs in Baghdad did, the Sovietologists saw Stalin's crimes as evidence of the danger he posed to the outside world. Parker Hart, the NEA assistant secretary in the late 1960s, says knowingly: "The Zionists can say what they want about Loy Henderson. But we needed someone like Loy Henderson in Baghdad in 1990. Someone discreet but tough. Someone who wouldn't mince words with Saddam, whatever the instructions."

An even more devastating historical comparison is with the U.S. diplomats who served at the embassy in Berlin in the early and middle 1930s, during Hitler's military buildup. These diplomats were as immersed in German language and culture as the Arabists were in Arab culture. On September 13, 1933, Ambassador William E. Dodd—a southern Protestant who spoke fluent German—exploded at German foreign minister Baron Konstantin von Neurath in a face-to-face meeting, chastising von Neurath for Nazi brutality against German citizens and the militant tone of Hitler's speeches. "Is it to be war?" Dodd challenged the foreign minister, a full six years before Hitler invaded Poland. The following month, at a meeting of the American Chamber of Commerce in Berlin, Ambassador Dodd again lashed out at German policy on an occasion when etiquette required him to promote U.S.-German trade. In July 1934 Dodd bluntly told his German counterparts that there could be no peace as long as Hitler remained in power. Dodd's commercial attaché, Douglas P. Miller, not only spoke fluent German but was married to a German woman. This, however, did not stop Miller from facing facts: during the winter Olympics in Garmisch-Partenkirchen in February 1936, Miller met with a group of

U.S. businessmen and tried, albeit unsuccessfully, to enlighten them as to the iniquities of Hitler's regime and why it was therefore not a wise idea to invest in Germany.* Rather than drum up business for Hitler and put his actions "into perspective," U.S. diplomats on the ground in Germany—none of whom were Jewish—were leading the charge to confront the Nazis long before it became clear that war was on the horizon. Measured by this standard, Arabists in Iraq not only failed, but their performance was a disgrace.

NEA's institutional failure had two exceptions, which in fairness need to be noted. In April 1990, four months before the invasion, Ambassador to Saudi Arabia Chas Freeman and his staff sent a three-part telegram to the State Department. Freeman is an intellectually intense and brilliant insomniac, who gets up in the middle of the night to bang out analyses on his home computer. He argued that the winding down of the Cold War would affect theaters beyond Europe. There would be "a collapse in the Horn of Africa" (which soon took place, with the overthrow of leftist regimes in Somalia and Ethiopia) and an upsurge in the expression of age-old local rivalries throughout the Arab world. The telegram specifically warned of the danger of Iraqi aggression against Kuwait. Freeman, by the way, is not an Arabist. He is a China hand, who translated for President Nixon during Nixon's 1972 visit to China and whose posting to Saudi Arabia was his first ever in the Middle East.

Kelly ignored the warning, perhaps because he had just tried and failed to change the policy toward Iraq and thus was somewhat fatalistic. Glaspie, however, thought Freeman's thesis worthy of consideration. Says one friend of Glaspie, "April is intellectually honest, loves a good argument, and is always willing to entertain another point of view." Tragically, the telegram did not alter her basic belief that trying to woo Saddam still carried less risk than getting tough with him. It is also questionable how much she focused on the telegram. Like most bureaucracies nowadays, the State Department and its officers are bedeviled by information overload. Thou-

---

* See Shirer entry in bibliography for the Miller meeting. See Dodd for all other references regarding U.S. diplomats in Germany.

sands of cables daily move between the State Department and its embassies and consulates abroad. One Arabist says, "If George Kennan sent his famous Long Telegram about Soviet intentions today, nobody high up would get to read it."

The other burst of insight came at the same time Glaspie was meeting with Saddam. After months of "missing signals because of all the smoke-screens being thrown up by the Kuwaitis and the Saudis," Barbara Bodine, the DCM at the U.S. embassy in Kuwait, and her ambassador, Nathaniel Howell, both Arabists, realized that Saddam wasn't bluffing, that his threats against Kuwait followed exactly the pattern of his threats against Iran prior to his invasion in 1980, and that Kelly's statement to Congress indicating that the United States was not bound by treaty to defend Kuwait would only encourage the Iraqi leader to carry out his invasion plan.

Bodine and Howell's cable arrived in Washington just as Glaspie was leaving on her holiday. On July 28, 1990, four days before the invasion, Bodine and Howell began destroying sensitive documents, including the Christmas card list, so that the Iraqis wouldn't be able to identify the embassy's Kuwaiti contacts. Howell and Bodine allowed all U.S. citizens and British nationals to hide out in the embassy compound. They sent out trucks to buy large amounts of food, diapers, and other items. When Iraqi troops besieged the embassy and turned the streets outside into a killing zone, the U.S. diplomats dug a well for water and used car batteries for lighting in order to save the generators to send coded communications to Washington. They grew their own vegetables and built their own bomb shelter by filling diplomatic pouches with sand and welding safe boxes together. It wasn't the first stellar performance for Howell and Bodine. They had worked together with Arabist Laurence Pope on the reflagging of Kuwaiti ships in 1988, a complex operation that succeeded without a hitch. And when Robert Spurling was first dragged away from his wife and children at Saddam International Airport in 1983, it was Barbara Bodine who initially made a nuisance of herself with Iraqi officials, demanding that they release the man. Yet when Bodine and Howell returned as heroes to Washington after the siege of the Kuwait embassy at the end of 1990, they got the impression that as far as job openings were concerned, they, like other top-notch Arabists, were not welcome at Kelly's NEA.

After waiting a decent interval following the Gulf War, Baker and Ross removed Kelly as NEA assistant secretary. They replaced him with Edward

P. Djerejian, the ambassador to Syria, a well-respected Arabist with out-of-area experience, who had been a protégé of Joe Sisco—in other words, a clone of Dick Murphy, the kind of guy they didn't want to work with in the first place. Baker and Ross had learned a hard lesson: that all their faults and failures notwithstanding, Arabists were still necessary for a successful Middle East policy.

Part IV
Redemption

Chapter 15

A New Species?

The irony of the Iraq debacle was that, in evolutionary terms, for NEA it constituted an aberration, not a trend. While the ambassador in Iraq, April Glaspie, was a member of the Arabist old guard, many of the other U.S. embassies in the Arab world were being stocked with a more contemporary brand of area expert. Here are the words of a U.S. diplomat assigned to an Arab country with which the United States also has had troubled relations:

"If the size of our mission staff had been cut down, I was next on the list to be sent home to Washington. I desperately, desperately wanted to stay on post. I'm Jewish. The Six-Day War was one of those defining moments of my youth, when I really identified with being a Jew. Radical Arab countries were like the dark side of the moon for me. To learn Arabic and serve as a diplomat in one of these places was just fascinating. How could I be expected to want to leave after just arriving?"

I'll call this diplomat Walter—he is an Arabist who may again serve in a radical Arab country and does not want his real name used in connection with his religion. He has been a political officer in both the Arab world and Israel. He is in his early forties, distinctly middle class, with degrees from the State University of New York at Binghamton and Stony Brook. This writer interviewed him at his mother-in-law's townhouse, in an unremarkable New Jersey development, where he was spending his vacation between overseas assignments.

Walter is typical of the generation of Arabists now moving into important positions. An increasing number of them have ethnic and suburban roots, have studied Hebrew, and have served in Israel. For example, Molly Williamson, an Asian-American who speaks both Arabic and Hebrew, was in 1991 named the U.S. consul general in East Jerusalem—perhaps the most sensitive of Foreign Service assignments because of the consulate's key role in Palestinian-Israeli peace negotiations and its past reputation for an anti-Israel bias that has put it at odds with the U.S. embassy in Tel Aviv. In several conversations Williamson revealed herself as someone who has gone beyond mere objectivity, to a point where she deeply intuits the angst-ridden thought processes of Arabs and Jews alike. The elevation of someone like her suggests how knowledge of both Semitic languages is a likely route to promotion in today's State Department.

These new Arabists stand old stereotypes on their heads. Alberto Fernandez, for instance, is a Cuban American in his mid-thirties from Miami. A graduate of the University of Arizona, he came into the Foreign Service by way of the U.S. Army, where he volunteered for Arabic training at the Defense Language Institute. "After growing up in an insular and suffocating ethnic society, I needed something completely different to define myself," he says. Because of his knowledge of Spanish and Arabic, Fernandez has served in Nicaragua, the Dominican Republic, Kuwait, and the United Arab Emirates.

Fernandez is critical of the older generation of Arabists. "It's true, Arabists have not liked Middle Eastern minorities. Arabists have been guilty in the past of loving the majority and the idea of *Uruba,* which roughly translates as 'Arabism.' I remember once going to a Foreign Service party and hearing people refer to the Maronite Christians in Lebanon as 'fascists.' I love and am fascinated by minorities: Maronites, Copts, southern Sudanese, Kurds, whatever. . . . I feel less strongly about the cause of the Palestinians than I used to. There are lots of injustices in the world, and self-determination is not something the Arabs want to apply anywhere else in the Middle East."

Yet Fernandez sees the Arab world embarking on a slow and convoluted path toward political modernization. "Just as there are Nazi skinheads in eastern Germany and fascists in Romania, there are fundamentalists taking advantage of democratization in Algeria. But fundamentalism may eventually crest. I see a post-Islamic phase as Arab societies hold more and freer elections and learn that fundamentalists don't have the answers, either. Already in Iran you see a disillusionment with fundamentalism." Other Arabists adumbrate Fernandez's point. Unable to predict specific developments a few months down the road, they draw the vague outlines of the future with more certitude. "The Saudis will, over time, rewrite their social contract without ever ripping up the old one," says Chas Freeman, ambassador in Saudi Arabia during the Gulf War. Jack McCreary, former press and culture officer in Baghdad, points out, "There is an enormous, widening gap between the [Arab] regimes and the people. Arabs see clearly that they are cut off from their own governments and that their press lies. Arab intellectuals trust Israel Radio's Arabic service more than their own stations. If Arab governments want to control their own populations in the future, they're going to have to tell the truth more often." Dovetailing with such political modernization, some Arabists say, will be a further breakup in the Arab world itself, with the Maghreb states of North Africa and the Gulf sheikhdoms increasingly consumed by their own regional problems.

Whatever the destiny of the Palestinian-Israeli relationship, it seems possible that the coming decades in the Middle East may be less traumatic for America than previous decades, a development that may lead to a reborn AUB, chastened by the lessons of the past and primed to help in health and educational projects that Lebanon so desperately needs. Also, the basic Arabist assumption of a middle-class-driven reform in line with Iraq's secular and urban character may yet, given enough time, prove accurate. If history teaches us anything, it's that nothing is permanent. But the metamorphosis will be frustratingly slow. "On account of what's happened in Eastern Europe, everyone demands instant gratification in the Middle East, and that's not in the cards," Chas Freeman warns.

Peter Rodman, a former top aide to Henry Kissinger and the head of the policy-planning staff under President Reagan, wonders whether the Arabists' best days actually lie ahead. "Since we will no longer have to look at the Middle East in East-West terms, it might be more appropriate, as Arabists have always urged, to treat the region on its own merits." In a new climate, in which various forces impel Arab leaders to focus inward on their own societies rather than on Israel, the interstices Arabists operate within should be wider and remain open for longer periods.

The importance of exploiting those interstices—pushing matters like food aid, cultural relations, and hostage negotiations forward before an opening disappears and then going back and starting over again—cannot be overstated, for it is in this way, rather than on the level of grand policy, that Arabists have always done their most effective work. Take, for example, Norman Anderson, who followed Hume Horan as the ambassador to Sudan. Anderson typifies another sort of new-breed Arabist: the multiarea expert, who speaks French, Russian, and Bulgarian as well as Arabic and thus has a much wider frame of reference than Arabists of the past. Anderson arrived in Khartoum, faced with an Arab government that did not want to send food to the famine-afflicted, non-Arab south of the country. So Anderson went to work befriending the defense minister, Majid Khalil. After a series of one-on-one chats in Arabic over the course of several months, Anderson convinced Khalil that the International Committee for the Red Cross (ICRC) could be trusted to keep relief supplies out of the hands of rebels fighting the Khartoum government. On December, 4, 1988, Khalil grudgingly allowed an ICRC airlift of food to starving peasants to begin.

Explains Anderson: "Foreign affairs has become so complicated and multilateral—with issues like drugs, the environment, and famine, as well as trade and military—that Washington can't know exactly how its policies are to be carried out in each individual country in every specific case. That is the job of the embassies. And it's hard to gather information on a country and do all this without knowledge of the language." Anderson adds that just as he was the only Arabic-speaking U.S. diplomat in Sudan at the time when a coup occurred, April Glaspie was the only Arabic-speaking U.S. diplomat in Iraq on the eve of the invasion of Kuwait. Although around two dozen U.S. embassies and consulates have multiple job slots requiring Arabic, Anderson notes that "in the same year [1990] in which we dispatched 500,000 troops to the Arab world, the Foreign Service field school in Tunis could graduate only half a dozen Arabic speakers." His implication is clear: if we had produced more of the latter over enough years, we might not have needed the former.

"We've got to stop degrading area specialists. Whatever their mistakes, they still offer the best chance of keeping the world at bay," says Chas Freeman. An affectingly cocky and opinionated man who can converse in German, Italian, Spanish, French, Portuguese, and Tamil besides Chinese and Arabic, Freeman gripes about a Foreign Service bureaucracy that now produces too much paperwork and too few language-proficient officers and a Washington foreign policy establishment that distracts everyone's attention with solecisms that don't relate to what the United States should or should not do, can or cannot do, in the field. "To focus more effectively on domestic policy, you've got to disengage politically from foreign policy while engaging in it at a more expert level on the ground overseas."

While the case for more and better Arabists is clear, it is by no means certain that the new species is entirely new or whether the Arabist community has adequately learned the lessons of the Iraq debacle. Bad habits have been far too ingrained to expect that they won't continue, albeit in an increasingly milder form, into the future. Explains one area specialist: "The intellectual training of Arabists is Levantine, since they learn Arabic from Arabs. And the Arab world is still characterized by a vacuum of information whereby every paranoid and crackpot rumor on the street has some currency. Some of this rubs off on Arabists who live in this environment. They take what Arabs say too seriously. That's why you had all those erroneous predictions from Arabists during the Gulf crisis, about how the Arabs were going to rise up everywhere in the street demanding that the Saudis kick our troops off their soil." Freeman puts it this way, "The price you pay for overspecialization is a failure of the imagination. Because Arabists know so much about the Arab street, they feel they have to play by its rules. A nonexpert can just say, 'I'll change the rules' "

Sir Hamilton Gibb, the late British Orientalist, describes the Arab "concept of knowledge as a closed circle," in which some Arabists may still be trapped. It is an open question whether Arabists, like Arabs themselves, fully comprehend the sterile emptiness and violence that lurks behind all the pretty phrases about Arab unity and Sunni Arab nationalism. Consider that for years one U.S. mission chief after another in Baghdad was a defender of the idea of Iraq's unity and territorial integrity, even though modern Iraq is a totally artificial state in which the Sunni Arabs, a minority of the population, tyrannize Kurds and Shiite Arabs. The tolerance and understanding with which Arabists have viewed the Baath party is particularly telling, considering that in Iraq Baathism means a fascist and racist ideology that oppresses non-Arabs.*

According to the former head of the policy-planning staff, Peter Rod-

---

* See Galbraith entry in the bibliography.

man, Islamic fundamentalism is now replacing Sunni Arab nationalism as the new focus of Arabist sentimentalism. Rodman warns that if the Arabist community persists in its tendency to concede a measure of legitimacy to fundamentalism—which the West is under no obligation to do—Arabists will "blow their opportunity" for the renewed respect that is being offered them in the post–Cold War era, since the wave of fundamentalism that is washing across North Africa and the Middle East could turn out to be just as tyrannical and threatening to U.S. interests as Sunni nationalism has been.

Horan says that Arabists, as well as other FSOs, must in the light of all their past actions take a hard, uncensored look at themselves in order to be ready for an era when covert intelligence and military power will give way to trade, development, and the propagation of ideas and technology— things that should in theory be a boon to diplomats. "An institution" like the Foreign Service, stresses Horan, "benefits from the very act of self-appraisal."*

In fact, the more immediate problems for Arabists in the 1990s are ones general to the entire Foreign Service: rampant shallowness and careerism and the sterilization of embassy life. The Foreign Service, after all, mirrors the society from which it draws its recruits, and these recruits are consumed with status and advancement and less concerned with the subject of their expertise than their predecessors were. Peter Bechtold, the head of the Middle East area-studies program at the Foreign Service Institute, remarks that during coffee breaks his students "now talk about their Peugeots rather than about things like the Shiite and Orthodox Jewish mentalities." Dick Undeland, who retired in 1992 from the Foreign Service after three decades in the Arab world, tells a story about a colleague who in 1964 wrote a four-and-a-half-page letter to his superior, explaining why he didn't want to serve in the U.S. embassy in Saigon. The superior remarked that "it was the longest resignation letter I had ever seen." In those days, Undeland explains, the Foreign Service was more like the military, and you just went where you were told, or you resigned. FSOs had a clearer sense of duty and patriotism and therefore complained less than their contemporaries, even though they had fewer rights. Nowadays, rejecting post assignments is not uncommon, and one's own interests plainly come ahead of national ones.

---

* *Foreign Service Journal,* March 1992.

Indeed, as middle-class life in America becomes more pressurized, the desire among FSOs for "pasha status" becomes more acute. There is a real motive for "protecting your empire," says one Arabist, which means staying abroad in a prestigious post where you and your wife have servants, while the U.S. government pays for your kids' private schooling. "You don't want you and your family to be thrown to the dogs—the rigors of a normal middle-class existence in America. So you fudge a political report when you have to. You don't say what you really believe if it is not the accepted wisdom, since using the Department's dissent channel is like taking a cyanide pill."

Yet even as the pasha life-style is pursued abroad, improved communications combined with the mania for security has made many embassies, as Ray Custis found out, mere extensions of the Washington bureaucracy and airtight cubicles of American community life divorced from the local reality.

A partial antidote to this dilemma may be the Peace Corps, an experience that an increasing number of Arabists and other area experts have had. The Peace Corps example, redolent as it is of foreign aid to the Third World, may seem hopelessly out-of-date in the current post–Cold War climate. But in terms of what the Foreign Service needs to improve its analytical skills and to adapt to this new reality, the Peace Corps has never been more relevant. Peace Corps graduates, adept at living and working in the bush on meager resources, are oriented toward a leaner Foreign Service that gets out onto the streets—embassy life and paperwork be damned—to find out what is really going on. Peace Corps people do not think in terms of high development budgets and military assistance to friendly regimes, but in terms of rural agriculture and education: the true building blocks of capitalism. The growing Peace Corps component among Arabists, and in the Foreign Service at large, runs parallel to the middle-class takeover of the formerly elitist State Department—a process begun in the 1950s that has now reached the point of saturation. A Peace Corps background in today's State Department carries the allure that an Ivy League education once had. More important, someone with a Peace Corps background is more apt to have an old-fashioned idea of service and selflessness that is at a premium in the State Department of the 1990s.

It may be nicely symbolic that the daughters of Bill Stoltzfus and Hume Horan served in the Peace Corps in Africa, Stoltzfus's daughter in the Central African Republic and Horan's in Zaire. It shows how Arabism in these two families is a form of compassion for, and interest in, the world-wide community of man that need not be confined to one geographical area and that is capable of continual evolution. Families like these—as well as that of the Peace Corps veteran Jack McCreary, which tried to show Iraqis "how free people think and behave"—showcase the American ideal and stoke the flame of freedom in darkened places.

Joe Sisco, the most successful NEA assistant secretary in the bureau's history, recalls a discussion he had years back with Moshe Dayan, the hero of Israel's Six-Day War. "Dayan told me," begins Sisco in his gravelly, recollecting voice, "that the more friends and influence America has in the Arab world [and elsewhere], the more secure Israel will be." That is as true now as it ever was. And as Arabs and Israelis try to negotiate peace with the help of a new generation of State Department Arabists, the time is past due for not just Arabs and Israelis but for Arabists and the Jewish supporters of Israel to bury the hatchet.

Bibliography

Antonius, George. *The Arab Awakening: The Story of the Arab National Movement.* New York: Putnam, 1938.

Baram, Phillip J. "A Tradition of Anti-Zionism: The Department of State's Middle Managers." *Essays in American Zionism, 1917–1948.* New York: Herzl Press, 1978.

Bell, Gertrude Lowthian. *The Desert & the Sown.* London: Heinemann, 1907.

Bird, Kai. *The Chairman: John J. McCloy; The Making of the American Establishment.* New York: Simon & Schuster, 1992.

Birmingham, Stephen. *The Right People: A Portrait of the American Social Establishment.* Boston: Little, Brown, 1958.

Blanch, Lesley. *The Wilder Shores of Love.* London: John Murray, 1954.

Bliss, Howard S. "The Modern Missionary." *Atlantic Monthly,* May 1920.

Bocage, Leo J. "The Public Career of Charles R. Crane." Ph.D. diss., Fordham University, 1962.

Bourne, Randolph. *The Puritan Will To Power.* 1917.

Brands, H.W. *Inside the Cold War: Loy Henderson and the Rise of the American Empire, 1918–1961.* New York and London: Oxford University Press, 1991.

Byerly, Anne. *See* Moore, Anne Byerly.

Byron, Robert. *The Road to Oxiana.* London: Macmillan, 1937.

Chambers, William Nesbitt. *Yoljuluk: Random Thoughts on a Life in Imperial Turkey.* London: Simpkin Marshall, 1928.

Clifford, Clark M. "Factors Influencing President Truman's Decision to Support Partition and Recognize the State of Israel." Speech to American Historical Association, Washington, D.C., December 28, 1976.

Coon, Carleton S., Sr. *Measuring Ethiopia and Flight into Arabia.* Boston: Little, Brown, 1935.

Coon, Carleton S., Sr. *Caravan.* New York: Henry Holt, 1951.

Coon, Carleton S., Jr. *Daniel Bliss and the Founding of the American University of Beirut.* Washington, D.C.: The Middle East Institute, 1989.

Crossman, Richard. *Palestine Mission.* New York: Harper & Bros., 1947.

DeNovo, John A. *American Interests and Policies in the Middle East, 1900–1939.* Minneapolis: University of Minnesota Press, 1963.

Dodd, William E. *Ambassador Dodd's Diary, 1933–1938.* Introduction by Charles E. Beard. New York: Harcourt, Brace, 1941.

Dodge, Bayard. "Must There Be War in the Middle East?" *Reader's Digest,* April 1948.

Dodge, Grace. *See* Guthrie, Grace Dodge.

Doughty, Charles M. *Travels in Arabia Deserta.* 2 vols. Cambridge: Cambridge University Press, 1888; reprinted New York: Dover, 1979.

Elon, Amos. *The Israelis: Founders and Sons.* New York: Holt, Rinehart & Winston, 1971.

Emerson, Steven. *The American House of Saud.* New York: Franklin Watts, 1985.

Feis, Herbert. *The Birth of Israel: The Tousled Diplomatic Bed.* New York: Norton, 1969.

Fernea, Elizabeth Warnock, and Robert A. Fernea. *The Arab World: Personal Encounters.* New York: Doubleday, 1985.

Finnie, David H. *Pioneers East: The Early American Experience in the Middle East.* Cambridge, Mass.: Harvard University Press, 1967.

Galbraith, Peter W. "The United States and the Kurds." Remarks delivered to the H. John Heinz III School of Public Policy and Management, Pittsburgh, November 5, 1992.

Georgetown University. The Association for Diplomatic Studies' Foreign Affairs Oral History Program. In particular, interviews with Carleton S. Coon, Jr., Hermann Frederick Eilts, Andrew Killgore, and Marshall Wiley.

Gibb, H. A. R. *Modern Trends in Islam.* Chicago: University of Chicago Press, 1947.

Graves, Robert. *Good-bye to All That.* New York: Anchor Books, 1929, 1985.

Graves, Robert. *Lawrence and the Arabs.* London: Jonathan Cape, 1927.

Guthrie, Grace Dodge. *Legacy to Lebanon.* Richmond, Va.: Privately printed, 1984.

Hitti, Philip K. *The Arabs: A Short History.* Princeton, N.J.: Princeton University Press, 1943.

Hocking, William Ernest. *Re-thinking Missions: A Laymen's Inquiry After One Hundred Years.* New York: Commission of Appraisal, 1932.

Hogarth, D. G. *The Life of Charles M. Doughty.* Garden City, N.Y.: Doubleday, Doran, 1929.

* Hooker, Edward W. *Memoir of Mrs. Sarah Lanman Smith.* Boston: 1840.

---

* David Finnie's *Pioneers East* (see Finnie entry) cites the recollections of some of the early Americans in the Middle East.

Hudson, Michael C. *Arab Politics: The Search for Legitimacy.* New Haven: Yale University Press, 1977.

Isaacson, Walter, and Evan Thomas. *The Wise Men.* New York: Simon & Schuster, 1986.

Laurie, Thomas. *Dr. Grant and the Mountain Nestorians.* Boston: 1853.

Kaplan, Robert D. "Tales from the Bazaar." *Atlantic Monthly,* August 1992.

Kedourie, Elie. *The Chatham House Version and Other Middle-Eastern Studies.* New York: Praeger, 1970.

Kerr, Malcolm. "Arab Society and the West." In *The Shaping of an Arab Statesman: Sharif Abd al-Hamid Sharaf and the Modern Arab World,* edited by Patrick Seale. New York and London: Quartet Books, 1983.

Khalid, Mansour. *Nimeiri and the Revolution of Dis-May.* London: KPI, Ltd., 1985.

Kinglake, Alexander. *Eothen.* Oxford: Oxford University Press, 1844, 1906.

Kipling, Rudyard. *Kim.* London: Penguin, 1901; reprinted 1987, with an introduction and notes by Edward W. Said.

Kissinger, Henry. *Years of Upheaval.* Boston: Little, Brown, 1982.

Knightley, Phillip, and Colin Simpson. *The Secret Lives of Lawrence of Arabia.* London: Times Newspapers, 1969.

Kraft, Joseph. "Those Arabists in the State Department." *New York Times Magazine,* November 7, 1971.

Lacey, Robert. *The Kingdom.* London: Hutchinson, 1981.

Lawrence, T. E. *Seven Pillars of Wisdom: A Triumph.* New York: Doubleday, 1926.

Le Carré, John. *The Little Drummer Girl.* London: Knopf, 1983.

MacKenzie, Richard. *The Case of a Colonel with Camera. Insight,* April 13, 1987.

Mansfield, Peter. *The Arabs.* London: Allen Lane, 1976.

Marty, Martin E. *Pilgrims in Their Own Land: 500 Years of Religion in America.* Boston: Little, Brown, 1984.

Mason, Alfred DeWitt, and Frederick J. Barny. *The History of the Arabian Mission.* New York: Board of Foreign Missions, Reformed Church in America, 1926.

McGilvary, Margaret. *The Dawn of a New Era in Syria.* New York: Fleming H. Revell, 1920.

———— *A Story of Our Syria Mission.* New York: Board of Foreign Missions of the Presbyterian Church in the U.S.A., 1920.

McPhee, John. *The Headmaster: Frank L. Boyden, of Deerfield.* New York: Farrar, Straus and Giroux, 1966.

Moore, Anne Byerly. *Lebanon's Child.* Tarpon Springs, Fl.: Privately printed, 1991.

Moorehead, Alan. *The White Nile.* London: Hamish Hamilton, 1960.

Parfitt, Tudor. *Operation Moses.* London: Weidenfeld & Nicolson, 1985.

Pelletiere, Stephen C. *The Kurds: An Unstable Element in the Gulf.* Boulder, Colo.: Westview Press, 1984.

Penrose, Stephen B. L., Jr. *That They May Have Life: The Story of the American Uni-*

versity of Beirut, 1866–1941. New York: The Trustees of the American University of Beirut, 1941.

Philby, H. St. J. B. *Arabian Days: An Autobiography.* London: Robert Hale, Ltd., 1948.

Pipes, Daniel. *Greater Syria: The History of an Ambition.* New York: Oxford University Press, 1990.

Pope, Laurence, "The Arabist Myth." *Foreign Service Journal,* January 1985.

Pryce-Jones, David. *The Closed Circle: An Interpretation of the Arabs.* New York: Harper & Row, 1989.

"Reviving Embers of the Past." *The Economist,* January 19, 1991.

Quandt, William B. *Camp David: Peacemaking and Politics.* Washington, D.C.: Brookings Institution, 1986.

——— *Decade of Decisions: American Policy Toward the Arab-Israeli Conflict, 1967–1976.* Berkeley: University of California Press, 1977.

——— "Lyndon Johnson and June 1967 War: What Color Was the Light?" *Middle East Journal,* Spring 1992.

Rand, Christopher, "Reporting in the Far East." *Nieman Reports,* 1965.

Randal, Jonathan C. *Going All the Way: Christian Warlords, Israeli Adventurers, and the War in Lebanon.* New York: Viking, 1983.

Rice, Edward. *Captain Sir Richard Francis Burton.* New York: Scribners, 1990.

Roosevelt, Archie. *For Lust of Knowing: Memoirs of an Intelligence Officer.* Boston: Little, Brown, 1988.

Roux, Georges. *Ancient Iraq.* London: George Allen & Unwin, 1964.

Rubin, Barry. *Secrets of State: The State Department and the Struggle over U.S. Foreign Policy.* New York: Oxford University Press, 1985.

Said, Edward W. *Orientalism.* New York: Pantheon, 1978.

Schwarzkopf, H. Norman, with Peter Petre. *It Doesn't Take a Hero.* New York: Bantam, 1992.

Seale, Patrick. *The Struggle for Syria.* Oxford: Oxford University Press, 1965.

Seikaly, S., R. Baalbaki, and P. Dodd. *Quest for Understanding: Arabic and Islamic Studies in Memory of Malcolm H. Kerr.* Beirut: American University of Beirut, 1991.

Shavit, David. *The United States in the Middle East: A Historical Dictionary.* Westport, Conn.: Greenwood Press, 1988.

Shirer, William L. *Berlin Diary: The Journal of a Foreign Correspondent, 1934–1941.* Boston: Little, Brown, 1941.

Smith, Eli, and H. G. O. Dwight. *Missionary Researches in Armenia.* London: 1834.

Stark, Freya. *East Is West.* London: John Murray, 1945.

Stephens, John Lloyd. *Incidents of Travel in Egypt, Arabia Petraea, and the Holy Land.* Edited and with an Introduction by Victor Wolfgang von Hagen. Norman, Okla.: University of Oklahoma Press, 1837, 1970.

Teymour, Mahmoud. *The Call of the Unknown.* Translated by Hume Horan. Beirut: Khayats, 1964.

Thesiger, Wilfred. *Arabian Sands.* New York: Dutton, 1959.

Thomsen, Mary Ellen. "Arabist Hume Horan: Fluency in a Difficult Language Takes Him Where the Action Is." *Harvard,* September–October 1977.

Thomson, William M. *The Land and the Book.* New York, 1859.

Truman, Harry. *Years of Trial and Hope.* New York: Doubleday, 1956.

Tibawi, A. L. *A Modern History of Syria.* New York: St. Martin's Press, 1969.

Van Dam, Nikolaos. *The Struggle for Power in Syria.* London: Croom Helm, 1979.

Weir, Ben and Carol, with Dennis Benson. *Hostage Bound, Hostage Free.* Philadelphia: Westminster Press, 1987.

Westrate, Bruce. *The Arab Bureau: British Policy in the Middle East, 1916–1920.* University Park: Penn State Press, 1992.

Wilson, Evan M. *Jerusalem, Key to Peace.* Washington, D.C.: The Middle East Institute, 1970.

Winstone, H. V. F. *Gertrude Bell.* New York: Quartet Books, 1978.

Zwemer, Samuel M., and James Cantine. *The Golden Milestone: Reminiscences of Pioneer Days Fifty Years Ago in Arabia.* Introduction by Lowell Thomas. New York: Fleming H. Revell, 1938.

Index

319